LIBRARY DISASTER PLANNING AND RECOVERY HANDBOOK

EDITED BY
CAMILA ALIRE

Neal-Schuman Publishers, Inc.

New York   London

Published by Neal-Schuman Publishers, Inc.
100 Varick Street
New York, NY 10013

REF
025.82
LIBR

Copyright ©2000 by Camila Alire

Printed and bound in the United States of America

Library of Congress Cataloging-in-Publication Data

Library disaster planning and recovery handbook / edited by Camila Alire.
     p.   cm.
     Includes bibliographical references and index.
     ISBN 1–55570–373–9 (alk. paper)
     1. Libraries—Safety measures. 2. Library materials—Conservation and restoration. 3. Morgan Library—Safety measures. 4. Academic libraries—Colorado—Fort Collins—Safety measures. 5. Library materials—Conservation and restoration—Colorado—Fort Collins. I. Alire, Camile A.
Z679.7.L53   2000
025.8'2—dc21
                                   00–020209

Table of Contents

Contents

Contents

Contents

Contents

List of Figures

List of Contributors

Camila A. Alire, *Dean of University Libraries, Colorado State University*

Joan Beam, *Associate Professor and Reference Librarian, Colorado State University*

Barbara Branstad, *Associate Professor and Reference/Collection Management Librarian, Colorado State University*

Carmel Bush, *Assistant Dean for Technical Services, Colorado State University*

Alan N. Charnes, *Executive Director of the Colorado Alliance for Research Libraries*

Donnice Cochenour, *Associate Professor and Serials Librarian, Colorado State University*

Nora Copeland, *Associate Professor and Catalog Librarian/Database Maintenance Specialist, Colorado State University*

Tom Delaney, *Coordinator for Interlibrary Loan and Document Delivery, Colorado State University*

Halcyon Enssle, *Associate Professor and Reference/Collection Management Librarian, Colorado State University*

James F. Farmer, *Coordinator for Access Services, Colorado State University*

Evelyn Haynes, *Associate Professor and Reference/Collection Management Librarian, Colorado State University*

Holley R. Lange, *Professor and Catalog Librarian, Colorado State University*

Naomi Lederer, *Assistant Professor and Undergraduate Instruction Librarian, Colorado State University*

Diane Lunde, *Coordinator for Preservation Services, Colorado State University*

George Machovec, *Technical Director, Colorado Alliance for Research Libraries*

Tom Moothart, *Associate Professor and Reference Librarian, Colorado State University*

Awilda Reyes, *Assistant Professor and Reference/Instruction Librarian, Colorado State University*

Joel Rutstein, *Professor and Coordinator of Special Events, Colorado State University*
Patricia Smith, *Associate Professor and Coordinator for Acquisitions Services, Colorado State University*
Teri Switzer, *Interim Assistant Dean for Administrative Services, Colorado State University*
Cathy Tweedie, *Director of Fiscal Affairs, Colorado State University*
Karen Weedman, *Coordinator for Library Technology Services, Colorado State University*
Lindsey Wess, *General Professional II, Reference Services, Colorado State University*
Julie Wessling, *Assistant Dean for Public Services, Colorado State University*

Acknowledgments

I want to acknowledge the entire Colorado State University Libraries' staff for their assistance, fortitude, perseverance, support, and understanding during our disaster-recovery process. This book is dedicated to all of them.

Thanks to Michael Mason for his assistance throughout the process. Thanks, also, goes to Linda Castor and Michelle Weimer for their contribution in preparing the final manuscript and to Teri Switzer for her review of the manuscript.

Preface

On Monday, July 28, 1997, at 6:00 p.m., it started to rain in Fort Collins, Colorado and on the Colorado State University campus. Although the city of Fort Collins experienced a flood—which is legally defined as an overflow of a body of water such as a creek, river, or lake—the University experienced a sheet flow of water coming down from the foothills of the mountains only a few miles away.

On Tuesday morning, we found Morgan Library's newly renovated lower level entirely submerged under water up to one-half foot above the ceiling tiles. A portion of the library's lower-level wall caved in from the pressure of the water beating against it. A flash flood rushed into the entire lower level of the library. The strong force of the water toppled row after row of shelves full of books. Our entire lower-level collection floated in murky, contaminated water.

Wednesday, the third day of the disaster, oversize pumps drained the water from the 77,500 square-foot lower level. Massive tubes from generators the size of small delivery trucks cooled and dehumidified the building immediately. Although we had major concern for all of our books lying underwater, we had equal concern for the one-half million volumes of materials on other floors of the building that were untouched by water. High humidity and the extreme temperatures of more than 95 degrees could have drastically affected these volumes and provided the conditions for a mold and mildew outbreak.

The disasters created the havoc; and librarians produced the response. The story and lessons of the Morgan Library grew into much more than one institution's catastrophe. A tale beginning with the ferocity of nature ends with a story of human determination. We hope your library will always remain free from danger. We offer our experience in The Library Disaster Planning and Recovery Handbook *as a way to prepare your library for a future filled with uncertainty.*

* * *

Our story is not hypothetical; it is about a real disaster at a real library. We are attempting to recover, replace, and/or rebuild our damaged collection—all bound journals and close to 500,000 volumes of monographs which made up half of our entire collection housed in Morgan Library. Our disaster-recovery techniques are based on the ongoing process occurring at CSU's Morgan Library. We based this viewpoint on actual experiences of what work is ongoing, what worked, and what did not work.

The Library Disaster Planning and Recovery Handbook provides the reader with details, advice, and recommendations on all aspects of library-disaster recovery based on lessons learned from the experience of Morgan Library. We thoroughly reviewed the specific literature available in each area of the library's restoration and set our experience within that context. The book is intended for readers primarily interested in library-disaster recovery. However, the reader does not have to be interested in *library* disaster recovery to learn from our experience; nor does the reader have to be interested in disaster recovery from only an *academic library* perspective. Because of the scope of this book, there is something for everyone—disaster-recovery administration, media relations, human-resource management, facilities, disaster planning, disaster-recovery efforts, and many other areas.

Much work lingers in Morgan Library disaster recovery. Nonetheless, there is something of value to learn from our experience for every professional on a library staff. It should be most helpful for anyone preparing or revising a disaster plan. The book doesn't anticipate what needs to be done, it details what actually happened and passes on to the reader lessons learned and provides advice for future disaster recovery considerations.

THE ORGANIZATION OF THE HANDBOOK:
A BLUEPRINT FOR RECOVERY

The Library Disaster Planning and Recovery Handbook is organized into six parts. Part I deals with a disaster from a management perspective. Part II focuses on disaster recovery from the public services perspective; whereas Part III reflects all of the technical services areas affected by disaster recovery. Part IV covers the major gift-solicitation processes. Part V is a unique and comprehensive account of every aspect of technical services—from materials restoration of special projects to tracking materials to quality control. Part VI covers the concept of resource sharing in disaster recovery. The book concludes with a bibliography of selected readings. These readings cover the scope of disaster recovery and disaster management not only from a broad perspective but also specific to libraries.

For easy reference, we have devised the following outline of the main topics covered in each chapter. Each chapter in *The Library Disaster Planning and Recovery Handbook* will show you how to:

Part I—Managing a Disaster

Chapter 1: The Administrative Response
- Manage internal issues: communications, command-center operations, time commitments, critical action points, operational plans, cost estimating, and address institutional issues.
- Work with external groups such as consultants and contractors.

Chapter 2: Human Resources
- Re-employ staff, provide alternative worksites, employ students, work on ergonomics, and deal with stress.
- Comply with institutional, state, and federal regulations relative to staffing, address new and/or temporary staffing issues, and develop new operations.
- Return to/re-enter the disaster site, environmental concerns, and insurance claims.

Chapter 3: Disaster Recovery
- Manage a disaster through a complete review of the literature.
- Stabilize the building for temperature, humidity control, and structural damage.
- Assess the damage to the collection, the pack-out process, treatment of materials, treatment-testing protocols for mold and bacteria, and communicate the treatment plan.

Chapter 4: Facilities
- Institute inspection and cleanup: disaster-recovery expectations, how to determine building contents and losses, risk management analysis, claims and settlement processes, and requirements for risk mitigation.
- Reoccupy the facility: environmental concerns, health and safety issues for staff, and security issues.

Chapter 5: Media Relations
- Devise a plan: the need for visual impact and controlling the message, maintain credibility, media training points, cooperate with other media offices, and external and internal perceptions of your organization during a disaster.

Part II—Public Services in Disaster Recovery

Chapter 6: Public Service
- Set up basic services: communications, establish reference services, set up processes for users to request materials, provide a work environment for staff, work with regional libraries for assistance, and rely on electronic resources.

Chapter 7: Circulation
- Establish communications, deploy staff, determine future implications for circulation services, and mobilize operations like fines/overdues, book returns, reserves, preventive measures.

Chapter 8: Interlibrary Loan and Document-Delivery Services
- Streamline current ILL practices and procedures to prepare

ILL services for a possible disaster. Use automation to make the ILL operation portable.
- Employ the necessary resources for ILL to operate in disaster recovery: partner, retrain staff and hire new staff and design new services.

Chapter 9: Library Instruction
- Revise user-oriented materials, adjust instruction lectures, and provide instructional data as a result of the disaster for the administration.

Chapter 10: Reference Services
- Find alternative sites for services, staff communication, and relations, assess the damage to the public-services area, and transfer electronic reference services and telecommunications systems to a remote site.

Part III—Technical Services in Disaster Recovery

Chapter 11: Technical Services
- Rethink technical-service activities, reassign/relocate staff, establish work flow, and contact potential partners.
- Restore, replace, or rebuild a damaged collection: recommendations on insurance issues, working with vendors, and systems design.
- Deal with total-loss items and factors related to total-loss recovery such as costs, audit requirements, working with collection-management staff, and opportunities for enhancing a collection.
- Re-establish technical-services operations, issues involved with returning to the library, and dealing with new demands made on technical services.

Chapter 12: Creating Data on Damaged Collections
- Pose the right questions and understand the criticality of using an integrated library system (ILS) to manipulate and generate data for management decision making.
- Know the historical capabilities of your ILS and discuss the specific requests that require exploring and manipulating data to generate precise data sets for decision making.

Chapter 13: Information Technology
- Take the initial steps for technology recovery.
- Replace damaged technology equipment, networks, wiring, and infrastructure and install new automation.

Chapter 14: Technical Services Operations
- Carry on business-as-usual and provide continuity to technical services staff.
- Discover the organizational and human dimensions of the activities following a disaster.

Chapter 15: Implementing the Processing Center
- Design and implement a processing center to play a critical role in recovering damaged materials and, ultimately, getting them back on the shelves.
- Select the management, determine the size of the operation and time frames, design the facility, find a workforce, determine training issues, and maintain communications.

Part IV—The Fine Art of Gift Raising

Chapter 16: Gift-Raising Project
- Replace damaged materials with donations.
- Coordinate early efforts, control and exploit the solicitation message, and establish the four phases of gift solicitation.

Chapter 17: Re-design of the Gifts Programs
- Re-design and detail the eight steps to set up the program.
- Create teamwork and good communications, control/accountability, and the importance of records and paperwork.

Chapter 18: Gifts from Donors
- Accept and process gifts.

Chapter 19: Processing Donor Gifts
- Accept donations verbally, shipping concerns/instructions, receipt of gifts, and storage challenges.

Part V—Great Expectations for Restoring the Collection

Chapter 20: Special Projects
- Initiate independent projects early on in disaster recovery.

Chapter 21: Restoring the Collection
- Conceptualize and design the processing of damaged materials.
- Organize for the planning effort: define goals, identify expertise, assemble the planning team, and relate the plan to contracts for services.

Chapter 22: Repurchasing Books
- Work with insurance companies, estimate repurchasing costs for total losses, develop a model for per-volume costs, and identify and process exceptions to a mass repurchasing project.

Chapter 23: Material-Recovery Reports
- Identify what data to track, create, store, and retain.

Chapter 24: Quality Control
- Create systematic, well-defined measures for the processing effort that involves contractors and large numbers of untrained staff.
- Establish standards with error rates and determine when to perform quality control and how it should be performed.

Chapter 25: Gift-Materials Procedures
- Unpack and sort materials, match gifts to library-item records, update your databases, physical processing, shelving and circulation, statistics and reports, and anticipate problems.
- Establish costs relative to gift materials not used to replace damaged titles.

Part VI—Resource Sharing

Chapter 26: Resource-Sharing Strategies
- Develop strategies for potential resource sharing and what to do if there is no formal interlibrary resource-sharing plan in place.

Chapter 27: Colorado Alliance for Research Libraries
- The role this organization played in developing a resource-sharing environment and resource-sharing assistance in CSU's Morgan Library's disaster-recovery efforts.

While every library needs to plan for disasters, we certainly hope you never need to face the challenge of recovering from one. *The Library Disaster Planning and Recovery Handbook* is designed so that you may use it in a variety of ways. You may read it cover to cover as a way to make prudent preparations with advice from disaster-recovery veterans. You may also focus on an area of special interest or your field of expertise. As a very practical feature of this handbook, each chapter ends with a useful bulleted list of seasoned, first-hand "Key Recommendations." We hope sharing our experience will help your institution create a more secure future. We trust our handbook will provide the benefit of all good insurance. We hope that your library becomes safer by learning our lessons and that you are never forced to find out first hand.

PART ONE

Managing a Disaster

1   What Do You Do When It Happens To You?: Managing A Major Library Disaster

Camila Alire

INTRODUCTION

As a library administrator, you probably haven't given much thought to facing a major library disaster. If you have, you probably have thought that a major library disaster wouldn't ever happen during your administrative tenure. Well, watch out! That disaster could easily sneak up on you when you least expect it and bite you on the behind.

So much happens during major disaster response and recovery. Much of those areas are covered in other chapters. This chapter focuses on administrative strategies necessary in disaster recovery, internal issues in library disaster administration, institutional/organizational issues in library disaster recovery, and the influence of external groups. All of this could be categorized as what an administrator needs to consider should a library disaster strike. The chapter concludes with recommendations and lessons from one administrator who was so rudely bitten!

PERSONAL ACCOUNT:
BAPTISM BY FIRE, OR WAS IT WATER?

I had just completed my eighth working day as the new dean of Libraries at Colorado State University (CSU). I was just starting to become familiar with the operations of the libraries and the library staff. I had been toured around to most all of the departments in the Morgan Library except, ironically, those which were housed in the lower level of the library. I was getting to know the folks in the administrative suite better. I had already been to one Council of Deans meeting on campus where I met the other campus deans.

When I left campus for the day at 6:30 p.m. on Monday evening, July 28, 1997, it was just starting to "sprinkle." I got the infamous call around 10:30 that night from the assistant dean for Technical Services. I was so new to the Libraries that no one yet had my new home telephone number in Fort Collins. The assistant dean informed me that there was flooding on campus. My new home was in Fort Collins, but seven miles from campus. At my housing area, only a very light rainfall had fallen since 6:30 p.m.

I got the second call from the assistant dean around 10:45 p.m. saying that the lower level of Morgan Library was totally flooded. She had assured me that the library had a disaster plan and a disaster recovery team in place.

I jumped in the car and drove to campus but could not get across the train tracks which go through campus because a train had derailed due to the flooding of Spring Creek. Luckily, the end of the train was nearby so I was able to wade knee-deep through the fast-flowing water around the train and to the library. That was the first mistake—little did I know that the flow of water included the overflow of the sewage drains! I read later on in our *Disaster Recovery Manual* (1996) the phrase: "Do not walk in flood waters—they may be contaminated."

When I arrived at the library it was very eerie. There was no electricity anywhere on campus or in the area. The rain had stopped, but rushing water flowed all through campus. The library alarms were all sounding off. The water level was already at the second tier of the lower-level stairs in the library.

Understand that the predicament I found myself in as the new library dean was extraordinary. Not only did I have the challenge of a major library disaster, but I also was challenged by the fact that I was so new to the university. As I drove to work the morning after the disaster occurred, I was unsure what my role in this whole process would be.

By 7:00 the morning after the disaster, all members of the Library Disaster Recovery Team (LDRT) had arrived. There was no time to feel sorry for ourselves or others. We were all operating on adrenaline. I was told not only had our preservation librarian just given a workshop on disaster recovery earlier that year, but also that the LDRT had been through at least one disaster recovery drill. You can't imagine how relieved I was considering that I had just come from heading an academic library which had been putting off doing a disaster plan for other "priorities" (a fact of which I am not exactly proud).

Challenges

One of the major challenges I faced was not knowing key players either in the library or on campus. I knew nothing of their personalities, work and/or administrative styles, or any other characteristics a library dean would already know about people with whom he/she worked closely.

Another challenge we faced was dealing with uninformed perceptions coming from outside the library. Much misinformation was going to and coming from campus administration. Within several days after the disaster, campus administration had heard two recommendations from various internal and external folks concerning library disaster recovery.

The first was a recommendation not to attempt to recover any of the damaged journals but to replace them all with microforms. The second recommendation was not to recover any of the damaged materials (journals and monographs) but to move towards a completely digital library. When I heard these two recommendations in several meetings, I almost went through the roof. When the LDRT folks heard these recommendations, they went ballistic!

Immediately, we called in our head of serials, who was not an original member of the LDRT, to assist us. She was asked to estimate the cost of replacing all our back holdings of journal titles on microfilm. She did a sample study and showed that the cost would be in the millions of dollars! Once that cost become known by campus administrators, the microform idea was dropped like a hot potato.

The other idea of becoming a virtual/digital academic library was the concurrent thought that we had to lay to rest. First of all, let me make myself perfectly clear: we were not and are not opposed to the concept of a digital library. In fact, CSU Libraries, along with other members of the Colorado Alliance for Research

Libraries, has embraced this concept; and we are moving more and more towards providing the digital library to all our users.

However, for some campus administrators to say that we can start the digital library by not attempting to salvage our close to half a million volumes of damaged materials was ludicrous. To end this discussion, I asked the head of serials again to provide information on what were the limitations of this access. The limitations were that most journal titles were retrospective three to five years only and that they did not include images, editorials, or advertisements. And what about all the monographs in the world? The commercial, digital world was not quite yet ready to resolve this matter of recovering 462,500+ volumes in digital form. I shared this information with the campus administrators.

Last, but not least, was the challenge coming from the university president. Our disaster occurred the week before summer session finals. The president met with key administrators involved in disaster recovery and informed us that we had to be recovered and in full operation by the time fall semester started. Not to do so could possibly result in the loss of enrollment. Fall semester was only four weeks away and the pressure was on!

WHAT'S IN THE LITERATURE?

Although there is voluminous material on disaster response and recovery in general, there is much less in the literature specific to management aspects of disaster recovery. This section highlights key contributions in disaster recovery administration.

Thomas Drabek's (1987) work deals with the characteristics necessary for emergency response administrators to be successful. He conducted a study where emergency response administrators in two groups—selected randomly and non-randomly—were polled. Drabek's goals were to explore possible differences and similarities among these administrators to determine which strategies were most used and to determine whether size of community made a difference in those strategies.

His results found that the strategies used by emergency response administrators are very similar to other non-emergency administrators. That is, two strategies—coping well with environmental uncertainties and using interagency linkages (resource-sharing)—were critical to their success and effectiveness.

Even though Colorado State University Morgan Library's experience was after the fact, the following strategies Drabek lists as the result of his study are strategies that would help any type of administrator to be successful. I took his strategies and used them, where applicable, as a self-assessment of my administrative performance in the Morgan Library disaster recovery.

1. *Meet with other unit heads.* In our case, we met with campus folks immediately after and during disaster response and disaster recovery. Administratively, the library was the most organized in these two efforts and was the only unit that had a disaster plan.

2. *Establish personal commitments and credibility.* As the new dean, I had to do this the day immediately after the disaster. However, it may be your experience that, as an administrator, you have already accomplished this.

3. *Use your past background.* This is assuming that you already had experience in a major disaster/crisis. I found that the use of my management style/practices was very useful in directing the library's disaster recovery up and beyond those efforts of our disaster team. You will be amazed at how many of your management skills come into play in disaster recovery.

4. *Engage in consensus-building activities.* Those who know my administrative style know that consensus-building is a strong component of that style. Because you are dealing with various units, internally and externally, at any one time, consensus-building was crucial.

5. *Seek to coordinate not to control.* This strategy was key in working with the LDRT and with external groups who agreed to assist the library. This is probably one of the most important strategies you should use.

6. *Establish media relationships.* Although I had been on the job only a few days, I had already met with the local community newspaper reporter. Knowing him was instrumental in our working together for public relations purposes after the disaster occurred (see Chapter 5). Media Relations, both

on and off-campus, are very important for basic communications during emergency disaster response and for telling your story.

7. *Continue professional development.* This has been a mainstay of my career as an administrator. You will be surprised at how much more you learn and develop professionally through recovery efforts.

8. *Establish a professional network.* Luckily, as a library administrator, my professional network was already in place and was used throughout our disaster response and recovery efforts. No doubt, your situation will be similar. Do not hesitate to call on your network to assist you in disaster recovery.

9. *Tenacity is essential.* This goes without saying in disaster recovery. Do not let your university/organization's administration railroad you in the decision-making process of what is best for your library and library services in disaster recovery. You and your folks are the experts; nobody else on campus knows more about library disaster recovery than you do. That is why your campus and/or other administrators will hire consultants. They want to make sure that what you are advising them and the decisions you are making are sound. Additionally, tenacity is necessary when dealing with the consultants. You want to make sure they understand what you are doing and that they are supportive.

When describing administrative characteristics found through his research, Drabek goes on to report that successful emergency administrators have a high tolerance for ambiguity, have a commitment to the organization's mission, and believe they can make a difference.

Quarantelli (1997) preceded Drabek in disaster recovery research relative to emergency management of disasters. He is one the first leaders in disaster recovery research and was a co-founder of the Disaster Recovery Center, which is the premier research center of this kind in the nation. He is adamant that readers realize the difference between planning and managing a disaster. Even though they are related, the principles of each are different.

Quarantelli provides the top ten techniques for good disaster management. I have taken the liberty to add comments relative to library disaster recovery to his strategies.

1. *Understand the difference between* agent-related *needs/demands and* response-generated *needs /demands.* Basically, agent-related needs are the result of problems created by the disaster with the agent being the disaster itself. For example, sandbags (need) are used for floods (agent). The needs vary depending on the disaster, and pre-planning can only be partially anticipated.

   Response-generated demands are produced by the responding organization's efforts to manage the disaster. These demands are common in all disasters, such as demand for personnel, resources, communication, decision making, and coordination. Pre-planning takes more of a strategic approach.

2. *Carry-out generic function in adequate ways.* These functions are generic enough that they don't depend on the type of disaster. An example of this would be trying to find temporary work sites for displaced library staff, whether the disaster was a fire, tornado, flood, or hurricane.

3. *Get personnel and resources moving.* To this list I would add *services.* The sooner this can be done, beyond the library disaster recovery team's emergency response, the better.

4. *Involve appropriate task delegation and labor division.* This technique is crucial in library disaster recovery. Even though the library disaster recovery team has tasks assigned during emergency response, it is imperative during disaster recovery that larger more complex tasks be divided and handled by the most appropriate staff person or unit.

5. *Allow adequate process of information.* Quarantelli says that the usual problem is not the content of the information but the process (information flow). Make sure that your communication process starts immediately, no matter what format of communication is available. If the telecommunication systems are all down (telephones and computers),

daily notices at a designated location at or near the library will suffice. You will find that throughout the chapters in this book, good communications is consistently mentioned.

6. *Permit decision making.* Quarantelli warns that over-worked/extended disaster recovery folks can make bad decisions. Nonetheless, decisions have to be made. Make sure that you have a mechanism in place to define the decision-making process. Because the Morgan Library Disaster Recovery Team met twice a day—first thing in the morning and last thing in the afternoon—most of the potential decisions were discussed and made in those meetings. Everyone leaving the meeting would be aware of the decision(s) and what their individual role might be in carrying out the decision.

7. *Develop coordination.* According to Quarantelli, control is not coordination and that the best model for disaster recovery is where mutual cooperation takes place to get the task done. If you don't remember anything else, remember this: As a library administrator in the midst of a major disaster, do not be preoccupied with whether or not you are in charge, per se. Managing a disaster does not allow room for egos. There is so much to do in disaster recovery that the library director cannot be in charge or in control of everything. Coordination and cooperation are the best practices.

8. *Blend emergent methods with established ones.* The emergent phenomenon appears in all disasters. Basically, this means that when something has to get done, people will attempt to do it; or, if something can't be done the usual way, folks will attempt to do it a new way. A good example would be neighbors organizing quickly to look systematically for injured people in the neighborhood. A good example in library disaster recovery would be setting up temporary services. If the service is critical and can't be done the original way due to conditions, staff will think of an emergent way to blend new activity with old activity to get the service up and operating.

9. *Provide the mass communication system with appropriate information.* Quarantelli refers to the CNN model of mass communication. That is, reporters like those from CNN, whose sole purpose is to provide the news, expect information immediately. With this technique, you must make sure that relevant details and accounts of your disaster are disseminated to the media immediately or else these reporters and their networks will send out inaccurate news. This is no different when you, as a library administrator, are responsible for media relations relative to your library disaster (see Chapter 5).

10. *Have a good, well-functioning command center.* Whether your library is the only unit affected by a major disaster/crisis or is one of several units that have been affected, a library command center is crucial. This command center should be staffed by library staff who are not part of the library disaster recovery team. The disaster recovery team will have enough to do. However, everyone needs to know that there is one place where the necessary staff and equipment are available to help in emergency response and in disaster recovery. This command center should serve as the major coordination point. Make sure that you have several places designated in your disaster plan as potential command center sites.

Probably the best, most comprehensive, and most recent book on library disaster recovery was written by Miriam Kahn (1998). Her book concentrates not so much on preparing a disaster response plan but more on the nuts and bolts of library disaster response and recovery. Having experienced a major disaster now, I can assure you that Kahn covers every aspect of disaster recovery; she left nothing out.

Because there is a tendency to use the terms disaster response and disaster recovery synonymously, Kahn makes a distinction between the terms. According to Kahn, disaster response includes all the activities and decision making occurring until the disaster clean-up is finished. Disaster recovery, on the other hand, entails activities and decision making necessary to resume operations, such as getting the damaged books processed and returned and library renovation. Even though Kahn makes that distinction, the reality is that both activities can be operating at the same time.

Kahn recommends that in disaster recovery you need to bring up the most important and critical services first. This was very true in our case. However, we had to do that simultaneously with disaster response. That is, while we were pumping our water from the lower level, we were also moving our critical services to remote sites until we could start on permanent disaster recovery. Many students and faculty were on campus during the summer to do research only, and library services were crucial to their tasks.

"The larger and more wide scale the disaster, the more everything and everyone within the institution is affected" (Kahn, 1998: 13). Kahn's section on emotional issues was on target. She writes that the adrenaline and high emotions that are experienced by the library director and library disaster recovery team are sure causes of stress and guilt. These individuals work long hours trying to achieve what amounts to superhuman efforts. She provides some methodology to remedy some of these emotions. Those suggestions include relying on staff outside the disaster area for assistance; using consultants and contractors to assume some activities and, thereby, relieving some of the stress; and providing counseling. Other areas covered by Kahn include dealing with consultants and experts, morale, sick building syndrome, and many more.

INTERNAL ISSUES IN LIBRARY DISASTER RECOVERY ADMINISTRATION

Although the administration of any major disaster covers so many areas, this section highlights only a few areas of internal library disaster recovery administration: the recovery team process, restoration of library services, and staff communications. Probably a whole book could be written on the administration of our disaster recovery alone.

Library Disaster Recovery Team (LDRT) Process

The role of the LDRT is a pivotal one, both in emergency disaster response and, soon after, disaster recovery. Whoever is involved in the LDRT process must understand that process, especially the library director or the head of any other agency affected by a major disaster. I say this because my life would have been much easier had I been familiar with the overall LDRT process. In spite of my lack of knowledge, the head of the LDRT and her supervisor did an excellent job of informing me on a daily basis of where we were in the recovery process to date and what needed to be done next on a short- and long-term basis.

Take the time to review your disaster plan with your management team at least annually. This could include a cursory reading of the plan or a review of the plan to see if anything needs to be updated and/or revised due to different circumstances. Different circumstances could include processes such as a major library reorganization, a new library building, and/or the addition of an off-site book depository.

After disaster recovery is completed, it is important that your disaster plan and the LDRT process be evaluated and possibly revised. Once that is done, the head of the unit that has been affected should make recommendations to his/her administration.

I recall when one of the members of our LDRT suggested a couple of months after our disaster that we should begin evaluating our disaster plan and process while it was still fresh in our memories. Although that made sense, the timing was not good, as many of the LDRT were still very much involved in their regular job responsibilities as well as with disaster recovery responsibilities. Nonetheless, arrangements should be made to provide ample time to review your disaster plan and the LDRT process should a major disaster occur.

Who's Taking Care of the LDRT?

During major disaster response and recovery, the LDRT experiences an extraordinary amount of emotions and is operating day after day on adrenaline. The LDRT and the library director will work long hours in trying to accomplish what amounts to superhuman efforts. If the recovery process is slow, there may be a sense of hopelessness. All of this leads to mental stress that can be manifested in terms of physiological problems.

As an administrator, you need to pay special attention to the

LDRT and to yourself. Make them take breaks; bring lunch and treats in; strongly encourage them to take some time for themselves and their family; and make them laugh! Remember that, for whatever reasons, there is usually a sense of guilt that the disaster happened. Let your team members know that the disaster was no one's fault.

Some LDRT members might be single; take their situations into consideration. Many of them may have pets which can cause problems when working extra long hours on a daily basis. Be flexible and give them administrative leave time to get personal affairs done.

If at all possible, do not schedule LDRT meetings and tasks during the weekends. This is more easily said than done, especially during the first several weeks of disaster response and recovery. However, depending upon the scale of the disaster, you will have more control of time and activities as disaster recovery progresses.

Most importantly, as the chief administrator, bring a positive attitude to work everyday. This may be hard to do day after day of long hours, little sleep, and much stress. However, you need to remember that the LDRT looks to you for setting the tone. This tone should reflect a sense of accomplishment; a sense of appreciation and acknowledgment, praising tasks and efforts accomplished; and a sense of humor.

Because disaster recovery may take months or years, remember to acknowledge publicly all those who continue to be involved in the recovery process. There may be a tendency to acknowledge staff during the peak of disaster recovery. However, you will have staff who have not only their regular responsibilities to do but also ongoing disaster recovery responsibilities added to their regular responsibilities. These staff members can easily be lost in the mundane process of disaster recovery if it goes on more than several months. Don't forget to acknowledge their efforts continuously.

So who's going to take care of you, the administrator? If you have a strong family behind you, draw on their strength. If you only have friends available, use them for your support system. But find a support system *outside* of the disaster arena and your workplace. Practice what you preach when supporting the emotional needs of the LDRT.

Remember that when you are trying to relax on the weekends, people will want to hear all about your past week(s) of disaster recovery efforts. If you can, explain events briefly, but don't feel bad about politely excusing yourself from not discussing it because you live disaster recovery all week.

Restoration of Temporary Library Services

Once staff whereabouts and safety are confirmed in a major disaster, the next order of business, along with emergency disaster response (e.g., getting the water pumped out of the lower level), is to establish temporary library services to minimize the interruption of business. Critical services should be restored. Your disaster recovery manual should identify the various coordinators involved in the LDRT and their specific functions in disaster recovery.

In terms of library services, critical functions for business service operations should include high-priority tasks, temporary operating procedures, facilities requirements, requirements for equipment, forms, and supplies, and minimum operational staff (Colorado State University Libraries, 1996).

Command Center Operations

Hand-in-hand with restoration of library services is the setting up of a central command center for LDRT operations. You will need this command center even if your institution or city/county has its own. This location should be central to all of your disaster recovery operations. All centralized communications should come from the command center. The command center should have appropriate telecommunications and other equipment installed. It should have all the supplies necessary to accomplish business operations.

The Morgan Library's command center was set up in an unaffected building next to the library. Although the size of the center was around six feet by twelve feet, it was equipped with a telephone, personal computer with e-mail capabilities, office supplies, message board, and mail service. It was staffed all hours of operation by members of the administrative suite staff. All LDRT members knew to check in at the command center each morning. Most of them had cellular phones with free services provided by a cellular company. All cellular phone numbers were recorded on the message board. The use of cellular telephones was very important and provided an invaluable link with staff and also gave us the capability to address disaster recovery efforts.

The command center staff had access to a photocopier and a fax machine in the host office next door. Until we were able to secure a conference room assigned exclusively to the library, we held meetings in chairs lined up in the hallway outside the command center. The staff and administration of our host office were very tolerant of invasion.

Communications with Staff

Without a doubt, this aspect of internal library administration in disaster response and disaster recovery is one of the most important areas to consider and to act upon. Any kind of major disaster which hits an organization can be devastating, even to those staff members not directly involved in the disaster response and recovery. In fact, their lack of involvement can work against good staff morale. Therefore, communicating with all library staff is critical.

In our case, because Morgan Library was off-limits to unauthorized library personnel for weeks, the first official communication process instituted was through our answering machine in Access Services, which provided almost a daily update of recovery status. Additionally, unofficial communication was occurring daily between the LDRT members and their respective coordinators. The intent was that the coordinators would then inform their respective staff.

However, it came to my attention several weeks after the disaster that, although most library staff were employed in remote sites or at home, and several had remote e-mail access, they were feeling disenfranchised from the recovery process. Immediately upon hearing this, we made arrangements for weekly meetings with the entire library staff to give them a complete update of recovery efforts and to listen to comments and concerns from staff. These meetings were extremely helpful in lessening the staff concerns on disaster recovery and in increasing the morale of the entire staff.

Do not assume that your internal communications process is adequate. Have plenty of feelers out to learn about any discontent or low morale that might be occurring. How the administration communicates during *emergency* disaster response (e.g., answering machine in Access Services) should differ from how the administration communicates during disaster *recovery*. During an emergency, it is understandable that staff communications may not be elaborate. However, once the LDRT and the library administration move into disaster *recovery*, the communication process for all staff should be more detailed and should be in a forum where information can be shared and where staff members can comment and ask questions. In fact, no matter how long disaster recovery should take, these regular meetings to update your staff are still very important. Kahn (1998) substantiates that low morale can be changed if the administration meets with the affected staff regularly.

Time Commitment

Depending on the extent of the disaster, time commitment could vary. However, never underestimate the time you, as the chief library administrator, and/or other deputy administrators will spend on disaster recovery. It is an unbelievable amount of time.

There are usually four demands on administrative staff time (director, associate directors, and other members of the regular, pre-disaster management team, as well as the coordinator of the LDRT) in disaster recovery:

- Emergency disaster response
- Disaster recovery activities
- Contract negotiations
- Insurance negotiations

Depending on who is involved in what, all of these demands on time can affect you and your administrative staff's regular duties, responsibilities, and workload. And, don't expect to get reimbursed for the time the staff spends on disaster recovery. Consultants can help with some of the activities; however, when they are gone, you might still be facing two to five years of disaster recovery. The time commitment is a critical factor.

The point to remember is that there are only so many hours in the day and week. Be cognizant of your administrative staff's commitments. Be able to prioritize in terms of the demands you make on their time, whether they are disaster related or regular work related.

At the time of publication, we will be almost through three years of major disaster recovery, with anywhere from two to three more years to complete our disaster recovery work. As the library dean, my chief concern is burnout of library personnel. Remember that all of you will be doing two jobs during this time: juggling your regular responsibilities and disaster recovery responsibilities.

INSTITUTIONAL ISSUES IN LIBRARY DISASTER RECOVERY

Institutional Coordination and Cooperation

Depending on whether or not a major disaster occurs to one unit on campus or within a community (e.g., disastrous building fire) or to an entire campus/community, there will be a need for intra-institutional coordination. Taking Colorado State University as example, where the disaster affected the entire campus, there was much need for intra-institutional coordination.

Be prepared to work within the framework where your library disaster, major as it is, will be but one of several units affected by the disaster. This complicates things greatly. You may find yourself having to get approval from teams such as a disaster finance team that is concerned about the fiscal implications of the disaster and insurance-related concerns. The purpose of such a group is to coordinate all disaster recovery efforts relative to fiscal affairs. It is a very critical team, and you need to make sure you understand the parameters, functions, and responsibilities of this team so that you can fiscally manage your disaster more efficiently and within the boundaries of the finance team.

As the director of your library/unit, you must establish a rapport with members of this group. You will probably already know all the members of this finance team, but it is necessary to re-establish rapport in the disaster recovery context.

Another possible intra-institutional team with whom you will need to coordinate could be the campus emergency disaster recovery team. Usually, this team is already designated in the campus disaster recovery plan. Some of the members could include representatives such as the campus heads of administrative services, facilities, academic affairs, campus security, personnel, risk management, or environmental health services.

If your library or unit is one of the most affected units by the disaster, negotiate to have your library represented at this team's meeting table, even in an ex officio or liaison basis. This did not occur in Morgan Library's situation. We never did determine who was adequately representing academic affairs (which is where the library belongs organizationally) on this team. Had we been sitting at the same table, some major miscommunications in the beginning could have been eliminated.

Be prepared for disaster recovery ad hoc committees. These will surface as recovery needs and demands change and will usually report to one of the main disaster recovery teams. Again, make sure that your unit is represented someway on these ad hoc committees. This is where your tenacity technique, mentioned earlier, is essential. To be involved in these intra-institutional teams is vital to good communications, coordination, and cooperation among all the units that are involved in disaster recovery.

Critical Action Points for the Library

Critical action points of disaster recovery for your library/organization refer to the messages you, as an administrator, deliver within your institution beginning in emergency disaster response and continuing through disaster recovery. This is more than internal public relations. This is critical action necessary to inform other campus administrators (campus deans, faculty governance, or faculty/students/staff) of exactly what steps are being taken to handle the disaster and to restore temporary critical services, and permanent services later on.

Once your plan of action is determined, you must prepare strategically so that these action points are disseminated immediately to the most appropriate audiences. During the first several weeks of emergency disaster response, we had two critical points of action. The first was explaining the effect of the disaster on library space and materials and exactly what measures the library was doing to address this recovery. The second critical points of action delivered concerned five areas of temporary service which would be in place on or before the start of fall semester (see Chapter 6).

The strategic preparation for sharing your action points should include key members of your management team, whether or not they are part of the LDRT. Your discussions should identify the key audiences, a succinct message covering your action points, and the timing of your message.

No matter how inundated you are in the response/recovery process, make time to do this. This is part of the communication process to get key points out to your campus community. It basically establishes your plans of action for you, other members of the library, your academic chief, and even your campus president/chancellor.

Operational Plans and Cost Estimating

In reviewing library disaster recovery plans and reading retrospectively about disaster response and planning, I found no reference to preparing operational plans and estimating costs for those plans.

In the case of having to provide alternative public services (e.g., *FastFlood* project—see Chapter 8) and alternative technical services (e.g., Processing Center—see Chapter 15), you must be prepared to design and present operational plans for these alternative operations and to include cost estimates for each plan. There is sound rationale for this.

First of all, you need to think and plan out exactly how these alternative services will be handled. This has to be done with such care and detail so that no cost factor is excluded. Having said that, I will add that, in some cases, you may only have several days to complete this process! Secondly, you need to affix some costs to these alternative services. This is extremely important if you plan to ask your institution and/or insurance representatives for additional monies other than those funds from your general base budget. Thirdly, your administration and/or insurance representative will scrutinize every activity and cost factor presented. Be prepared for frustrating, sometimes demoralizing, discussions with these groups.

To do this, you need to consider the following factors:

1. *Activities.* These need to be identified and completely and clearly defined because they are what drive all the other variables.

2. *Personnel.* Will additional personnel need to be hired to complete these activities? If so, have all job responsibilities and descriptions developed. Administration and/or insurance representatives will review these with a fine-tooth comb.

3. *Equipment/supplies.* Do these alternative services require more equipment, telecommunications needs, and supplies? Your plan should include supply minutiae needed such as additional book trucks, desks/chairs, staplers, etc. Always keep in mind that your general operating budget, like most libraries, is probably inadequate as is, so every additional disaster recovery-related cost should be identified and listed.

4. *Space.* Is additional space needed to conduct these activities? If your building will be unavailable for a long period of time, this factor could be extensive and costly.

5. *Partnerships.* Are there other units on campus and/or external agencies that need to be involved to provide these alternative services? This is a very important factor. If partnerships are necessary, get your partners to agree to the relationships, describe them in great detail, and affix costs, if any.

6. *Outsourcing.* Is it more efficient and economical to outsource part or all of a particular alternative service? In order to determine this, your staff will have to find the time to do some type of comparative analysis, because either your administration or the insurance people will want to see the comparison.

7. *Costs.* Once you have addressed all the factors mentioned, what are the costs to provide your alternative public and/or technical services?

8. *Documentation.* Make sure to keep a record of everything during disaster recovery. This documentation is critical when dealing with campus administration, insurance representatives, and *finger-pointers!*

You may also find yourself preparing your operational plans without having adequate or any information. If that is the case, spend enough time with the appropriate members of your management team to develop clear assumptions on which to base your services and their factors. This is not an easy task because, as administrators, we are not used to working with such unknowns when trying to determine services and cost estimates.

In our case, what we are doing, in terms of recovery of almost a half million damaged volumes, has never been done. There was no one to call to find out *how they did it.* We found ourselves determining assumptions almost on a daily basis.

Also, be prepared to defend your operational plans and cost estimates to lay people who have no idea about libraries, library operations, and library services; who think that putting a book back on the shelf does not require any technical services component and costs; and who will question every item and related costs in your plan. Also be prepared for the need for validation. This could be in the form of statistical validation to support your position or in the form of hiring consultants, auditors, and/or vendors to provide appropriate information and/or financial figures to prove the feasibility of your plan.

In our case, we hired vendors as consultants to work out pricing models. We employed experts from our statistics department to assist us in our random sampling efforts. Additionally, we hired a rare-book expert as a consultant to help us determine how to assess *loss value* to a volume. All of these people were hired to validate our plans with university administrators, the disaster recovery finance team, and the insurance representatives.

All of this may be the most frustrating experience you will ever have. However, never lose sight of your ultimate purposes to provide temporary alternative services to your primary clientele and to provide appropriate technical services to complete disaster recovery.

Organizational Culture and Politics

I thought long and hard about whether or not to include this topic in this chapter. However, organizational/campus culture and politics is a fact of life everywhere. So, the fact that campus politics should occur during a disaster and its recovery process should be of no surprise. Almost all library administrators are already aware of the leadership and political culture of their parent organization, such as: Who are the strong campus administrators? Who are the insecure ones? Who are the power hungry? Who can be trusted and who can't? Who believes in laissez faire? And so on.

During disaster recovery, much of your organizational culture will not change except that the characteristics seem to escalate. If, like me at the time, you don't have a clue about the organizational culture and politics, it can prove for some very interesting moments during disaster recovery.

Understand that the cultural characteristics and politics will intensify. Be prepared for some folks to try to position themselves at the most inopportune time—even in the midst of major disaster recovery. Pray that your library/unit's disaster is not the paramount one (that is, the most costly in recovery efforts and the most extensive in terms of time) for your university or organization. And, most of all, pray that the administrator to whom you report is a strong leader in the organization.

If you are politically and culturally savvy within your organization, you should be able to work with and work around some of these institutional characteristics. Just understand that they will surface.

EXTERNAL GROUPS

Consultants

"Seldom are we prophets in our homeland" (Drabek, 1987: 250). The use of consultants can be helpful in advancing proposals, ideas, or methodology that you might not be successful in doing.

Even if the LDRT thinks that they can handle disaster response and recovery, consultants do not have the emotional ties to your collection/services and, consequently, can provide objective choices and options. Consultants can be used to work with your LDRT and help relieve the day-to-day stress of the director. They can prepare proposals, recommendations, and overall cost estimates for disaster recovery. They can write bid specifications for subcontractors and supervise your library clean-up, as well as work with insurance representatives (Drabek, 1987; Kahn, 1998).

If your disaster recovery plan does not have a list of consultants available for library disaster recovery expertise, it should. It is not hard to check the library and preservation communities to get names of reliable consultants.

As with probably any disaster, the consultant phenomenon was alive and well at Colorado State University. The university hired a consultant to manage the first few weeks of emergency disaster response for the entire university; and he hired a library consultant. FEMA (Federal Emergency Management Agency) hired library consultants from the Library of Congress and the insurance companies hired a consultant who knew nothing about libraries! Our contractor for the Processing Center hired four consultants who were preservation experts, and, as mentioned, we hired a consultant to help us determine a loss value process for damaged volumes.

Part of the consultant phenomena you may need to prepare for is the resentment that your staff may feel about any one of the consultants, especially if some of your staff members are considered as experts in the same area. What can be most frustrating to some members of the LDRT and/or staff is when it takes a consultant to affirm all their work and plans to your administration.

However, as the library director, you need to think more broadly on how the consultant can further your own agenda in disaster recovery. Because hiring a consultant with recognized expertise is a commonly used strategy in disaster recovery, accept that if they are not hired by the library, they will be hired by others.

Another part of the consultant phenomena will be that top-level administrators in your institution or city/county government will believe almost everything a consultant tells them as the gospel truth. If that is the case, then use the consultants to your and your library's benefit. I strongly recommend that you develop a good communicative relationship with each consultant. Library consultants speak the same language you and your staff do and want to be helpful. Their reputation depends on it. How a library consultant performs in your estimation is what counts. Fellow library administrators around the country are not going to call your university/organization administration for a reference on a library consultant; they are going to call you or your staff.

When appropriate, don't forget to remind your administration after the consultant's report or advice has been submitted that those were the same results your folks had originally reported to them. Believe it or not, it will at least make your staff feel better!

What about consultants who are not library professionals? How do you and your staff work with them? My recommendations are no different than what has already been mentioned. However, I would add one word of caution: You may not have any influence in their work or their recommendation if they are declared *off-limits* to the library staff and/or administration. This could happen. If it does, and you disagree with their findings, make sure to go on record explaining those areas with which you disagree and why. As an example, our major contractor and a member of the university's Disaster Finance Team went to great lengths to keep key library personnel from submitting questions/information to meetings with a group of preservation consultants prior to their releasing their report. We have a record of our response to the consultants' report.

Contractors

Your disaster recovery plan should include the names of library disaster recovery contractors and how to contact them. Remember that you may be restricted by bidding requirements. There should be something in your disaster plan that covers institutional procedures in case of an emergency. Also, remember that your insurance representatives may want a say in the selection of disaster recovery contractors.

In our case, we needed to hire a contractor to provide the equipment and services to stabilize immediately our temperature and humidity levels. We estimated the contract to cost around $250,000 and did not have the time to complete a bid process. Twenty hours after the disaster occurred, I had an emergency meeting with the university's Disaster Finance Team to get permission to hire the contractor. I provided them with the facts and rationale for an exception to normal contracting processes. It was granted. In a subsequent campus meeting, the Disaster Finance Team recognized that emergency purchases for large amounts of money might be necessary and told everyone that all emergency disaster recovery expenses had to be approved by the chair of the finance team.

Contracting or outsourcing disaster recovery projects can be very beneficial to your library. It relieves the stress of an overworked staff; it makes someone else responsible for temporary personnel issues; and, in many cases, it can be more efficient and less expensive.

In terms of the contracting process, keep the following tips in mind:

1. Make sure the contract specifies to whom the contractor reports and answers. More importantly, make sure that, if the contracted work is for library disaster recovery work, the designated administrator is responsible for the contract and the contractor's performance. In our case, because we thought I had signed the contract with our major contractor, we assumed he reported to the library. When disagreements occurred between the contractor and the library, we discovered that the vice president for Administrative Services ultimately was responsible for the contractor and that my signature was for contract text approval only. Because of this, the contractor's reporting line continues to be a bone of contention for the library.

2. When time allows, follow the normal contracting procedures established by the institution. However, in emergency disaster response, you may not have the benefit of time. Coordinate appropriately with the powers that be to hire the much-needed contractor.

3. Have the appropriate addenda included in the contract, especially if certain specifications are crucial to contract compliance.

4. If the contractor must hire subcontractors, be sure that the library has a strong voice on determining duties, responsibilities, work specifications, quality control, etc. The same type of involvement stands for the contractor's hiring of consultants.

5. Make sure to include the role of the library in monitoring the contractor's work. Because of this, you need to insure that you have something systematically in place to monitor your contractor's work and quality control.

LESSONS LEARNED

The intent of this chapter is to guide any library administrator through the real nuts and bolts of managing a library disaster. This chapter focuses on administrative strategies necessary in disaster recovery, internal issues in library disaster administration, institutional/organizational issues in library disaster recovery, and the influence of external groups.

In the review of the literature relative to library disaster recovery, few authors have been in a position to write about disaster recovery *after* the disaster. As the chief library administrator during this major disaster recovery process, I now have the opportunity to share 16 key lessons I have learned, so far. The chapter ends with the following general recommendations for administrators from one colleague to another.

LESSON 1. Don't think this will never happen to you!

LESSON 2. As the chief library administrator, make sure to rely heavily on your in-house experts. They know best how to handle the situation and what to advise for further action. Having said that, realize that you will have to work with the external consultants and be prepared to maintain the peace between them and staff.

LESSON 3. Be willing and ready to take proposed actions for the appropriate institutional/insurance approval. If you think the proposed action is critical for safety and/or emergency recovery, be very assertive and don't take "no" for an answer.

LESSON 4.   Do not dwell on snafus or mistakes made. Fix them, if possible, and discuss what needs to be done to prevent them from happening again.

LESSON 5.   Deal with any misinformation immediately and provide the necessary data to insure all institutional parties are well-informed. Perceptions and misguided advice can seriously damage recovery efforts.

LESSON 6.   Set up regularly established meetings with your library disaster recovery team and make sure that, as the chief administrator, you are included in key campus/institutional meetings.

LESSON 7.   Keep excellent lines of communications open. This prevents any misunderstandings, mistakes, and rumors.

LESSON 8.   Keep your immediate supervisor or his/her representative apprised of all issues, concerns, and/or successes. Make sure he/she is represented in key meetings and/or negotiations.

LESSON 9.   Keep all library personnel informed at the beginning of emergency response by designating one individual to channel information to those not involved in emergency disaster response.

LESSON 10. Hold frequent meetings of all staff to keep them informed and to answer questions/concerns, no matter how busy you and other members of the recovery team are.

LESSON 11. Keep the disaster recovery team fed because of the extended hours they will work and have plenty of *emotional* health or junk food available.

LESSON 12. Keep a positive attitude for the rest of the team and for the staff. They will feed off your spirit.

LESSON 13. Maintain a healthy sense of humor. Show folks you are human too.

LESSON 14. Don't forget to share your appreciation of all efforts with your disaster recovery team and to thank them at the end of each day.

LESSON 15. Realize that disaster recovery efforts continue even after the emergency response phase. Continue to acknowledge all staff involved in any aspect of disaster recovery.

LESSON 16. Do not take anything personal! People throughout your campus/organization are all under a lot of stress.

Library Disaster Planning and Recovery Handbook

KEY RECOMMENDATIONS

Disaster Management

- Make sure that your library anticipates readiness by having a disaster plan and library disaster recovery team in place.
- Be prepared to respond to well-intentioned, higher-level administrators' misconceptions of what can and should be done in library disaster recovery.
- Understand that your president or chief executive officer will have enormous pressures in seeing that your campus/organization recovers quickly. Support that individual.
- Enlist *every* administrative/leadership skill you possess to assist you through disaster recovery management.
- Coordinate efforts; do not try to control them.
- Use your professional network, as appropriate, to help your library through the recovery process.
- Communicate, communicate, communicate.
- Be concerned about the library disaster recovery team's mental, emotional, and physical health during disaster recovery.
- Be flexible or you will go crazy!
- Make sure to coordinate recovery efforts with other units/individuals on campus.
- Be prepared for unreasonable requests and deadlines for activities such as providing operational plans and cost estimates. Just do it!
- Understand that there will be external folks who will be involved in your disaster recovery efforts at one point or another; accept that and work with them.
- Be obnoxiously involved in any contract development, specifications, and negotiations relative to library disaster recovery work.
- Make sure contractors doing exclusively library disaster recovery work report to the designated library administrator in charge of disaster recovery.
- Realize that you and your staff have a life beyond disaster recovery and beyond the workplace regardless of the conditions there. Live it!

REFERENCES

Colorado State University Libraries. 1996. *Disaster Recovery Manual*.

Drabek, Thomas E. 1987. *The Professional Emergency Manager: Structures and Strategies for Success*. Boulder, CO: Institute for Behavioral Sciences, University of Colorado.

Kahn, Miriam B. 1998. *Disaster Response and Planning for Libraries*. Chicago: American Library Association.

Quarantelli, E. L. 1997. "Ten Criteria for Evaluating the Management of Community Disasters." *Disasters* 21, No. 7: 42–51.

2 Human Resources Implications in Disaster Recovery

Teri Switzer

INTRODUCTION

Human resource involvement in crisis management is extremely important; however, it is usually overlooked until a crisis occurs. In the event of a disaster, the human resource unit has a two part role: a responsibility for its internal operations and staff and the development of close ties with outside sources (Barton and Wellheiser, 1985). The exact role human resources plays in the disaster recovery effort can vary, depending on the organization and the disaster. In general, human resource specialists serve as resource consultants and as advisors to three critical areas of disaster recovery: people, information technology, and facilities (Strouse 1995).

Once a disaster hits, the human resource specialist has to pull out these different hats and start wearing them as necessary. While there are no definite dos and don'ts, there are several tips that can make a hectic period more organized and efficient. This chapter gives several tips and pointers to implement when dealing with personnel issues during the aftermath of a disaster.

WATER, WATER, EVERYWHERE

Following the July 28 disaster, the realization of the importance of being prepared hit as hard and fast as the waters did. It's common that most people don't think a disaster with a magnitude as great as the one that hit Colorado State University would ever occur. But, it did, and although a disaster plan was in effect, it certainly has not been a substitute for the real thing.

To me, the most unsettling aspect of Morgan Library's disaster recovery operation was that when the rampant waters broke through the building, I was impatiently awaiting a flight to central Illinois that was already five hours late. Even when I arrived at the small nursing home at 6:00 a.m., where my sister lay dying of cancer, I didn't know of the devastation that had occurred in Fort Collins. However, within minutes of my walking through the door, I received two shocks: the realization of how gravely ill my sister was and the news of the devastating event in Fort Collins. My hometown for 25 years had fallen under Mother Nature's spell. The news media painted a dismal picture and not being able to get through to either my home or to the library clouded my hazy thinking even more, and anxiety set in. What happened at home? What happened in the library, the university? Where was everyone? How could I help from 1,000 miles away?

The news reports kept me at bay, and after reaching my Colorado family in the early evening, I was back on track. Phone contact with the library finally occurred August 1st and my mind was more at rest. By the time I returned to Colorado State University on August 5th, things were well under control and I was able to hit the ground running, knowing that our staff members were being taken care of.

PEOPLE, PEOPLE, EVERYWHERE: RE-EMPLOYING STAFF

During the summer of 1997, the University Libraries employed 75 support staff, 34 faculty, and approximately 75 students. All but three support staff and seven students were employed in the main campus library, Morgan Library, and all but these ten staff were affected by the disaster at Morgan Library and needed a place to work and a job that could be done given the obvious constraints.

In any disaster or crisis situation, the human resource specialist has several tasks. The first, and most obvious, is the placement of staff in alternate worksites that still give them the ability to perform their assigned tasks. Within four days of the disaster, alternate worksites for permanent staff had been arranged. Interlibrary Loan was housed in a community college library four miles away and in a small, on-campus classroom that was wired for Internet access. Reference services first went to the Veterinary Teaching Hospital Branch Library then moved to a computer lab on campus. Cataloging, the preservation lab, acquisitions, and government documents found space in the on-campus book depository. Library technology services and administration were housed in unused offices elsewhere on campus, and special collections took their operations to a staff member's home.

ALTERNATE WORKSITE CONSIDERATIONS

The task of arranging worksites for more than a couple people normally proves to be an arduous one. Most libraries are short of space, and finding unused office space on university campuses can be difficult. Some suggestions to keep in mind are:

1. Know what kind and how much space you absolutely must have.
   - Don't even think of providing office space for everyone. Double and triple the staff in each office available.
   - Pair people either by "function," main responsibilities, and/or by amount of time spent in the office area. Consider pairing a high use on-site employee (e.g., secretary, personnel, accounting) with someone who can do some of their work from home, such as materials selector/bibliographer.

2. Determine what positions or which staff have to be centrally located.
   - Reference
   - Interlibrary loan
   - Circulation/Reserve
   - Administration

3. Determine those tasks that can be done remotely.
   - Database maintenance
   - Government document processing
   - Cataloging
   - Acquisitions
   - Gifts and exchange

- Electronic reference
- Interlibrary loan (if remote access is available).

4. Do you need telephone lines? Can you use cell phones?

5. Is Internet access needed? Can laptop computers be used?

6. Is it possible to retrieve equipment/furniture from the disaster site?
   - Consider using rental agencies for tables, chairs, and lamps.
   - Use furniture from personal homes.
   - Contact the campus surplus unit and arrange for desk, table, and chair "loaners."

Student/Hourly Staff

Student and hourly staff also need to be considered in the setup of temporary office space. Most student and hourly employees depend on working a given number of hours weekly in order to meet their bills; so when a disaster hits, it's important to consider temporary placement of hourly employees. The July 1997 disaster occurred only two weeks before the end of the twelve-week summer session, and many student staff take off a week between the end of summer session and the start of the fall semester. However, not all of the Morgan Library student staff had planned on being gone, and missing two to four weeks of salary was potentially devastating to these students.

Most libraries are capable of offering their normal services in a disaster, but these services might need to be pared down and staffing needs could be a fraction of what is normally needed. This is where creativity must be used and departments should be encouraged to consider all tasks that could still be done. Some examples of alternate placement of students for you to consider include:

- Use students who have personal computer equipment to word process those long-awaited pathfinders and bibliographies at home.
- Assign students to staff the doors or perimeter of the disaster site to field questions and accept returned books.

- Contact other campus departments and offer them extra help. If possible, split the salary with the hiring department.
- Enlist students to help in setting up temporary offices, carting materials across campus, and/or making hand deliveries of library materials to patrons.
- Set up information booths around campus to field questions and direct campus visitors to buildings and parking.

Although the relocation of displaced temporary employees seems effortless, it very likely won't be. There are several tips that should be followed to make the alternate placement a success:

- Have a readily accessible, up-to-date listing of names, addresses, and phone numbers of current student staff. Each department head/supervisor should have a list of the students working for them. If possible, keep a list at home as well as at work.
- Take the time to call each student with information about what happened and to make alternate work arrangements. Keep them informed.
- Assure the students that they will not lose their jobs unless absolutely necessary.
- Be proactive and seek ways in which student staff can be used. Most students will be more than happy doing anything, as long as they are working and making money.
- Try not to decrease a student's hourly pay rate, even though lesser duties are being performed.
- Work with campus and community offices to ensure that students will be paid either the same pay rate or one as close as possible. If feasible, contribute the difference in the pay rate.
- Consider setting up a care package of gift certificates, coupons, food items, etc. for students whose personal belongings might have been affected by the disaster.

ERGONOMIC CONCERNS

The University Libraries has worked diligently during the past ten years to ensure that staff practice proper ergonomic principles. Along with the relocation of Morgan Library staff was the need to consider steps to take in order to maintain the practice of proper workstation placement. In fact, a few staff specifically requested that ergonomics be addressed in the alternate worksites. Although it may be difficult, or even impossible, to set up temporary offices as they should be, do the best that you can. Keep these suggestions in mind:

- Position the monitor so it is 19-29" from the front of the operator's body.
- Body should be positioned at a 90° angle.
- If at all possible, use an adjustable chair. Bring a chair from one's home office, or retrieve chairs from the worksite that have been undamaged.
- Use blocks of wood, phone books, binders, etc. to raise the monitor to the proper height.
- Take frequent breaks when working at a workstation that can't be properly adjusted.
- Provide task lighting. Use pole lamps, clip-on lights, or battery-operated camp lanterns for areas that have no power or have inaccessible electrical sockets.
- Adjust the chair and monitor when getting ready to work.
- Remind staff to adjust the workstations. Many staff aren't used to sharing a personal computer with others, so they may need to be shown how to adjust the chair and move the monitor up or down to the proper height.

A FLOOD OF EMOTIONS; DEALING WITH STRESSED STAFF

Let's take a look at what took place at Morgan Library following the July 28th disaster. Seven staff lost their offices, including personal papers and effects that were kept at work, and 120 faculty and support staff and approximately 75 student staff were unable to return to work due to lack of power, water, and the fact that the campus was under water. In addition, six permanent staff lost part of their homes or cars in the disaster and one staff member witnessed the books and the work space where he had just been working on his doctoral dissertation destroyed under eight and a half feet of water and sludge.

As described above, the disaster directly impacted all library staff; some more than others, but everyone felt the effects. This brings us to study how employees are affected by crises and/or disasters. Generally, when crises occur, physical, as well as emotional, distresses are created. Those people who are impacted by a crisis often suffer from some kind of stress. One type of stress is "crisis stress," which is better known as traumatic stress (Blythe, 1992). Traumatic stress occurs in any potentially life-threatening event that causes people to experience unusually strong emotional reactions and pushes them beyond their normal coping abilities and interferes with their ability to function (Blythe, 1992). Nearly every one of our staff members suffered from some sort of stress, and interpersonal relationships among some staff were strained.

Organizational Intervention : Internal

In the event staff appear to exhibit traumatic stress or a breakdown in effective working relationships due to the crisis occurs, it is important to get professional help immediately. Most often, disaster plans don't provide measures for recognizing or treating traumatic stress or interpersonal issues. Although only one library employee appeared to be suffering from traumatic stress, the need for organizational intervention was present. Not having had the experience dealing with traumatic stress, the subsequent handling of this staff member was not as caring as it could or should have been. If confronted with possible traumatic stress, these steps are recommended:

- Offer sympathy and support.
- Encourage, and if needed, demand that the individual seek professional assistance from the agencies' workers compensation provider (mental health care specialist is preferred).
- Ensure staff that any time lost from work will be considered either administrative leave or fall under workers' compensation allowances.
- Give assurance that the employee will not be terminated.

In general, traumatic stress is rare, but it can, and does, occur. Nevertheless, it is important to address stress-related disorders. Some symptoms of stress are headaches, problems sleeping, changes in appetite, feelings of anger, suspicion, and irritability.

Kerry Grosser (1985) has written several articles about stress and organizational intervention and has developed a model that divides organizational solutions for solving stress into three sections:

- Those aimed at changing organizational characteristics such as policies and procedures and programs.
- Those aimed at changing role characteristics such as reducing workload.
- Those aimed at changing task or job characteristics such as job redesign (Grosser, 1985).

Using this model, it is advisable to put the following measures into place:

- Relax policies and procedures. Let staff wear comfortable clothes, drink coffee at their desks, or hold potlucks on the lawn.
- Reduce workloads and consider changing how some tasks are done. Try a rotation schedule and schedule staff in shifts. This will lessen the burden of trying to find work space for everyone and will also give some staff the ability to work more independently than normal.
- Redesign jobs where appropriate. Put cross-training and job-sharing to use (Switzer, 1998).

As stated earlier, crisis planning in organizations generally focuses on material objects such as computers, data, systems, paper, and books. Seldom is the survival of the employees addressed. It is advisable to make sure the personnel/human resources side of your library is involved when drafting a crisis management plan, and make sure intervention programs should be identified before a crisis occurs.

Organizational Intervention: External

Another aspect of dealing with stress is teaching coping techniques (Bunge, 1989). Most universities, colleges, city agencies, and large corporations have employee assistance programs (EAP). These programs offer systematic and organized advice, counseling, and assistance for employees (Berridge, et al. 1997). Typically, there are two types of employee assistance programs: on-site counseling services, provided by either the employing agency, or counseling services that have been contracted out. Colorado State University has an on-site EAP for faculty and classified staff and a counseling program for students. Because of the large number of classified staff and faculty in need of counseling following the July disaster, the student counseling service opened its doors to the university's permanent staff.

Occasionally, counseling is seen as taboo or only for those who some deem as "really messed up." It is too often misunderstood or viewed in the negative. In the hope of making counseling programs more attractive to staff, offer the services in two ways: group counseling sessions and individual sessions. At Colorado State University's Morgan Library, the counseling sessions were grouped by department or individual work unit. For those staff wanting more private sessions, individual appointments were made. Confidentiality was important, respected, and enforced.

A third counseling service, made available to university personnel as well as to community citizens, was Project Rebound, a special project designed to assist people affected by the disaster. Sponsored by a grant from the Federal Emergency Management Agency (FEMA), Project Rebound was housed in the county mental health center and staffed by two counselors. Project Rebound was not available to deal with the initial stages of loss and depression, but it was able to pick up the pieces three months post-disaster. It provided information and referral on finding help for disaster-related problems and crisis counseling for individuals and groups to help cope with the stress of the disaster. Services were offered in both English and Spanish.

Some considerations to keep in mind in order to assist staff in dealing with traumatic stress include:

- Recognize the initial symptoms of depression and stress.
- Be supportive.
- Immediately contact the on-site EAP or off-site counseling service.
- If your organization doesn't have provisions for either of these services, inquire about counseling services available through workers' compensation.
- If possible, use administrative leave for time missed from work to attend counseling.

- Arrange for department/group sessions as well as personal/ individual sessions.
- Maintain confidentiality.
- Arrange follow-up counseling sessions.
- Give time off so staff who are relocated and expected to work a regular eight-hour day can take care of personal losses.

NEW STAFFING ISSUES

Two weeks before the library building was deemed habitable, staffing discussions were underway. Contrary to logic, these discussions were about hiring approximately one hundred people to process and return gifts and damaged materials to the shelves. Initially, this seemed to be a rather simple exercise. Within a day however, it had proved to be an exercise with several insurmountable hurdles.

State and University Regulations

State of Colorado personnel rules have clear and distinct hiring guidelines. In short, these rules stipulate that temporary hourly employees can be employed for a maximum of only six months. Because this is a constitutional provision, a waiver was impossible, even in light of a natural disaster. Given this, the one-hundred-plus staff needed for the Processing Center could only be hired for a six-month period of time (see Chapter 15 for more description on this issue). This was an unrealistic expectation. Training alone could easily take several weeks, and having to re-hire and retrain one hundred people every six months would be very inefficient and impractical.

In addition to state rules, the University Libraries is also bound by university hiring procedures. These procedures stipulate the kind of appointment longer-term temporary employees can have. Because additional staffing was limited by the six-month temporary hourly rule, consideration was given to hiring these people as temporary faculty, something that has been done regularly when a faculty member takes a sabbatical or while we have been recruiting for a permanent faculty member. However, because the individuals who were to be hired did not possess an MLS, a temporary academic faculty appointment was out of the question. Instead, special permission from both the director of University Human Resource Services and the university provost was obtained and we were able to hire key supervisory staff for the document delivery program as temporary administrative professionals. This is a type of faculty appointment, but isn't considered academic faculty because the educational qualifications are different. The key to this type of appointment was the kind and level of duties to be performed by these temporary staff. If the positions these staff were to hold were comparable to ones that our faculty/librarians would hold, the administrative professional classification was approved.

Internal Revenue Service Regulations

In addition to knowing state and local staffing rules, Internal Revenue Service (IRS) regulations also had to be followed. Namely, attention had to be paid to employer-employee relationships as compared to contractor-employer relationships. Section 530 of the 1978 Revenue Act provides that if a taxpayer did not treat an individual as an employee for any period, then that individual would not be deemed an employee unless there was no reasonable basis to the taxpayer's treatment of the person.

Revenue Ruling 87-41 (1987) contains a list of twenty factors to use as guidelines in determining whether an individual is an employee or not:

1. *Instructions.* Does the service recipient have the right to require compliance with instructions as to when, where, and how to perform the work?

2. *Training.* Must the worker go through training to ensure that the work is performed in a particular manner?

3. *Integration.* Is the work such an integral part of the business as to indicate that the worker is subject to direction and control?

4. *Services rendered personally.* Must the worker perform the services and tasks personally?

5. *Assistants.* Does the service recipient hire, supervise, and pay any assistants?

6. *Set hours of work.* Does the service recipient set the hours of work?

7. *Location.* Must the work be done on the service recipient's premises, even if it could be done elsewhere?

8. *Order or sequence.* Does the service recipient have the right to control the order or sequence of the work?

9. *Oral or written reports.* Is the worker required to submit regular oral or written reports?

10. *Payment.* Is the worker paid by the hour, week, or month rather than by the work accomplished or by commission?

11. *Expenses.* Does the service recipient pay or reimburse the worker's travel and business expenses?

12. *Tools and materials.* Does the service recipient furnish significant tools, materials, and equipment?

13. *Investment.* Does the worker lack a significant investment in facilities used in performing the services, other than those typically maintained by an employee?

14. *Realization of profit and loss.* Is the worker subject only to the normal risk of nonpayment for services and unable to realize a profit or risk economic loss?

15. *Continuing relationship.* Is there a continuing, even if irregular, service relationship between the worker and the service recipient?

16. *Full time work.* Must the worker devote substantially all of the worker's time to the service recipient?

17. *Multiple service recipients.* If the worker performs services for others, are they limited to either *de minimis* services or services performed as part of the same service arrangement?

18. *Availability of services.* Does the worker refrain from making his or her services available to the public?

19. *Right to discharge.* Does the service recipient have the right to discharge the worker without cause?

20. *Right to terminate.* Does the worker have the right to terminate the relationship at any time without incurring liability (Revenue Ruling 87-41, 1987)?

A "yes" answer to any of the above questions may indicate that the worker is an employee and not a contract provider. However, the IRS tends to focus on the overall situation rather than one or two factors. If a worker is classified as an employee, the employer is liable for employment taxes and is subject to withholding requirements. Failure to meet either of these requirements could result in penalties to the employer. This regulation was extremely important when considering staffing for both expanded services and new services.

Existing Operations

Staffing for existing, yet expanded, library services was critical. However, state, university, and IRS regulations had to be followed. The most critical need for additional staff was in Interlibrary Loan for its expanded document delivery operation. In typical years, the University Libraries hires approximately 220 students to work during the academic year. Interlibrary loan, a department that normally consists of a department head, two support staff who are supervisors, three non-supervisory support staff, and approximately ten (three full-time equivalent (FTE)) student staff, found itself in need of an additional six FTE supervisors and more than 40 full-time staff! Because state and university regulations put an undue restriction on the type of employee allowed to be hired, the document delivery program was in peril. Several brainstorming sessions were held and "thinking outside the lines" in terms of staffing became the norm. Taking all issues into consideration, it was ultimately decided that students who could work at least twenty hours each week and six supervisors classified as temporary administrative professionals would be hired. Blessed with a student population who scrambled for these jobs, the vastly expanded document delivery service was in business.

The department was also re-engineered in order to fit this immediate need. Because one-fourth of the collection was not usable, the interlibrary loan lending operation was suspended and those staff were shifted to the borrowing section. Creativity and flexibility were, and continue to be, key elements in continuing to operate and offer patrons what is needed.

Although a gifts and exchange unit had been a part of acquisitions for many years, the operation was a very small one, consisting of only one support staff. The July 28th disaster brought not only a torrent of water, but also an outpouring of donations of monographs and journals from around the world. Much like the interlibrary loan document delivery service, the gifts and exchange section found itself in need of hiring several additional staff. Unfortunately, the staffing restrictions were the same and alternate hiring options were used. Luckily, however, there was light at the end of the gifts tunnel because the expertise needed was primarily clerical and organizational. Three librarians were reassigned to the unit to provide leadership and collection development expertise, three hourly workers were hired for six-month terms, and four student hourly staff were hired for the academic school year to provide clerical and receiving assistance.

When faced with the possibility of reorganizing a unit due to a disaster, consider these ideas:

- Use all the skills of the staff, not just those needed for a particular task or job.
- Temporarily place staff in other departments to help in getting over the "crunch time" or to work semi-permanently.
- Keep the integrity of the job classification. Don't expect support staff to work higher-level duties indefinitely without being compensated accordingly. If additional compensation is warranted, work with the appropriate administration in arranging for supplemental pay.
- Investigate union, local, and state regulations. Know what is and is not acceptable regarding changing one's duties or job description.
- Consider contacting retired faculty and support staff to assist with the operation. Most will enjoy becoming involved and using their skills.
- Use personal contacts for the temporary hourly hires. Con-

sider spouses and friends who have the clerical and organizational skills.

- Unemployed librarians living in the area can provide the expertise needed and most relish the thought of getting their foot in the door. (We were able to appoint these people as temporary academic faculty because they had an MLS; therefore, they were able to work for as long as needed.)
- Seek out area librarians living in the vicinity who want to "moonlight."

The downside of hiring temporary assistance is that in many cases, such as ours, the employer can hire someone for a maximum time period of six months, and the employee generally receives no benefits other than salary. In our case, it was unavoidable and the hiring of six-month temporaries was a necessity. However, not all state or city/county regulations are as narrow, so becoming very familiar with state and local hiring regulations is a necessity before any disaster hits.

Developing New Operations

Even though we had already expanded existing departments, we realized that what was going to be done within the next 18 to 24 months amounted to staffing another medium-sized university library. A myriad of questions went through our minds. The most prevalent was how would such an operation be staffed and where would it be housed? Although the human resource specialist is involved in both of these questions, the one that will be discussed in this chapter is staffing issues of the proposed Processing Center.

Outlining the proposed Processing Center was mind boggling, with the primary concentration being the receipt of the water-soaked materials from the drying plant in Texas. An anticipated monthly shipment of 24,000 items was the basis of discussions for staffing considerations. After taking into consideration how long, on the average, it takes to receive, unpack, inspect, prepare forms, and get nearly destroyed volumes back on the shelves, it was decided that there had to be at least two shifts of nearly a hundred workers each shift solely to process the materials. It was out of the question to try and run the proposed Processing Center ourselves. There were too many hiring restrictions, so outsourcing this operation was the only solution.

Because IRS regulations prohibited us from serving as our own contractor, the next step was to make inquiries of private jobbers or contractors who could run an operation of this magnitude. In order to determine what was out there, inquiries were made around the library community in Colorado. Regional resource agencies were too small to take on such a large project; consequently, the agency the university originally contracted to provide emergency disaster response for the entire campus was able to put together a satisfactory proposal that would satisfy IRS, state, and university regulations. With guidance and consultation from the Libraries' Technical Services Division in the design of the Processing Center, the contractor began screening and hiring personnel with the computer and library expertise needed for the large-scale operation.

Ironically, the processing of the returned disaster-damaged items proved to be the least of our concerns. Within a week of the disaster, the Libraries' director of development had started a gift donation drive (see Chapter 16). Soon there were 900,000 exact matches, duplicates, and unique items received. While the University Libraries was able to provide staffing for the soliciting and receiving components of the gift operation (see above), the processing of these items was far more than our catalog services staff could handle alone. Once again, help was needed from the contractor's umbrella, the gift-processing component was born as an extension of the Processing Center.

The development of new operations, however, was not yet over. As an off-shoot of the gifts donation effort, an augmentation plan to add unique materials to our existing collection was approved and funded by the university administration. Once again, within a year of the disaster, another new operation was conceived.

There are several important considerations that have to be investigated when faced with the need to establish new operations relative to human resources implications:

- Possess a thorough knowledge of state, local, and national (IRS) hiring regulations.

- Think outside the box; be creative. Brainstorm and consider all options of hiring.
- Explore all local and regional sources for assistance.
- If considering outsourcing, detail the expertise needed in order to make the operation a success.
- Be realistic about what can be done. Remember that most, if not all, of the outsourced workers will not be catalog librarians. In fact, many will have only remedial knowledge of libraries.
- Prioritize your short-term and long-term needs. Be aware that you may need to accept somewhat lower skills and products if short-term/immediate needs are more important. However, don't compromise the integrity of the collection or the online catalog.
- Be willing to offer advice or consultation as needed and encourage its acceptance.
- Be willing to take as active a role in the expanded operation as possible.

HOME SWEET HOME

Almost four weeks to the day of the disaster, the library building was deemed habitable. Although there was no telecommunications access (including phone and LAN/Internet), the electricity and water were on and the building environment, namely the air, had been extensively tested and pronounced "safe."

Environmental Concerns

As expected, the library staff were concerned about the building environment. Was the air safe to breathe? What about mold? The university's environmental health services unit provided a thorough analysis of the mold spore content inside the building and, to make staff more at ease, the director of the environmental health services unit was invited to several open forums and discussed environmental issues associated with the building. Just prior to returning to the building, staff were given a copy of the policy and procedures for reporting environmental concerns and encouraged to follow them. The steps taken to prepare staff before re-occupying the building worked well. Some steps to consider relative to re-entering the building include:

- Keep staff apprised of what is going on with the building and when they might be expected to return.
- Provide expert opinion on the building environmental issues.
- Arrange a Q&A period for staff to meet with the environmental experts.
- Provide staff with procedures for reporting environmental concerns. Keep the reporting procedure simple (see Appendix 2-A).
- Keep alternative placement options open in case some staff experience health symptoms. Everyone reacts differently to molds and humidity, so don't expect all staff to react the same.
- Work with the environmental health specialists and workers' compensation physicians to assure timely treatment of reactions to the environment, if any.
- Encourage staff to seek counseling from the Employee Assistance Program if needed.
- Continually reassure staff that the building is safe.

Insurance Claims

Once back into the building, Morgan Library staff had an opportunity to take an assessment of what was lost. Although it was readily apparent that everything in the lower level was destroyed, this didn't become a reality until the building was reopened and staff who were housed in the lower level realized that there was nothing left. Because the library wasn't the only building on campus impacted by the disaster, the university set up a procedure for claiming insurance coverage for lost items. Both personal and library/university property were covered. It's important to make sure all staff who lost personal items complete a reimbursement form. Although only a fraction of the true costs of the items will be realized, everything should be claimed, including plants, paintings/pictures, office lamps, books, and other personal items. On the flip side, be prepared for some questions and some disappointment regarding the reimbursement process. Not everything will be covered, nor will full reimbursement be realized.

AND THE BEAT GOES ON

The disaster recovery operation is not yet completed and very likely won't be until the year 2000. The human resources implications of the disaster most likely will go on longer. However, from chaos arose a staff that didn't give up and pulled together to reinforce why Colorado State University Libraries' staff excel in service and in providing researchers with appropriate access to information. From a human resources perspective, a lot was learned, and the most prevalent lesson has been to communicate, communicate, communicate. The care and nurturing of staff should not take a back seat to the bricks, mortar, bytes, and books. Be flexible, be sympathetic to staff needs, and trust your staff to do the best they can. Most of all, never underestimate the indomitable spirit of the human being.

Library Disaster Planning and Recovery Handbook

KEY RECOMMENDATIONS

Human Resources

As discussed, crisis management can be planned to ensure that each issue is covered prior to an actual disaster. Even though several suggestions have been given, by keeping in mind the following key recommendations, the human resource issues will be under control.

- Spend time thinking of alternate work-sites for both permanent and temporary staff before a disaster strikes, and have more than one option in mind.
- Keep wellness issues, such as ergonomics, in mind when relocating staff.
- Take steps to address the mental health of staff who are personally and/or professionally affected by a disaster.
- Become familiar with campus/local employee assistance programs that will decrease time spent on identifying these agencies and allow for more time to be spent in relocating staff and revising staff job duties.
- Be open to doing some tasks differently because very likely the same procedures will not be able to be followed. As long as the end result is what is wanted, the path to getting there can be changed.
- Look into all federal, state, and local regulations if hiring of additional staff is needed. In fact, it might be wise to become somewhat familiar with your local regulations prior to an actual disaster.
- Address environmental concerns when returning to the "home" office or building.
- Know who your local environmental health specialists are and consult with them to ensure that the building is safe (both structurally and environmentally) for occupancy.
- Assist staff in filing insurance claims and arrange for insurance representatives to meet with staff.
- When the disaster clean up is completed and things are back to normal, evaluate what worked and what didn't, so you can be better prepared in the future.
- Last, but not least, keep everything in perspective, and as the director, the department head, or the human resources officer, take time for yourself. The last thing the library needs is to have their administrative team frazzled and not capable of making the best decisions they can given the circumstances.

APPENDIX 2-A

COLORADO STATE UNIVERSITY LIBRARIES BUILDING ENVIRONMENT PROCEDURES

During the past several months, Morgan Library employees have been subjected to a wide variety of building inconveniences such as crowded offices, occasional dust particulates, noise and odors. We have done everything we could to ensure that construction related concerns were kept to a minimum and were dealt with in a timely manner. Now, however, our patience and flexibility is once again being tested. After being closed for three weeks, Morgan Library is open to staff and will soon be open to the public. As we all know, a lot has happened in Morgan Library these past three weeks. Even though the building has undergone several environmental tests and has been found safe to work in, a few of our employees may experience some discomfort. In the event that you are negatively affected by either the building construction or the basement recovery and clean-up, please follow the following guidelines to better help the Libraries administration track and remedy the situation. In an emergency situation, follow the prescribed emergency procedures as detailed in the disaster plan.

Procedures:

1. Inform your supervisor of the concern. Your supervisor will access the situation and will take any action that he or she deems necessary.

2. The supervisor should notify Halcyon Enssle by phone of the concern and any action taken and follow-up with an E-mail message. Send a copy to the services coordinator, Betty Espinoza, Teri Switzer and the appropriate assistant dean.

3. If the condition is such that you are unable to continue to work in your assigned work area, your supervisor will make arrangements to find an alternate worksite for you. If

the alternate placement is anticipated to be long term, the Flexplace Request Form, DO:21a, should be completed and routed through the proper channels.

4. Halcyon Enssle and/or Teri Switzer will report back to you, your supervisor, the services coordinator and the assistant dean what action was or will be taken regarding your concern.

5. In the unlikely event you experience an on-going adverse reaction to the building due to the construction and removing yourself from the building does not alleviate the symptoms, you may want to consult the University's workers compensation provider, Poudre Valley Hospital, Occupational Health Services. To have this visit covered by workers compensation insurance, report forms will need to be obtained from Libraries Personnel Services, completed and returned to Libraries Personnel Services within three days of your visit to the physician.

Tips:

1. If there are odors or other environmental concerns that bother you, take more frequent, but shorter, breaks and eat lunch outside of the building. Staff should consult with supervisors before taking actions that are not in line with state, university, or library policy.

REFERENCES

Barton, John P., and Johanna G. Wellheiser. 1985. *An Ounce of Prevention: A Handbook on Disaster Contingency Planning for Archives, Libraries and Record Centres.* Toronto: Toronto Area Archivists Group Education Foundation.

Berridge, John, Gary Cooper, and Carolyn Highlye-Marchington. 1997. *Employee Assistance Programmes and Workplace Counselling.* New York: John Wiley and Sons.

Blythe, Bruce T. 1992. "HR . . . Home Run or Strike Out?" *HR Focus* 69 (April): 13–14.

Bunge, Charles A. 1989. "Stress in the Library Workplace." *Library Trends* 38 (Summer): 92–102.

Grosser, Kerry. 1985. "Stress and Stress Management: A Literature Review, Part III." *LASIE* 16 (July/August): 2–23.

Revenue Ruling 87-41. 1987-1 C.B. 296.

Strouse, Karen G. 1995. "What If Your Office Vanishes? Practical Advice on What To Do if Disaster Strikes." *Industry Week* 244 (July 3): 60.

Switzer, Teri R. 1998. "The Crisis Was Bad, But the Stress Is Killing Me!" *Colorado Libraries* 24 (Fall):19–21.

3   The Disaster-Recovery Process For Collections

Carmel Bush and Diane Lunde

INTRODUCTION AND PERSONAL ACCOUNT

My thoughts flashed back several months to a meeting of the board of the Colorado Preservation Alliance (CPA) as I (Lunde) reacted to the horrible news that the lower level of Morgan Library was inundated by water. At that meeting, we discussed various potential program topics for the annual meeting, and I had strongly suggested disaster preparedness. It had been ten years since the last state-wide workshops on disaster preparedness and recovery had taken place. This fact and the forthcoming trial of the Oklahoma City bombers slated in Denver had everyone's mind on disaster preparedness. The suggestion was enthusiastically received and, with the instrumental help of the Denver National Archives and Records Administration staff, a well attended two-day workshop was held in May 1997. My part in the program was to be twofold: as part of a panel relaying my experience responding to the many small disasters at Morgan Library during our recent construction and renovation and as the "dirty wet book" demonstrator during the pack-out practice session. Part of my job was to encourage workshop participants to get their hands wet practicing washing the dirty wet books and preparing them for pack-out. Now, instead of a simulation exercise involving a few books, I will be seeing hundreds of thousands of wet volumes.

With this thought, I contemplated my next steps and realized that I had the Libraries' *Disaster Plan Quick Reference Guide* at home, but that the complete disaster manual was in my office on the second floor, as was my copy of the staff directory. After several calls to directory assistance, I notified preservation staff and made final arrangements for several experts who had worked on disaster response/recovery in various Denver metro libraries to come to the library at 10:00 a.m. the next morning. With sleep disrupted, and in the intervening lulls between phone calls, I mentally ran through the possible scenarios I might find in the morning and the usual procedures for responding to a water disaster. While the nature of the disaster would determine the exact response, the underlying processes for rescuing water-damaged materials have been well documented. Despite confidence about the general processes of how to proceed, I still found myself wondering just what I would find with so many volumes involved.

After years of planning and two years of construction and expansion, the 1997 disaster damage to the newly constructed and refurbished Morgan Library was heartbreaking; however, the damage to the collection was monstrous. The deluge impacted all books in science, business, political science, law, sociology, social work, education, and music. In addition, the waters covered nearly 19,000 sets of bound journal titles. Newspapers among other materials were scarcely recognizable—almost paste.

This chapter addresses disaster recovery for collections, including disaster response (notification, stabilization of the environment, assessment of damage, and pack-out of the collection) and the beginning recovery of the damaged collection up to the point of receipt of the materials back for further processing. Through the emphasis on the Morgan Library experience and decision making, the chapter illustrates the key facets of response and recovery for large-scale water disaster.

REVIEW OF THE LITERATURE

Disaster Planning

The genesis of the recovery process is in the disaster plan. In the plan, a library anticipates risks, addresses preventive measures that reduce risks and outlines the means to minimize damage. Major books by Cunha (1992), England (1988), Fortson (1992), and Morris (1986) provide excellent guidance to libraries on disaster planning and include sections on water damage. *Procedures for Salvage of Water-Damaged Library Materials* (1975) by Peter Waters is the pre-eminent practical text on recovery from water damage. Amplifying these works are bibliographies by Murray (1987) and Henry (1988).

The plan is the basic tool for managing and responding when disaster strikes. It may be tempting to take a quick and dirty approach by adopting another library's plan, but Cunha (1992: 545) describes this as a "foolhardy" approach. England (1988: 14) emphasizes that emergency preparations "can be significant if before and after disaster actions are to be the most appropriate for survival and optimal recovery." Sound management requires a comprehensive and responsive approach to emergencies that is not naive. Wrotenbery (1972: 227) advises "assume that the worst might happen and service might be limited."

Considerable agreement exists among experts about the general elements of a disaster plan. These elements are prevention, organization and management for disaster, and policies and procedures for responding to a disaster.

The plan anticipates risks for disaster. It includes determining risks; considering their effects upon library services; deciding on acceptability of risks; weighing acceptable risks vis a vis the tolerable period of downtime for services; and the affordability of reducing the level of risks by taking measures to eliminate or alleviate consequences (Levitt, 1997). For water damage, Morris (1986) outlines knowing the water hazards of the area; performing surveys aimed at preventing fire and water incidents; setting up a program for maintenance in air handling systems; knowing water damage potential of plumbing, sprinklers, and rooftop air conditioners; knowing draining patterns; checking materials shelved on the floor or low shelves; and considering earthquake measures.

A review of related preventive measures supports disaster preparedness. Library storage practices; heating, ventilation, and air conditioning operations; and security measures are but a few of the type of procedures that are linked to a library preparation for disaster (Spawn, 1979; Morris, 1986).

How the library coordinates its staffing makes a difference to recovery. Waters (1993: 1) emphasizes that the best preparation for major water damage requires "being familiar with the necessity of having to make a series of interrelated decisions promptly, understanding the effects of any particular course of action on subsequent ones." England (1988) proffers two teams for disaster—a prevention team and a recovery team. The former assesses and measures risks, establishes priorities for collections, provides training, and has a policy role. For the latter, the author prescribes a minimum of five staff who would be responsible for 1) management of the recovery, 2) leadership of work crews, 3) record keeping, 4) damage assessment and training, and 5) backup services. Crossover of membership on teams is deemed likely.

Regardless of the number of teams or the numbers of their membership, staff involved in a disaster should be assigned specific responsibilities for responding and recovery. Reinsch (1993: 4) stipulates that team members "should be skilled library managers with demonstrated abilities in problem resolution." For water damage, Waters (1993: 6) advises a leader who "has had practical experience and understands the effects of different environmental conditions on water-soaked material of all types, conditions and ages." Underscoring the need for expertise, Mileti and Sorenson (1987) summarize studies that show that mobilization is more effective in disaster for organizations whose staff have normal duties that resemble their disaster-tied roles, a dispersed decision-making structure and little role conflict among staff members. Roles for disaster response and recovery may include procurement decision making, insurance monitoring, public relations, collections priorities, bibliographic management, conservation measures, service arrangements, inventory control, security, vendor liaison, training, logistics management, facilities, documentation of disaster, and evaluation of the plan (Kahn, 1998; England, 1988).

Assignment of responsibilities to staff must be followed up by training. "Staff member should read and have access to the disaster plan" according to Murray (1987: 12). The Preservation Directorate of the Library of Congress (*http://lcweb.loc.gov.preserv/prepare.html*) advocates convening "regular meetings of an organization-wide emergency management team." Another option is to center "decisions of all procedural details affecting disaster prevention" as a part of regular staff meetings (Fortson, 1992: 81). Testing the plan through role playing and simulation exercises is an important component of training. Rothstein (1990: 510) states "there should be an explicit test plan defining test strategy, standards, methods, assumptions, expectations, and criteria." In addition to the design of the exercise, Page (1993: 8) states that there should be "sufficient time allowed for comments and evaluation of the drill." The value of such training is underscored by Moon (1981: 43), who observes that, although exercises are artificial, these "lessons learned leisurely can be applied effectively."

There are several basic procedures which should be in place for disaster. Multiple means to notify staff of impending disaster or disaster in progress should be established. Keeping phone numbers and e-mail addresses of staff and contacts for emergencies up-to-date and at off-site locations is recommended for disaster team members and administrators (Northeast Document Conservation Center Technical Leaflet: *Emergency Management*). Fortson (1992), among other major book authors, recommends a telephone tree to facilitate a rapid response. Kahn (1998) and Fortson (1992) offer checklists for services that might be contacted in disaster. Examples include key library vendors for regular operations and special vendors for emergencies such as freezer, freeze-dry, air handling, cleaning services, and other specialists who may need to be contacted. For libraries without resident expertise for disaster, the services of outside consultants or assistance of consortia partners may be necessary. Cunha (1992: 527) supports "reaching an understanding (in writing) with the selected specialists" for services in advance and comments that "it is a sensible goal that will provide big dividends some time in the future."

Primary among procedures are the evacuation and safety measures for staff and users to observe. Ric Rea, human resources manager for the Oklahoma Metropolitan Library System, offers training to staff in the procedure for cutting off water and gas valves and the master electric breaker (MetroNetwork Workshop on Emergency Preparedness, 1998), echoing an earlier statement by Morris (1986). When possible, powering off computers in standard fashion is recommended. Personal safety is paramount. For example, in natural floods, contaminants are present and there can be serious risks for infectious organisms. The Occupational Safety and Health Administration (OSHA) recommends protective wear, frequent hand washing, and precautions in using water (CPA Alert, 1993). Another safety consideration is the procedure for determining re-entry to the library. The plan should define when a safety inspector or building engineer is required. There should be on-hand emergency supplies and methods to procure additional supplies quickly.

Priorities for salvaging collections and other vital resources must be documented. In setting priorities, a library recognizes its valuable collections and identifies the salvage order for all collections by department, location, or format. Fortson (1992: 82) emphasizes as a top priority "materials that are difficult or impossible to replace or replicate and that are either essential for the ongoing operations of the institution or of some larger body, such as a state agency; or have prime research values; or have significant monetary value." Insurance coverage and ability to replace material influence the setting of these priorities (Insurance for Libraries, CAN no. 20). In addition to collections, salvage priorities for computing equipment, fiscal records, and other key operational documents should be made (Kahn, 1998).

Security procedures that address off-site storage of backups, computer files, equipment inventory, vendor contacts, and the disaster plan facilitate the disaster response. A library should include alternate site locations for computing operations (Cerullo and Cerullo, 1998).

Included in the basic procedures are inspections that update the status of conditions for the building and emergency controls. Sprinkler systems, fire alarm system, and water detectors are among the systems whose operability must be checked. Regular conduct of staff drills on emergency responses assures "that process, experience, environment, and knowledge are up-to-date" (Rothstein, 1990: 52). There should be provision for updating the disaster plan on an ongoing basis and linking it to organization and governmental jurisdictions that also have responsibility in a disaster response.

Disaster Recovery in Libraries

According to Kahn (1998) recovery has three phases: notification, assessing the situation and damage, and beginning rescue and recovery of the collections. Reinsch (1993) describes a response phase and recovery phase. Barber (1983: 153) reinforces the collective approach to notification in the response phase to "make sure that senior and other appropriate staff are informed so that as much emergency action as possible is carried out by informed persons." This may involve administrators and professionals outside the library's disaster team, including the pre-contracted consultant for advice that "may direct or influence further salvage and reclamation work" (England, 1988: 91).

Waters (1993) states that the next step of the assembled disaster recovery team members is to establish the nature and degree of damage. For disasters in which structural damage is suspected, the first assessment is to have facilities staff identify potential deficiencies and provide temporary measures to protect life, property, and belongings, and clean and repair structures' roofs and roof draining systems in order to protect the building from future storm damage (National Park Service, 1993). No inspection should occur by library staff until assured that the building is first safe to enter; Buchanan (1981) also advises careful assessments of contents to be able to make wise decisions. In the assessment, consider how the disaster impacts people and processes and the consequences of these impacts (Levitt, 1997). Document the damage and note the immediate recovery actions. Griffith (1983) emphasizes the restoration of minimal service in the short-term goals for recovery. It may be necessary to establish an alternative site for a command post. Pre-existing arrangements for alternative space to house staff will enable a smooth transfer.

Using the inspection data, the collection maps, collection demographics, and team member expertise, the team determines the scale and scope of damage. This determination will direct the extent to which recovery can be sustained by the library. Very large scale disasters—such as the 1988 fire and water damage of the U.S.S.R. Academy of Sciences Library, the 1966 flood in Florence, and the 1986 fires and water damage of the Los Angeles Public Library—have required multiple and extended forms of assistance to meet the long-range goals for recovery (Waters, 1990; Lenzuni, 1987). Small disasters, characterized by Kahn (1998) as involving less than 500 items, may be handled by the library staff depending upon what is damaged and the type of treatment required for the recovery of materials.

Cunha (1992) posits speed as a primary requirement in the recovery operation. Once the assessment is made, it is essential to activate the plan according to what is pertinent to the disaster. In a large scale disaster, the object, according to Henry (1988), is to recover the collection as a whole and to minimize damage. For large numbers of wet materials, freeze stabilization is recommended by experts in order to inhibit growth of mold and give more time to make decisions about subsequent care. A comprehensive outline on how to pack-out materials is offered by Walsh (1988) according to formats and the packing methods for each. Waters (1993) provides practical guidance on the organization of teams for the packing process and the removal of items. The admonition for pack-out is to "be extremely careful when handling wet materials" (Walsh, 1988: 2). Identifying boxes with the objects they contain is advised for insurance and tracking; however, in medium- to large-scale disaster, the effort can be questioned. One lesson from the flood at Stanford University, involving damage to 50,000 volumes, is to "not be overly concerned about numbering each box. For us it was nearly a total waste of time" (Leighton, 1979: 458). Waters cautions that packing of material should take into account the "drying method to be used" (1993: 2).

Buchanan (1992) succinctly describes the five ways to dry wet books and records: air drying, dehumidification, freeze drying, vacuum thermal drying, and vacuum freeze drying. Choosing the right technology suited for the disaster is a key decision. In major floods, recovery will almost certainly involve vacuum freeze drying (Henry, 1988: 8).

Mold is the danger with wet materials. Depending upon climate, the time frame can be relatively short, 48–72 hours, before an outbreak of mold. Establishing environmental controls that keep heat in check and humidity low are recommended by Kahn (1998). Chemical and gamma radiation treatment are still the subject of research. Formerly used chemicals such as thymol and ethylene oxide have been found to have adverse health effects. Research on radiation indicates damage to paper at higher dosage levels and has not been conducted on large numbers of volumes (NDCC Technical Leaflet: *Protecting Book and Paper Against Mold*).

Cleaning the debris and dirt not only helps bring the building back into service but also removes contaminants and contributes to stabilizing the building environment because of the water retention properties of some debris. Typical cleaning includes furniture, fixtures, carpet, shelving, and removing ceiling tiles and cleaning of duct systems (Harrington, 1993). Professional cleaning services can be hired for this purpose (Cunha, 1992). It is important to take precautions with the ventilation system when cleaning. Depending upon the extent of damage debris, removal may involve a contractor, preferably one selected in advance. A contract should include provisions for emergency loading and hauling that details haul distances, fees, and other specifications (O'Connor, 1988).

During the initial response and recovery period, the library should have a spokesperson on the disaster. Kamer (1997/1998: 28) advocates a short-term communication plan that includes "the key messages, key facts, identifies spokespersons, and the next day's needs." On the staff side, Reinsch (1993) subscribes to a central message unit with staff instructed to direct outside inquiries to the spokesperson of this unit.

The library- and emergency-related literature provide a wealth of information on disaster planning and recovery. The bias that preparation girds the library for decision making and action is well-founded. Large-scale disasters present challenges; however, no plan can adequately address them all. For these contingencies, a library disaster team will have to work with its parent organization or other constituencies or consultants to make the judgments with the best information at hand.

"SAY IT ISN'T SO!": DISASTER RESPONSE AND INITIAL RECOVERY STEPS

Notify and Convene the Disaster Team

Roles require review in the first meeting of the Library Disaster Recovery Team (LDRT) after notification that disaster has occurred. The initial rules of operation for the team must be outlined and assignments changed as warranted. Large-scale disaster also involves tapping other library staff to take on specific tasks for response and recovery for collections.

In the case of the Morgan Library's disaster, the telephone tree worked well, and the LDRT was scheduled to meet on Tuesday morning at 7:00 in the lobby of the new entrance. On the way to the library, the preservation librarian stopped to buy two disposable cameras to record initial impressions. Photographs and video recordings substantiate insurance claims for disaster.

Upon arrival, team members walked the perimeter of Morgan Library. Evidence of tide marks showed that the water had begun to recede, but the wake of its path showed awesome destruction. On the west side of Morgan Library, the lagoon area just north and behind the Lory Student Center was under several feet of water; the terrace leading to the library's lower level was completely filled. From the outside of the library, water could be seen up to the level of the upper-most stack shelves with UFOs (unidentified floating objects) in the water. It appeared that the collection was still within the library. From inside the building, only the dark water could be seen in the staircases leading from the first floor to the lower level. There was no electricity, air conditioning, or ventilation. Temperature and humidity conditions approached that of a sauna.

The meeting of the LDRT set the tone for the weeks to follow. Members reviewed the general organization of the LDRT per the disaster manual. Because of the scope of the disaster, the dean of Libraries assumed the role of head of the disaster team. In any large-scale disaster, the interplay of the library within the parent institution and community disaster response and recovery officials requires leadership at a level commensurate with those directing disaster operations. With so many tasks to be accomplished, team members suggested calling in additional staff for assistance; and the dean directed these assignments. The dean reaffirmed that the preservation librarian would take the leading role for collection assessment and determining initial recovery steps for them. Coordinating with other team members and consulting with selectors and other staff, the preservation librarian first concentrated on the immediate response for the collections.

Among the obvious first steps to recovery of the collection would be pumping the water out of the building and establishing temporary humidification and ventilation controls. Everyone was cognizant of the 48–72 hour period for mold to grow.

What everyone was not cognizant of was the university-wide disaster recovery plan and the roles that a number of individuals had been assigned for large-scale disasters. This plan made a difference in that the recovery for the library was under an administrator other than the one reported to in the normal university hierarchy. This proved to be one of the most challenging relationships of recovery and emphasized the importance discussed by Mileti and Sorensen (1987) of making sure staff have normal duties that resemble their disaster-tied roles, a dispersed decision-making structure, and little role conflict among staff members. The determinations made by this individual would profoundly affect library efforts throughout the recovery.

Stabilize the Building

Large-scale disaster may prohibit an immediate inspection of the damage to collections. The waiting time, however, can be used to coordinate action with the parent institution's disaster response team for displacing water, establishing services for air handling, reviewing environmental conditions, and reviewing options for recovery once the go-ahead is given.

PUMP OUT WATER

How do you remove 4.9 million gallons of water? "Lake pumps," was the answer when staff queried the construction crew. A subsequent meeting with the university facilities department confirmed their efforts to rent lake pumps. Besides obtaining the pumps, decisions had to be made about where to pump the water. Avoiding further damage to that already experienced by 36 of the campus buildings was a chief concern. Quick study of the drainage status resulted in a plan that designated Morgan Library as a priority insofar as the drainage sequence pattern permitted. This proved frustrating but intractable for library staff concerned about collections, given the projection for mold growth.

STABILIZE THE BUILDING'S TEMPERATURE AND HUMIDITY

While the one-and-a-half days of pumping proceeded, the LDRT made its decision about which company would supply drying, air conditioning, and ventilation. Lack of electricity and destruction of heating and air conditioning systems (HVAC) left the building bereft of any controls and effected a sauna-like environment. With three other floors of book stacks, protecting the rest of the collection was a paramount concern, especially forestalling spread of mold or other biological contaminants.

Pre-established arrangements for disaster service facilitates response. When large-scale disaster strikes, however, no calls may need to be made. Disaster relief companies monitor Web news reports and know within minutes of the occurrence of a disaster. Company representatives for air drying, cleaning, and specialized recovery assistance such as technology recovery will appear on the doorstep in less than a day, each vying for business. What is important in selecting an emergency service is the company's process, their experience working with libraries, and their effectiveness in providing monitoring and reports. The Libraries had no prior arrangement, but received permission to enter into a contract with a vendor within two days.

For Morgan Library, the vendor supplied portable refrigerant units and trailer-mounted desiccant dehumidifiers with flexible ducts to force air through the upper floors of the building. Large knee-high air tubes wove throughout the building supplying air to counteract the outside, higher-temperature air, thus lowering the temperatures in the building the accepted measure for combating the growth of mold. Because of the water in the lower level, it became necessary to cordon it off with heavy sheets of plastic in order to attain optimal temperatures and relative humidity in higher-level floors.

As a corollary action, assigned preservation staff routinely checked out the upper floors of the library looking for evidence of the collection reacting adversely to the conditions. Monitors placed in various positions in the floors provided readouts of temperature and relative humidity. This proved important in detecting a problem with the dew point, which began to affect the wavering in paper. In addition to refining controls, it became necessary to coordinate the action of the vendor with the activities of the university's facilities department and other emergency support workers in the building. Fortunately, airborne measures showed that no mold migrated to the upper floors from the lower level. For air drying arrangements, the vendor should supply daily measurement and monitoring of conditions with reports to staff assigned to monitor conditions. (See Chapter 4 for additional information on recovery of the building.)

STABILIZE BUILDING STRUCTURE AND ASSURE SAFETY PRECAUTIONS FOR ACCESSING COLLECTIONS

Before disaster team members or other individuals entered the lower level, LDRT wanted to assure safety. Immediately after the pump-out, engineering and construction specialists inspected the library to assure structural soundness. Despite the huge gaping hole in the lower-level wall, the building was pronounced fit for access by authorized individuals. Additionally, staff contacted university Environmental Health Services (EHS) regarding a potential hepatitis risk because of the contaminated water from a sewer line overflow. Although EHS did not consider hepatitis a risk, they advised that staff wear protective gloves and boots and wash hands frequently if touching items. Measurements of water quality and wall surfaces in the lower level indicated 11 microbiological contaminants, reinforcing the hand-washing strategy. Air drying and conditioning by the vendor extended to the lower level following an initial fumigation for contaminants at the completion of pumping.

Assess the Damage and Make Decisions On What to Save

The initial inspection documents the general damage to the collection. It is not reasonable in large-scale disaster to canvass the collection and detail the damage. Advanced setting of priorities for collections in the disaster plan saves time in determining what items do not justify the cost of salvage.

INSPECT THE COLLECTIONS TO RECORD DAMAGE

At Morgan Library, the force of the water knocked over and twisted shelving and cannoned volumes off the shelves, particularly in the monographs for music and social sciences located opposite from where the wall broke in the building exterior. Unlike usual flooding, in which the water rises leaving most materials on the shelves, many of the CSU volumes in the collection were forcibly thrown off the shelves and became UFOs. Serial and monographic volumes still on the shelves, especially bound journal volumes on compact shelving, had absorbed water such that their expansion created a fanning of the volumes rising from the shelves. Damage to volumes included extensive swelling, wavering, and distortion of text blocks and coverings, discoloration visible from edges, and moderate to heavy deposits of silt. Debris from fallen ceiling tile remnants and destroyed furniture and equipment had mixed with volumes on the floor. Getting rid of the debris would be a challenge in order to work in the space to rescue materials.

In addition to the collection, staff areas for Gifts and Exchange and Binding were totally destroyed, along with a computer lab and nearly all book trucks for reshelving. By only one-and-a-half inches, networking cables in cable trays above the ceiling tiles escaped harm; however, the power and telecommunications closets were destroyed. The saturated carpet and sheet rock contributed to an environment perfect for the mold soon noted to be growing on materials and walls.

APPLY PRIORITIES FOR COLLECTION SALVAGE.

The Libraries' disaster plan contained appendices for collection priorities, noting critical bound journal volumes and monograph collections in science and technology. All were in the lower level and most had been reviewed by selectors with lesser-used volumes transferred to the storage facility. Overall, the selectors affirmed the priorities previously set and wanted to save these materials; however, a few collections served as exceptions to rescue. Based upon their condition and limited retention period, staff decided to discard newspapers and replace them with microfilm versions per standing order for these titles. Only one local newspaper title would be replaced so that the library could microfilm it.

Besides the newspapers, staff declared two other collections as total losses because of the heavy destruction: the Current Awareness Collection and Curriculum Materials Collection. The Current Awareness Collection consisted of mass-market paperback books of subjects of current interest and as such deemed easily replaceable. Also slated for replacement was the Curriculum Materials Collection, conceived as a revolving collection to support teacher education and field experience.

Based upon these few exceptions, the first significant decision of recovery was to save as much of the original collection as possible. Because of the scale of the disaster, no decision of this sort should be made without extensive consultation. There are many unit costs associated with freezing, conservation treatment, and subsequent processing and valuation measures that will be associated with what will be saved. Substantial financial resources are required for response and recovery operations. The decision to salvage materials should be discussed with administrators and insurance representatives to gain their approval.

Packing-Out the Collection to Stabilize it by Freezing for Later Freeze/Vacuum Drying

There is only one means to begin to salvage a large-scale wet collection: freeze it. Securing the services of an emergency vendor experienced with library materials is key to appropriate handling, transportation, and storage. Quality control is an essential role of library staff in this process.

SECURING VENDOR SERVICES FOR INITIAL RECOVERY

Once the decision is made to salvage collections, securing recovery services is the next step. Vendors who specialize in the treatment of library materials can be found in *The Librarian's Yellow Pages* as well as disaster manuals including Fortson (1992). Arrangements made at the time of disaster require knowledge of appropriate questions to ask prospective vendors. What experience does the vendor have working with library disasters? What size of libraries and what type and size of disasters? How much feedback/input does the vendor expect/want from the library staff as the pack-out progresses? Will the vendor ask questions if faced with unseen circumstances? What, if any, conditions must be met before work can begin? How does the vendor staff and organize for pack-out? Who will be designated the primary contact through the duration of the pack-out? Are staff who supervise or train temporary staff hired on the spot or are they permanent employees of the company? What type of training is given the workers? How quickly can they begin pack-out? What is the method of pack-out and what materials are used? What records are made of packed materials? What is the rate of pack-out? Does the vendor own its own equipment that can be quickly mobilized or must the equipment be rented? Does the company clear debris and what precautions are exercised if they do? Does the vendor include dumping of debris? What arrangements are made to transport materials? What cold storage facilities will be used? What are the conditions of the cold storage, and how close are they to the disaster location? What are the vendor's prices? How does the vendor expect to be paid and how quickly (on the spot)? Are there additional security requirements? What precautions will the vendor take for the collection and the workers in regard to environmental and health concerns? What reporting is provided to the library on a daily basis? Does the vendor also offer drying facilities and/or services?

A major question that a library will have to answer in developing an agreement with a vendor is the size of the collection to be packed out. At CSU, the team calculated the number of volumes in the lower level from the number of linear feet of shelving and the average number of volumes per linear foot. This method was initially chosen because the shelving of material into newly constructed space was underway just prior to the disaster and staff had the latest information on the fill rate of shelving and the location of classifications. The number was later compared to the number derived in the online public catalog for materials located in the lower level and allowed for deduction of materials checked-out at the time of the flood. Adjustments were made to account for miscellaneous materials such as materials brought by patrons from other floors of Morgan Library to the lower level and volumes in the binding office.

According to calculations, approximately 462,500 volumes were damaged, including all bound periodicals and the monograph collection in the Library of Congress classification ranges of HG-M and Q-Z. These volumes represented the prime Libraries' collection, as 30 percent of the older, little-used collection had been relocated to an off-site storage facility over the past 20 years. Using these numbers, the LDRT and a prospective vendor constructed a cost for the pack-out process in order to submit them for approval to the university Disaster Financial Team.

PACK-OUT PROCESS

Once the vendor agreement for the pack-out was concluded, hiring day laborers and setting up the pack-out became the priorities for the vendor. The pack-out started at the bottom of the lower-level stairs, about in the middle of the east wing, and progressed systematically toward the north and west wings. Because of the number of volumes and extent of debris and damage, the pack-out took 14 days. As part of the standard shelving was twisted and compact shelving was off its track in many places or not operable because of damage to the system, the crew had to disassemble shelving as the pack-out progressed. The crews also cleared the area of debris and deposited it in dumpsters rented by the university.

On the positive side, the closed compact shelving units prevented volumes from falling off the shelves to the floor. With the exception of collections deemed not salvageable or individual items already turned into paste and sitting on the floor, all damaged items were boxed in the lower level. To get the boxes to the ground level, conveyor belts were constructed up the staircase. The boxes were marked as much as possible with the contents (monograph or periodical) and a general call number range. If the volumes came off the shelves, this was fairly easy; but if the volumes were off the shelves and on the floor, such information was impossible to determine. Once outside of the building, the boxes were organized onto pallets which were numbered consecutively.

Over 7,000 pallets were loaded onto semi-trailer trucks for delivery to temporary storage at cold storage lockers. Initial shipments were frozen inside trucks by using refrigeration units. This process was replaced midway by liquid nitrogen pumped into the trailers and circulated through the trailers' refrigeration units in order to speed the process. The fleet of semi-trailer trucks moved in a steady stream from the library to the locker facilities and back to the library for another load. Arrangements for the pickup of the pallets by semi-trailers required special permission from the campus police department to change a one-way street so that the trucks could maneuver in the space.

THE LONG AND WINDING ROAD: OFF-SITE TREATMENTS

With the decision to salvage materials and freeze-dry them, development of strategies for treatment of materials begins in earnest. Restoring salvageable materials to their pre-disaster conditions is the aim insofar as possible. The complexities and interrelationships of treatments to subsequent processes, coupled with the significant costs that large-scale disaster entails, argues for the advice of experts. Testing is a prerequisite to deciding what treatments to use in further salvaging of materials.

Working with an Emergency Management Facilitator as Contractor

Recovery from large-scale disasters requires expertise in conservation, library processes, and automation systems that handle bibliographic and other data. These experts do not provide long-term management for disaster recovery, and they do not operate as a business that can handle the fiscal and legal issues associated with labor pools and entering into subcontracts. Libraries that suffer damage on a large scale and do not have sufficient staff to direct efforts themselves will require a contractor with the expertise required for recovery.

The university hired an emergency management facilitator (contractor) to coordinate the campus disaster recovery efforts, including water removal, providing air and dehumidification service to damaged buildings, clearing out debris, cleaning and fumigation services, and a host of repair problems. The company's contract was extended to include the recovery of Morgan Library. The contractor worked with the vendor for pack-out and hired a consultant in library preservation. The latter provided input to the library on the plans for off-site mass treatments and worked directly with our preservation librarian and other experts and staff in determining conservation treatments for damaged collections. The advantages of working with an emergency management facilitator are especially evident for recovery of buildings and the ease with which the contractor hired staff and avoided the bureaucracy of purchasing. The disadvantages are lack of knowledge of library operations for materials and lack of experience in working with systems that libraries use. While the facilitator contributed operations management ideas on a large scale, extensive efforts were required on the part of library staff to fill the facilitator's deficit of knowledge about general library operations.

Based upon the CSU experience, a library involved in disaster recovery should hire experienced librarians to coordinate and/or assist in library recovery efforts if they cannot dedicate sufficient permanent staff to this effort. The library should seek third party means to hire labor if their employment regulations limit hiring temporary labor. Once beyond the initial response of recovery related to the facility, emergency management facilitators should only be hired for further recovery tasks if they employ qualified professionals with expertise in disaster recovery of library collections.

Determining and Applying Off-Site Treatments for Damaged Collections: Working with Consultants and Vendors

Developing protocols to provide mass off-site treatments involves using proven treatments, identifying options for chemical or physical treatments if mold, bacteria, or yeast is found, and testing options and determining protocol for treatment. In deciding upon the protocol, consultants in conservation, paper chemistry and environmental health services play an important role.

INITIAL ASSESSMENT OF PACKED-OUT VOLUMES

Volumes evidenced every kind of physical damage, mold, and associated odor. Initial assessments by CSU Libraries' staff and several consultants estimated the damaged collection as 20 percent total loss (the volume would be totally unusable in its post-disaster condition) and 80 percent recoverable. Of the recoverable materials, 20 percent would need page repair and 80 percent would need replacement pages and/or rebinding. The emergency management facilitator, his library consultant, the recovery service company, and our preservation librarian drew upon their visual inspection of the materials in the pack-out phase to project this estimate. Consultants from the Library of Congress, who served in that capacity via FEMA, examined a sample of frozen volumes to check the quality of packing and the range of conditions of the volumes and concluded that 10 percent of the packed-out materials would be "beyond hope."

Based upon these initial assessments, restoration would include treatment of the volumes by freeze-drying for mold and odor. The odor related to the mold permeated the air. No one wanted hundreds of thousands malodorous volumes returned to the lower level. Hence, odor joined mold as a significant issue slated for further investigation.

ESTABLISHING THE PROTOCOL FOR FREEZE-DRYING

Immediately after assessing the extent of the water damage to your materials, you need to establish the protocol for freeze-drying. This will set the course for your first phase of treatment of the materials.

During an August 1997 visit to the facility of the recovery services vendor by the emergency management facilitator, the Library of Congress consultant, and the CSU Libraries' preservation librarian, a protocol was outlined for freeze-drying. Efforts would be made to save every volume, no matter how bad it looked coming out of the pack-out box. Each volume would be thawed in filtered water and washed to remove the dirt and to reshape the volume if necessary. Volumes would then be refrozen and freeze-dried at 4 torr of pressure and temperatures not to exceed 105° Fahrenheit in a special chamber. The actual time of freeze-drying would depend on the amount of water in the volume and the type of paper and cover. As an example, drying occurs more quickly for a mass-market paperback than for a heavy clay-coated hardback volume. Once dried, the volumes would be repacked in clean boxes to be returned to the library.

Although not related to the freeze-drying process, the group also drew up general guidelines as to the acceptability/ nonacceptability of damage caused by the disaster; for example, discoloration from the running of inks and dyes was acceptable unless it affected the readability of the text.

REVIEWING THE FIRST SAMPLE OF PROCESSED MATERIALS

It is very important to review a sample of processed materials. Doing this will give you your first picture of how the process is working. Doing the first review early in the process will help identify any problems which may require tweaking the process.

In October 1997, the library staff viewed the sample of materials dried according to the protocol. The sample of 128 volumes met with the fanfare of a celebrity. Representatives of insurance, the insurance brokerage, the recovery services company, library, university, FEMA, State of Colorado Office of Emergency Management, and the emergency management facilitator convened in Fort Collins to review the sample.

All volumes were identifiable except one. Barcodes remained in the volumes, so quick checking of the volume in the integrated library system would be possible—older OCR labels fared poorly and were unreadable. Mold was very much in evidence, especially on covers, end sheets, and the first and last 10–20 pages of volumes. For volumes that appeared to have ended up on the floor, mold was widespread throughout. Earlier estimates concerning page replacement and binding was supported by the review of the sample. The total loss estimates at 20 percent appeared reasonable in analyzing the sample for volumes with extensive mold damage or paper degradation and for volumes that were completely blocked, i.e., pages fused together. For most representatives viewing the materials, the finding for total loss was central to their evaluating the earlier decision to salvage and bolstered their confidence in the protocol.

For the LDRT, the issue of odor as a problem was reinforced by the review of the sample. It was also clear that the question of how far to go in repairing a volume before declaring it a total loss had particular perspectives. The insurance representative's position is to pay the lowest cost for restoring the collection. Definition of pre-flood conditions of materials is key. The LDRT addressed longer-term requirements for usability, longevity, and retention of critical titles. Because of the differences in perspectives, the determination of total loss versus repair issue underscored the importance of hiring experts for the insurance brokers to negotiate with insurance companies when large settlements are pending and to involve them at all stages of decision making.

ESTABLISHING TESTING PROTOCOLS FOR FURTHER TREATMENTS

To help address all the concerns about the potential treatments, it would be helpful to prepare a list of questions to be answered concerning the following: the possible treatments, including a review of the treatment and its past use in libraries; the short- and long-term effect on the users of the materials after treatment and the potential short- and long-term impact on paper; pros and cons for each treatment; and the need for monitoring of the collection after it returns to your library. It is important that the testing be done using a statistically valid sample technique with exact step-by-step procedures outlined.

At the October 1997 meeting, key issues identified for further action included refining the existing treatment protocols using a statistically representative sample; odor elimination; the parameters for declaring a volume a total loss instead of salvaging it; and treatment for mold. Testing was indicated in several of these areas to establish appropriate protocols.

A later meeting was held to discuss the protocols with university administrators and officials from EHS in order to receive approval for testing. It also identified what treatments, such as the irradiation proposed for eradication of mold, might have public relations components because of the user and staff concerns.

Refining Treatment Protocols

Every disaster would require a different treatment protocol and/ or a combination of treatments. Be prepared to explore all the available treatments. Do not be pressured to accept a certain protocol without adequate testing. This section will describe the testing completed for our library materials.

CLEANING AND FREEZE-DRYING

A trial of thawing volumes in their original packing boxes showed that the timing needed to be improved from point of freezing to cleaning in order to minimize potential additional mold growth on materials. Close monitoring was needed on the volumes as they were thawing so that the number of boxes in the thawing pipeline matched the staff available for cleaning to avoid creating a backlog of thawed volumes. Dipping volumes in water before cleaning was dropped to limit further water exposure for volumes. The reviewer also reconfirmed the decision to provide cold storage to materials already freeze-dried to avoid the creation of micro-climates within the boxes because of the warm Texas climate (where the recovery center was located).

MOLD

A CSU microbiologist joined efforts to explore means to combat mold. The first step was to establish baseline data for what would be considered normal conditions in order to determine what were acceptable levels for library volumes. With guidance from the preservation librarian, a random set of volumes on the upper floors of the Morgan Library were sampled using Malt Extract Agar Rodac plates to determine fungal populations. Measurement of colonies followed incubation of the plates. Of the 55 books sampled, only five had positive mold counts with a mean count of 0.152 fungi/ square centimeter with a standard deviation of 0.168 or 19 colonies per 25-square-centimeter plate. In other words, the books in the collection were rather "clean" in terms of mold spores.

With this benchmark, options for treatment were identified to test efficacy in reducing or eliminating the presence of mold and bacteria to acceptable levels. Initial testing following washing and freeze drying showed that volumes had spore counts above acceptable levels; hence further treatments were indicated. Sample volumes were subjected to one of the following treatments: ozonized water wash/airborne ozonization; ozonized water only; quaternary ammonia and orthophenylphenol (OPP) disinfection; and gamma sterilization. In considering these processes, the effects of the treatment process on paper and possibly health were of upmost concern. We did not want processes that would produce contact hazards or off-gassing, and we did not want to further degrade the paper.

OZONIZED WATER WASH WITH AND WITHOUT AIRBORNE OZONIZATION

A two-step decontamination process consisted of ozonized water, a fungal and bactericide, and airborne ozonization. Ozone is frequently used for deodorization, although risks exist for paper because it is an oxidant. This test involved rinsing contaminated materials in ozonized water at a solubility range that neared saturation. The second step, airborne ozonization, followed freeze-drying and exposed materials located in the chamber to concentrated levels of ozone at 300 torr of pressure via generation while the chamber was under vacuum and left overnight. As a variation of this protocol, only the ozonized water wash was done prior to refreezing and freeze drying.

DISINFECTION: QUATERNARY AMMONIA AND ORTHOPHENYLPHENOL (OPP)

OPP and quaternary ammonium are characterized as gentle and broad spectrum chemicals in their killing of contaminants, albeit involving time-consuming protocols with attendant off-gassing. Manufacturers of the chemicals were consulted for dilution rates so that the concentrations were effective in terms of disinfection time. To expose all of the contaminants to the first chemical wash, it was necessary to immerse or to pressurize wash materials with the quaternary ammonia or OPP disinfectant in solution after thawing. It was also necessary to perform a final rinse with clean water to evacuate residual contaminants.

GAMMA RADIATION

Gamma radiation is designed to physically kill contaminants through sterilization of the affected materials subjected to exposure at controlled levels of gamma rays. It involves "radioactive materials and requires a specialized facility with appropriate shielding and monitoring apparatus, as well as highly skilled operators" (Wellheiser, 1992: 41). Studies indicated a range of 4.5 Kilo Gray (kGy) to 18 kGy is needed to kill fungi with the irradiation process taking one to five hours. As no residues are created by the process, gamma radiation poses no health problems, although paper may degrade and become slightly weaker as a result of treatment that would result in making the paper vulnerable to future exposures to contaminants. Ethylene oxide was not selected for testing because of health risks associated with it. A subcontractor specializing in sterilization using gamma radiation was engaged for the testing.

TESTING PLAN

In the testing, volumes would be sampled to demonstrate efficacy of the individual procedures. This involved using Redditch plates with 17mL of Malt Extract Agar pressed against covers and

FIGURE 3–1
Treatment Options: Effect on Mold, Yeast, and Bacteria

	Airborne Ozonization	Gamma Radiation	OPP	Quaternary Ammonium	Ozonized Wash
Average Change in Yeast	61.9	169.9	120.6	131.3	-72.4
Average Change in Mold	25.1	26.9	30.2	26.3	24.4
Average Yeast/Mold Change	86.9	196.8	150.8	157.6	-47.8
Average Change in Bacteria	5.2	16.9	28.7	20.2	-44.0
Percent Yeast/Mold Reduction	27.5	100	53.3	56.4	-22.0

pages of sample volumes before and after treatments. Reports would be based on number of yeast and mold per square centimeter from these samples.

TESTING RESULTS

Figure 3–1 demonstrates the results of confirmation testing showing gamma radiation to be most effective, producing a total kill as expected from the sterilization process. Chemical washes produced a more than 50-percent kill rate; airborne ozonization, less than 30 percent. Ozonized water wash proved to be totally ineffective in killing the mold, yeast, and bacteria. In fact, there was an increase in yeast and bacteria rather than a reduction.

ODOR

Many volumes had an unpleasant odor—described by some staff as "dirty gym socks"—even though they had been treated with ozone in the testing. Odor perception is highly variable, and in the industry it is known that the odor would diminish over years; yet the concern was the interim effect upon users. Beyond the use of ozone, would odor be reduced if binding covers were removed? Their removal at the time of treatment was already under consideration because of problems with distortion of the text block and the desire to improve drying time. Later, a commercial bindery would have to recover almost all of the salvageable volumes, so why not remove the covers now? This question would be discussed with experts hired to review the treatment and recovery process.

From the beginning of the disaster, library staff had requested the assistance of experts to consult on treatment options and their effects. With the completion of the testing, a panel of experts was finally hired by the contractor to review the protocol for off-site treatments and recommend changes to the protocol. The panel consisted of individuals who had experience in large-scale library disasters, conservation, and paper chemistry. As part of their review, the experts visited the emergency service provider, the subcontractor for gamma irradiation, the Morgan Library building, and the contractor's gift processing plant. Based upon their inspection of damaged materials, they summarized that volumes were in a significantly weakened state as a result of the water damage and extended length of the pack-out. They found the off-site treatment processes to contribute insignificantly to further damage of the materials and agreed that the removal of book covers, gamma irradiation at low levels, and ozonization were appropriate steps given the nature of the collection as a working, rather than a rare, collection. Overall, the administration of off-site treatments was given a thumbs up by the experts. They did, however, express concerns about the environment to which volumes would return because of the sensitivity of paper attributed to irradiation and ozone treatments.

In addition to the treatment options, the experts questioned the options considered as alternatives to restoration of damaged materials. This question illustrates a valuable lesson for institutions in which the contractor reports to a university administrator instead of a library administrator. Experts can only provide helpful guidance insofar as they are *correctly and completely* appraised of circumstances. Since the panel of experts were not allowed to meet separately with the library staff as requested, they only had partial information from the emergency management facilitator contractor and other non-librarians. This led to a fundamental misunderstanding of the aims for recovery of the collection. Hence, their review was not elucidating in this area, although it did underscore that avenues had not been overlooked.

REVAMPING THE TREATMENT PROCESSES

Following the experts' review, further testing involved removing of binding covers early in the treatment process for a 500-volume sample. This testing showed that removal of covers at the washing stage reduced wavering of text block. For these volumes, a comparison of the dosimetry readings for volumes, with and without covers, was undertaken to check the uniformity of irradiation among volumes, showing the treatment to be within specifications. The experts also recommended that there be additional inspections of materials during the process to determine salvageability of volumes. This would allow volumes that were a total loss (totally blocked or unidentifiable gooey mess) to be removed from the treatment process and discarded. As a result of the testing, the protocol for treatments was revised. The protocol incorporated the removal of the covers at the time of washing and two inspection points of the volumes for total loss—at the point of thawing and after freeze drying. Figure 3-2 outlines the treatment process.

Communicating the Treatment Plan

It is extremely important to communicate the treatment plan to various groups. Do not underestimate this communication process. Various groups, especially library staff, will be concerned about the treatment plan. If you have to hold off telling them about the final plan while testing is being completed, that is fine; but tell them why.

DECISION MAKERS

With the revised treatment protocol in-hand and examples of materials treated according to this protocol available, a forum was planned to present the revised protocol to insurance, insurance brokers, FEMA, State Office of Emergency Management, and other university officials, along with the general plan for processing once the treatments were completed. Their approval was necessary for continued support of the protocol.

FIGURE 3–2
Initial Recovery Processing by Vendor

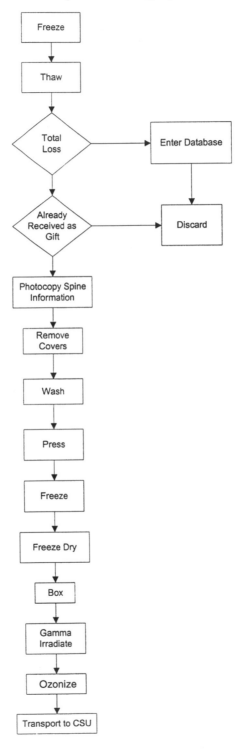

In preparation for the meeting, sample volumes were also assessed by faculty, students, and staff in order to determine the layperson's acceptability of treated volumes. The preservation librarian held a meeting with evaluators to explain treatments and the sample that they would view. Unfortunately, the only rebound volumes available for review were those that needed no repair or replacement pages, so *raw* volumes with those conditions were also used. Evaluators were asked to picture the volume with a new cover and all repairs/replacement pages done and make a judgment based on that viewpoint. All volumes were reviewed for appearance, usability, readability, ability to be photocopied, and odor. Results showed a high level of acceptance of most volumes, with odor showing the widest variance of acceptability.

With data from users and the testing results, the decision makers responded favorably to the revised treatment plan. In order to avoid expenditures on treatments, it was agreed to accept the recommendation to screen volumes against those already replaced by gifts before processing and to capture data for volumes deemed a total loss at the emergency services vendor. Databases would be developed to support the screening and capture activities at the emergency services vendor's facility.

LIBRARY STAFF

Open meetings were held with library staff to describe the treatments and to respond to their questions. Condition of paper and health risks proved to be the chief concerns. EHS staff responded with detailed explanations, in particular on gamma radiation.

LIBRARY USERS

Having the same information available for everyone is important in communicating status in disaster. To accomplish this, the Libraries added a description of the general process to the Website. This site is connected to the university's public relations Website, which had responsibility for communicating the status of the disaster.

Ongoing Vendor Treatments

With the off-site treatments determined, a subcontract was finalized by the contractor with an emergency services vendor for the treatments. As part of that contract, the inspections for total loss and screening of volumes already replaced by gifts were incorporated. Third-party clearance testing of work performed by the vendor was recommended, and specifications included in an amendment to the emergency management facilitator's contract.

CONCLUSION

The decision to salvage materials rests with a knowledge of the collection that has been water-damaged and is the first of many important decisions a library will make in recovery. The nature of the collection dictates whether salvage is warranted. Once salvage is determined as one of the routes for collection rebuilding, a host of questions and actions arise, leading to a bevy of business relationships with contractors, vendors, consultants, and other agencies.

Establishing treatment protocols can require months of effort when large numbers of volumes are damaged. Pack-out and freezer storage provides the time to make informed decisions about treatments. Aside from well-established cleaning and freeze-drying processes, other treatments require testing. No large-scale protocol should be undertaken until evaluated and the pros/cons weighed for the collection and its users. These treatments are a first phase in the recovery of collections, but not the end phase.

Because large-scale disaster has monumental costs, the decisions at each step require ratification from all parties involved. Consultants play a valuable role in helping shape the recovery plan and providing the independent assessment that insurance companies seek. Underlying the success of the recovery of collections is the

Library Disaster Planning and Recovery Handbook

KEY RECOMMENDATIONS

Disaster-Recovery Process

- Although a disaster plan is essential to recovery, do not expect it to provide all the answers if your disaster is on a large scale. Be flexible—the disaster plan is a working document and should be used as a guide.
- Rely on staff with prior experience and training with disaster-recovery actions because this provides a solid basis for staff to step into roles for recovery from the beginning of the disaster.
- In the parent institution plans, seek to have authority delegated to the library for all phases of recovery in order to facilitate the process. If this cannot be accomplished because of the fiscal implications of large-scale disaster, prepare to take an active role in influencing the recovery of the collections through meetings, reports, and documentation.
- Expect emergency service vendors hired for collection salvaging to have library experience; however, do not rely on past performance as an indicator of success for your recovery. Include quality measures in the agreement for service.
- Pay acute attention to the nature and priority of the damaged collection, as this will be the major factor in deciding recovery actions. There are many possibilities for rebuilding a collection; salvage is just one of them.
- Count on mold if you have a large-scale disaster and if mobilization and pack-out require more than three days. Because there are chemical and physical options for combating mold, investigate and test candidates before embarking on a large-scale treatment protocol.
- Keep parent institution administrators, insurance, and other agencies involved at the key decision steps that will have an impact on costs. They will have a vested interest in decisions for recovery.
- Contact consultants in large-scale library disaster at the early stages of disaster recovery in order to benefit most from their expertise.
- Know what roles individuals in the parent institution will have in the event of large-scale disaster.
- Remember that disaster recovery is a cooperative effort involving a variety of skills and talents. It is not a one-person job, but a job for the library as a whole.
- Take two aspirin daily.

plan and knowledge of library staff regarding priorities of collections and appropriate actions to take. Leadership to keep on task and on target makes a difference over the lengthy process associated with a large-scale disaster.

REFERENCES

Barber, Giles. 1983. "Noah's Ark, or Thoughts Before and After the Flood." *Archives* 16, No. 70 (October): 151–161.

Buchanan, Sally. 1981. "Disaster Planning." In *Disasters: Prevention & Coping; Proceedings of the Conference.* May 21–22, 1980. Stanford, CA: Stanford University Libraries.

Buchanan, Sally. 1992. "Drying Wet Books and Records." *Northeast Document Conservation Center (Technical Leaflet).* Andover, MA: Emergency Management.

Cerullo, Michael, and Virginia Cerullo. 1998. "Key Factors to Strengthen the Disaster Contingency and Recovery Planning Process." *Information Strategy: The Executive's Journal.* 14, No. 2 (Winter): 37–43.

Cunha, George Martin. 1992. "Disaster Planning and a Guide to Recovery Resources." *Library Technology Reports* 28: 533–624.

England, Claire, and Karen Evans. 1988. *Disaster Management for Libraries: Planning and Process.* Ottawa: Canadian Library Association.

Fortson, Judith. 1992. *Disaster Planning and Recovery: A How-To-Do-It Manual for Librarians and Archivists.* New York: Neal-Schuman.

Griffith, J.W. 1983. "After the Disaster: Restoring Library Services." *Wilson Library Bulletin.* 58, No. 4 (December): 258–265.

Harrington, Gary. 1993. "Flood! Or, Disasters Always Happen on a Weekend." *Southwestern Archivist* 16, No. 4 (Winter): 1, 4–5.

"Health Concerns for Flood Recovery." 1993. *Colorado Preservation Alert.* 3 (4) (Winter).

Henry, Walter. 1988. *A Brief Bibliography on Disasters.* Palo Alto, CA: Stanford University Libraries.

"Insurance for Libraries: Part II." 1985. *Conservative Administration News (CAN)* 20 (January): 10–12.

Kahn, Miriam. 1998. *Disaster Response and Planning for Libraries.* Chicago: American Library Association.

Kamer, Larry. 1997/1998. "Crisis Planning's Most Important Implement: The Drill." *Communication World* 15, No. 1 (December/January): 27–30.

Leighton, Philip D. 1979. "The Stanford Flood." *College & Research Libraries* 40, No. 5 (September): 450–459.

Lenzuni, Anna. 1987. "Coping with Disasters." *Preservation of Library Materials*. Conference at the National Library of Austria, Vienna, April 7-10. *IFLA Publication* 2: 98–102.

Levitt, Alan. 1997. *Disaster Planning and Recovery: A Guide for Facility Professionals*. New York: Wiley.

Mileti, Dennis, and John Sorensen. 1987. "Determinants of Organizational Effectiveness in Responding to Low Probability Catastrophic Events." *Columbia Journal of World Business* 22, No.1 (Spring): 13–19.

Moon, Myra Jo. 1981. "A Report on the Colorado Disaster Prevention and Preparedness Workshop." *Colorado Libraries* 7, No.3 (September): 39–43.

Morris, John. 1986. *The Library Disaster Preparedness Handbook*. Chicago: American Library Association.

Murray, Toby. 1987. "Don't Get Caught With Your Pants Down." *Records Management Quarterly* 21, No. 2 (April): 12–41.

National Park Service. 1993. Untitled. Preservation Assistance Division (July): 11–15.

O'Connor, Patrick V. 1988. "Debris Removal: Planning for the High Cost of Post-Emergency Cleanup." *Emergency Management Quarterly* (2nd Quarter): 2–3.

Page, Julie A. 1993. "Exercising Your Disaster Plans: A Tabletop Drill." *Conservation and Administration News* 54 (July): 8–9.

"Protecting Book and Paper Against Mold." 1994. *Northeast Document Conservation Center* (Technical Leaflet). Andover, MA: Emerging Management.

Reinsch, Mary. 1993. "Library Disasters and Effective Staff Management." *Conservation Administration News* 55 (October): 4–5+.

Rothstein, Philip Jan. 1990. "Put it to the Test." *Contingency Journal* 1, No. 3 (July-September): 51–52.

Spawn, Willman. 1979. "Disasters: Can We Plan for Them? If Not, How Can We Proceed?" *A Manual of Archival Techniques* 71–76.

Walsh, Betty. 1988. "Salvage Operations for Water-Damaged Collections." *WAAC Newsletter* 10, No.2 (May): 2–5.

Waters, Peter. 1975. *Procedures for Salvage of Water-Damaged Library Materials*. Washington, DC: Library of Congress.

Waters, Peter. 1990. "Requirements for an International Center for Preservation of Books and Manuscripts." *Bollettino dell'Instituto di Patologia del Libro* 60–84.

Waters, Peter. 1996. *Bibliography on Disasters, Disaster Preparedness and Disaster Recovery*. Tulsa, OK: Murray.

Wellheiser, Johanna G. 1992. *Nonchemical Treatment Processes for Disinfectation of Insects and Fungi in Library Collections*. London: K.G. Sauer.

Wrotenbery, Carl R. 1972. "Recovery from Disaster: The University of Corpus Christi Library Recovers from Hurricane Celia." *Libraries and Archives Conservation*. The Boston Athenaeum's 1971 Seminar on the Application of Chemical and Physical Methods to the Conservation of Library and Archival Materials: 221–227.

4   Why Can't Facilities Fix This?

Halcyon Enssle and Cathy Tweedie

INTRODUCTION

In the spring of 1994, Colorado State University's Morgan Library was approved for a major capital construction/renovation project which would add 109,000 square feet to the physical structure and bring the infrastructure to the cutting edge of technology. The project was scheduled to be completed in October 1997. The final phase of the renovation was about to begin: the completion of the final portion of the lower level. We were in the process of moving the last books out of the area to be renovated and up to the second floor. The compact shelving in the lower level was completed and housed all of the journal collection and the entire science monograph collection. I (Enssle) had been serving as construction project director for the Libraries from the beginning and was looking forward to seeing the completion of what had become a truly beautiful building.

On the night of Monday, July 28, 1997, I was at home. I did not have the television news on; so, although it was raining heavily at my home in the foothills west of Ft. Collins, I was not aware of any special problems until my husband called at about 9:45. He told me that the rain was extremely heavy and that he was worried about making it home from campus where he was working late. We agreed that if he had any problems he would spend the night at a motel and call me in the morning.

The first time I was aware of problems at the library was at 10:15 p.m. that evening. I received a call from our assistant dean for Technical Services telling me that there was water in the lower level of the library, and that I should be prepared to come in at

7:00 the next morning. I received a second call at 4:15 a.m. through the university building proctor notification system. The next morning, the news on the radio carried the story of a disastrous flood which had wiped out a trailer park with several people still missing. Driving into campus from the west, I was amazed at how few people I saw. The campus seemed deserted. There were no police monitoring entrance into campus and hardly any cars in the parking lot. It was not until I actually walked along the west side of the library and saw the lower-level window well filled with more than eight feet of water that I realized the true extent of the catastrophe.

WHAT CAN YOU EXPECT IN A MAJOR DISASTER?

What Really Happened

A flash-flood warning for eastern Larimer County was issued at 9:06 the evening of July 28th. "In some parts of the city, the rain had been falling continuously since the previous afternoon. The town's irrigation and storm water drains were filled. The rain continued to come down" (Hayes, 1998). A second flash-flood warning was issued at 10:03 p.m. The main campus received 6.51 inches of rain, but the flash-flood waters that roared in from the area west of campus did most of the damage.

A little after 10:00 p.m., a custodian in the library noticed water coming through the roof where the new building met the old, an area that had not yet been completely sealed. Water had also started leaking into the building through the lower-level doors on the west. At about 10:30, the pressure of tons of water caused a portion of the west wall of the lower level to give way, allowing the water to cascade in. Unlike a normal flood, where water slowly rises, a flash flood raged through the lower level. Later, estimates by the city indicated that the water entered the building at 5,000 cubic feet per minute—flood stage on the local Cache La Poudre River is measured at 3,000 cubic feet per minute.

At 7:00 a.m. on Tuesday, July 29th, the library disaster team gathered in the main foyer of the new building. Looking down the main staircase of the old building, we could see the water above the lower-level ceiling, with books floating in the staircase.

At the height of the flood, the water in the lower level was 8' 6", which meant that the lower level was filled with 658,750 cubic feet of water, equaling 4,928,109 gallons, or 41,106,000 lbs.

Inspection and Cleanup

By Wednesday at noon, the water had been pumped out and I (outfitted with huge construction boots, hard hat, and a flashlight) accompanied representatives from our facilities services department and the contractor into the lower level to assess the damage. As the water level receded below the dropped ceiling, soaked ceiling tiles fell onto the books lying below. As we penetrated further into the lower level, it was difficult to avoid walking on the piles of books covered with sodden ceiling tiles. The true nature and horrifying extent of the damage became more and more evident. The force of the water was such that the steel shelving directly in the path of the initial surge was toppled and twisted, and books were driven onto the floor where they lay in heaps. I saw books in the fans in the mechanical rooms, and stacks of ceiling tiles waiting to be installed had been lifted up and thrown on top of books. One look at the first photograph below gives a clear snapshot of the immediate conditions after the water was pumped out from the lower level of Morgan Library.

In our compact shelving area, further from the initial force of the water, many more volumes remained on the shelves, but the end panels had been forced off the stacks by the swelling of these books. The force of the water was so severe that one main air handler was completely lifted off its pad. Later, as demolition took place, books were found under the air handler itself. Our initial, possibly too pessimistic, estimation of recovery of the collection was 50 percent—if we were lucky. The photograph on the next page illustrates the unique position of tightly packed books after they became swollen with water and then expanded when they dried (also known as the *fat factor*).

REVIEW OF THE LITERATURE

In reviewing literature dealing with disasters and disaster recovery, I found that the overwhelming majority of the articles dealt

Force of the water toppled shelving and books.

with preparation for potential disasters and the development of disaster plans and manuals. There is a great deal of information on recovery of damaged library materials, but little dealing with recovery of the physical infrastructure of the library building itself. There have been few major disasters involving massive physical destruction of a library's infrastructure in which the library was occupied during the reconstruction. In the case of the Los Angeles Public Library building, the main library was relocated for more than five years while reconstruction and renovation took place. One article by Gary Harrington (1993) provides an account of a similar type of disaster in microcosm. Barry J. Varcoe (1994) outlines the essential steps for a disaster recovery plan for physical facilities and Bill Larkin (1998) gives an overview of the precautions needed to deal with possible contamination when dealing with areas that have been damaged by water.

With regard to insurance for libraries, most of the literature concentrates on the need for pre-disaster planning: risk assessment, loss prevention and control, and options for insurance coverage (Brawner, 1993; Fortson, 1992; Inland Marine Underwriters' Assoc., 1994; Sherbine, 1992; Ungarelli 1984). The general business lit-

Swelling and expansion of the books after water damage.

erature also offers a perspective on the importance of business interruption insurance in disaster planning (Paradine, 1995; Urbani and Satinsky, 1997). Marcia J. Myers (1991) surveyed actual insurance practice in major research libraries for the Association of Research Libraries Office of Management Services, and published the results as a SPEC (Systems & Procedures Exchange Center) Kit. She found that "ARL libraries appear to have adequate coverage," that only 14 percent had experienced losses of more than $25,000 in the past five years, and that only one respondent out of 86 had indicated they had had any problems with insurance coverage.

However, there is little to guide one through the detailed experience of claim preparation, negotiation with insurers, and settlement—in either the library or the general literature. We found only one reference that described the claim and settlement process for library materials. An article by Naslund and George (1986) describes how they were able to calculate loss of value for a number of damaged volumes and thus arrive at a favorable insurance settlement.

WHAT YOU CAN EXPECT IN A MAJOR DISASTER

It is essential that your administration and insuring party have in place standing contracts with the major players providing disaster recovery services that are reviewed on a yearly basis. Valuable time can be lost while determining who can authorize recovery companies to begin work.

Immediate issues on that first day of the CSU disaster included clarification of which recovery vendors would be approved by the university. By noon, there were many representatives of companies specializing in disaster recovery, de-humidification, and paper recovery vying with one another for our business. Because we as a library were not authorized to sign contracts for the university, our dean met in emergency sessions with university officials to obtain authorization for at least the first step, the drying of the portions of the building not under water. By the next morning, de-humidification equipment was in place to ensure that the remaining collections would not be subject to mold.

In a disaster of this magnitude, you are not in control. While it is essential to have a disaster plan, you may find that your plan simply doesn't work for a variety of reasons. You will be at the mercy of your central administration, the insurance companies, and outside contractors for the help you need in saving your collection and restoring your building. Make sure in advance that your administrators are well-educated in the special problems faced by libraries when disaster strikes.

No one from the library should attempt to enter the building until it has been cleared by the police, fire department, and your environmental health staff. There is the danger of electrical shock if the power has not been turned off, and there may be health hazards from backed-up sewers.

When you do enter the disaster area for the first time, there is no way you can prepare yourself or your staff for the impact of seeing the collections and facility—which you have labored to create and maintain—damaged or destroyed. Both you and your staff will experience emotional trauma. Work with the professionals and be sure that help is available for anyone needing it following a disaster (see Chapter 2 on human resources).

Be prepared for your organization's facilities department to be totally overwhelmed. Your catastrophe may exceed the capabilities of your existing campus or organization's facilities operation to handle. There needs to be a great effort made at organizational flexibility and the services of outside contractors will be necessary.

In our situation, a new contract for immediate emergency repairs was drawn up with the same contractor who had been doing the construction and renovation. Since they were on-site, work could begin very quickly. This was a great advantage, as we knew all of the sub-contractors very well, having worked with them for the better part of two years.

Don't be shy. If you have responsibility for the building, make it your job to find out who is in charge of any given aspect of the cleanup and recovery and introduce yourself. Offer your services in helping them become more familiar with the building and where the contents and the collections were stored.

The communication between the university and the library concerning which disaster recovery contractor would be doing what and when was not completely satisfactory from our point of view. We had information about the building and the collections which only we could provide and which would make the work of packing-out the collection and cleanup easier. We found, however, that we simply had to go to what appeared to be the main site of the contractors, introduce ourselves, explain who we were, and offer our services. Once we had done this, communication became much easier and we were better informed as to what was happening. This was particularly important in working with the contractor who was charged with maintaining humidity levels within the un-flooded portion of the building.

For example, we had developed a floor plan of the compact shelving which showed where each call number in the collection was located. This was of great help to the recovery contractor when they began to pack-out the books. Keep in mind, they are the recovery experts; but you are the expert on your building and its contents.

HOW TO DETERMINE YOUR BUILDING AND CONTENTS LOSSES

Picture the reality of the aftermath of a major library disaster. You are not allowed access to your building for safety and health reasons. You can't inspect the disaster area to judge the extent of the damage. Salvage is being carried out by contractors who answer to the insurance company, not to you. Much of the material is unrecognizable anyway. Even if you were able to inspect, how would you be able to judge what is usable; what is repairable; and what should be written off immediately?

Be prepared to respond to unreasonable demands and deadlines for building contents information. What you will be asked for, and what you need to be able to come up with in a hurry, is a detailed listing of the building contents and estimates of how much it will cost to replace or repair them. Your records may be destroyed or merely be inaccessible, likewise your computer. You will need to be able to defend and justify your estimates to hard-nosed insurance adjusters.

Fortunately for us, this task proved to be manageable. Typical of a floor in a university library, the damaged area contained book stacks, reading areas, an electronic classroom, staff offices, and some storage rooms. A substantial part of the lower level was still under renovation, and there was also a large section dedicated to mechanical and electrical space. The stack areas contained thousands of linear feet of shelving, including 40,000 linear feet of electrically-operated, movable compact shelving; and there was lounge, table, and carrel seating for several hundred readers. Some of the furniture was brand new, some was more than thirty years old. As part of the renovation, the book collections were in the process of being moved, and the furniture was also in a transitional state. The electronic classroom contained 25 student computer stations and a state-of-the-art instructor's station. The staff offices, which belonged to the two departments of bindery and gifts and exchange, included all the in-process gift and exchange materials and all the binding records, as well as the usual office furniture and equipment. The storage rooms were crammed with shelving components and furniture awaiting relocation at the end of the renovation.

Use what records you can find, and enlist the aid of staff with institutional memories. You may find you have the pieces you need to break this seemingly insurmountable task into components as we were able to do (see Chapter 12).

We were fortunate to have records that were retrievable, and the ongoing building project actually made things easier. We had accurate floor plans of all the areas and accurate measurements of the shelving. The compact shelving had been installed only a few months before. In preparation for the renovation, we had created a detailed inventory of all the existing public furniture in the building; and we also had accurate records of the furniture recently installed in the renovated areas. This was fortunate because central inventory records are not maintained for furniture. Our computer support staff were able to furnish details and serial numbers of all the computer equipment, and there were central inventory records available as well. The staff involved were able to provide complete details of the contents of their offices. Only for the storage areas were we forced to make some educated estimates.

When the insurance representatives come back with questions pertaining to your building contents inventory and estimates, be able to document the standards you used to estimate replacement value, and, where possible, show them photographs or actual examples of the contents being replaced.

Again, luck was on our side. The building project also helped us to estimate replacement costs quickly with some degree of confidence. Even though much of the furniture and shelving was old, we had recently purchased new furniture of equivalent quality, and we used these prices to estimate replacement value. The new compact shelving had only just been paid for. Since we knew how much standard shelving we had, we were able to obtain a budget estimate for replacement fairly easily.

Review your library's and your institution's inventory systems for both capital equipment and furniture. Make sure you keep your lists updated at least once a year. As with other documentation discussed in other chapters, keep a copy of this outside of the library. Your inventory should be in a database that should allow you to download to a disk which can be kept off-site.

We had another reason to be pleased that our records were complete. The building contents, other than the collections and the computer equipment, were almost immediately declared a total loss, and we never saw them again. The various salvage contractors who removed the contents had kept partial listings of what they had handled, recording inventory numbers where these existed, otherwise merely listing a description and in many cases an estimated value. Insurance and university personnel had the unenviable task of trying to reconcile these pack-out lists with both the content lists we had supplied and the university's capital asset records. Without our detailed knowledge and records it would have been next to impossible.

Some parts of the building may not be your responsibility. Construction, mechanical, and electrical areas are not usually considered part of the library space. In our case, these areas contained equipment belonging to the general contractor and several subcontractors, as well as to the university. These areas were included with the building reconstruction which is discussed below. The contractors were responsible for their own insurance claims.

ANALYZE YOUR LIBRARY'S RISK-MANAGEMENT SITUATION

How Adequate is Your Insurance Coverage?

If you haven't already, review coverage with the appropriate officials within your parent organization. Not many libraries are in the position of independently arranging their own insurance. Most share in the parent organization's insurance, which is usually managed through its risk management office.

The risk management office is responsible for assessing risks—choosing which ones to insure against and deciding which coverage and limitations are acceptable. As with one's personal insurance decisions, the cost of insurance in terms of premiums must be balanced against the consequences of the possible losses. It is the risk manager's job to keep the library insured, but it is prudent for the library management to review the coverage provided for the library and work with the risk manager to make sure the possible losses specific to the library and to the collections are understood and adequately covered.

Institutional insurance arrangements vary from commercial coverage to self-insurance, in the case of some government agencies. Colorado State University is insured through the state of Colorado. The State Risk Management Office negotiates a commercial insurance policy that covers all agencies and institutions of the state with a few exceptions. The policy is not with just one insurance carrier—several layers of coverage are involved, each covered by one or more different carriers. The layers are for the first $5 million, the next $30 million, and so on. The *stop loss* is the limit of the state's insurance coverage for any one loss. At the time of the Colorado State University disaster, the stop loss had just been raised from $150 million to $250 million—fortunately, as it turned out.

Losses Covered

It is helpful to review what *losses* are covered by insurance and what *hazards* or *perils* are included in that coverage. A library's insurance needs obviously include the building and its contents, which includes all its collections. An important risk management choice is whether to insure for *full replacement cost value*. It seems to be generally accepted that this is advisable.

A Systems & Procedures Exchange Center (SPEC) survey by the Association of Research Libraries (ARL) indicated that this was the most common type of coverage for research libraries (Myers 1991). Other possible choices are *agreed value per item* and *actual cash value*. Colorado State University's buildings and contents were insured for *full replacement cost value*. Either of the two other types of coverage would require difficult procedures for valuation on an ongoing basis. At the time of loss, they could make it very difficult for a library actually to replace its collection.

As well as repairing the building and replacing its contents, there are other risks that a library needs to be aware of. One is *business interruption*. For a library, direct business losses might include revenues from fines, lost materials fees, photocopying, and other service charges. These revenues often are counted on to help pay for library operations. We stood to lose thousands of dollars in commissions from our copy service vendor; not only was the building closed for a month, but there were also no longer any bound journals from which to copy. Additionally, as a net lender, we had to stop all interlibrary loan lending and stood to lose these payments and credits.

Another loss to consider covering is reconstruction of valuable papers and records. This is the coverage that you would need to rebuild critical paper or electronic files—or reconstruct the library catalog from the backup tapes. To our relief, this was one loss that the Morgan Library did not have to face.

It is important to consider whether separate coverage is needed for rare books and special collections. Some libraries carry *fine arts* or *valuable papers* coverage specifically for these collections. In our case, they are covered under the university's general coverage. Fortunately, our Special Collections and Archives department was housed on the second floor of the library and was not affected by the disaster.

Make sure that the institution has adequate *extra expense* coverage. In the event of a major disaster, money has to be spent immediately in order to provide emergency supplies and equipment, and to pay the expenses of setting up a temporary workplace with equipment, phones, and network connections. Later, there are the substantial costs associated with getting services to patrons up and running quickly.

Colorado State University opened for fall semester on the scheduled date of August 25, 1997. The most significant and costly service the library had to provide immediately was a greatly expanded interlibrary loan service. At the time of writing, this expense continues and will extend for many months to come (see Chapter 8).

In the ensuing time, numerous other expenses, both small and large, have been necessary. Without insurance coverage, it would have been impossible to meet these costs from our operating budget and still maintain essential library operations. By far, the bulk of the university's "extra expense" costs have been in providing library services.

One limitation of coverage that may only appear in the event of a major disaster is the existence of ceilings on coverage. For example, limitations on coverage are likely to exist for *business interruption* and *extra expense*. As we discovered, it is quite possible that the extra expenses involved in providing access to missing materials—interlibrary loan and document delivery services—throughout the entire disaster recovery period may take the organization's claim beyond the insurance ceiling. There is one consoling factor in all this. Our university's insurance provides for a $1,000 deductible per claim. Since the entire disaster constituted one claim, the $1,000 deductible still applied!

One last thing: personal property of full-time, part-time, and/ or student employees is almost certainly not covered by your institution's insurance. And yet many people keep their own books, journals, papers, and other treasured possessions in their offices. Be prepared for personnel who may lose personal possessions and suffer this additional devastating blow.

What Hazards are Covered?

All insurance is based on balancing assessed risks against the cost of insurance. Each library or institution must make its own risk management decisions and insure accordingly. Commonly, perils include fire, lightning, other weather-related acts of God, as well as theft and mysterious disappearance.

A major disaster may reveal weaknesses in some of the decisions made. In our case, the state agency had made the decision to limit flood coverage to an amount that would not have covered the university's claim. Fortunately, it was established that the Colorado State University disaster was not, in fact, a "flood" in the strict insurance definition—but there were some anxious moments in the interim.

The Importance of Valuing the Collection

Why is it important to have an up-to-date valuation of the collection? In the case of a research university, apart from the actual buildings, the library's collections may be the single most valuable asset the institution owns. Just as the buildings and contents are valued as capital assets, so should the library collection be valued.

However, if the collections are insured for *full replacement value*, the cost of replacement or repair will be paid, whatever that cost is, just as it will be for the buildings and their contents. It is important to be aware that your insurance coverage is not limited by the valuation placed on the collection. Nevertheless, having up-to-date valuation data on file is of great utility in the event of a major disaster. The first thing you will be asked is, "What was damaged and what will it cost to replace it?" The aftermath of a disaster is not the ideal time to begin working out a methodology for establishing these costs. Furthermore, the cost of replacing research collections is likely to be much greater than anyone, particularly outside the library, realizes. Again, having current data on file will help in negotiating with insurers and perhaps educating senior members of your own institution.

It is crucial to keep your library collection valuation up-to-date to assist your risk managers in maintaining adequate coverage. According to the National Association of College and University Business Officers (NACUBO, 1990), the value of a library collection determined for insurance purposes must reflect resources required, in current dollars, to replace the collection in the event of a catastrophic loss. The method recommended in the *Financial Accounting and Reporting Manual for Higher Education* uses an inflation index to recognize the fact that the cost of replacing a substantial portion of the collection would cost much more than the original acquisition costs.

The formula is:

[Base Value + Processing Cost x Inflation Index] = Replacement Valuation
(average purchase (average costs of (change in (value of library
cost per number processing average costs) collection)
of items acquired library holdings)
per category of
library holdings)

This formula recognizes that the costs of acquiring and processing replacements should be added to the estimated purchase costs of replacement materials.

In the case of Colorado State University, our Risk Management Office had, just a few months before the disaster, become concerned that the value of the collections in the University Libraries was approaching the limits of the state's insurance coverage. As a result, the state-wide coverage limit for a single claim was raised significantly. Had this not been the case, the state's insurance may not have been adequate to cover the 1997 disaster.

We had recently furnished to the Risk Management Office an annual updated valuation based on our indexed average cost per volume in 1997 dollars. We had also provided an estimate of the average cost per volume for acquisition and processing. The process we use is not difficult and can be updated annually using standard acquisitions and cataloging reports.

However, this methodology alone is not adequate to use as the basis for a claim settlement. What you will need to do to establish replacement costs in a particular loss will depend very much on the materials that have been damaged. These may or may not be typical of the collection as a whole, on which your average costs were based. The processes involved in establishing a valid replacement cost model are discussed in detail in Chapter 11.

CLAIMS AND SETTLEMENT PROCESSES

Who are All These People? And Whose Side are They On?

Within 24 hours, disaster recovery contractors and consultants will arrive on every available doorstep. In addition, if you have several insurance carriers, they will all be on the scene, each with its own officers, consultants, and contractors. Even after the initial confusion is sorted out, and official contractors are appointed, it will be very difficult to keep track of the various individuals and organizations who have their hands in the process.

In addition to the insurance personnel, be prepared for your parent organization to appoint a number of consultants of its own. Don't be naive enough to think that they will not want a library consultant. They will. Be prepared with a list of certified consultants with their specialties identified to submit to your administrator. Your parent organization may leave the appointing of library consultants up to library administrators.

If your parent organization has an insurance broker, that person will also play a critical role throughout. Each party naturally has its own interest and agenda to pursue, and they are not all on your side. In a nutshell, the interest of the insurer is to settle the claim quickly for as little as it can, and walk away. The institution's interest is to recover every cost that it possibly can, or if it sees that its best bet is an early settlement, to make sure that it gets enough money to cover all the costs, foreseen and unforeseen.

If you or your staff feel very strongly about a decision that is made, you need to be insistent about your displeasure and provide sound rationale for your disagreement. Decisions about what to write off as total loss and what to repair are basically made by the insurers on the advice of their contractors and consultants. They may not always be the best decisions from your perspective.

One example at Colorado State University was the repair and replacement of computer equipment. One of the insurers brought in a firm that specialized in restoring computer equipment and insisted that the university accept the restored equipment instead of replacing it. The library refused and eventually received approval to purchase replacements. We had the dubious pleasure of saying "I told you so" as restored equipment failed in other university locations in the ensuing months. On the other hand, there is nothing to be gained by making exaggerated claims, and your guiding policy throughout should be to make recommendations and decisions that are completely defensible and based on good business principles.

Use caution and prudence in dealing with questions from outsiders. In a major disaster, the administrators responsible for the parent organization's financial affairs will probably be the ones who will negotiate directly with the insurers. You will be asked frequently to produce all kinds of information, usually on short notice, and often over and over again by the same or different officials, consultants, and so on. It is again important to realize that not everyone is on the same side; consequently, you should err on the side of caution in giving out information.

Be aware of rules and constraints on the use of your own staff in disaster recovery tasks. You may need to consider seriously the use of outside contractors. Note again that insurance should cover not only the purchase costs associated with your claims, but also the costs of the extra labor that has to be hired to respond to the disaster and to complete the disaster recovery processes.

More problematic, however, is the time spent by the regular staff in disaster response and recovery. For example, apart from overtime, our insurance will not directly cover the countless hours spent by library faculty and staff in planning and carrying out disaster recovery activities.

Be prepared for a flood of paperwork. Throughout the claim and settlement period, the importance of keeping careful records cannot be overstated. Until the entire claim is settled, it will be necessary to keep extensive records and to produce them on demand for the insurance and Federal Emergency Management Agency (FEMA) auditors.

Within days of the Morgan Library disaster, the university had set up special financial procedures to ensure that all disaster-related expenditures received specific approval and to keep the accounting for these expenses separate, well-documented, and easy to identify. Unfortunately, this meant that everything had to be done on paper and not through our well-established automated systems.

Requirements for Risk Mitigation

There may be requirements for risk mitigation by either your insurance carriers and/or FEMA. Understand that these requirements may be well beyond you and your parent organization's control.

The recovery plans for our library called for the lower-level floor to be restored to its pre-disaster condition and for the half-completed renovations to be finished as originally planned. That meant that the lower level would continue to house 50 percent of the collection. As a precondition to its agreement, FEMA required the university to build a mitigation wall on the western side of the library building to reach a foot higher than the highest point of the July flood. This was completed within a short time with financial assistance from FEMA. This was one cost that was not covered by insurance.

Assess the building's structure and infrastructure. An immediate assessment of the cost of building repairs will be required. This is a task for your facilities department or an outside consultant. The initial assessment may have to be made before it is truly safe or even possible to inspect the damage. In our case, the library's lower level was still under water.

A number of approaches can be used effectively; the fact that we were in the midst of construction at the time once again made the task a little easier. One approach is to get an estimate from a suitable construction company—our facilities project manager naturally requested a figure from the contractor who had been on the site for the past two years; and this was obtained within a few days. A second approach, which we also used, is to compile an estimate of reconstruction costs per square foot, basing your judgments on the institution's expertise, records, history, and experience. Again, the existing library construction contract and its schedule of values proved a useful source. You can also, with caution, use standard estimating books; our project manager used these as a reality check rather than a primary source. Of the two approaches, the figure produced by the second estimating method came closer to the actual costs.

At the same time that initial assessments are being compiled, the actual work must begin. The process will be even more complex and frustrating than a normal building project. You must expect constant tension between the critical need to carry out repairs without delay and the necessity for controlling costs and obtaining approval for every step.

RAMIFICATIONS OF THE DISASTER

Environmental Concerns

It is critical that you protect the portion of your building and the collections not affected by the disaster from conditions such as high humidity and mold, which can rapidly spread if precautions are not taken. Experts in these areas of disaster recovery must be on the job as soon as possible. Portable air handling units need to be brought in and temporary ductwork should be run throughout the building to provide movement of air and control of humidity.

Once the cleanup of Morgan Library began, concern about safety was paramount. Mold began to form very quickly, even in the dry climate of Colorado. There was concern both for the collection and for the workers involved in the cleanup. To mitigate the effects of the mold, the lower level was fogged for microorganisms several times. By August 6th, the contractor was requiring all subcontractors to wear masks when working in the lower level. This was in contrast to advice given to us by our environmental health experts, who said that their testing showed that masks were not necessary. However, the contractor said that their insurance representatives were requiring this precaution. To protect our staff, no one was allowed into the lower level without clearance from the dean of Libraries.

Because of delays in beginning the pack-out of the material and an additional delay when the original contractor was fired by the university and a second one brought in, the pack-out of the material was not completed until August 14th. This delay meant that mold developed on a good portion of the material being packed-out and covered walls in the lower level. To keep mold spores from migrating to upper portions of the building, air handling units on the roof were set to force air down to the lower level and out the hole in the west wall. This created an air lock which pushed the air out of the lower level and did not allow it to come to the upper floors. The building was also kept very cold with refrigerated air to help inhibit mold growth, and de-humidification equipment ran 24 hours a day. Lab samples were taken daily to monitor air quality. Environmental Health Services (EHS) was a critical player in this portion of the clean up. The building could not be re-occupied without their approval.

While pack-out and demolition are taking place, you will need to monitor the moisture content of the existing collection carefully. Arrange for measurement several times a day and make adjustments to the levels of de-humidification and temperature to assure that the remaining collection is not adversely affected by the humidity and mold from the area that was flooded.

In our case, maintaining the temperature just above the dew point was a difficult balancing act. If dew point was reached, then the non-damaged books would begin to re-absorb the water which was being drawn out by the de-humidification equipment.

Your staff will be very concerned about health and safety issues. Be vigilant about air quality issues; use the resources of environmental health experts and ask for testing, testing, testing. Meet as frequently as you can with all staff members, both prior to the reoccupation of the building and after occupation, to field all their questions and assuage their fears. They have experienced a trauma and have legitimate concerns.

The safety of staff was of paramount concern once the building could be re-occupied. Aside from the structural safety of the building, which was quickly established, staff expressed concern that the mold which had developed in the lower level would migrate into the upper levels of the building and create health hazards. Frequent meetings were held with the staff to share test results and explain what had been done to assure that such migration had not taken place. Tests just prior to reoccupation showed that the mold spores were confined to the lower level and that there was no evidence of mold spores from the first floor up. By the time of reoccupation, tests showed that the mold and spore count in the upper levels of the library were no different from exterior levels in the rest of Fort Collins.

Safety and Security Immediately Following the Disaster

Expect some surprises regarding safety and security in the immediate aftermath of your disaster. There will be a great deal of confusion; and depending upon the type of disaster and its effects on your building facilities, your building and its contents may be exposed. In a disaster in which many surrounding buildings are affected, the normal response that can be expected from security and safety experts is not readily available (Enssle, 1998).

During our first two days, security was not a major issue. Since the disaster team was meeting in the area inside the main entrance of the library, we served as the security team. No one could enter the library without our knowledge. The real concerns began as the water was pumped out, leaving the gaping hole in the west side of the building unsecured. There were hundreds of recovery contractors coming on the scene, setting up de-humidification equipment and beginning to remove debris. Insurance representatives were walking the building making assessments of losses; Colorado State University environmental health personnel were touring the building; and volunteers were appearing to offer their help. We felt we were losing control of access to the building.

Your institution needs to have in place a plan for handling the numerous volunteers that will appear wanting to help. In most cases, even staff members will not be allowed to enter the disaster area of the building, let alone volunteers. In our case, the best we could do was to direct them to the temporary employment agency which was supplying labor for the recovery contractors. They would be paid for their efforts and covered by the typical employment insurance, thus assuring that questions of the University Libraries' liability would be handled. However, there should be a central office to which the volunteers can be directed so that efforts can be coordinated. In some cases, and in other areas of the campus, volunteers were allowed to help where the devastation was not as severe.

In the event of a widespread disaster, be prepared to take matters into your own hands to secure your building for the first few days. Campus police and authorities will be concerned with life safety issues for the entire campus. Building security, while important, is not their first priority. You may find yourself providing band-aid security until your library can be properly secured.

In order to maintain some semblance of control, personnel from our Access Services Unit were set up as monitors at the front entrance. They maintained their posts from eight a.m. to six p.m., checking all entrances to the building and physically opening and closing the doors for those legitimately coming and going. (Since we had no electricity, the electrically operated sliding doors did not function.)

By the fourth day, when removal of debris and pack-out of books began in earnest, a further security issue arose. In order to pack-out the thousands of boxes of books, a conveyor belt was run through doors on the south side of the building. Since this could not be removed and reinstalled during the brief down periods at night, it meant that access to the building through these doors would be unmonitored. Amazingly, by the time the water had been pumped out, the university police were able to provide security into the area where recovery was going on and provide around-the-clock patrols on the campus, giving us some reassurance as to the safety of the building's contents. In addition, the university issued badges to all of the hundreds of workers assisting in the recovery, making identification of those authorized to come and go into the affected areas much easier.

These conditions prevailed until the pack-out of the material was completed on August 14th when we were again able to secure the doors on the south side of the building. However, it was not until August 22nd that demolition work in the lower level was complete, and the hole in the west wall could be boarded up. Surprisingly enough, we suffered no known theft from the building during this period.

How to Continue to Operate When Your Building Can't Be Occupied

Make sure that in developing a disaster plan you also include contingency plans for space outside your building if you are unable to occupy it. You will also need to arrange for basic office furniture and equipment if your temporary space is vacant and unfurnished. And, be sure that you have computers with necessary basic software available for transfer to temporary locations and that arrangements for cell phones can be quickly implemented.

Once the safety of the remaining collections and the pack-out of the flood damaged material had been dealt with, an immediate concern was the need to find space, other than the main foyer of the library, where the disaster team could meet and work. Although air circulation was being provided to protect the collections, we had no lights, phones, or telecommunication capability. The first priority was to find a space where the administrative and essential service units could be housed to provide basic functions. We identified circulation, reference, and interlibrary loan as the main functions which would need to continue to function even before the library could be re-occupied. Space for the library administration was also critical, since communication with the rest of the campus and the outside world was essential.

We were lucky in that an adjoining building had escaped the disaster and we were kindly offered the use of several vacant offices as well as a conference room and a small office in which we set up a command center to field the numerous calls which were coming in. However, we were very much on our own in obtaining this space. The university administration had its hands full with the devastation of the rest of the campus.

Take projections of repair and reconstruction with a grain of salt. You will find that initial estimates of how long repairs will take are made without a comprehensive knowledge of the extent of the damage. As the contractors move further into demolition and can more fully assess the need for repairs, time lines will be inexorably extended.

Make sure you have a representative on the team managing the reconstruction. Communication problems arise no matter what. However, by having a library representative on the team, such problems can be minimized.

On August 6th, we met with the construction team to begin to assess the damage to the building. The plan was to conduct a system-by-system review of the wiring, main switching gear, feeders, controls, fire alarms, telecommunication, plumbing, and sewer systems. The first priority was to restore air and power to the west wings which had the only air handlers that were not in the lower level. The second priority was to restore air and power to the new east wing which contained the majority of services—circulation and interlibrary loan—that would be needed to open the building to the students. The third priority was the administrative portion of the building. Generators were brought in to provide power for the building until wiring was pulled and replaced. Our short-term goal was to have the building minimally operational by August 21st, in time for the fall semester. At this briefing we learned that, while four of our six mechanical systems were destroyed, the two units on the roof were operable and would be set to bring 100 percent outside air into the building to aid in the de-humidification process. The electricians were working around the clock to get temporary power into the building because the main switch gear was unsafe and the transformer dead.

At the disaster remediation meetings which we attended, the initial estimates of repair to the air handling equipment were very optimistic. The initial goal for occupation of the lower level was August 1998. This was delayed by the decision to locate the Processing Center in the lower level (which was eventually moved out); final occupation was re-scheduled for January 1999—a year and a half later!

In the same way, but for different reasons, repairs to the mechanical systems took much longer than estimated. The largest air handling unit suffered major structural damage. It was estimated that each of the other three would need, at a minimum, new motors, supply fans and dampers, and that the ductwork would have to be completely cleaned.

Repairs to the elevators, initially estimated to be done by late September, dragged on with one elevator finally placed in operation on the 29th of October. Repairs to the freight elevator and two other passenger elevators stretched out until mid-January. The initial goal for repair of what appeared to be the least severely damaged air handler was September 9, 1997. Final repair of this unit was achieved in January 1998. Similarly, the goals for final completion of the other units were delayed by a variety of complications; with 100 percent completion of all mechanical systems achieved in February 1998.

OCCUPANCY/RESTORATION

Plan for a Staged Reoccupation.

Once the building is declared safe to occupy, everyone will be eager to return and start trying to restore order to their working lives. As the preceding account shows, the fact that the building is able to be occupied does not by any means imply that everything is in proper working order. It may mean simply that you have power and water, and the bacteria are thought to be under control. You may not be able to open the doors to the public and pick up where you left off.

Ideally, the library's staff would be given plenty of time to put the building in order and prepare to re-open; but, if our experience is typical, there will be pressure to re-establish service as soon as humanly possible. There will be frustration to come, however, because restoring the infrastructure of a modern, technologically complex library building is a long process and is influenced by many factors that are quite beyond the library's control. Moreover, there will be huge demands throughout the institution for restoration of essential services, and the people in charge of the facilities restoration will be forced to set priorities. Library services may not be at the absolute top of the priority list.

At Colorado State University Libraries, everyone had had enough of working out of makeshift quarters by the time the library was declared safe to occupy. However, the reality was that we had lights and power (mostly), we had clean water, some of the phones worked, we had part of our data network, and one of the six mechanical units was supplying air. We had no hot water and no elevators, and the fire alarm system only worked within the building. A vital missing link was the data network—until this was restored, key services continued to operate from temporary locations. But that wasn't all; we had drying units with two-foot diameter plastic tubes entering the building through fire exits and windows and snaking around the floors to pump warm air into the library to reduce the humidity. And we were re-occupying a building where two of the non-damaged floors had large areas still under construction. We also had a plentiful supply of goodwill and patience on the part of the library patrons, and goodwill and ingenuity on the part of the library staff.

Be prepared for many of the building systems which you normally take for granted to be functioning in an emergency mode well after the eventual occupation. Identify responsible individuals within your organization to help monitor the building and notify you of problems during periods when your building is occupied.

You *can* exist without what we consider the basic amenities of life in our climate controlled existence. We brought in fans and space heaters according to the need. The same recovery contractor providing air and heat for the de-humidification of the lower level ran their equipment into staff areas to keep these areas at least bearable most of the time. Your staff will probably surprise you. There will be grumbling; but for the most part, your staff will take the initial less-than-desirable conditions in their stride. Most will be delighted to be back at work. The disaster will be hardest on those staff who are not directly participating in the recovery process and who have to sit at home and wait.

Be very assertive about security. Once the building is reopened and still under repair, security will continue to be a constant concern. You may find that your building is literally wide open; doors and windows could be missing. All your emergency exits will be in constant use by contractors, causing issues of identification and authorization that you may never resolve to your satisfaction.

Attempts to have all authorized contractors wear ID badges may be only partially successful, problems will arise with on-site enforcement, and compliance will become more lax as time goes on. (It was almost impossible for us to tell whom each recovery group reported to—the only certainty was that they did not report to the library administration.) Your police services may be stretched past their limits and unable to provide additional services inside the building.

In retrospect, we should have planned to handle the security issue more assertively from the start—either by posting our own staff to watch all vulnerable spots or by insisting that the university hire security professionals. While there were no serious incidents or major thefts that we have yet discovered, it would have improved the peace of mind of everyone working in the building to know that security was being handled in a more thorough way.

Understand that the restoration of the damaged space may take many months. Like us, you may have no sensible choice but to reoccupy the habitable part of the library building. There may be no feasible alternative in your circumstances. Even though this may well be your best option, recognize that it will mean many months of inconvenience while repairs are completed.

Living through a disaster reconstruction where every building service has been damaged means that unforeseen problems and breakdowns can and will occur unpredictably as the repairs progress. Systems and equipment may be repaired, only to fail in some unforeseen way a few days later. Different systems also interact in complex ways; coordination will inevitably be less than perfect. For the already stressed library staff, frustration may well pile upon frustration because of the effect such equipment and system failures will have on the work environment.

SPACE FOR DISASTER-RECOVERY PROCESSING: THE PROCESSING CENTER

In a major disaster that affects library collections, an initial determination will be made as to whether the collection should be salvaged and repaired or written off as a total loss and replaced. If the number of volumes involved is large, there will be a requirement for a processing facility, either to repair the damaged books and do the necessary adjustments to library records and/or to order and process replacement volumes. Very few libraries would have space available to handle an operation that might be several times larger than their existing technical services operations. This was certainly the case for Colorado State University. See Chapter 15 for more details.

Begin the planning process immediately, but expect the unexpected. Within a few days of the disaster, the disaster team needs to establish a preliminary plan for the reprocessing/repurchasing operation and an estimate of the space and facilities requirements.

Space estimates for planning purposes can be arrived at by following the planning guidelines available in the standard space planning literature (Leighton and Webster, 1986), once the type of operations and an estimate of the labor requirements are known. Ideally, the space would be on campus or close by, and not require lengthy renovation to make it usable, since time is of the essence. Costs should also be reasonable and acceptable to the insurers.

At Colorado State University, the facilities department could not identify the required 30,000 square feet of space in any building owned by the university, so we went to a commercial realtor to see what kind of warehouse/processing space was available in a small city. Suitable space of this type is not easy to find, and it does not come cheap—we were able to locate a vacant retail warehouse/storefront that had most recently been an appliance store, several miles away from campus. Working with facilities staff, we produced estimates for renting and setting up this space for book recovery operations and submitted estimates on August 17th, as requested.

Because of the state of repair of the library's lower level and the projected schedule for its renovation, we had not considered the space in the lower level of Morgan Library as an option. However, on August 20th, the library learned that there was a new plan, developed by facilities department personnel and a consultant without the library's knowledge. The Processing Center for restoring the collection was going to be set up in the lower level in about 18,000 square feet of space that underwent only enough reconstruction to make it safe and habitable, with sufficient power and telecommunications for the work at hand. Reconstruction of this space was fast-tracked, started immediately, and scheduled for completion in a month's time.

Consider the pros and cons of having the processing center onsite. If you find yourself in a position where temporary disaster recovery processes are located in your existing library structure, there will be some advantages. Your space has the necessary facilities, and the work required to bring it to an acceptable standard can probably be accomplished in a reasonable time. Your space probably has easy access to power and telecommunications, which may have been a problem with a remote site. There will be no rental costs and communication will be easier. However, the temporary operations may pose more problems than solutions. Based on our experience, security, indoor air quality, and space will be major concerns.

Be prepared for further security issues after re-occupation. Your security issues may not be completely solved with the occupation of the building. Depending on the damage to the infrastructure of your building, many of the support functions of the building, such as the fire alarm system, may be operating manually. This can create a potential safety problem.

We suffered such a problem. We therefore had to operate in a *fire watch* mode with instructions to staff to manually pull an alarm station and call 911 if there were problems. The fire alarms were not fully operational until January 1998.

Having temporary employees automatically creates its own set of security issues. Early on, you will need to meet with that staff, library staff, and the police to review security concerns. Emergency response, evacuation plans, key control, and entrance and egress will need to be discussed. You may need to have your temporary staff wear identification badges at all times. In addition, officers may need to be hired to patrol the temporary worksite.

In our situation, with two shifts of one hundred people each, the Processing Center immediately created a security nightmare for the library. The instructions to wear an identification badge at all times quickly went by the board, despite best efforts by the supervisors. The fire-tower door leading from the lower level to the outside, which was to be their only egress from and access to the building, could not be locked during hours which the center was staffed as it was needed for exiting during meal times and for breaks. Staff from the center also soon discovered another exit which was open because of the reconstruction of the rest of the lower level and made free use of it.

Because the building was not fully recovered from disaster damage, the air handling systems were not completely operational. To improve air flow in the lower level, processing staff propped open fire-tower doors. This, of course, was soon discovered by students and others who found that they had access to, and egress from, other parts of the library through the fire-tower stairs. Material was delivered to our loading dock on a daily basis, and the doors leading into the area with the freight elevator and a rear exit were constantly left open and unsecured.

MORE ADVICE

Stay flexible! (You will be bending over backwards a lot.) In case there were questions concerning the title of this chapter, here's an explanation. During the eight months of reconstruction of the disaster damage, we were constantly receiving inquiries from both the staff and the public as to "why isn't this working yet?" When the response was given "it's because of the disaster," we were frequently given looks of disbelief. They could not understand why everything was taking so long. "Why can't facilities fix this?" It was difficult to explain the complicated labyrinth of requirements which had to be met before any work could even begin.

After the initial euphoria of being back in the building, the lack of heat and air conditioning will begin to grow wearisome. We had complaints coming from both staff and patrons. Our reference staff probably had the worst of it. They were living temporarily in an open space designed for reader seating prior to the disaster. This space was in an area served by the air handler that was the most badly damaged and took the longest to fix. Temporary cooling and heating provided by a recovery contractor was not sufficient to maintain a truly comfortable working atmosphere.

Brace your staff for ongoing post-disaster inconveniences, some relative to the insurance issues. Your insurance process itself could cause delays. Replacement will be interpreted literally. For example, no work can be started until proposals for replacement parts and pricing are given to the insurance companies. If the part to be replaced is not exactly what had been destroyed by the disaster, justification needs to be made as to why a different part is being proposed (the original part was no longer being manufactured, etc.). If the insurers feel that the price is out of line, then either the price has to be justified or an appropriate and less expensive alternate has to be found. Once approval has been given for the work to be started, then the parts must be ordered. Unfortunately, you will find long lead times before parts can be delivered and installed.

Keep your cool. Attend meetings with the contractors, the insurance representatives, and your facilities maintenance staff. Make it your business to understand exactly what is being planned, when it is expected to be completed, and why it is being delayed.

Explain to the staff, in as much detail as you think can be absorbed, exactly where repairs stand, what is causing the delay, and when the completion date is expected. When that date comes and goes and it's still not fixed, explain again why it didn't happen and when the next completion date is anticipated. Delays will inevitably happen. Our best advice is to smile and deal with it to the best of your abilities. Inform the appropriate people—your library administrator, the staff, and/or the users—of the complications and their possible ramifications, and persevere in maintaining two-way communication.

CONCLUSION

In many cases, a major disaster brings out the best in people. When we look back at what was achieved at Colorado State in restoring library facilities, everyone involved has a strong sense of pride in achievement. Though day to day we tended to be disheartened by the innumerable crises, discomforts, and dangers to the well-being of our staff, facilities, and collections, the broader view shows that a major six-million dollar reconstruction project was completed in a very short time and very efficiently by industry standards. Though the building did not suffer major structural damage, all of its complex electrical, mechanical, and telecommunications systems required extensive repairs. Yet we re-occupied within a few weeks and had completed most of the reconstruction of all available areas and systems by August 1, 1998. It then took until November 1, 1998 to reconstruct the area that had been occupied by the Processing Center for nine months.

In major part, the successful outcomes can be attributed not to good advance planning, which was not in great evidence throughout the university, but to some good choices by the university in its appointment of recovery contractors. Mostly, however, success was due to consistent and ongoing teamwork and communication among facilities staff, the construction contractor, the library, and the many other players in the drama.

Library Disaster Planning and Recovery Handbook

KEY RECOMMENDATIONS

Facilities

Before Disaster Strikes . . .

- Review your disaster plan and be sure to include contingency plans for responding to a major disaster.
- Review your risk management situation and be satisfied that all potential losses are adequately covered.
- Review possibilities for mitigation of potential disasters.
- Make sure you have in safe keeping the data you will need to document and justify an insurance claim.

After The Fact . . .

- Deal with the complications as they occur—apply your disaster management principles.
- Understand that predicted dates for the stages of disaster recovery will probably not be met.
- Do not take problems personally. Much of what is done regarding facilities and disaster recovery will be out of your control.
- Be assertive about finding out what you need to know from the right people. Don't rely on either the chain of command or the grapevine.
- Expect unique security problems in the aftermath of a disaster.
- Communicate early and often and again and again.
- And finally—keep your sense of humor!

REFERENCES

Brawner, Lee B. 1993. "Insurance and Risk Management for Libraries." *Public Library Quarterly* 13: 5–15.

Enssle, Halcyon. 1998. "Security Following a Disaster." *Colorado Libraries* 24, No. 3: 16–18.

Fortson, Judith. 1992. "Disaster Planning: Managing the Financial Risk." *The Bottom Line* 6: 26–33.

Harrington, Gary. 1993. "Flood Recovery in Oklahoma City." *Conservation Administration News* (CAN) 54 (July): 10–11.

Hayes, Kathy, and Mark Minor. 1998. "The Flood." *Colorado State Alumni* (Winter): 2.

Inland Marine Underwriters' Association Arts and Records Committee. 1994. *Libraries and Archives: an Overview of Risk and Loss Prevention.* Inland Marine Underwriters' Association and Society of American Archivists.

Larkin, Bill. 1998. "After the Deluge." *Safety and Health Practitioner* 16 (July): 46–47.

Leighton, Philip D., and David C. Webster. 1986. *Planning Academic and Research Library Buildings.* Chicago: American Library Association.

Myers, Marcia J. 1991. *Insuring Library Collections and Buildings.* SPEC Kit # 178. Washington DC: Association of Research Libraries Office of Management Services.

NACUBO. 1990. *Financial Accounting and Reporting Manual for Higher Education.* Washington, DC: National Association of College and University Business Officers.

Naslund, Cheryl, and Susan C. George. 1986. "Insurance Settlement Negotiation." *C & RL News* (May): 325–328.

Paradine, T.J. 1995. "Business Interruption Insurance: A Vital Ingredient in Your Disaster Recovery Plan." *Information Management and Computer Security.* 3: 9–17.

Sherbine, Karen. 1992. "Closing the Book on Library Losses." *Best's Review* (August): 64–68.

Ungarelli, Donald L. 1984. "Insurance and Prevention: Why and How?" *Library Trends* 33 (Summer): 57–67.

Urbani, Cynthia and Martin J. Satinsky. 1997. "After the Flood: Helping Clients Handle Disaster-Related Business Loss." *Journal of Accountancy* (May): 39–41.

Varcoe, Barry J. 1994. "Not Us, Surely? Disaster Recovery Planning for Premises." *Facilities* 12 (August): 11–14.

5 Media Relations

Camila Alire

INTRODUCTION

This chapter on media relations includes a personal account and a review of the literature relating to media relations during a disaster and/or crisis to include specific examples of what we did during our disaster. It also covers the importance of the "Library Advocacy Now" media training offered by the American Library Association (ALA), which is strongly recommended. Additionally, the importance of cooperating closely with the university's Media Relations Office is discussed. Because perceptions are always evident in situations like ours, this chapter includes a discussion on addressing both internal and external perceptions of the disaster recovery process. Last, but not least, are some tips for the reader.

PERSONAL ACCOUNT

Did I ever think in a million years that I would be interviewed on all three national television networks, CNN, National Public Radio, and all the Denver television affiliates? With the print media, I was interviewed on several occasions by the local Fort Collins newspaper and the two Colorado regional newspapers. Some of these interviews and photographs were then carried over the wires and printed in major newspapers across the country, as well as in *USA Today*.

The Tuesday immediately after the Monday night disaster, we were assembling the Library Disaster Recovery Team (LDRT) in the main foyer of the library. The head of Access Services had made arrangements for some of his staff to sit at the front doors to the building to keep folks out except for team members and campus facilities personnel and administrators. We had no air conditioning or electricity.

Although the media was on campus that same day, they didn't show up at our doorstep until Wednesday. I had yet to meet the campus media relations folks, but knew that since the library and the Lory Student Center were the two most impacted buildings, it would only be a matter of time before they and the media would be wanting interviews.

The university Media Relations Office handled all media relations on Tuesday; they had just enough information to share with the television crews for the evening news. However, everyone knew that, as the preliminary assessment of damage was being conducted by campus facilities staff involved in each of the impacted buildings, the media people would want up-to-date, daily information.

The day after the disaster I had to assess who could serve as the library's spokesperson. The only name that came to mind was our associate dean, who had just finished a year's stint as the interim dean of libraries. She, however, was on vacation during the first part of disaster recovery. I knew that our two assistant deans would have their hands full with disaster response and recovery efforts in their two areas: public services and technical services. That left only one person—*moi*.

Although I was ready for this challenge, I am not sure that the Media Relations Office was. Remember that no one in that office knew me or vice versa. They didn't know whether I was capable of handling the media or not.

When Media Relations contacted me and asked who would be doing the interviews, I think they were quite surprised when I said I would be doing them. Consequently, on the first several interviews, the media relations staff was right there. I think they were pleasantly surprised how well I did. In fact, after proving myself, they did not feel it necessary to continue accompanying the television crew to the library for interviews. I had passed that test.

Why did I do so well? "All potential spokespersons . . . should be media-trained in advance." (Wexler, 1993: 30). Several years before, I had gone through the American Library Association's "Library Advocacy Now (LAN)" training and had served as a LAN trainer in several states. One whole section of that ALA LAN training dealt with working with the media. Thank heavens I had received this training. I was ready for this assignment!

The facilities coordinator/librarian, who was the key person in the renovation and building additions, was my alternate. She was also the designated tour guide along with one of our library technology staff members. Having been on the job only eight days, I knew that I didn't know enough about the library facilities (nor had I had a comprehensive tour yet) to do this. Nonetheless, I accompanied them on all the tours. What I did know was what had happened from the disaster on.

MEDIA RELATIONS AND THE LITERATURE

Unlike most topics dealing with disaster recovery and libraries, there was a considerable amount of information written on disaster recovery and media relations. What I will be doing in this section of the chapter is to insert, where appropriate, what we did at Morgan Library relative to what the literature says should be done. It gives true meaning and concrete, real-life examples to points covered in the literature.

One of the best accounts written that reviewed the role of the Public Information Office (PIO) was completed by Federal Emergency Management Agency (FEMA) in one of their basic public information courses. FEMA characterizes a disaster as that which causes a disruption in local operations where there is poor or no communication systems, and the people involved fall into categories of victims, responders, managers, and policy makers—all of whom are overwhelmed, stressed, and confused by the disaster. The PIO's areas of concern include the public, employer, media, and employees (FEMA, 1996: 4).

Colorado State University's Media Relations Office was the established PIO on campus. What we did in the library relative to media relations was a subset of the Media Relations Office. First of all, the public was not as important to the library as were the other three areas: our parent organization, the media, and our employees. The general public was not affected directly by the campus disaster, as was the Fort Collins public who were flooded out in some areas with the overflow of Spring Creek which runs through the city. My only concern was public perception of the campus and library status.

This public perception was driven by our concern for our parent organization/employer, Colorado State University. FEMA states that, in any disaster or crisis, the employer wants the organization to look good. We knew that the president of the university was concerned about public perception of the campus given that the new academic year was to start less than one month after the disaster. There was concern among campus administrators that we not lose much student enrollment because of the disaster.

Concern for the employer—that is, Colorado State University—is a primary concern of mine. This was a very important challenge when dealing with the media. The other area of concern for a PIO was officially dealing with the media. I relied on our university Media Relations Office to identify the needs of the media during disaster recovery and to inform me when they needed my involvement. Consequently, when the television crew called to say they wanted an interview, I assumed that they had already cleared this with the Media Relations Office. Mistake! Do not make this same assumption. Even to date, I am still unsure which television interviews I gave were sanctioned by our media relations people and which might not have been.

Concern for the employees was the other area mentioned by FEMA; staff always want to be a part of a winning team. In the first week or so, those of us on the LDRT were so involved in emergency disaster response measures that the best we could do for our employees was to give an up-dated report via Access Services' taped message and to try to get as many staff re-employed as soon as we could.

When I was reminded by a recovery team member that some of the staff were feeling left out or disenfranchised because they were not part of disaster recovery, we moved expeditiously to handle internal public relations with our staff. We started holding staff meetings almost on a weekly basis to inform them of our progress, challenges, and whatever accomplishments we could claim at the time. Dealing with the staff by keeping them informed was a smart move and made them feel that they were again part of the organization.

In reviewing the literature concerning media relations during a disaster, there were eight recurring themes that surfaced. The first theme was to make sure to have a media relations plan prior to the disaster. The second theme was to have one spokesperson. The third theme was that television would always be there, which leads to the fourth theme: a need for visual impact. The fifth theme was the quick delivery of the information to the media. The sixth theme was controlling the message. The seventh theme was developing a relationship with media personnel which leads to the eighth and last theme of credibility. These themes are explained in detail in the remainder of this chapter.

Theme 1: Media Relations Plan for a Disaster/Crisis

Most articles I've read mentioned the need for a media relations plan to handle a potential disaster or crisis (Davies, 1990; FEMA, 1996; Hudgins, 1996; Kempner, 1995; Zerman, 1995; Zoch and Duhe, 1997).

As the spokesperson for Morgan Library, I assumed we did not have a media plan because no one brought one forward. In our disaster planning manual, we never mentioned a media plan. However, I was confident that I could serve well as the library's spokesperson based on the media training I received through ALA's LAN training. Many of you may not be so lucky if you have not had some type of media training. So please consider signing up for a media training seminar or workshop.

Lustberg and Silverberg (1995) provided the simplest crisis management planning to include working with the media. They call it the *Nine Step Plan*. I am mentioning it here because I will respond to their plan after each step. Also, since the library is a subset of campus media relations, I can't respond for the Media Relations Office in terms of whether or not they have a media disaster plan.

The first step in the *Nine Step Plan* is to have an emergency response team and designate a chief spokesperson. Luckily for Morgan Library, not only did we have a disaster plan in place, but we also employed several librarians who had the expertise in disaster recovery and had presented workshops on the topic. And, a spokesperson was already named.

The second step in the plan is to establish a command center. About a week after the disaster, we established a 6' x 12' command center in an unimpacted building adjacent to the library. This command center, as small as it was, was equipped with all telecommunications: telephones and desktop computers for e-mail and word-processing, a message board, listings of staff hours, and mail delivery. Our host, the Office of Instructional Services, allowed us the use of their copy and fax machines. At all times, the command center had three full-time people working with the rest of the disaster recovery team using the center as necessary.

Identifying goals is the third step in the media plan. These goals should deal with safety and with returning to normal operations and service. We identified these goals immediately, which included the packing-out of the damaged materials, opening the library for staff's return to work, getting the library operational by the start of fall semester, and reprocessing the damaged materials back into the library.

The fourth step is anticipating crises. Find out how other organizations have handled a similar crisis; learn from their experience. This step was a challenge for us. No other library had suffered a disaster at the magnitude relative to the total number of materials damaged. We discovered this when we called various libraries that had suffered water and/or flood damage for assistance.

Identifying your audience is the fifth step. We were able to identify our key audience: the public, to include students, potential students, and parents of those students, and the community. Included in the audience was the media (and its role in getting our message disseminated to the public), the campus, and library staff.

The sixth step concerns developing the message. In our case, we decided that there would be two main messages and that those messages would be sent electronically. One message would have general information for the Website and the other message would be one that I would send to key groups from whom we would need assistance, such as the Alliance Member Council and the Association of Research Libraries (see Appendix 5-A).

The seventh step is establishing methods of contact. The authors mention that your administrators and boards should have the information first and that the staff answering the telephones needed to be adequately trained to handle preliminary media calls. Our staff working the command center were excellent at understanding the media relations process and what to say or not to say. Additionally, the campus administrators were the first to know of any updated information, as we met almost on a daily basis.

Conducting a drill is the eighth step. What can I say? For me, the drill was the actual disaster. This was no time for us to conduct a media drill.

The ninth step is evaluating the plan. We will officially be doing this soon; but in reality, we are unofficially doing this almost on a daily basis.

It would appear to the reader that this *Nine Step Plan* is just a lot of common sense; however, I urge you to review your disaster plan and if you do not have any mention of a media component to that plan, amend it to include one. Do not assume that you will remember all of this when a disaster hits. Even our preservation librarian had to review our disaster plan the night of the disaster.

Theme 2: Need for One Spokesperson

Along with the need for one spokesperson for the organization, there needs to be an official alternate. Using one spokesperson eliminates confusion and avoids misunderstandings. Additionally, it lessens the chance for facts being exaggerated or interpreted incorrectly (Lustberg and Silverberg, 1995). The spokesperson needs to be able to translate technical information to the layperson (the public) on the one hand, and then be able to explain to his/her administrators who may not know the operation very well (Davies, 1990).

Kempner (1995) and O'Mara (1991) will tell you that the appointed spokesperson should know the organization, be considered very credible, and feel comfortable with the press. Well, in my case, one out of three was the best we could do. Having been in my new position only a few days, I hardly knew Morgan Library and was not around long enough to have established any local credibility. However, I was comfortable with the press.

Theme 3: Television is Always There

Don't think it can't happen to you. No matter how small the community or how remote the area, when a disaster or crisis occurs that is newsworthy, television reporters and crews will be there! In a poll taken several years back, it was determined that 78 percent of the public get their news from television (Gallup, 1996: 117).

Will you be ready? Will you have designated an official spokesperson? Will you have effective sound bites to use relative to your disaster or crisis?

Theme 4: Need for Visual Impact

The audience needs to feel visual impact. That is, you can read it in a newspaper or journal article, or you can see it visually through a photograph or television. Even with television, however, visual impact may not be available. What if, for safety reasons, the television crew cannot get in to film the disaster area? What kind of visual impact can the spokesperson provide?

Sound bites will work just fine as long as the audience can visualize them. Sound bites are covered in more detail later in this chapter under ALA media training.

Here is an example of a sound bite with visual impact. In a previous position, where I wanted my audience to understand the impact of student workers in the library and the need for more money to employ more students, I had mentioned that our circulation of books the previous year had doubled—which meant that we needed more students to shelve the books. I knew that the point was not strong enough as stated; so I added that if we took the number of books we shelved the previous year and lined them up end to end, we would have shelved 57 miles worth of books, which equated to books lined up from Denver to Boulder, Colorado, and back! Mouths dropped open! That was a sound bite which provided the necessary visual impact I needed without a picture.

In the disaster interviews, when I mentioned that the over 400,000 items in the library were damaged and packed-out, I knew that information really didn't have much visual impact on the audience. So the sound bite that I added to that statement was "that includes all of the bound journals we own and one-half of the entire collection housed in Morgan Library." There was the visual impact!

Theme 5: Quick Delivery of Information

Information has to be timely. This is particularly an issue with the media who are in competition with each other. The media will be very pushy in trying to get the story first. You need to be able to accommodate their schedule and to do it with finesse. The university's Media Relations Office was excellent in doing this.

Theme 6: Control the Message

You cannot control the media, but you can control what, when, and how you share your news. The spokesperson needs to know what information to release. You can collect and organize the information for the media and help shape the media coverage (Lustberg and Silverberg, 1995; Wexler, 1993).

On the day the television crews and newspaper reporters showed up, we had just placed some staff at the entrance to Morgan Library. Their job was to keep all people out other than LDRT members, campus administrators, and contractors approved to start working. They were literally our gatekeepers.

I knew that one of the first things I needed to do was to inform staff and the LDRT that no one was to talk to the media and that all media were to be referred directly to me. With the staff sitting outside of the library, it would have been real easy for any reporter to come up and ask them questions which, unless otherwise told not to do so, they would be more than willing to try to answer. Even though the staff were situated at the front door, they knew nothing about LDRT discussions or decisions.

I also knew before I was told that we would need to project a positive image no matter how grave the situation. Consequently, I needed to make sure that the only message coming out of the library was a message I could control with the help of the university's media relations staff.

Additionally, and once we had clearance to go down into the lower level, I had to make sure that everyone understood that all tours had to be cleared by me even if the request came from the Media Relations Office. I designated two other people—our facilities librarian and one of our telecommunications employees, both of whom knew the lower level well—to be tour guides with me. Doing this was a must because I hadn't even visited the lower level before the disaster. Also, when I wasn't available, either one of them could then give the approved tour.

Again, this helped tremendously in alleviating any pressure exerted by external individuals being placed on our gatekeepers and on our recovery team to have unauthorized access to the building and to the damaged area. It also helped in keeping the traffic to the lower level limited to those authorized to work down there and to authorized tours.

Another example of controlling the message occurred within the first several days of interviews. The reporters and the television crews were chomping at the bit to get into the lower level to film and take photographs. I had to keep telling them that we couldn't do that just yet because we could not guarantee their safety; that we were still having facilities staff determine the physical soundness of the structure; and that the lower level had been contaminated. I gave them examples of shelves toppled over on each other and of books and ceiling tiles still hampering safe walking.

Theme 7: Establish a Relationship with the Media

You will, hopefully, have already established a relationship with some of the media, especially locally. With organizations like large public libraries, city governments, and universities who have media relations offices, you can bet that the staff in those offices will have already developed the appropriate relationships with the media.

Luckily for me, on my second day of work at Morgan Library, I was involved in an interview with a reporter from our local city newspaper so, at the time of the disaster, he and I were already on a first name basis. He was very instrumental later on in doing follow-up articles on disaster recovery in the library. I knew I could count on him to cover an event in the library with just a phone call.

Theme 8: Maintain Your Credibility

This theme was mentioned in almost every article I read. V. Lavoyed Hudgins (1996) provided the best advice to maintaining your credibility. He called them the *Six Cs*: be concise, candid, conversational, clear, correct, and compassionate. I cover credibility in more detail later on in this chapter.

Besides the aforementioned eight themes, David Zerman (1995) provided the best and most succinct article on dealing with the media during a disaster or crisis. He provided ten procedural elements to consider during such stressful times:

1. Have one authorized spokesperson and an alternate.

2. Don't delay when the crisis hits. Go out of your way to help the media.

3. Provide media access to the disaster area.

4. Don't deny that the disaster exists.

5. Do not provide information on any victims until their families have been notified.

6. Do what you can to console the victims and reassure your community.

7. Set up a media center that is properly equipped, if possible.

8. Have a plan in place for monitoring the media.

9. Make sure to provide information on any developments for employees, leaders/administrators, etc.

10. Always thank people who have helped or offered to help.

I can honestly say that we followed most of the elements that applied. Luckily, we did not have any victims who were hurt and, if there was a media center on campus, this was handled by the university's Media Relations Office. It was also this office that monitored the media.

ALA "Library Advocacy Now" (LAN) Training

"If 'Murphy's Law' is a fact, then a crisis will happen when we least expect it, at the worse possible time, and when we could definitely do without it" (Zerman, 1995: 25).

Having gone through ALA's advocacy training and become a trainer myself, I cannot emphasize enough how the portion of the training dealing with media relations was a lifesaver for me as the official media spokesperson for Morgan Library during the disaster. The overall training speaks to becoming an advocate for libraries. The ALA themes for advocacy may change as each ALA president comes in; however, the one consistent component of that training should be media relations. I learned and then taught all the media basics covered in the LAN training.

Let me review some of the basic tenets of LAN media training and how they applied to our particular situation.

TALK IN SOUND BITES.

A *sound bite* is 12–20 seconds long and is something that is quotable, as it should provide some useful impact albeit verbally (ALA, 1994). I had my sound bites ready for each interview. For example, for the first television interview, I knew that we would not be able to film it in the lower level because they were still pumping out eight feet of water. However, I needed to provide the viewing audience with a visual impact of our disaster. So my first sound bite was "the water level in the lower level rose as high as eight and a half feet which is comparable to six inches above a standard drop ceiling; our book shelving is 90" high. So all our books were underwater." This sound bite definitely provided the visual impact needed.

I used another sound bite later to help the viewing audience with another visual impact when I was being interviewed by a local newspaper reporter. I described the size of the hole in the lower-level wall caused by the weight of the water outside the building as "looking as if my red Miata drove through it!" Not only did this sound bite make it into the local newspaper, it made it into *USA Today*.

Do NOT SAY "NO COMMENT"; HOW TO MAINTAIN YOUR CREDIBILITY; AND HOW TO HANDLE DIFFICULT QUESTIONS

LAN training states that there is the possibility of an interviewer asking a difficult question to get to some good information. This indeed happened. One of the pieces of information television reporters wanted was some mention and/or confirmation of monetary damages.

Although we had completed a very preliminary analysis of damage to Morgan Library in terms of building facilities, cost of materials recovery, and costs of alternative services, the president of the university had requested that we keep that information confidential until further notice. Almost immediately, in a television interview, a reporter asked me about damage cost estimates for the library. I knew from my training that I couldn't respond with a "no comment" because of the viewing audience's perception that I was trying to hide something. I also knew that I couldn't fabricate something (nor did I want to) because that would affect my credibility. As a result, my response was "the President's Office will be handling all information dealing with damage cost estimates." That worked just fine.

BE PREPARED TO LOOK YOUR BEST ON CAMERA

I remembered in our LAN media training that how we looked on television mattered. The irony is that looks are the last thing any administrator involved in a disaster wants to worry about when her/his workday starts at 5:00 a.m. and ends after 10:00 p.m. Proper attire in disaster recovery work for standing in front of a television camera was the last thing on my mind at the beginning.

As we continued to wade through contaminated water and debris for days after the storm, the only proper dress code was blue jeans and cool summer tops. Remember, we had no air conditioning in the library and the stench from the contaminated water was unbelievable. Nonetheless, starting on the first Wednesday morning immediately after the disaster, I made sure that each day

I was wearing something presentable, at least from the waist up, and had more than adequate make-up on.

BE POSITIVE AND SMILE DURING AN INTERVIEW

This was probably my biggest challenge from media training. Although I looked fine—clothes and make-up—and I always verbally projected a positive image of the library and the university, there was nothing to smile about. In fact, friends and colleagues who saw the various interviews said I looked terrible. I think that my not smiling during an interview affected my appearance. I just could not get myself to smile into the camera knowing the devastation we just experienced and the ongoing personal trauma the library staff were enduring.

BE READY FOR INTERVIEWS WHETHER OR NOT YOU HAVE A MEDIA
RELATIONS OFFICE

Although many of the large, urban public libraries have their own media relations offices, most of us do not have the funds to staff our own office. Many of us have parent organizations that do support media relations offices. However, remember that television crews want to talk to the victims (as in the university's case, mostly people from Morgan Library and from the Lory Student Center).

If you are a library director or some other type of administrator, be prepared; you may find yourself the spokesperson during a crisis.

For example, although what we experienced at Colorado State University was a natural disaster, any one of you could experience a censorship or First Amendment-type of dilemma and/or crisis. How you handle the media in that crisis is similar to handling the same media during a natural disaster.

If you are an assistant director or library manager or if you have a certain expertise—archives/special collections, library network services, preservation/conservation—be prepared. You will never know when being the official media spokesperson for your library may be *delegated* to you or when you will be asked to do an interview because of your expertise.

To all library directors, if you and key staff members haven't already gone through some type of media training possibly sponsored by your city government, school system or college/university, please do so. If that opportunity is not available, please take advantage of ALA's library advocacy training. It is usually offered at every ALA annual conference and many states already have LAN trainers residing in them. The ALA Public Information Office has a list of all the trainers listed by state. The only costs you should incur are the costs to get a trainer in your state to your library. I recommend that you try to get public libraries and/or college libraries from your surrounding areas to attend one main training session. Trust me, it is well worth the time and effort.

COOPERATION FROM YOUR CAMPUS OR COMMUNITY MEDIA RELATIONS OFFICE

As was previously mentioned, many libraries have parent organizations that support a media relations office. If you already know the key players in your media relations office, great. If you don't, begin to develop a relationship. Think about what might be happening in your organization and call media relations folks to introduce a potential story.

Call the director of media relations and invite him/her to lunch. You don't have to have an excuse for lunch other than you would like to get to know the person better and share possible updates about what is going on in your library.

Most organizations write newsletters for alumni and/or for the campus. Call that unit of media relations and see about the library being included in the next issue. Try to develop an excellent relationship with the entire staff. They are great people and will be extremely helpful in disaster recovery efforts or through other crises that may occur.

The media relations office can also be very instrumental in arranging for follow-up interviews with area newspapers to present a positive picture of your library's efforts in disaster recovery or after a crisis has subsided. Media relations staff are usually always available to answer any questions, receive any suggestions, and/or provide guidance when requested.

Make yourself accessible to the media relations office for providing updated information and for whatever media assignment they might want you to be involved in. One other area that they are involved in are various tours of government officials and legislators. If your library is usually not considered on the usual legislative tour route, suggest to the head of media relations that it be considered. Be prepared to tell the head person why.

If you are part of the legislative tour, or are included after your suggestion, be full of sound bites. Have your "Tour the Library" segment down to the exact time you are given by the media relations office. If you have 15 minutes, be sure to include certain important components. If you have only five minutes, get it down to covering the areas providing the most impact on the tour group. This will be extremely helpful to legislators who are instrumental in their recommendations to the entire legislative body to grant your institution more funds, if that is the purpose.

By the way, LAN media training worked hard to dispel the intimidation factor of meeting with legislators. Months after the disaster, I was on first-name basis with the state legislature's Capital Development Committee and the local legislative representatives from the Fort Collins area.

Remember that working with your media relations office prior to a disaster or crisis will only help solidify your relationship with these folks. Don't wait for a crisis to get to know them well.

PERCEPTIONS OF THE CAMPUS AND LIBRARY DURING A DISASTER

External Perception

"All language used should be as positive as possible to convey the message that the company expects to resolve the situation favorably" (Kempner, 1995: 46).

How the campus or city/county government and your library is being perceived by the public after the disaster should always be on your mind. Understandably, for an academic environment (higher education or K–12), the key administrator's concern should be that your disaster should have as minor of an impact on students and faculty and on enrollment as possible.

Given that scenario, and from impressions gained doing discussions in various campus meetings of disaster recovery folks, you will all understand that the image you portray with the media would be critical to the perception of campus readiness for students.

Consequently, determine your party line before you are interviewed; a party line should always include a statement that your library will be opened and operational by the date that is settled by top administrators internally on campus or within your city/county government. The reality is that you may have no control over your statement! That is, you may have no control over what recovery efforts need to be completed by your facilities folks and outside contractors. What will be in your control is the development of alternative services for your users as well as alternative services for those doing research during disaster recovery.

However, rest assured that your top administrators, due to public perception, will develop a time frame for disaster recovery and will assume you and other administrators affected by the disaster will follow the same party line.

Internal Perceptions

The first folks you should be concerned about immediately after the disaster in terms of communications are your library staff who are not part of the recovery team. You may find that in your disaster, officially, your campus may be off-limits to all staff except for *essential* employees. In your library's case, that would probably be only your disaster recovery team designated by title in your disaster recovery plan. If you don't have a disaster recovery plan, then your essential employees will probably be your management team and department heads.

What is important is to maintain some type of public relations with your staff. Most of the members of your library disaster recovery team will probably also be managers. It is through them that you will gradually be able to re-employ some of your folks either at remote sites on campus or at home.

In terms of internal perceptions of your disaster recovery efforts, you want to keep your staff from feeling disenfranchised and not part of the team. Remember that your staff are definitely victims of the disaster, and they deserve attention and accurate information to prevent any misunderstandings or rumors.

If possible, organize weekly staff meetings in an alternate site on campus or within the city. This will allow you to communicate to your staff any updated information, changes, new dates, etc.

As important to your library will be the perception of your disaster recovery status with internal campus people; or, for public libraries, your colleagues in other government agencies. You need to work hard to get the message to campus personnel through your staff campus newspaper and also through the student newspaper about what you are doing to recover from your disaster and about possible alternative services and resources.

Let folks know of your plan for recovery and the time frame you are anticipating. If you have to deviate from your original recovery plans, inform the campus or other city employees as well as the public about this change.

Having said that, I need to say that you need to be prepared for the perception from some folks who only have the original recovery plans in their minds. That is, they will forget about the second major message about the deviation in recovery plans and only remember what was delineated in the original plan. I say this because your faculty and students, who have the original message in their minds, will start inquiring about why you haven't been able to move back into your library or why there aren't more materials on the shelves. Make sure that your subsequent media messages are developed with that thought in mind. They must be strong enough and noticeable enough to change the original perception in most minds.

What to Do When the Information Is Not So Good

You may find yourself in a predicament where the updated information you have does not look very positive and may have a negative impact on your institution's party line; and yet, internal folks (faculty, for example) are asking for updated information because they have the "right to know and know now!" How do you handle this internally?

Agree that they have the right to know but also remind them of possible external implications and that the top-level administration would have to approve the release of such information. Not only will you be faced with some angry and frustrated faculty, but you will also be faced with the pressure of external implications if any negative message gets out without your institution's administration knowing it.

You will also realize that your credibility and integrity will be in question if you do not respond honestly to the faculty concerns. Be prepared for major damage control at best.

First, share your situation and concerns with your immediate supervisor. Lobby this person hard for him/her to talk to the president and his/her cabinet (or in a public library situation, your city manager or mayor and the library board of trustees) about getting the accurate and informative message out. You need to convince your supervisor that it is better to deliver the bad news and that there may be some way to turn this negative into a positive (be sure to have some examples). Remember that the concern of most top administrators is the external perception. For example, in an academic setting, that concern could be the effect any negative news would have on student enrollment and/or faculty recruitment. Additionally, work with the head of media relations to draft an internal press release that would address your negative issue in a positive way. Then work hard to have your supervisor get the approval to release that internal message. In the long run, it is very important to get the message out, but remember you can control or spin the message. In doing so, you have maintained your credibility and that of the institution.

CONCLUSION

This chapter provided a personal account and a review of the literature relating to media relations during a disaster and/or crisis. It also covered the importance of getting media training and of cooperating closely with your media relations office. Because perceptions are always evident in disaster situations, this chapter included a discussion on addressing both internal and external perceptions of the disaster recovery process.

Let me conclude with one appropriate quote:

> Each time we deal with the media, it should be seen as an opportunity to get our message across to the public in the most professional way. For us to lose those opportunities can destroy our credibility as a public servant (Hudgins, 1996: 52).

Library Disaster Planning and Recovery Handbook

KEY RECOMMENDATIONS

Media Relations

- Don't think something like this or some other crisis couldn't happen to you. Be prepared before it strikes.

- Get media training. The head of your organization and key folks within your organization should go through some type of media training.

- Have some type of media plan in place before a crisis occurs.

- Based on that plan, have a trained spokesperson (and an alternate) designated for your organization.

- Don't forget to communicate with your staff to eliminate any rumors or misunderstandings. The staff is your public also.

- If your parent organization has a media relations office, work very closely with that staff to communicate and coordinate the flow of information and interviews.

- Control the message to the media.

- Remember that your credibility and your organization's credibility are always at stake. Do nothing to affect your credibility negatively.

- Keep your administration abreast of all events and updated information.

- Remember to remind yourself that you will get through this also.

APPENDIX 5-A

MORGAN LIBRARY E-MAIL MESSAGE TO
ARL LIBRARY DIRECTORS

TO: ARL Directors
FROM: Camila A. Alire
SUBJECT: CSU Disaster
DATE: August 5, 1997

First of all, let me give you a brief recap of the extent of the damage caused by the flood. ALL of our bound journals [A-Z—humanities, social sciences and sciences] have been damaged and removed for possible salvaging. ONE-HALF of our entire monograph collection housed in the building has also been removed. They anticipate that it will be at least 2 years [or maybe more] before our whole collection is back.

We have estimated [based on library consultant's advice] that 80% of the damaged materials can be saved. We will not have access to major book collections in the following areas: all of sciences [Q]; all of education [L]; all of music [M]; all of our vet science, agriculture, forestry and soil science [S]; all of engineering [T]; all of medicine [R]; all of poli sci [J]; all of military science [U-V]; all of library science [Z].

Other partial monograph areas impacted are business [HG, HJ]; sociology [HM, HN, HQ]; Urban/Cities [HT]; Social Work [HV]. Additionally, 11 of our 13 "areas of excellence" (only collections in the state) are totally damaged. We also lost a state-of-the-art [and new] Electronic Instructional Lab full of PCs and other A-V equipment.

This list of damaged and unavailable materials is enough to make anyone shudder! I suspect most of you are now thinking "there but for the grace of God go I." However, I know that all of you are thinking of us here at CSU and will be willing to help us in some way.

We are still not in the building and are operating out of a 5x10 command center in a nearby building. However, I have folks working out of the depository and from home. They have all been real troopers!

The final box that was "packed-out" was yesterday eve and all the materials packed-out will be going to freezers in Texas. We had a severe outbreak of mold/mildew late last week as the workers who were cleaning out debris were finally able to get to the back part of the lower level. However, they contact sprayed a fungicide Saturday and Sunday nights. We are checking our regular collections on the other 3 floors twice daily and so far, so good. [The building has already been fogged].

After much discussion/brainstorming with staff, here are our ILL needs for your consideration:
1. No charge for ILL/photocopies*
2. Priority ILL status for CSU
   –No bumping
   –Fed Ex delivery [where available]
   –Ariel delivery [where available]

*Includes medical/law specialties.

For your information, we are aggressively pursuing setting up Ariel workstations at 6 remote sites [based on journal collections] in academic libraries for document delivery—4 at Alliance libraries in Colorado; and 2 out-of-state. We received approval from the insurance company to provide all the necessary equipment and FTE for the 6 libraries to operate. As soon as those sites are confirmed, I will pass that information along.

What I need to know is what each of you would be willing to offer in terms of our stated ILL needs. Mary Jackson has most graciously agreed to coordinate your responses and deliver them back to CSU. Please e-mail your responses directly to Mary at: *mary@cni.org*

As you can imagine, time is of the essence for us. We are planning to be back in the building, once power and telecom. are restored, a few days before the start of Fall semester [Aug. 25]. The president wants everything in place [!] by the time students and faculty arrive. So I plead for your immediate attention in this matter and thank you so much for your consideration.

Besides the subject areas listed above, I would like to share with you the 11 subject areas of excellence [collected for the entire state] that are damaged and unavailable: animal reproduction and biotechnology; biochemistry and molecular biology; chemistry; environmental toxicology and technology; infectious diseases; meat science; natural resources ecology; neuronal growth and development; optoelectronic computing systems; radiological sciences and cancer research; and water resources. [whewwww!]

Here is what we would need:
* priority on discards [list of those materials by author/title for books and vol/year for journals would be extremely helpful]
* contact faculty for long runs of journal titles
* contact CSU before posting on DEU [Duplicate Exchange Union]
* hold these materials you plan to send until CSU finds appropriate space

There is a listing of the journal titles and monograph titles that we are most specifically interested [but we are interested in more than those on the list] on the Alliance WEB SITE at: http://www.coalliance.org/

Joel Rutstein is coordinating this gifts effort. He can be reached at 970-491-1838 or *jrutstein@manta.library.colostate.edu*

Also, the CSU president will be sending your presidents a formal letter.

Nonetheless, I again thank you for your consideration of our request.

Your colleague and friend—CAMILA ALIRE, Dean

REFERENCES

American Library Association. Special Committee on Public Awareness. 1994. *Americans Can't Wait—Library Advocacy Now!* (Training notebook).

Davies, Jean S. 1990. "Crisis Management: Working in the Media." *The Camping Magazine* 62 (April): 30–34.

Federal Emergency Management Agency. 1996. "Basic Public Information Course." Chapter 1, page 4. Available at: *www.garlic.com/oes/pio.txt.*

Gallup, George, Jr. 1996. *The Gallup Poll: Public Opinion 1995.* Wilmington, DE: Scholarly Resources.

Hudgins, V. Lavoyed. 1996. "Crisis Management and Media Relations for Small Agencies." *The Police Chief* 63 (February): 50–52.

Kempner, David. 1995. "Reputation Management: How to Handle the Media During a Crisis." *Risk Management* 42 (March): 43–48.

Lustberg, Arch, and Beverly Silverberg. 1995. "Sending the Right Message When Crisis Strikes." *Association Management* 47 (July): 3–4.

O'Mara, Lisa. 1991. "Openness and Quick Response Critical When Working with the Media in a Crisis." *Occupational Health and Safety* 60 (March): 28–30.

Wexler, Jim. 1993. "Using Broadcast Television to Control a Crisis." *Communication World* 10 (November): 30–31.

Zerman, David. 1995. "Crisis Communication: Managing the Mass Media." *Information Management* 3: 25–28.

Zoch, Lynn, and Sonya Forte Duhe. 1997. " 'Feeding the Media' During a Crisis." *Public Relations Quarterly* 42 (Fall): 15–18.

PART TWO

Public Services in Disaster Recovery

6   Public Services: Holding Up the Storefront

Julie Wessling

INTRODUCTION AND PERSONAL ACCOUNT

It rained all the way back from Colorado Springs that afternoon, but nothing seemed unusual about the storm. I carried on a lively conversation with my colleague from the Fort Collins Public Library, discussing follow-up plans from the LSCA evaluation meeting we had just left and then moving on to explore ways we might collaborate on projects, stretching a bit to identify mutually beneficial possibilities. Little did I know just how soon we would be collaborating with the benefit exclusively for Colorado State University users. Fort Collins Public Library was among the first libraries to get in touch and offer Colorado State University's Morgan Library assistance in the hectic time to follow.

It was eleven o'clock that same evening when I got the first clue that this was not a normal storm, at least not near the university. A quick call from the assistant dean for Technical Services alerted me to the escalating problem in the library; her words, "you'd better be thinking about alternative places for offering services" were still haunting away normal sleep when the phone rang at 5 a.m. This time it was the associate dean announcing that the campus was unsafe; staff should not come to campus; and the phone tree notification system should go into place immediately. It would be a long time before any of us would again entertain thoughts of normal sleep patterns.

It is difficult to describe the range of emotions during those first few days and weeks. There were the stories about the incredible bravery of our staff on duty at the time—and how very close some staff came to being swept away when the lower-level

149

wall gave way and the water first rushed in. The relief that no staff were injured kept the magnitude of the damage to the collection and to the building in perspective, helping us focus on the immediate demands. Still, it was overwhelming. No building, no electricity, no computers or network connections, no working phones, and no safe access to the parts of the collection not damaged by the disaster. How could we provide any services? With a week of classes still remaining in the summer session, the first day of classes for fall semester was less than one month away. In a normal year, this is a very busy time in which we revise all the instructional guides and library instruction courses in preparation for the onslaught of new students in the fall. This year everything was under revision to reflect the anticipated changes soon to be in place. We were approaching the completion of a four-year building construction and renovation project that essentially doubled public space in the building. Plans were underway for the grand opening to occur early in the fall semester with all service areas and collections finally in their permanent configuration. The staff, finally able to escape the distraction, smells, dirt, and noise of construction, were ready to focus on exploiting the architectural and technological features of the new building. The disaster really couldn't have happened at a worse time; but, then again, maybe that's what helped us to all come together so quickly. This chapter provides an overview of issues to consider when you redesign library services to minimize the impact of a disaster.

REVIEW OF THE LITERATURE

Library disaster articles focus extensively on protecting the collection, and on salvaging and restoring the volumes which are damaged. Much less is written about providing library services in the face of disaster. Indeed, there are few disasters in library history in which a large and significant portion of the collection is damaged and unavailable for an extended period of time. Articles which do touch on services focus primarily on brief, temporary relocation of service following building damage to the library. A useful article by Miriam Kahn (1994) outlines the specific responses of several special libraries faced with disasters which made their main facility unavailable for a number of weeks. It includes practical suggestions for setting up a command center, keeping in touch with staff and users, and restoring computer services after a disaster strikes. In addition, it shares the things each library would do differently if such a disaster happened again and addresses elements to consider in putting together a plan to improve ability to respond to disasters in the future.

Robert Chadbourne (1994) reminds the reader about the silver linings that may follow a disaster, especially if focus remains on the users during the most difficult recovery periods. In Chadbourne's particular case, the damaged public library was restored in a temporary location near the downtown, which placed it near city officials and decision makers, resulting in increased visibility and ultimately resulted in funding for an expanded, new facility. Long-term political benefits will be the last thing on your mind during the early days of a disaster, but when you are presented with alternatives for a temporary service location, it is prudent to consider long-term opportunities.

As you face the reality of running a library based solely on remote access, you won't find a "how to" resource for your dilemma, but you will be able to find a number of articles which ponder the merits of purposely tipping the scales, perhaps dramatically, in the direction of access. I enjoyed reading Laura Townsend Kane's (1997: 59) description of the hypothetical library based solely on access; it would

> become more of a business, an "information broker," cold, and impersonal. Logic would dictate that these libraries could obtain monographs through ILL and access to journal articles through online, full-text e-journals on various networks or the Internet. The first major problem crops up when libraries begin to rely solely on ILLs for monographs requested by patrons. If interlibrary loans were filled at all in this situation (where there is no reciprocal service), patrons would be forced to wait months for a book they requested. Libraries would be at the mercy of those who actually *owned* the information. . . . A second ominous problem is one of cost . . . there is no free service; someone pays; will the library be able to absorb the cost of ILL and database searching? . . . Further pitfalls would be speed of access and elimination of browsing. It would be naive to believe that library patrons would accept such radical changes without complaint. . . . The success-

ful library of the future will consist of a delicate balance between materials that are owned and those that are accessed. The quality of these future libraries will not be determined by size but, rather, by how effectively they fulfill the needs of the patron.

I think Kane has it right. The unprecedented experience at Colorado State University's Morgan Library provided a test case of a "library based on access" in action. In the early weeks before the building opened, the service at the library depended exclusively on access. Even after the building was accessible, our library users continued to depend on access for all journal articles older than two years (most bound journal volumes had been shelved in the lower level) and for all monographs in call number ranges of HG-HZ, J, K, L, M, and Q-Z. Kane's cautionary notes are important ones to keep in mind as you put together a package of service options for your users following a disaster.

SETTING UP THE BASICS

Daily crises and unexpected happenings are the norm in library public services, and staff are trained to be flexible to meet the needs of library users. This is just not the same as coping with a major disaster. It is difficult to be prepared for losing a major portion of your collection and having the building not accessible for a lengthy period of time. Planning ahead for responding to a major disaster is essential and can provide an anchor during the ensuing chaos. Somehow, library service must go on in the face of any disaster. In fact, it is likely that business will increase since many people who lost their personal libraries or information resources now look to you for assistance.

Communicate With Each Other

Communication is the first priority. It is essential to target key staff to assist with planning and organizing, but you cannot focus exclusively on staff with management responsibilities. Be sure mechanisms are in place to get basic information out to all staff. Public services typically includes a large percentage of the total staff. At the library, more than 60 full-time staff are in public services, and there are many student assistants. Despite the implementation of daily voicemail updates and several library-wide staff meetings followed by divisional and departmental gatherings, some staff still felt they lacked information. This was a major problem during the weeks the building remained closed at CSU. The most important element in helping staff cope is to be sure they have specific assignments and a well-equipped space to work. This may be easier to achieve in areas such as Reserve or Interlibrary Loan, in which processing activities may be continued at a remote, temporary location. Reference and Information staff may be scheduled at temporary service stations; however, they will also need some accommodation to tend to other duties. For us, it was impossible to find regular work space for Reference/Information staff; when not scheduled for "desk" duty, many staff members worked from home. This separation from other staff was unfortunate and added to the stress of the situation for these individuals. Perhaps no amount of communication is truly enough in this situation, but every attempt should be made to minimize a feeling of separation or non-involvement.

Establish a Reference/Information Base

From a service perspective, the first challenge is to identify a base from which to offer users information, and we were able to build a temporary framework for providing as many library services as possible. During my restless night, I had briefly considered sharing space in area libraries. I quickly moved to favor setting up a main base in one or more of our branch libraries or possibly identifying other available space on the main campus where we would have more local control and our users would have more convenient access. Early conversations with public service managers confirmed this direction.

Each service area has unique space needs, equipment requirements, and staffing restrictions which need to be considered when evaluating the options for housing temporary services. It is important to balance the needs of staff and users when allocating use of available space. In order to evaluate space options, it is important to identify essential elements for each service area. Focus on two or three distinguishing priorities for each. Common needs will not help you determine the best use of available space.

You may not know how long you will be displaced from your regular facility. It is desirable to identify space which could accommodate services for an indefinite period of time. Moving an operation is time-consuming, stressful for staff and confusing for your users. However, it is not always possible to work with just one temporary location. You may decide an interim move is warranted if the first space fails to meet your need and better space is identified. Or, you may be forced to move when the space is no longer available for your temporary service. Once you have set up an initial temporary site, you can make any subsequent moves from a position of experience.

Minimal reference service requires phones and access to a print or electronic ready-reference collection. The facility should be easily accessible to your users and provide staff and user space. It should have computers with network connections or modems to access your library online catalog (as soon as it is available), as well as other library catalogs and any networked databases or available electronic resources and the Web.

At Colorado State University, the branch library at the Veterinary Teaching Hospital emerged as the first choice for providing information/reference assistance. Although it was almost two miles from the center of campus, it offered some user space and had several fully equipped terminals and a solid, basic reference collection on-site. However, this is a small, one-room facility, and it was quickly apparent that it would not satisfy reference needs for the entire campus very long. The distance was a real problem for users; most queries came by telephone, with very few users arriving in person. Also, the space was too small to accommodate very many staff members at one time. The first priority is to provide a suitable reference location for users, but a good temporary facility should also provide a core of staff work space to support the off-duty tasks of reference staff.

Better space was identified on the main campus, and the reference operation was moved to a centrally-located building on the campus, where space included a computer lab setup and classrooms equipped for hands-on computer instruction. It still wasn't *home*, but this second choice for a temporary reference facility offered more than 20 terminals for users to access the library online system and networked databases. Reference staff had more access to e-mail, word processing, spreadsheets, and other tools. With the addition of ready-reference tools, which were retrieved from the library, staff were able to meet most basic reference needs in this temporary facility.

Reference service using electronic resources and access to a ready-reference collection will likely be the pieces you can put together first. You may need to provide reference service for an extended time using a greatly-reduced collection. In this case, it is useful to negotiate referral options for your users to receive in-depth reference assistance at area libraries. This could include a combination of e-mail reference, telephone reference, and on-site assistance at another library by appointment. Some libraries may prefer that a reference query be mediated by local reference staff; others will encourage direct interaction with your users. It is important that you provide guides and assistance to help your users identify the most appropriate library for handling in-depth reference needs that cannot be met by your local collection.

Provide an Immediate Method for Users to Request Material

After a disaster, ILL suddenly becomes the primary option for users to access materials. At the library, the ILL program is one of the most heavily used services since the disaster. In the first year of recovery, there were more than 130,000 interlibrary loan requests to borrow materials, rather than the 24,000 handled in a typical year. Setting up an immediate way for users to request material and for library staff to process the requests is essential. Equal attention should be given to the convenience of submitting requests and the infrastructure available to process requests and then deliver requested material to the users.

Creating a work environment for interlibrary loan staff requires identification of physical space with workstations and connectivity to support your normal communication modes with other libraries. The environment must also allow staff to have a reliable way to receive user requests, respond to questions about the status of requests, allow mail and/or courier delivery from supplying libraries, and support a mechanism for delivery of both loaned and photocopied material to users.

Staff training will be the first order of business, and significant time should be set aside for it. More staff will be needed to handle the increase in requests; the numbers are likely to be huge when interlibrary loan is the only access to library materials. You may be augmenting your staff with a combination of reassigned library staff (including retraining of the lending staff in your regular interlibrary loan operation) and new hires. (See Chapters 2 and 8.)

Setting up the user loop

User convenience should be the top priority. In an environment which requires total reliance on interlibrary loan for accessing books and journal articles, users will need a clear and easy method to communicate information about the materials they need. The more automated an interlibrary loan operation is at the time a disaster strikes, the more options there are to restore interlibrary loan services quickly. Libraries with an electronic request system already functioning can focus on restoring the computer server where the program is stored or on activating back-up plans for installing their basic request program on a temporary computer server. Libraries without an interlibrary loan electronic request service may wish to consider accepting requests from users on e-mail and will need to provide a conveniently located physical location, open for extended hours, where users may place requests.

Plans for delivery of requested material must consider both loaned and photocopied items. When feasible, focus on delivery directly to the user rather than limiting pick-up to one physical location. This is a time which calls for creativity to help bridge the tremendous loss your users are facing with no on-site collection. In a campus environment, you should focus on delivery to individual departments or offices. Loaned material presents the greatest challenge; it demands some sort of local courier system to take materials to users or to designated retrieval sites. As a last resort, you may offer pick-up of loaned material from one site and play the convenience card by offering extended hours, including evenings and weekends. Photocopies should be faxed or transmitted electronically to the user. Mail or courier delivery should be used as a last resort.

SETTING UP THE STAFF WORK ENVIRONMENT

Efficient interlibrary loan is heavily automated. Your temporary environment needs to include all the technology used in your normal work routine; if resources allow, also add programming and technology support staff to further automate processing for handling the increased demand. But technology is not enough. There must be a corresponding change in workflow and processing routines. This is the time to eliminate any procedures, policies, and practices which were developed in an era of manual operations. It is widely reported in the literature and recognized by many interlibrary loan staff that early procedures were developed to control workflow and minimize the workload of staff rather than to optimize the effectiveness of the service for the user. Staff may not have taken the time to step away from hectic workloads to examine the effectiveness and efficiency of procedures. In the face of disaster and escalating demand, it is essential to strip out all the unnecessary steps, design a process to address the bulk of requests rather than to accommodate exceptions, and take the time to refocus all workflow around speed, efficiency, and user convenience.

DEPENDENCE ON OTHER LIBRARIES

Any significant increase in interlibrary loan activity puts a corresponding load on the libraries that lend you materials. This impact is exasperated by the fact that you are no longer in a position to be a lender; the same libraries to which you are turning for extra help also must fill the void you have left. When a disaster hits a large lender, the impact on its regional and consortial partners can be enormous. It is essential to review your new demands with other libraries and work out solutions cooperatively.

A large disaster that lasts more than a few months will require ongoing communication about offers of assistance and sensitivity to the need to redistribute requests on a regular basis. Generosity and cooperation from other libraries have played an enormous role in the library's disaster recovery services. Libraries of all sizes and from all regions of the nation came forward quickly to offer interlibrary loan preference by expediting requests and eliminating fees. (See Chapter 26 on Resource Sharing.)

A TAILORED APPROACH AT MORGAN LIBRARY

Immediately after the disaster, the library considered using UnCover as the main journal article service to provide access to material damaged in the disaster. However, based on the history of journal checkouts for the impacted volumes, the estimated cost of this option would have approached $300,000 per month. This was prohibitively expensive and encouraged us to design a custom system for providing convenient, fast access to the articles in the damaged journal collection.

FastFlood, the custom article delivery model developed at the library, combines the best of technology with radical changes in staff processing procedures. However, the most important ingredient in its success is the cooperation and dedication of staff at six partner libraries who willingly share their library resources using radically modified procedures and protocols.

Provide Options for Users to Return or Retrieve Material

While the building is not available for use, an alternative location should be identified for users to return material they currently have checked out. You will want to encourage users not to return materials until you have space to store and process items safely. Local libraries may be willing to accept returned material from your users and store it for a limited time. You may need to explore other types of local sites which would be willing to accept returned books from your users on a temporary basis and could offer convenient access for this purpose.

You may need to provide a location to retrieve material when you offer page-only service to a selected portion of your collection or when you continue to retrieve material from a storage facility not impacted by the disaster. Paging may be integrated into your interlibrary loan delivery plan with emphasis on direct delivery to the user or, alternatively, may be offered as a walk-in service in temporary space for information and reference services.

Academic course reserve services may need special attention.

Depending on the time of the semester, you may need to provide a site for faculty to bring materials they wish to place on Reserve or provide easy user access to available course reserve items (see Chapter 7).

If your online system is functional, it is advisable to renew all checked-out material in order to minimize fine and billing problems when the library returns to normal. Your patrons will appreciate your efforts to reduce confusing library notices which seem to ignore the existence of a disaster.

Once the library building is available, location assistance will be an important service if any materials need to be housed in temporary or changing locations. At Morgan Library, based on experience gained with roving assistance during a recent renovation project, the library hired student assistants after the disaster to help users locate material which was housed in temporary locations. Students are available whenever the library is open to help people locate material or services and, when necessary, to page material from inaccessible areas. This service, based at the main information desk, provided the main access for our disabled users during the weeks when elevators were not functioning.

When material is in temporary locations for an extended period, or when it is necessary to shelve material in confusing sequences, it is important to consider a comprehensive paging system. This may be designed as a recovery service, but long-term implications should be considered. Your users will like this service; data gathered during any temporary paging will provide you with valuable information should you decide to implement a long-term paging service for user convenience. Some online catalog systems support a request feature for retrieving an item from the local collection. Disaster recovery is a good time to try out this option and identify the staffing requirements for providing the service on a regular basis.

Set Up Links to Regional Library Resources

You may want to consider providing shuttle service to area libraries. A shuttle service should be designed to provide your users with convenient, inexpensive (or free) access to nearby libraries known to hold materials which match your users' needs. It is difficult to estimate demand for such a shuttle service, so it should be planned to allow schedule and route adjustments in response to actual experience. Key elements in setting up a shuttle service include appropriate and accurate publicity; clear instructions about how to use the service; use of a reservation system to avoid disappointed or stranded passengers; planned routes and schedules to match building hours at destination libraries; modification of schedules during intersession or holiday periods; and good communication with destination libraries to clarify expectations and respond to any problems or concerns.

After the disaster, Morgan Library set up a shuttle service to five neighboring university libraries. University Motor Pool operated the service using 15-seat vans driven by student employees. Use of the shuttles was low. The slowest routes were cut back during the first semester of operation with service during the second semester remaining for only one library of the original five. Shuttle service ceased completely after the second semester. Shuttle service is expensive to operate, and it is staff-intensive for responding to problems and concerns which may involve stranded passengers who require late night rescue or expect reimbursement for unexpected overnight stays. Area libraries reported a great deal of use by Colorado State faculty and students, who mostly preferred to use private cars for transportation.

Information sheets about resources in area libraries are useful to help direct users to the appropriate library; you may wish to mount information about area libraries on your Web page as well. Useful items to cover include information about the collection; driving directions to each site, and parking information; checkout privileges extended to your users; on-site photocopy facilities and costs; and information about the online catalog and electronic resources. For the Web version, this should include a link to the library's homepage and online catalog.

COMMUNICATE WITH PATRONS

Following any disaster, your users will want to know exactly what is going on and what they can expect for the immediate time period, as well as plans for long-term disaster recovery. Utilize all communication options available to provide service information.

Initially, this may be limited to posting signs indicating the status of the disaster and information about any available services. It is essential that this information be kept up-to-date. You will also want to engage the media early on to help reach users with basic information. (See Chapter 5 on media relations.)

The Web is invaluable for providing up-to-date information that can be offered in layers, allowing your user to select the level of detail desired. You can move from a key list of services available and contact information to comprehensive information about how to utilize specific local services; and you can also offer help to interpret the services and collections available at other libraries.

Another option is a voicemail system which provides details on a select group of services. This is easy to keep up-to-date and provides a low-tech option for your users to keep current about services and any existing restrictions or limitations. It is advisable to use no more than six selections, fewer if possible, and the categories should remain constant. You will want to include one option for recent changes which is updated at least weekly.

Library building signs and up-to-date maps and location guides are essential. Light-weight, portable easels with whiteboards can serve as visible, easy-to-read tools for directing users to temporary service or collection locations. At the library, we had frequent moves of the call number sequences as a result of a combination of disaster recovery activities and completion of the building renovation project. The best tool for dealing with this frequent change was a colored, printed locator guide indicating exact building location for specific call numbers; each new update was clearly dated and produced in a different color so that the latest iteration could be identified. Disaster-damaged call numbers were clearly marked with the reminder that some items in these ranges escaped damage by being in alternative locations at the time of the disaster or by being checked out. (Status information about specific items was available on SAGE, our online catalog, where the record indicated if an item had been damaged by the note: *Flood - See ILL*.) The paper locator guide was complemented by additional guide cards added to the ends of the stacks.

Communication with users is a two-way street. It is just as important to provide alternatives for your users to ask questions, give you suggestions, and let you know about their concerns. It is im-

possible to anticipate or be aware of all the frustrations your users may be feeling during disaster recovery; the more options you
can make available to hear directly from users, the better. Give
high priority to restoring any communication channels patrons are
used to having available, including telephone answering/voicemail
systems and suggestion boxes.

An electronic suggestion box using basic e-mail or accessible
from the Web on your library homepage is ideal for receiving regular feedback from your users. The more you hear from users, the
easier it will be to gauge the success of your temporary efforts
and verify that you are directing your energy to the most valuable services. Users will be powerful cheerleaders for you during
disaster recovery. Provide them with up-to-date, accurate information about what is happening, and they will reward you over
and over again with praise and support for your efforts. Also, they
will be much more understanding when you are not able to meet
all their needs for a temporary period. Staying flexible and adjusting to user needs is a given for any public service staff; the
main difference in a disaster recovery environment is the time
frame. You will find yourself making rapid changes that might have
been reviewed by a task force for several months in normal times.
One of the positive legacies we are realizing at the library is a
new willingness among many staff to embrace change more easily and to recognize their own ability to make things happen
quickly.

SEIZE OPPORTUNITIES

Promote Transition to Electronic Resources

A disaster which damages a significant portion of your print collection may offer an opportunity for both staff and users to explore the full strength of electronic resources. It is likely that a
library will have opportunities for the temporary addition of many
electronic databases and full-text resources. See Chapter 26 on
Resource Sharing and Chapter 27 on Colorado Alliance Consortium for details on the gift acquisition of databases for the library.
The sudden existence of many new databases—perhaps offering
hundreds of individual options within a variety of packages—pre-

sents a tremendous challenge to reference staff to keep up with what is available, let alone master the full searching capabilities of each database. Reference and collection development staff will need to develop an approach which will allow them to keep up with the frequent additions; they should also address a plan to review the long-range usefulness of specific databases under consideration for permanent purchase.

It is important to clearly identify any temporary databases as "gift" or "trial" databases on your public menus in order to minimize disappointment and confusion about their long-term accessibility. You will want to include ways for your users to let you know which of the temporary databases are useful to them and which ones they would most like to see retained on a permanent basis. Some database vendors will be able to provide you with use statistics. You may wish to augment any vendor-supplied numbers with tailored data gathered from your local homepage. This could include a brief questionnaire on a Web page users must pass through before or after they search the database; or you might use a program designed to track which terminals are being used or capture basic information about the person searching, gleaned from their patron record stored in the online catalog system.

In addition, actively solicit comments from your users about any temporary products. Some comments will come through your regular suggestion box options. Formal and informal instruction sessions will offer opportunities for staff to gather both anecdotal and prompted responses to available products. Focus groups may help you gather input about selected databases. These are all standard approaches under normal circumstances; the main difference in disaster recovery is the enormous number of new databases presented to your users simultaneously. You may never again have an opportunity to compare the virtues of such a wide array of databases at one time.

Your instruction program during this time should highlight the strength of electronic resources. Disaster recovery is a golden opportunity to help any reluctant users test the electronic waters and perhaps be more willing to adopt an electronic alternative in place of, rather than in addition to, a print resource. Temporary access to JSTOR at the library is a good example of this phenomenon. The original 26 journal titles included in JSTOR at the time of Colorado State's disaster included a high proportion of history titles. The history department includes faculty who are especially reluctant to use electronic resources. The opportunity for them to experience the strength of this retrospective full-image journal database and to see the ready acceptance by the students in their classes is significant and will most likely influence their library use long-term.

Plan For Long-Term Integration of Improved Services

At the Morgan Library, ILL operations will benefit from the automated processing routines which have been programmed into request handling, and ILL will be in a position to maintain top-notch service on an ongoing basis. The Ariel workstations placed across campus have set up a network of equipment which will continue to speed delivery of articles for the foreseeable future. This high-tech solution required extensive programming to support the user interface and also to streamline the processing behind the scenes. Although it was designed to meet our immediate needs during disaster recovery, it also builds on existing automation in a way that will support permanent improvements in ILL services.

The popularity of the ILL article delivery service has raised long-term user expectations for desk-top delivery. The ability to maintain this level of service beyond disaster recovery will provide a lasting, positive legacy of the disaster. Sample comments from users at Colorado State include:

> I appreciate all the extra work this system (*FastFlood*) creates, but it is probably more convenient for me overall than having the journals on the shelf. I think this system would serve as a good model for a permanent method of accessing periodicals.

> I've been using the library's service for delivery of articles that appeared in journals that were damaged by the flood. I must say that this is a great product. The library staff is sure going the extra mile to keep up the standard of service in spite of all the damage that was done. I would like to suggest that this service be maintained even after the journals are replaced. I can't speak for the rest of the faculty/staff here, but I would certainly be willing to pay a small premium for the convenience of requesting the item online and having it delivered to my mailbox here in my department.

Another service introduced at Colorado State on a trial basis during the recovery period is Shop-on-SAGE (SOS). Shop-On-SAGE fully activates the request feature in the online catalog (using the Innovative Interfaces, Inc., platform) and allows users to request local items electronically for retrieval by circulation staff. The material is pulled and held at the loan desk for convenient retrieval. This pilot project, introduced to help off-set the inconvenience of the disaster, will provide valuable data on the need to continue this approach on an ongoing basis.

CONCLUSION AND TRANSLATION TO THE FUTURE

The new emphasis on convenience for putting needed materials in the hands of users—ILL delivery to campus mailboxes, staff retrieval of electronically requested circulating items held in the local collection, and student staff to accompany users to the stack areas to help locate materials—redefines our face to the user and impacts everything from instructional programs to staffing of service points. As a public service staff, we have evolved beyond the need to debate whether we are "spoon-feeding" our users by retrieving materials for them or by delivering items directly to their desktop. Firsthand experience has shown us that our users better appreciate our expertise as teachers and information navigators when we remove the barriers to putting their hands on identified resources.

Staff and users alike have had access to a rich array of electronic databases and full-text resources. Jointly, we have benefited and are much better positioned to make the difficult choices facing all libraries as we develop collections with an appropriate, affordable balance of print and electronic resources. Formerly reluctant users of electronic options among our staff and users alike are more experienced and now much more willing to give serious consideration to electronic alternatives. Conversely, the most radical champions of electronic options in the same two groups have been tempered by reality—when the opportunity presented itself, electronic resources could not come close to substituting for a research collection built over decades of planned acquisition. It's hard to imagine a more effective training program for preparing us for the twenty-first century.

Library Disaster Planning and Recovery Handbook

KEY RECOMMENDATIONS

Public Services

Services
- Focus on convenience for the user.
- Stay flexible and refine services based on users' suggestions and comments.
- Seize opportunities to introduce new or expanded services.

Communication
- Keep information up-to-date.
- Use multiple outlets—both high tech and low tech—to let users know what is happening and status of services.
- Provide easy options for users to give comments and suggestions.

Staffing and Space Issues
- Keep staff at all levels fully informed.
- Staff training, and retraining, needs to be top priority.
- Space should address a balance of staff and user needs.

Assistance from Others
- Keep area libraries informed about your status.
- Negotiate expectations with other libraries who assist your users.
- Provide tools to help your users identify appropriate libraries to use.

REFERENCES

Chadbourne, Robert. 1994. "A Post-Disaster Primer: Elba on the Rebound." *Wilson Library Bulletin* 68 (May): 24–25.

Kahn, Miriam. 1994. "Fires, Earthquakes and Floods: How to Prepare Your Library and Staff." *Online* 18, No. 3: 18–24.

Kane, Laura Townsend. 1997. "Access vs. Ownership: Do We Have to Make a Choice?" *College and Research Libraries* 58 (January): 59–67.

7 Circulation: When the Heart Stops Beating

James F. Farmer

"The circulation of its books is like the circulation of the blood, passing constantly back and forth from the heart to the members of the body" (Tinker, 1948: 79).

INTRODUCTION AND PERSONAL ACCOUNT

"How can you be so calm?" With this question I knew I was in for a rough time. Never before had I considered that my job—all of the jobs in Access Services—could completely change overnight. On Monday, July 28, 1997, beginning at 9:30 p.m., it did.

The Access Services Department of Colorado State University's Morgan Library has a department head, four mid-level managers, and seven full-time staff who report in various configurations to these supervisors. In the summer, we employ approximately 20 students—less than half of what we do during a fall or spring semester. Our Loan/Reserve Desk is managed by the students. Desk managers, or monitors as we call them, are trained and paid at higher levels to handle the hour-to-hour situations which arise at our service point. The full-time staff and supervisors supplement these efforts by also working at the desk (see Appendix 7-A). Staff typically work either a Sunday–Thursday, Monday–Friday, or Tuesday–Saturday shift which includes some openings and some closings. The individual on duty July 28th was a supervisor.

The rain had been frequent that summer, and it is no surprise that the ground just couldn't hold another ounce on the night it poured down on campus. I was at home—approximately three miles away from the university. The rain was drizzling. I received a phone call from a staff member who informed me that the water was pummeling her neighborhood. The water was over the curbing. Alarmed, she wondered what was happening on campus. I decided to phone the library and ask. It was amazing that I was able to get through. For hours, staff on duty had been trying to deal with some roof leaks over Reference. Our building, Morgan Library, which had been under construction for over 24 months, was not quite watertight from above. The skylights were letting in enough water to soak part of the reference collection housed on the first floor. Books were being fanned everywhere on the first floor, and it was a mini-disaster in itself. The supervisor told me that things seemed to be in control but that if extra hands were needed, she would phone me. I hung up and called back the staff member at home, filling her in. The conversation was short. My voicemail indicator told me I had another message. I just knew it was from the supervisor on duty before I checked the message.

Listening carefully to the message, I heard that the overhead leaks had worsened, and more books were affected. My extra hands were indeed needed. I grabbed my raincoat and headed outside. By now it was approximately 9:50 p.m. I could hardly believe that this drizzle outside my apartment was causing mass commotion at work. I drove my truck south toward the university on College Avenue. With each passing second, the weather worsened. I drove through all of the intersections which, just minutes into the future, would be raging rivers. Rivers which would kill five people. On campus at 10:00 p.m., I parked in a downpour near the building directly adjacent the library. I ran to the south doors of the library knowing that if I tried to make it to the north entrance I would be soaked. So far so good.

I got inside, and the building was nearly deserted. We close at 10:00 p.m. in the summer, and the last building closure announcement had just been made. I made my way to the loan desk to see what was happening. The supervisor greeted me and told me that efforts to fan the books were futile.

The campus security officer was trying to hail his supervisors by radio. I suddenly realized that this was more than a simple heavy rain. The students on duty wanted to get home, but the west parking lot had flooded and many feared their cars were underwater. Custodians reported on conditions in the lower level.

It was hard to believe when someone shouted that a wall had collapsed and there was water pouring into the lower level. You cannot picture this in your mind. I certainly couldn't picture it in mine. Even the next day, it was hard to mentally reconstruct an event where enough water to fill the entire 77,454-square-foot lower level was pouring into an open hole as I was standing above it on the first floor.

My immediate thought was to wait until our assistant dean for Technical Services could arrive to issue instructions for the reference collection and subsequent lower-level flooding. Being a member of the disaster team, I knew that there was a plan for managing a water emergency. Phone lines were erratic and nearly useless. The supervisor on duty had put through calls to the assistant dean and others on the team before it became difficult to call out.

Havoc broke out. Almost simultaneously, the fire alarm exploded into action as the overhead lights went out. Emergency-generator lighting quickly replaced the darkness and the remaining staff scrambled for flashlights. The plan changed. Evacuation was the only order of business now. We grabbed the three or four flashlights available to us and headed out into the rain, leaving only the campus security officer to wait for instructions on how to handle the alarm situation. Across the plaza, the student center alarms were blaring. Our only choice was the nearby Clark Building. Time had become hazy. It was between 10:15 and 10:45 as we found shelter inside the Clark Building on the first floor. All of our student employees were waiting for the rain to let up before heading home. I sat with them and contemplated the next step. "How can you be so calm?" someone asked. I replied something to the effect that, "There's not much we can do right now but wait and see."

Our assistant dean arrived on the scene shortly thereafter and asked the custodial crew on duty for a phone. She had been briefed by other janitorial crews nearby that the lower level was bad. So bad, in fact, that little could be accomplished that night. By now, the other students and staff had drifted off to find a way home. Since the supervisor had walked to the library, I offered her a ride home. The magnitude of the flood was still not apparent to us. We couldn't see the west-side lake where we now stood—east of the library. We informed the assistant dean that we were leaving and she said she would be in touch later.

I made it back to my apartment at 2:00 a.m. Time for a hot shower and a little sleep before the 5:00 a.m. wake-up call from our assistant dean, assembling the disaster team.

The morning television news told me everything I hadn't already figured out. Here it was, 21 years after the area's Big Thompson River flooded on July 31, 1976, when I was 13 years old. The major difference was that now, as a responsible adult serving the largest employer in the county, I was not helpless—I intended to make a difference by facing the immediate challenges by being solutions-oriented.

The diagnosis was not good at the library—as Tinker would say, the heart had stopped beating; there was no circulation. Emergency resuscitation was required and fast. Unfortunately, I didn't have a job description for the duties ahead. In retrospect, I should have paraphrased Bones McCoy, the physician from the original *Star Trek* series, to inject some humor in the dismal early hours: "I'm a department head, not a doctor!" When all was said and done, we all became doctors trying to fix our wounded circulatory system.

The "Lost August"

As recounted before, all of the staff was out of Morgan Library from July 28th until August 22nd. I refer to this as our "Lost August." What would normally be a time when we were finishing up summer tasks and gearing up for the start of a new school year was spent in reaction mode. How we could cope with the tragic event was top priority as we began each morning. We inched forward at a pace which I can only describe as slower than slow motion. Each successive day after the disaster involved new challenges and stressors. It was almost as if we had decided to open a brand new library within a month and had just started to plan.

Our experiences during the "Lost August" have helped me compose this guide to assist you in planning for a disaster which hopefully will never come. We were lucky in that we had done some planning ahead and were ready to roll from day one. And, yes, we made some mistakes too. The bottom line is we survived. In fact, we have flourished and now offer more client-focused services than before.

In order to paint some different strategies for you to consider, I have divided this chapter into four major sections: Scenario I: Worst Case; Scenario II: Next-to-Worst Case; Scenario III: Better Case; and Scenario IV: Best Case. The emphasis will be on Scenario II: Next-to-Worst Case, since that is what we experienced. Worst case, of course, would have been a total loss—all collections and an entire building. The loss of even one human life would make any disaster a worst case scenario, in my opinion.

The Next-to-Worst Case scenario may be a partial loss of a building and/or collections such that your building is closed and you must find a way to offer service through other means. My intent is that, as you pass through this chapter, we will go from a bleak situation to a more sunny outlook. Our Access Services Department passed through all three of the stages I describe to get back to normal.

SCENARIO I: WORST CASE (INSTANT DEATH)

The worst case, or instant death, scenario is what no one wants to face. You lose everything: building, collection, and maybe even staff. Susan Curzon, dean of the University Library at California State University-Northridge, tells me the 6.8 earthquake disaster they suffered on January 17, 1994, was,

> About as bad as could be. We were out of the building for seven months—at that time, we returned to the center of the building. The two wings of the building were torn down and are being restored as I write this. Everything (was a constraint). No electricity, no plumbing, no wiring, no phones. We spent the first week in an open field in the pouring rain, then we moved to tents, then trailers and plastic domes (Curzon, 1998).

When something this devastating happens, there is no easy way to start a resurrection. Dean Curzon explains,

> The most immediate question was how to bring back library services. Our campus president, in spite of the damage to all 52 buildings on campus, decided to re-open within four weeks of the earthquake—a decision we applauded. Given that, how can you have a university without a library? We had to use every gray cell in our heads to create and provide service under those conditions (1998).

In order to literally get off the ground, Curzon wrote that CSU-Northridge library staff just rolled up their sleeves and got to work. Once they decided how to proceed, they called staff back appropriately and they launched the services. From here, the CSU-Northridge Access Services/Circulation group took many of the same steps we did to return services to users, as you will read about in the next section.

SCENARIO II: NEXT-TO-WORST CASE (WHAT TO DO IF YOUR HEART STOPS BEATING)

Establishing Communications

Following a disaster of such a grand scale where you are left without a building or are otherwise away from your service point, you will be in a position of asking yourself, "What do I do first?" Invariably, people are social beings and the need to share feelings with others will be of utmost urgency, such as speculating on what will happen or gossiping about who will have to do what. Because of this need to connect, you have your first opportunity to establish some communication links among your employees. If you do nothing else right, you must have near-perfect communication following a disaster. Otherwise, you will be managing two disasters. Before reading ahead, please refer to Appendix 7-A to acquaint yourself with the structure of the Access Services department at Colorado State University Libraries. The actions I recommend may have to be altered to address variances in your individual structure and circumstances.

Pre-planning is essential. All staff members, especially supervisors, should have a list of every employee's home phone number. We have gone so far as to ask staff to keep a duplicate copy in their automobile in case an accident prevents them from making it to the library to open the building. Having at least two departmental cellular phones is also a wise plan. If a disaster strikes, then this should be at the top of your list for immediate acquisition. The department head should also wear a pager or have voicemail on the cellular phone because you will not want to miss any incoming messages.

The first order of business after your disaster will be to establish phone communication. While you can plan this to some degree, it is likely that in the heat of disaster recovery you may need to delegate this responsibility.

I do not recommend a phone tree. It is better that important messages are consistent. The only way to insure this is to have one person from each department make the calls. It will most likely not be a person on your supervisory team because those individuals will be managing other post-disaster aspects. Everyone will be on the telephone and employees will most likely hear from more than one person unofficially very soon after the disaster. Pick someone who enjoys phone work and can aggressively get the word out.

Because we are speaking about the next-to-worst case scenario, your employees are going to be scattered. First, many will be at home. Expect your library administration to establish some policy for on-call status which will help you reach all those individuals at home who are waiting to receive work assignments.

For Access Services, workflows are established in phases. Since the primary mission of circulation is customer service, it will take some time to set up satellite service points and associated work details. Until staff have a place to go, their homes are their work sites.

At some point, usually about one to two weeks after the disaster, the phoning will become cumbersome. If your campus has telecommunications service, you should consider a voice bulletin board. This way, your entire library staff will phone in to get essential messages. At Colorado State University, our library as a whole used this method to learn about library-wide meetings and other important information. As the head of Access Services, it was my job to update this telecommunications bulletin board daily, and all staff were required to telephone in after 6:00 p.m. to retrieve information and instructions for the next day.

Deploying Staff

Getting employees to work is the next order of business. If you have a mix of salary and hourly employees, your task is tricky. Hourly/work-study employees, mostly students in an academic setting, are paid only if they work. Your organization may grant administrative leave for salaried employees for the duration it takes to establish satellite service. Your hourly employees will count on you to find work as soon as possible (see Chapter 2 on human resources).

Before managerial decisions can be made, you must establish a communication plan for your supervisory team. In our operation, our favorite method of making decisions was impromptu meetings at a local bagel shop. Plenty of food and coffee for all involved! The supervisory team needs to be cohesive from day one. The department head should set the tone for action, but no one person can do it all. Your team must not only help you fill conceptual gaps but also carry out directives on your behalf. If you are on the library's disaster team, as I was, you will have many responsibilities beyond your own department. It is important that your department is operating effectively during the times you are diverted to other administrative, disaster-related tasks.

So far, I have noted how you can begin to communicate with staff. Another task is to begin to establish communication with your users. If you are allowed on campus, you may be permitted to set up a duty station at the front entrance to your library. If your entry is affected, pick a spot where you are likely to encounter walk-up questions from sightseers and concerned patrons. If campus access is denied, consider a highly visible location to establish your station nearby—again, where you are likely to encounter person-to-person questions. This direct contact is important. Even if you can only say, "I don't know what will be happening next," at least your users can physically see a familiar face. Using your hourly employees is a perfect way to establish a link to the outside world. This is your first satellite operation.

Special concerns arise when you establish a duty station. Safety is of tantamount importance. You will find that attention to this detail will carry over into all other strategies you pursue. Your staff must feel safe, and they must be safe. The door crew needs at minimum a cell telephone to be able to telephone police if a security threat arises. The crew should always be scheduled in teams of two. If possible, don't schedule anyone after dark. If the disaster happens at a time when the outdoor weather is very cold, you will need to consider other requirements to keep your staff warm and healthy. Bitter weather conditions may prohibit this type of outdoor activity altogether. If that is the case, try to find a well-trafficked indoor area to begin your customer outreach.

Formulating Strategies: The Brain Isn't Dead Yet!

Once you have begun your service resuscitation with communication, it is time to begin formulating strategies for dealing with other aspects of disaster recovery. This is a two-fold process. First, you must continue to get the work force involved in service recovery. This is an essential step, not only in the healing process, but also because the work increases daily as more things need to get accomplished. Second, all of the patron-related operations you perform need to be examined and put on track for when you are again fully operational. Customer service takes on a new meaning because, for awhile, you are in a reactive mode. Instead of looking to what service you can provide your clients to maximize their expected outcomes, you are looking at ways to minimize the potential, negative effects of the disaster. Remember that a community disaster is a blow to everyone, not just to those who work in the buildings which were damaged. Since both of these concepts—re-establishment of services and public/user relations—go hand-in-hand, they will be co-mingled in my discussion of them.

In an academic environment, students and faculty are probably facing enormous pressures following the disaster. For many, time is money, and frustrations seep in very quickly when a research library is devastated. At Colorado State University, we were approaching the start of the academic year during the emergency response and recovery; however, a disaster could strike in the middle of a school term or semester. Either way, the heat is on.

Circulation Transactions: Snapshot and Suspension

First and foremost, I recommend that you take whatever steps necessary to take a "snapshot" of your circulation transactions at the time of the disaster. By snapshot, I mean a picture of all your circulation transaction and user data at one point in time. This could be a download from your system right after the disaster—a master list of all items checked out and the link to the patron who has the borrowed items.

If your circulation system does not allow you to make this snapshot on your own, inquire immediately to your system administrator or the vendor. An accounting of what materials were checked out at the time of the disaster helps in many regards. Besides being an inventory to help sort out replacement information for insurance purposes, it gives you a basis for accepting or denying future claims of returns. For example, if a user in the future claims to have returned a book before your disaster, you can quickly verify whether that book was indeed checked out at the moment the event took place. Another user may inform you that a book was lost at home as a result of the community disaster. The list will help you track the losses. Once you have the list, secure it. The list will not be of much benefit at the beginning because I simultaneously recommend that you temporarily suspend all inquiries about replacement, bills, and fines.

I recommend this suspension of inquiries for a number of reasons. If you collect your own money for bills and fines, you will find that it is a burden which is not worth the time spent on it. There will be plenty of time to settle accounts later. Establish a policy of no fines for the duration of the initial recovery. If you allow your campus bursar to collect the money, you will find that they will be under the gun to handle other pressures. Perhaps their office was also affected by the disaster. Suspension of fines for overdues (for both books already past due and those which will reach the due date during recovery) is an opportunity to establish your first reactive policy. Not only will it ease stress on all parties involved, but it will also set a positive customer service tone for the future.

Taking this policy a step further, consider renewing all books which are checked out. At Morgan Library, we did this very thing, and it was an enormous success. It enhanced our customer-service policy. For an employee, it makes a difference in providing positive service to our users. I recommend that, if at all possible, you establish another satellite operation based on these book renewals. For example, an undamaged branch library could be used for space and access to your online system so that renewals can be made.

Advertise the number where your users can get information on circulation operations. It is wise to spread the duties of renewal and telephone monitoring to many individuals on a rotated schedule to prevent burnout. At the two-week mark following our disaster, we had two operations running smoothly: the front door team to greet users and prevent unauthorized entry into Morgan Library and the renewal/telephone receipt operation at our Engineering Branch Library.

Renewing all books also negated a workflow for which we were not prepared at that moment—book returns. If your building is damaged, you want to encourage your users to keep the books they have. Unless you suspend bills and fines and implement a renewal process, you will have to begin to deal with physical pieces. Eventually, you can establish a satellite operation for book returns, but initially it is wise to ward this off for as long as possible.

Mobilizing More Operations

BILLS AND FINES

Now is the time to begin negotiations with your billing office. Concerning bills and fines which accrued before the disaster, you must find ways to lessen the impact of users wanting to pay their balances. In many academic settings, the registrar will block students from enrolling in classes due to financial obligations. By arranging with the registrar for temporary release of these blocks on student accounts, you establish goodwill among your clientele; and you further lessen the workload of colleagues in another university office. It is hopeful that such negotiations are possible, but your own individual organization may have rules governing the flexibility of such recommendations. If you collect your own bills and fines, you may have more control over the process. For samples of the forms we used to handle "claims returned" status items see Appendices 7-B and 7-C.

RESERVES

The faculty has needs too. Following a disaster, there may be a call for enhanced reserve services to support faculty courses. The university bookstore was severely damaged in the disaster, so our reserves staff geared up to handle the processing of textbooks.

Many faculty members gave us examination copies or excerpts from their course materials enabling students to have access to their readings at the start of the semester. I recommend that reserve services be kept a top priority in your disaster recovery, regardless of whether your bookstore is affected or not.

Depending on when your disaster happens and how accessible your library building is, you may be faced with reserve difficulties. Materials which were already on reserve for the term may not be salvageable, depending on how bad your library was damaged. In this scenario, you may want to prepare a computer printout listing of materials presumed lost in order to begin emergency replacement. Many libraries still operate with a manual reserve system. If this is the case, your course listing may be manually produced and maintained using course listing forms submitted by instructors. If this is how your reserve system works, I highly recommend keeping a copy of your manual listing somewhere off-site in case a disaster does strike.

Reserve is a big operation requiring space to process materials and shelve materials for student check-out. Depending on how long your main building is unavailable to you, you may find that you need to rent space or ask your university to accommodate your operations in an empty classroom or facility. Estimating space requirements can be a chore because there will be many uncertainties regarding the duration of your satellite reserve operations. Planning for the short term or long term will make a difference in how much space you need. Further complicating space needs will be decisions regarding reader stations. If your traditional course reserve features materials that circulate for one or two hours and must remain in your library, you may have to rethink this in lieu of your new situation. You may have no choice but to allow materials to circulate out of the building/room you are occupying—especially if there are no copy facilities available. Policies regarding checkouts, overdues, fines, and bills will have to be re-established which may not parallel your regular circulating policies during this post-disaster time period and are influenced by factors like space, high-demand, and/or low-supply nature of your new, temporary reserve system. Other policies come into play as well: Do you rush process textbooks? Do you allow submission of photocopies outside of your regular copyright policy?

Computer hook-ups are required if you are processing materials into your online system. You may choose to revert to a manual reserve operation for the duration of the disaster recovery; however, there are advantages to maintaining computerization. First, you don't have to establish new procedures and training regimens. Thinking manually, however, can be difficult in the computer age. Second, you want to be ready for the return to normalcy. Staff will appreciate that you are trying to keep familiar processes intact—it will help reduce the traumatic effects of the disaster. Plus, your materials are ready to circulate and will not require reprocessing later. If you cannot be 100 percent computerized during this interim period, I recommend that you process your materials as far as you can toward computerization so that manually-circulated materials can easily be processed online later. For example, affix barcodes to materials and flag manual items so they can be easily identified later as being unprocessed.

Once you have your reserve satellite location established, you will want to inform your campus community of the location, hours, information, and cooperation needed to make the effort a success. Each of us in the academic library field is used to many open hours of service. If your satellite is in a building which closes earlier than you are traditionally used to, then it will be very important to mention this critical fact in your press releases, e-mails, Web pages, etc. Faculty dropping off materials to be processed, as well as students checking out materials, will need to be informed as much as possible to prevent frustrations. Here is where it is nice to make a leap in customer-service attitude. Cellular telephones are excellent for helping panicked faculty and users. Consider setting up an information hotline with voicemail if telephones are not readily available. This is a good way to take calls, because, as the disaster recovery unfolds, you may be asked to make changes in locale (maybe even return to your library building) on short notice. Responding to voicemail messages quickly is important since the person on the other end will experience some aggravation at not being able to speak to someone directly.

A disaster should not be motivation to begin an electronic reserve operation—at least not right away. Trying to establish such a process in the aftermath of a catastrophe is not using good business sense. Purchasing new software and then implementing a new system would be overwhelming to staff already dealing with post-traumatic stress. Make a mental note to pursue an electronic reserve system on a brighter day. Stick to the basics, and you cannot go wrong. If you have an electronic reserves strategy in-place before your disaster (preferably one accessible via the Internet), you may find that it will ease some of the problems of finding space, etc. Again, consideration must be given to policies regarding copyright. If equipment (such as scanners, Web servers, etc.) is not available, electronic reserve recovery may be a moot point.

BOOK RETURNS

Once all of these other essential operations are in place, you can return attention to book returns. Even if you have put out the call to your library community to not return books, some users will insist on returning them anyway. Again, some of the items may have suffered disaster damage at the home of the borrower. Being good Samaritans, individuals want to bring in the items for proper care and recovery—especially if they know you are performing a mass recovery of your main library items.

From the very beginning of the book return stage, strategy is extremely important. I recommend you start by deciding whether you want all book returns to come to a central location or whether it is best that you offer your users the ease of returning materials to one of many sites, such as:

- Branch libraries
- Local public libraries and their branches
- Other designated book drop points

If a central site is selected, you must look at space requirements needed for accumulating and sorting the items before and after check-in. If you were successful in securing space for course reserve operations, you may be able to piggyback with that function. Perhaps a single branch library has space to shelve your returned materials temporarily.

I would recommend that you try to stick to one location only unless you have a robust courier service for when you re-open. Remember, you have to return these materials to the main library eventually. If you elect to go with a multiple-library return policy, you may want to meet with the different staff members who will be handling your returns. Are these branches simply going to be pseudo-storage facilities until your main branch re-opens, or will you allow the branch to re-circulate your materials?

The issues of what to do if a book has a hold on it will come up, and you need to be prepared. Similarly, books which have been billed or fined will also require attention. Decentralization means you will lose some control over these functions, but you may not have a choice. Do as much planning as possible before you implement any check-in program. I have found that one of the most frustrating gaps in good customer service often evolves from poor check-in management.

Finally, your mobilization should include a fleet to transport materials among your satellite operations. These may be books, but it will most likely be supplies—especially in the area of reserve. If you have a library vehicle undamaged by the disaster, you are set. If you didn't have a vehicle beforehand, or if your vehicle was damaged, you may want to inquire with your organization's motor pool to see whether a van or some other large, covered transport truck is available. Following a disaster, you will find that local businesses may also be willing to donate or loan various forms of disaster recovery items—including transportation.

It is hoped that eventually you will be able to re-enter your building. If the damage was so great that construction of a new facility is required, then the ongoing management of your satellites will evolve into a more complicated array of policies, processes, and procedures. Your ad hoc way of life will become more permanent. More care can be taken to solidify communication channels and operations. Student-employee staffing may require a different budgeting plan, and perhaps new organizational models will develop. But, if estimates indicate your time outside your main facility is short-term, it is better to keep the public spotlight on your temporary setups while preparing for reentry offstage. What this means to me is that you keep customer service as a primary but simple goal. Don't establish elaborate satellites which will require many days to break down and relocate back to the main facility when it reopens. At most, your break in service to move home should be no more than four to eight hours. This is vitally important if you are in the middle of an academic semester or quarter. Preparing for your grand reopening may seem daunting, but it could be no more complicated than being ready for the first day of classes in September or January. There will be many factors which you cannot control, so the exhaustive task of keeping up morale doesn't stop here. Know your hours of operation; have staffing patterns ready to meet these hours and make sure the satellites are synchronized for the collapse back to the main site.

Dealing With Special Challenges

Special problems may arise beyond the first day back in your building. Again, the facilities will improve day by day. If computer wiring is affected, you may need to use manual systems for awhile. Some integrated library systems provide laptop software for times when your system is down. If this is the case, you may consider storing daily data on floppy disks which can be uploaded into your system at night. Other trends will become apparent as days pass. Reserve statistics are likely to increase dramatically while monograph statistics may fall if your library collections took a severe hit during the disaster. Users may not be comfortable using your facility at first, and the accommodations you made to allow course reserve materials to circulate outside your normal reading areas may have to continue after you have moved back. Facilities reconstruction will be distracting, and some patrons may continue to get service at your branch libraries, which means your systems for transfer of materials will have to continue to handle this workload.

A return to normalcy is on everyone's mind. Where users were patient before with your satellite services, they will now expect a higher level of satisfaction with the return to familiar territory. Normalcy is also on the minds of other officials and administrators. This means you should be close to sorting out procedures for financial transactions relative to circulation matters. The bursar or accountants will want to know that procedures are sound and in-line with audit requirements. The readiness mode you found yourself in directly after the disaster as you coped with quickly changing environments will not subside now. Time will take care of the hectic pace, but mentally you will find great relief to be in familiar surroundings. This is akin to being discharged from the hospital and returned home. You aren't ready to go jogging just yet, but your heart is starting to beat with a better rhythm and some color will return to your day.

Up until now, I have talked about the intensive care approach to a disaster where you are in a "near death" experience. In Fort Collins, only part of our city was affected by the rushing flood waters. The community's focus on recovery was intensified on very specific areas—our campus being one of them. It could very well be that your disaster will keep you out of your community or off of your campus until the disaster subsides. Some disasters, for example, last for days and weeks. The approaches I have noted may not begin on day one after your disaster, as it did in our case. Nevertheless, important work can be done wherever you are. Preparing communication channels, collecting ideas, assembling teams, etc., are all administrative functions to which to attend.

SCENARIO III: BETTER CASE (KEEPING THE HEARTBEAT YOU HAVE)

Assessing service in reaction to a mini-disaster (which I define as one where you do not have to evacuate your primary facility) is very similar to the steps outlined in the worst-case scenario. Communication becomes a primary consideration. Again, employees need to know what happened and what will happen, to the best of your knowledge. They need to know how they will fit into changing service strategies as you develop them. The public will have questions with regard to their circulation transactions. You will also field questions about the disaster, and your university and library administrators may want that function standardized with a common message—just as before.

In most cases, a mini-disaster will result in work-arounds which are apparent from day one. For example, even a small flood could be powerful enough to knock out computers and computer connections. Manual circulation procedures may be required until those systems can be repaired. The damage, for whatever reason, may cause a reduction in the number of service hours. You will have to tinker with schedules and staffing patterns. It may be that formerly open stacks areas will now be closed and a new service of retrieving materials for patrons may evolve. Will you need to alter reserve services? If hours of operation are reduced, you may need to consider establishing a satellite reserve site where the hours can mimic your former hours. Space requirements will need to be estimated, and decisions made regarding reading space. Book returns may pose special problems. How do you handle returns in the call-numbered areas affected by your localized disaster?

A February 3, 1998, flood at the Cecil H. Green Library on the campus of Stanford University could be described as an example of a localized disaster. While their disaster recovery, as a whole, could be considered just as serious as our flood (mostly due to the fact that staff were involved in pulling wet, muddy books and shelves from the affected areas), the Access Services aspect was more manageable due to several factors, as explained by Joan Krasner Leighton, chief of Access Services:

> The building (Green Library) was closed for approximately five days. But 100 feet away from Green is the J. Henry Meyer Memorial Library. Staff accepted patron requests for Green via the nearby Meyer Library. Access staff did the paging and someone was stationed at the adjacent library to help with service. All staff were employed (Leighton, 1998).

Once Green reopened, users had full access to the building except the lower level. The paging service continued as described by Joan,

> Access Services and temporary staff paged materials from the lower level of Green Library, first twice per day and later every four hours. Approximately ten FTE staff participated in paging duties although none on a full-time basis (Leighton, 1998).

Another role taken on by the Access Services department in the aftermath:

> One-seventh of the materials shelved on the lower level of Green Library were taken to a local freezer. While the need to move very rapidly on this in order to save the materials precluded an inventory during the packing process, a method was devised to determine which items were taken to the

freezer and to indicate that in the online catalog (Leighton, 1998).

Thus, even in a better-case scenario, there is much work to be done and flexibility is equally important as in other scenarios.

Potentially, a small disaster may affect only staff work areas. In this situation, a new panorama of problems is exposed. If your reserve-processing materials and workspace are affected, you will be faced with not only establishing temporary work space to recover this operation, but you will need emergency replacement of supplies. If Reserve Services is automated, computers will be needed for processing. I recommend that you keep detailed inventories of supplies used for Reserve and other operations in Access Services. The loss of equipment and supplies is relatively easy to replace—if you don't have to spend lots of time deciding what it is that you lost. Keep a copy of your inventory in a safe place off-site, perhaps at a branch library.

Small disasters should be taken just as seriously as large ones when evaluating, modifying, and, most importantly, planning your short-term circulation services. Just because the heart is beating this moment does not mean that it can't stop altogether in the next instant. Operations may seem to be running smoothly for days, but suddenly a structural engineer informs your administration that everyone must vacate the premises for an unknown length of time. Would you be ready? Take the time to put telephone trees in place. Assign emergency roles to staff in the event you are shut out of your main building. Use supervisory team meetings to discuss "what if" scenarios. You could hold a work session and have staff simulate their response to the worst case situation by brainstorming solutions. A mini-disaster, like a heart murmur, is a wake-up call to take action for better health.

SCENARIO IV: BEST CASE (PRACTICING PREVENTIVE MEDICINE)

Usually your biggest enemy is time. When things are sailing smoothly you don't have spare minutes to dwell on how horrible things can go. You take comfort that your library has a disaster plan in place and that it would tell you what to do when the sky falls. This statement is not entirely true.

As I learned at Colorado State University Libraries, there was no manual available to say do this . . . and then do that. Even this chapter and this book cannot meet that need for anyone who reads it. Your situation will be completely different from ours. Just as the heart attack of a 50-year-old man in New York will be different from the heart attack of the 38-year-old in London, you can't prescribe the exact same set of steps to save both of their lives. Looking at it from the patient's perspective, each might not have prevented the heart attack, but they could have taken *some* preventive measures. This is what I recommend you do.

As mentioned before, you should talk about strategies, formulate simulations which require you to come up with solutions, and exercise your department's collective mind power toward preserving your mission should the bottom drop out from underneath you. Yes, it will take time, and that time is hard to find. Had I spent even a fraction of the time in preparation that I spent in departmental recovery after our disaster, I could have saved myself a lot of stress. The amazing thing was that we found we were prepared in several key areas! Keeping contact with staff was a cinch due to the layers of communication we had put in place for years before the disaster hit. Building upon what you have— even in small increments—will pay off and will be time-effective.

More Good Medicine: Going the Extra Mile On the Treadmill

As long as you are exercising to keep in good health, here are some things we either learned after the disaster and/or things that were reinforced that will make a difference when you are in the middle of a crisis.

Face-to-face contact is important. Your users are used to seeing you in the best of times; and when those times take a turn for the worse, you still need to be there for your clientele. For many years leading up to the disaster, we accepted reserve lists and course materials at our Loan/Reserve Desk whenever they were dropped off. Sure, we had face-to-face contact with these instructors, but every semester they would likely see a different face. With our satellite reserve operation, our patrons saw one set of faces. Questions could be asked on the spot. The hustle and bustle of a busy service point did not deter them from offering specific processing instructions for fear that they were holding up the line. Brand new professors to the university could be coached in our procedures and given accurate information on expected completion dates. Staff enjoyed meeting the people who had previously only been a name on a reserve form or on a reserve screen. Customer service for reserve became fun. Many other post-disaster scenarios brought home the fact that face-to-face, personalized service is second to none. Having re-learned this valuable lesson, we now set up a special location to receive materials for approximately two weeks before, and four weeks after, the first day of classes for each semester. It is a win-win situation for both staff and users.

Change is a friend. I don't know how many times my department has organized and reorganized into different configurations. The bottom line should always be geared toward the ultimate goals of superb internal teamwork and excellent external customer service. Our pre-disaster structure was good, but after the disaster we found that it had to be bent a lot. New employee strengths emerged and, likewise, new employee weaknesses had to be addressed. While we kept our skeletal structure intact, we worked and molded different muscle groups to meet the quickly changing environment with which we were faced. A good leader will allow this development to progress naturally. In many cases, you will personally feel you have no control—and that will exactly be the case. But those are the exact moments that you are growing and learning and simultaneously your staff are also growing and learning. Truly, when the sun shines again you are better, stronger, and more cohesive than ever before. Give up some control and marvel at the results!

Views are forever changed. The way you look at your department will never be the same as before your disaster. Every new challenge you face will be subjected to some, if not all, of the raw energy you felt when starting over. Barely two-and-a-half months after our disaster, we had another chance to practice our coping skills. A large snowstorm moved through the Rocky Mountain front range region dropping 18–26 inches in the vicinity. Fort Collins was spared the heaviest of the snows, but the unfortunate aspect of this storm was that it hit on a Saturday. While the city,

county, and state closed offices and shut down, the library remained open due to the fact that the campus snow emergency
procedure is implemented only on weekdays. Access Services was
ready. We had our telephone trees in place and, for many years,
had required every student employee to say whether or not they
lived close enough to campus to get to work on a snow day.

YOUR FRIEND, THE ELECTRONIC PACEMAKER: THE FUTURE OF CIRCULATION

Long after the disaster, the bad memories will start to fade. Somewhere during the recovery, you may have been in the position of
kicking yourself because you always wanted to implement that
one thing that would have made the recovery more bearable. Don't
ever let these memories pass into the netherworld. Keep them
close to your heart. Many of the ideas will likely focus around
the notion of an electronic future for circulation. Perhaps your
integrated library system vendor isn't as modern as you would
like. Maybe that electronic reserve system would have made a difference if it were up and running before the fire, hurricane, or
earthquake hit. What about those patron self-services? Or e-mail
links to users? Even voicemail! All of these are commonplace and
easily implemented—why didn't you do them?

By keeping those feelings of dread in the forefront of your mind
you will be able to better mold the future of your circulation department. Sure, you will first have to concentrate on rebuilding
to where you were before the disaster, but as big an accomplishment as that is, it is not enough. It may be that in your lifetime
that library will never again be subjected to such horrific damage
and loss: but what if . . . ? It is ironic that the electronic pacemaker
keeps alive the very organ from which love and caring emotes.
No matter how high tech your library body becomes, don't leave
out the high-touch component. Connect with your patrons even
more. Find ways to build upon your customer service. Your efforts will not go unappreciated, and you will reap major rewards.
Finally, look inward. Your staff has survived a major ordeal. Sharing thanks and kudos are critically necessary to regain health. Nour-
ish the team by taking lots of positive action. Celebrate small gains
and really celebrate the big ones. You will see smiles again.

Library Disaster Planning and Recovery Handbook

KEY RECOMMENDATIONS

Access Services

- Before a disaster happens, pre-plan and practice using your plan. Use small disaster situations (like a heavy snowfall day) to test your plan in a live situation.
- Establish communication within the department using telephone trees or a single person to make telephone calls. Later, consider a voice bulletin board for announcements.
- Deploy employees as soon as possible. Hourly employees are depending upon you for an income. Salaried staff want to make a difference during the recovery.
- Establish communication with your patrons. Keep these connections throughout the recovery process.
- Consider safety always—protect your staff.
- Keep your supervisory team cohesive by having regular meetings and strategy sessions.
- Make decisions regarding your online circulation-system data. Take a snapshot of data. How will you handle books which are overdue or will come due soon? What will you do about fines and bills?
- Establish other satellite operations and hours of service. Set up a site for users to get information by telephone or walk-in. Course reserve is a special consideration requiring space. Consider computer needs. Find a way to handle book returns.
- Set up a transport fleet to shuttle people and materials between your sites.
- Keep looking ahead—consider long-term options for satellites if your main building will remain unavailable. If the building will become available soon, plan for the collapse of satellites and level of service back at the main branch.
- Strive for excellence/maximum performance and always recognize work well done.

APPENDIX 7-A
ACCESS SERVICES ORGANIZATION CHART

	CIRC	N/W, RESERVE	RECORDS	AT-LARGE
SUPERVISOR	Library Tech II	Library Tech II	Library Tech II	Library Tech II
STAFF	Library Tech I (2)	Library Tech I (3)	Library Tech I (3)	
STUDENT STAFF	Monitors and students--hours/week vary based upon time of year and budget; approx. 40-45 students on the payroll per Fall/Spring semester.	0 hours per se. Shared students with Circ LTII.	20 hours/week	
PRIMARY DUTIES PERFORMED UNDER DIRECTION OF LTII (List is not necessarily all-inclusive)	1. Desk duty 2. Hiring, scheduling, training monitors/students 3. Loan Desk management 4. Lockers 5. Courier 6. Phone station management	1. Desk duty 2. Reserve management 3. Hiring, scheduling, training monitor/students 4. Night/weekend Loan Desk management 5. Branch requests/Ariel (SHARED W/ RECORDS) 6. High plains courier returns 7. Recalls	1. Searching 2. Fiscal management 3. Printing daily notices 4. Statistics 5. Weekly manual file (overdues) management 6. Patron database maintenance (SHARED W/ JIM FARMER) 7. Holds 8. Supplies/Equip req. 9. Branch requests/Ariel (SHARED W/ RESERVE) 10. Faculty study carrels 11. Faculty authorizations	1. Special projects implementation 2. Cooperative efforts with other public service points 3. Departmental support duties as assigned

NOTES TO APPENDIX 7-A

The cross-unit duties listed below will still require cooperation and participation of staff from all units in Access:

Phone duty
Desk duty
Pager duty
Intersession schedule coverage (weekends included)
Nights/weekends

Even though night/weekend coverage is reduced, it is highly recommended that everyone do some desk duty each semester in order to keep up on the duties (and keeping current with procedural changes) at the desk. Keeping current on opening/closing duties also applies.

APPENDIX 7-B
FORM FOR NON-RETURNABLE, FLOOD-DESTROYED ITEM CLAIM

PLEASE PRINT:

NAME _____ID NUMBER_____

ADDRESS_____

CITY, STATE, ZIP_____PHONE ( )_____

LIBRARY STATUS (CIRCLE ONE): FACULTY   STAFF   STUDENT   COMMUNITY

I am unable to return the following library material to the library for the following reason pertaining to the July 28,

1997 Fort Collins flood: _____

_____

_____

TITLE OF BOOK_____

CALL NUMBER_____

BARCODE NUMBER_____

By my signature below, I state that I fully accept the following terms of this agreement:

1.   I understand this book will be taken off of my account and will be declared missing.

2.   I understand any charges accrued for the item will also be taken off my account.

SIGNATURE_____DATE_____

OFFICE USE ONLY:

HEAD, ACCESS SERVICES SIGNATURE_____DATE_____

DISCHARGE DATE_____Was the item billed at the time of discharge?_____

Recorded on last check-out list_____BR_____L/S_____

COPY TO: HEAD OF ACCESS SERVICES; PATRON; BILLING TECHNICIAN II

RETURN TO:
  HEAD OF ACCESS SERVICES, COLORADO STATE UNIVERSTIY LIBRARIES, FT. COLLINS, CO 80523

APPENDIX 7-C
FORM FOR RETURNABLE, FLOOD-DAMAGED ITEM CLAIM

PLEASE PRINT:

NAME _____ID NUMBER_____

ADDRESS_____

CITY, STATE, ZIP_____PHONE (___)_____

LIBRARY STATUS (CIRCLE ONE):   FACULTY   STAFF   STUDENT   COMMUNITY

I returned the following library material to the library in a wet/damaged condition following the July 28, 1997 Fort

Collins flood.

TITLE OF BOOK_____

CALL NUMBER_____

BARCODE NUMBER_____

By my signature below, I state that I fully accept the following terms of this agreement:

1.   I understand this book will be taken off of my account and will be declared missing.

2.   I understand any charges accrued for the item will also be taken off my account.

SIGNATURE_____DATE_____

OFFICE USE ONLY:

HEAD, ACCESS SERVICES SIGNATURE _____DATE_____

DISCHARGE DATE_____Was the item billed at the time of discharge?_____

Recorded on check-out list_____BR_____L/S_____

COPY TO: HEAD OF ACCESS SERVICES; PATRON; BILLING TECHNICIAN II

RETURN TO:
HEAD OF ACCESS SERVICES, COLORADO STATE UNIVERSTIY LIBRARIES, FT. COLLINS, CO 80523

REFERENCES

Curzon, Susan. 1998. E-mail correspondence with author, October 6.
Leighton, Joan Krasner. 1998. Telephone interview with author, October 6.
Tinker, Chauncey B. 1948. The Library. In *Readings for Liberal Education*, edited by Louis G. Locke, William M. Gibson, and George Arms. New York: Rinehart and Company.

8 There Is No Normal Anymore: Interlibrary Loan / Document-Delivery Services During Disaster Recovery

Tom Delaney

INTRODUCTION

In some ways, Interlibrary Loan (ILL) is already a form of disaster recovery in some academic environments. There are academic libraries which perceive the need for ILL service as the sum total of failures of collection development, a flaw in the librarian-liaison system, and the aftereffects of a failed security system through which the most in-demand material has disappeared. There are other academic libraries that see the role of ILL as modestly supportive, indicative of budgetary constraints, or as a means of selectively supporting the marginal academic programs.

These views of ILL are, in fact, disasters waiting to happen. In the environment that we found ourselves after the CSU disaster, one of the first realizations that we had was that ILL would play a fundamental role in disaster recovery. We also realized that the model of ILL that had evolved at CSU over the last several decades was one that saw its role as a program striving to develop services to meet user expectations as a rapid, reliable delivery service. When the disaster that damaged so much of our collection occurred, the need to structure this model into a fully developed service moved from the theoretical to the essential. We survived because we had always been a department that considered itself unfinished and was willing to experiment with newer, faster, and higher-quality delivery processes. This made the disaster, as dramatic an event as it was, an opportunity to expand the scope of experimentation in the face of necessity.

197

ILL, as most of us know it, has generally been considered a supportive service. When a library user cannot locate the material to conduct research or teach class material, ILL has frequently been the "Solution of Last Resort." Because of the academic environment, and because of the specific nature of ILL functions, usage of this service has been most beneficial to that part of the community conducting long-range research projects or those engaged in long-term teaching/planning. The plain and simple fact is that ILL is a slow, inefficient, and time-intensive means of providing the user with the materials they need. Colorado State University has long recognized—actually, has long admitted—that this is the case; ILL is not a primary service. It cannot provide the academic community with materials for short-term class assignments, undergraduate class projects with short due dates, be a quick source of information to conduct day-to-day business, or be a rapid source of access for material to subsidize studies for exams and tests.

While I don't recall the specific thoughts in my mind on the morning of July 29, 1997, I think they could have been summed up by condensing the internal jumble into a summary statement much like that above. I also knew that, like it or not, the faculty, staff, students, and administrators across campus would establish a new dependency on ILL, and that this relationship would play a short-term role in the credibility of the library as a campus institution. From the top of the stairway looking down into "Lake Basement," I was reminded of the town inundated at the creation of our local reservoir: during particularly dry years, the old church steeple and a few house peaks are seen rotting under the muddy waters of an engineered lake. I wondered, at the time, if (or even when) our complete collection of bound journals, science monographs, and a significant portion of the social science monographs would peek their moldy, cruddy spines out of an equally murky lake. It was both a disaster and an opportunity, and ILL would play a large role in determining the perception of this event in the collective campus memory.

We were simultaneously overwhelmed and enthused by the challenge presented by the CSU disaster. Over the years, ILL at CSU has escaped much of the common theoretical ruts that could have driven the ILL environment into a process-ridden time sink.

This thinking has been built into a systematic approach to resource sharing that represents a procedural continuum. Rethinking ILL has assisted us in overcoming the delusion that ILL is the same now as it was in the early 1960s. Methods, policies, procedures, and technology have contributed to provide dramatically enhanced service.

Since the early 1970s, the ILL department at CSU has been willing to introduce innovative techniques that enhance speed and quality of item delivery. The philosophical intent is *not* to maximize the efficiency of ILL as much as it has been to minimize the impact of its inefficiencies for the users. The plan has been to build from a core, and manufacture a process that provides the fewest hurdles for the users and the fewest number of times that material has to be handled by the staff, thus minimizing staff intervention.

The immediate pre-disaster goals of the ILL department can be consolidated and outlined as:

- Provide access to all ILL requesting functions and information 24 hours a day.
- Whenever possible, conceptualize information as electrons rather than paper in every phase of the process.
- Never be fooled into thinking that ILL is the service of choice—it is always the service of last resort.
- Minimize the inconvenience of ILL use.
- Recognize that if any added service or convenience results in increased demand, it is a signal that ILL has been incapable of providing needed services prior to the inception of the convenience.
- Have the user be an accountable agent in the ILL process.
- Minimize the need for intervention in the ILL process.
- Understand that technological equipment is a large front-end expense, but in the long run is far less expensive than staff time. (To state as a corollary: Nothing is more expensive than staff time.)

Were these my thoughts that morning as I looked down at the lower-level lake that was as unsuitable for drinking or swimming as it was for studying? Not precisely—but if any ideas could be culled out of the emotional morass, these would be at the core.

In retrospect, these ideas formulated the thinking that created the conceptual environment in which ILL would need to function. It was too late to change any of it. If we had been right in how we were organized and how we thought, we'd survive. If we had been wrong, life would be more than a little unpleasant. If ILL was going to provide a useful primary service during the coming year(s), it would have to be based on these fundamentals—they were really the only ways that we knew of to do business, and it was too late to rethink any of it. At the same time, we all knew that what we had come to think of as normal would never be the same again. In the long run, these fundamentals have served us well.

THE CONCEPTUAL VERSUS THE PRACTICAL

In the initial days following the disaster, we were not able to sink into a state of shock suitable for the occasion. Classes were just a few weeks away, the library was not habitable, the campus bookstore was gone, and the world was not going to wait for a long-term recovery plan. In many ways, we were pre-prepared for just such a crisis. Standard careful planning and a solid long-term set of goals left ILL in a surprisingly good position. Much of what we had done in the previous 25 years had provided a foundation that prepared us for the adaptability necessary for this catastrophic event.

We had introduced remote electronic requesting in 1994, and it was an instant success. In 1995, we utilized the protocol provided by the Online Computer Library Center (OCLC), which is a library bibliographic utility, to implement the OCLC Transfer Program for transferring user-centered electronic requests to the OCLC system for local staff handling. This allowed us to transmit the requests to OCLC and have the user-generated information put directly into an OCLC format so that we did not need to re-key the request. The result was immediately reflected in time-savings for the staff. We had been eager to jump into the ILL electronic request arena, unlike many libraries at that time.

The question about electronic requests that we most frequently fielded was, "Hasn't this caused users to increase the number of

FIGURE 8-1
ILL Requests 7/97 Through 12/98

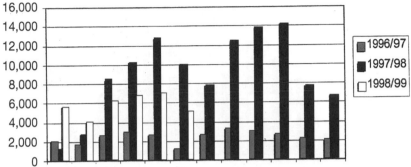

requests they make?" The standard answer reflects one of the primary ILL corollaries listed above, and which prepared us for the post-disaster arena: "It doesn't matter." If there was a need for information, we would be irresponsible to not find innovative means to meet that need—even if it results in a greater number of requests. Secondly, such a notion reflects thinking that has also been responsible for the perception of ILL as slow and lumbering. We have always thought out-of-the-box in designing new services, which is vastly different than trying to squeeze services into tired and overcrowded boxes.

Figures 8.1 and 8.2 demonstrate a month-by-month breakdown for the period of January 1996 through December 1998. Figure 8.1 shows a comparison of ILL borrowing transactions starting the month of the disaster (July 1997). Shown are: the pre-disaster year (1996/97), the disaster year (1997/98), and the post-disaster year (1998/99). The figure indicates a marked increase in ILL borrowing transactions once the *FastFlood* operation began. The month of April in the disaster year shows more than 14,000 transactions (an average of 3,500 per week)!

Figure 8.2 shows pre-disaster and post-disaster ILL borrowing transactions for 1996 and 1997. However, at the bottom of the graph are the actual number of transactions for comparing between pre-disaster and post-disaster months.

FIGURE 8-2
ILL Requests 1996/97 and 1997/98

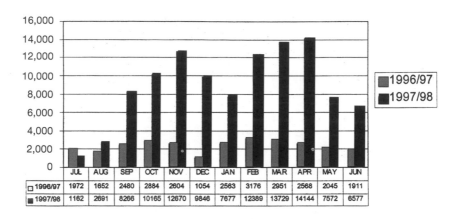

	JUL	AUG	SEP	OCT	NOV	DEC	JAN	FEB	MAR	APR	MAY	JUN
1996/97	1972	1652	2480	2884	2604	1054	2563	3176	2951	2568	2045	1911
1997/98	1162	2691	8266	10165	12670	9846	7677	12389	13729	14144	7572	6577

PLANNING EXPANDED INTERLIBRARY LOAN SERVICES IN DISASTER RECOVERY

Your ILL policy should dictate that staff cannot labor in the self-delusion that ILL is an attractive service. It isn't. It never has been. It never will be. The best ILL can do is to minimize inconvenience to the user and decrease cost to the library—and you can do both simultaneously. This approach will provide you with a pre-adaptive strategy in which, as in the case of a disaster, your ILL department will be able to become convenient and efficient overnight. This is essential because you will have to address the needs of a brand new audience and make your services available to undergraduates on a classroom and examination-ready *on-demand* basis. Your ILL will be able to survive as long as you are willing to discard the traditional in favor of generating new standards. In the days immediately following a disaster, you will need to be prepared to fight a two-front war: plan for the inevitable demands to be placed on ILL in the long run and become an immediately viable and available service while your library may be closed during the recovery period.

If your long-term recovery strategy is pre-aligned with your long-term goals for ILL, this will serve you well. In our case, through a combination of both need and a long-range strategy, we invested a huge amount of time in creating an automated department. This will serve the needs of any ILL department well. We had adopted an attitude premised first on "the future is coming, and we need to be prepared," and, second, "nothing is ever more expensive than staff time." Your ILL processes need to be built on the construct that data is portable. It will make your department lean in terms of staffing; that is, a small number of people in this environment can perform a huge number of tasks without being overstressed or overworked. Moreover, the premise that data is portable will save your lives in disaster recovery.

In this disaster recovery process, you will have to address our two immediate needs: how to make your services available immediately to a needy audience, and how and where to completely relocate your services. All of this should be transparent to the users. Your dependence on automation will also prepare you for the needed portability to make your ILL services available to your user community, even in disaster recovery.

Automation

All of us in the library world are dependent to some degree on automation. In fact, we may not like to admit it, but many of our users are aware of the limitations of library services because they are becoming more familiar with the principles of information access, transfer, and retrieval than we are. They are more familiar with using computer-available information and databases and have more experience in a variety of platforms and search engines than we do. This position is not one that has met with popular approval among information professionals, but the simple fact is that, especially among the faculty and graduate-level students, it is a true statement. We don't provide information to users, rather we provide information to users when their experience, time demands, or familiarity with new databases fail them. Our goal in ILL has been to stay close to meeting the expectations of our users based on *their* experience.

The historical trend at CSU has been to find the means to utilize technical innovations to enhance service. When the former ILL coordinator was promoted to assistant dean for Public Services, the continuation of this policy was ensured as a means of always providing at least the minimal service that our users anticipated.

I hope to make it clear to you how automation positioned us to be able to respond with immediate services after such a large-scale disaster. By the start of 1997, approximately 80 percent of our requests were submitted electronically. Our ILL program was an ASCII-text based program running on our own UNIX server. The time savings were substantial. With the bulk of requests submitted electronically, we did not have to re-key those requests. The ILL borrowers could search and send the requests directly from the OCLC command line. This provided us with the opportunity to focus our attention on providing a maximum fill rate and provided us with the time to encourage the campus community to utilize ILL services. Our fill rate has traditionally been in the 94–97 percent range, which is astonishingly high. It also provided us with the opportunity to maximize convenience for the user. By 1996, we had an automated, menu-driven, e-mail notification system; we were experimenting with fax deliveries direct to users and had established a small pilot to send requests to academic departments via Ariel electronic transmissions; and we were mailing articles directly to users. There seemed to be little that we could do to improve on these services.

Our borrowing unit has been used as an ILL model for establishing efficient service. However, in addition, our lending unit was also extremely capable. In early 1997, we had established a simple automated program to search our OPAC for call numbers for lending titles/ISSN numbers. This had eliminated the need for approximately 80 hours of student help that were transferred to other units in the library that were desperately in need of staffing.

We had become as dependent as possible on Ariel and fax delivery. When the administration provided support for the acquisition of two high-speed scanners, we were able to transfer our Ariel and fax capabilities from four-pages-per-minute devices to twenty-eight-pages-per-minute devices. After a steep learning curve on the computer-fax driven software, we were able to again re-evaluate our staffing. We had gone from eight hours a day Ariel and eight hours a day faxing down to two hours each. The savings of student staff time to the tune of 12 hours per day allowed us to save the equivalent in the cost of the new scanners and workstations in one year. After that, we were coming out way ahead (remember, there is *nothing* more expensive than staff time!). We also made certain that there was at least one computer terminal for each and every staff member. At the time that we did this, we were one of the first units in the organization to provide this level of hardware support. However, given the set of circumstances outlined above, this policy met with administrative-level support; and we were able to move fully into an electronic environment.

In both the borrowing and lending arenas, the trend towards utilizing technology was a bimodal strategy: first, to provide a more efficient and more effective service, and, second, to reduce the high cost associated with interlibrary loan. There is no point to improving ILL services unless the improvements are passed along to the user.

In June of 1997, ILL officially adopted a policy of no longer accepting written requests. All users were required to type them into computers (either their own home/office computers, the OPAC terminals in the building, or in terminals in the ILL office dedicated to user requests). We received only two complaints, both from older faculty members. I explained to both of them that when they typed the requests we could provide faster service for everyone since we then did not need to re-key them. We also used a comparison to the card catalog. Card catalogs are labor-intensive, require a lot of maintenance time, and are slow to be updated. The same fundamentals applied to ILL requests. I don't know if this explanation left them satisfied, but we did hold our ground. Our users continued to use ILL, and we made certain that we always had staff available to assist users with any questions on how to appropriately fill out the form.

Finally, in June of 1997, we also started to use a new software package to track ILL statistics for both borrowing and lending. We officially switched to Clio in May of 1997 (in favor of our previous homegrown package and, later, Aviso). Clio provided us with the functionality to become essentially a paperless office. We no longer filed records for lending; we had no paper records associated with borrowing; and the number of printouts that we made for various reasons kept reducing.

Since we had been gradually moving into a mode where our users accessed our services remotely, the ILL department had become, essentially, an on-demand service that our users could access 24 hours a day, 365 days a year. Many of our regular ILL customers were not even aware of the fact that we had moved our offices in October of 1996!

Portability

In moving towards a paperless environment, we had also inadvertently become almost fully *portable*. We had no files or no paper records to move. What we did have to do was become careful (almost paranoid) about maintaining solid backups of all of our records and programs. The plan was to maintain all records in three physical locations so that we would never be caught off guard in the event of an electronic catastrophe.

ILL departments striving to be paperless and portable need to be running almost solely off of Internet connections, local PCs, and electronic communications. This will give the department a great deal of portability. In the event of a disaster, there will be nothing to move except machines and people. Our records and our connections could be accessed from anywhere that we had the capability to plug-in to the Internet. In fact, two days after the disaster, we were training staff to send on OCLC from a dial-up connection in my home.

The other important factor that will allow your ILL to be fully portable, if your building becomes uninhabitable, is to have your own UNIX or NT server so that you can relocate your main user-to-ILL connection wherever you can plug into an Internet connection. This was essentially the state of affairs in our ILL on July 28, 1997. We felt like we had been preparing for The Future— but we did not expect The Future to be a disaster happening the next morning!

RESOURCE REQUIREMENTS

You may be in a position, should a disaster occur, to not be able to use your library building for a long time. Your first thoughts should be directed towards the recovery process. You need to create a plan to reestablish an ILL presence for the university community. Whether or not your building may be severely damaged and/or your collection seriously compromised, at least for the short run your ILL will be the complete link between the users and research/resource material. It may be several weeks before you know the absolute long-term implications for ILL, or how profound and long-lasting the impact of the disaster may be.

If your ILL service is portable, then you will only need two immediate items to begin providing ILL service: labor to move your equipment and an Internet location to plug in and begin acting as ILL.

Your time frame could be very short and your resource demands immediate. However, due to reliance on electronic requests only, your users will have connectivity within a day or two, and you will be prepared to meet the demand.

You will need to develop a list of priorities to establish connectivity and service for the immediate future and, simultaneously, begin a long-range plan to provide recovery service. What you will discover in this process is that your ILL department will be already poised to meet at least the initial demands.

In our disaster recovery efforts, space for ILL would be a long-term consideration. We met our immediate goal when our associates at the Front Range Community College in Fort Collins offered us space for our ILL borrowing staff in their library during the remainder of the summer break. This gave us a start; and on Friday, August 1st, we moved our equipment in and hooked up to the Internet via their connection. Our technology support staff also moved rapidly, moving our server (undamaged) from the library to the university's engineering building. The server was hooked up and we started receiving electronic requests almost the minute that the server was online.

Since we were in no condition (in terms of the collection and with a pending staffing crisis) to lend materials, our staff involved in lending became "distributors." We established a network of students and our lending supervisor established a rapid-delivery process to minimize handling material and expedite the time it took for us to process and distribute the material. Since we had no "library," the distribution operation took place out of our library's storage depository. All needed materials were moved over and delivered to the depository, and by Monday morning, August 4th, we had enough of a procedure in place to distribute materials through the mail or in-person to campus academic departments.

Our borrowing operation had a temporary solution for at least the first few weeks of the crisis, and our lending operation completely changed its orientation and was relocated for the short term (a relocation that would last seven months).

The portability that comes with being electronic and paperless was perhaps the biggest benefit to immediate service: we were fully operational and developing and implementing projects within two days after the disaster.

Staffing Requirements

The library had long been considered unique in our approach to utilizing student staff. We have argued long and hard with other ILL colleagues (mostly unsuccessfully) that most large institutional ILL departments would benefit from using students as staff members. Their contribution is invaluable; and it is counterproductive for you to consider students as "envelope addressers," or "mail openers."

Employ your students to be full participants in the ILL process. Beginning students can start off with elementary tasks; but by the end of their first semester, they should generally be full-fledged OCLC senders or fully responsible for collecting material and marking it for lending. This will provide you with a tremendous volume of labor that begins unskilled but quickly learns to participate in a full teamwork environment.

This approach will provide you with staff who are willing and capable contributors. Your first, and most immediate, need in disaster recovery will be for more staff to handle the number of incoming requests. Reliance on students will pay off not only in terms of economics and department morale in the pre-disaster environment but will also provide you with a core of pre-trained and ready employees.

The dependence on student assistants, as well as the drive to automate ILL, left us in a unique position. Our online program, the first of its kind nationally and the first program to create a direct interface with OCLC, was the result of a complete reliance on student programmers. While these programmers had long-since graduated, they were familiar with the field and with the demands of ILL. The library administration immediately moved to reincorporate these former students into a full-time staff mode. Luckily, we were able to rehire them to build a disaster recovery program.

Given that some of your ILL services will become works-in-progress in a crisis environment, it is essential to maintain a core flexibility in order to maximize the contributions that you place on your students. Cross-train as many students as possible in the initial recovery period. You could have several students sending on OCLC, learning the ins and outs of Internet document delivery, learning how to use your database, and how to track and update requests. While you may have an initial excess of people, the complicated nature of the training process dictates that you bring in as many student staff as you can and rely on supervisors, full-time staff, and other already-trained students to become invested in the training process.

Your second staffing demand could be an increased number of students to process requests in one form or another. Your borrowing and lending unit supervisors should begin to hire a large number of students immediately and initiate the training process as soon as possible in your recovery process.

Equipment Connection Requirements

The most obvious demand that your ILL department will be faced with is the need for equipment. Even if you have your own server, you should anticipate that it will be stressed to the maximum in order to handle the volume of requests. An increase in volume may demand not only an increase in the number of staff available to assist with the anticipated requests but also an increase in the necessary terminals to accommodate the increased volume. In addition to the straightforward PCs that ILL will need to survive, you will have to think in the short run as well as the long run.

Secondly, you may need to get over the mindset that a computer requires constant human intervention to run. This should not be the case, and most libraries are slowly beginning to realize this. A computer can print out documents transmitted via the

Internet with the only need being to occasionally replenish the paper or change the ink cartridge. This understanding, pre-built into your ILL department's structure, will be one of the most effective of all preparedness strategies. Computers can do work—people just need to manage the output.

Tangentially to this, you need to realize that the increasing amount of equipment will not be useful without adequate connectivity for your ILL department. At Morgan Library, this was the first situation in our disaster that was most difficult for which to plan. We had inadvertently anticipated the *how* but not the *where*. Who could have anticipated that our entire building would become temporarily uninhabitable?

In the long run, we were fine. CSU ILL had, as most ILLs need to do, planned ahead. When our ILL area was designed, we had included 54 LAN drops. Without this connectivity to prepare for the need to move information digitally, we would not have survived the disaster; and ILL would have been an artifact during disaster recovery. Most of the material would have been moved via paper and would not have provided an acceptable delivery time for the bulk of our users. This would have reduced research to nothing more than bus-riding students between campuses and a volume increase for document suppliers sending 200 x 100 dpi fax transmissions.

But, in the short run, it was difficult to find a location that had anticipated the need for Internet connectivity. We immediately began training staff members to send ILL requests via telephone and modem. The day after the disaster, we were sending requests from my home on a PC/modem connection. Our immediate plan was to use this approach indefinitely and provide staff with laptops and have a fleet of telecommuters until the building was open.

Our biggest immediate need was staffing—due to the gradual move towards making ILL a paperless operation, several full-time and student hours had been reallocated to other departments. Fortunately, we have made it a policy to train student staff to be full active members of the department and to contribute by performing the same functions as full-time staff members. By the end of their sophomore year, the student staff is fully trained to send on OCLC, process incoming requests, and maintain the ILL database. This gave us a ready pool of staff from which to draw. We have several students who had graduated from CSU who were looking for permanent full-time positions. Given the emergency nature of the situation, we were able to bring them on as fully trained members of the department.

With connectivity and staff, ILL became fully functional and became capable of handling the volume of requests within a few days of the disaster. Our technical support staff prioritized hooking up our ILL electronic request server, and we were fully on line by Thursday—two days after the disaster and about three weeks before the library was again able to open its doors.

In terms of being prepared, ILL had inadvertently become capable of being the "Solution of First Resort." In the long run, due to the strategic design and carefully engineered evolution of the ILL department, CSU Libraries was fortunate enough to have had the long-term foresight to see ILL as a means of collection augmentation. The disaster and the recovery would increase the visibility but not the functionality or design of ILL.

DISASTER STRIKES: THINK FAST!

Once a disaster strikes, you are going to have to reassess your ILL operations at lightning speed to determine how you can best meet the needs of your users. If your library materials are so damaged and/or your building is so damaged you can't get to the materials, then the first assessment you need to do is determine your ILL operational strengths and weaknesses. Based on that assessment, you will have to move quickly to think of innovative methods of getting materials to your users given your programmatic strengths or limitations.

There are three steps to consider in light of this kind of disaster:

1. Partner with other libraries.

2. Retrain staff; hire new staff.

3. Design new services.

In our disaster, our operation was scattered across two different campuses; our central ILL server had been relocated to a third part of campus and users were returning to the campus to prepare for fall studies. We had immediately realized that ILL would have a new and different audience. Our primary constituency would no longer consist of faculty and graduate students but the entire campus population. We had no choice but to build a program with services and delivery methods designed to meet their needs. With all of our bound journals damaged, and half of our monographs in the same state, our situation was critical. Fortunately, we were prepared not only to meet user expectations of providing materials in a damaged environment, but also to quickly design programs that would meet user expectations of ILL as a complete, short-term library service.

Step One—Partnering

This step relies on your partnerships with other libraries and/or organizations to assist you in providing emergency assistance. If access to your materials is the major problem, then you will want to work out partnerships with other libraries to have some type of access to their materials. In this step, you will find that immediately after your disaster, the word of your situation will spread rapidly. Offers of assistance will pour in, especially for enhanced ILL service from other libraries throughout the country.

In our situation, Step One was the easiest of them all. Before we even had access to our computers, word of our situation spread rapidly. The resource-sharing specialist with the Association of Research Libraries (ARL) coordinated all the offers of assistance. She spent many late evenings on the telephone relaying offers, requesting updates of the situation to present to ARL libraries, and providing advice. Before we were out of the gate, we had offers of enhanced ILL service from over 50 libraries. They are too numerous to list here individually, but the ILL relationships fostered through being a net lender to libraries for so many years was more than returned to us overnight by libraries from coast-to-coast. We knew that we would survive.

Step Two—Staffing

Again, depending on how your ILL services will differ in disaster recovery from ours, you will find that you will not only have to retrain your staff but you may also have to hire new staff to handle your program redesign and other activities.

It was our experience that Step Two was much more complex than Step One. Our borrowing staff and our lending staff had to immediately develop new ways of cooperating and sharing different types of information. Our lending staff had to be retrained to become the Materials Delivery Unit until our collection returned to normal. This staff had to discover the ins and outs of traversing the campus to deliver materials. The scale was as awesome as the task, and its implementation was tied into Step Three—the design of a new program that developed rapid access to journal articles.

Step Three—Designing

In ILL services, this step calls for some kind of new program design to help you meet your users' needs for library materials. If the basis for your new program is access to journal materials ordinarily owned by you but heavily damaged, you are probably looking at a new service/program design for short-term access to those materials. In preparing to think, talk, and design such a new, temporary service, make sure your ILL folks think "out of the box." The emergency of your situation will require thinking in this manner. Emergency response to a disaster is not the time for your staff to think traditionally. If that means bringing in an innovative ILL methods expert to help shape the thinking, then it is well worth the expense.

In our pre-disaster situation, we were reliant on electronic delivery of documents through Internet transmission systems. We had been one of the initial test sites for document delivery through Ariel and immediately saw the potential for rapid, high-quality document delivery. This became our third step: to design an emergency service based on our previous experimentation and willingness to think "out of the box." Our experiment in the early days of document transmission had evolved into a reliance of Ariel as an essential part of our service; this left us in a position to depend on Internet delivery as the primary source of receiving materials. Our assistant dean for Public Services devised a disaster recovery plan for document delivery that would encompass the entire campus and would provide ILL with the flexibility to deliver documents quickly to strategic academic departments.

The plan called for 15 Ariel receiving stations, to be placed at geographically-distributed buildings around campus, and a fleet of 15 students to staff the machines two hours a day to sort and deliver articles directly to department mailboxes. Our initial goal was to have a turn-around time of three days on journal requests that were part of the damaged CSU collection. This called for a series of negotiated partnerships with cooperative libraries. Our need consisted of finding libraries who were also willing to think outside the box of traditional ILL, of creating a computer program that would provide some form of rapid access to those titles that were damaged in the disaster, and of creating a complex electronic network that was easy to access for both the CSU community and the libraries we would need to cooperate with us.

The key, as with any large endeavor, relied heavily on cooperation from a variety of sources. We had to be willing to create and implement a design and be able to communicate the functionality of the design to the technology and library staff who would actually route the material. Our campus networking specialists offered to install and distribute the computers necessary for this project. We were able to quickly establish cooperative relationships with six other libraries to assist us with filling these requests, and our database specialists were able to create a digital list of titles that we needed to be able to access on a rapid basis. With this in place, the *FastFlood* request system was ready to go. Within a month, the system was fully operational; the success that we have been able to achieve with this system has led us to seek funding to expand this service as a permanent, two-way delivery system for articles.

FASTFLOOD: A NEW DESIGN FOR ILL

FastFlood is really an extension of the processes that we had been designing for a number of years. Requests would be accepted only through electronic means, high-end rapid delivery would be required rather than optional, and delivery to mailboxes across campus would be the norm. *FastFlood* was designed to be the equivalent of an on-campus collection; the only service that we could not duplicate was the ability to browse a local collection. This turned out to be a minor concern for the serious users and not a concern at all for the students in need of quickly retrieved material for tests/papers.

The program was designed to function as a database rather than a free-text ILL request program. We built a database of our old journal titles, and from these we sought out libraries with collections that would mirror our own collection. Once the networking equipment was in place, and the programmers had completed the Web forms to make the system available, we launched the service.

Our assistant dean for Public Services negotiated with six libraries to establish a partnership with them. We agreed to supply high-end Ariel workstations and to pay for student staff to retrieve, photocopy, and scan articles. We did ask them to provide training and supervision for the staff, and all of them generously agreed. The six partner libraries—The University of Colorado at Boulder, The University of Northern Colorado, Arizona State University, The University of Denver, Colorado School of Mines, and Cornell University—have performed flawlessly.

We were able to create programs that search these libraries' catalogs and extract holdings, location, and call numbers. Armed with this information, our programmers designed a database search engine that allowed users to browse titles by word or by ISSN (an unusual search, but very specific). Thanks to the programming expertise that ILL had fostered over the years (due solely to our reliance on student help), our database was on-line and active before the hardware could be installed. Our first official day of *FastFlood* database availability was October 6th, and within hours we had received our first requests—even before the campus listserv announcement could be posted. Within three days, we were receiving over one hundred requests per day. By semester's end, we had received up to 300 *FastFlood* requests per day; and because of our long-term commitment to Ariel/document delivery and technology, we were able to provide at least a photographic "image" of our damaged collection.

Statistically, the results were impressive—our successful fill rate was 97 percent in three days or less. Conceptually, the results have been even more impressive. We found that we were finally able to start meeting user expectations by raising our standard of service. The long-term administrative support given to ILL provided the impetus to quickly design and implement a new model that was functional because the staff was already trained in the functional aspects of the technology. ILL, already seen as a "Solution of Fast Resort," set the stage for expanding service rather than trying to respond to a crisis. Our user expectations have increased, and we are in a mode to continue to try to meet the demand while the collection is in the recovery process. The long-term results of this process are providing the motivation to move into new arenas of service that are possible in an environment completely driven by user expectations.

The disaster recovery process has driven us to evaluate the functionality of ILL in light of extreme demands. While the ultimate goal of any institution is to have a perfect collection, access to any collection at all is not guaranteed under disaster circumstances. With the tools available to you, it is possible to utilize and build off of readily available technology and establish a "virtual connection" between your library and your patrons. This is not only possible, but is also essential to prepare for any eventuality.

CONCLUSION

We were able to create programs that search our partner libraries' catalogs and extract holdings, location, and call number for the items held by these libraries that were formerly in our collection. When our users initiate a request, they search a database of titles; when they find a title that was in our collection, they launch a request and ILL routes it to the appropriate library.

The program has been a huge success—we have received approximately 94 percent of the articles in two days or less. A comparison of our post-disaster borrowing transactions demonstrate 20,000 pre-disaster transactions for one year as compared to 130,000-plus borrowing transactions in the subsequent, post-disaster year. The turn-around time, accuracy, and quality of the transmissions has impressed both the library and the end-users alike.

Given our ability to quickly jump into an "out-of-the-box" mode,

ILL has been able to assist in the disaster recovery efforts by providing nearly uninterrupted service for our local users.

In the Long Run

While we are still unable to lend materials to other libraries, our lenders have become adapted to a new function as on-campus delivery facilitators. In order to minimize the inconvenience of the temporary loss of materials, we have a sweeping campaign to get materials to the users as quickly as possible. We deliver to office, mail to home, or provide whatever option for delivery notification that they choose. This approach has enabled even faster turnaround times for ILL items.

What we are learning in this process is that ILL is not raising expectations, but rather we are finally meeting expectations. Our users know what our capabilities ought to be—and this crisis has pushed us into evaluating what we do in order to meet their needs. In the long run, our disaster recovery ILL module will have an impact on how we perceive the role of ILL.

We are educating an entire generation of students to understand and use ILL. From that first day incoming first-year college students arrive on campus they are initiated into the role and function of ILL. We are one of their primary sources. We don't expect them to forget the availability of this service as materials come back to the shelves. The feeling is that ILL is not an exceptional service, but a part of the everyday library environment.

We welcome new users, and hope to continue to find new means to continue to address their research needs quickly, efficiently, and inexpensively.

Library Disaster Planning and Recovery Handbook

KEY RECOMMENDATIONS

Interlibrary Loan

- Think "out of the box."

- Rethink your staffing patterns and use student workers as you would regular employees. They learn quickly and are very capable.

- Automate, automate, automate—use technology for almost every aspect of ILL operations.

- Making your ILL portable enables you to move the operation elsewhere on short notice.

- Review your resources: staffing, equipment, and electronic connections.

- Develop partnerships to help you during ILL disaster recovery.

9 Library Instruction During Disaster Recovery: Why is it Needed?

Naomi Lederer and Awilda Reyes

INTRODUCTION

Library instruction provides an opportunity to introduce users to materials and services available in a library, and it plays an important role at the Colorado State University Libraries. An instruction librarian position was created to focus on the library and other research needs of undergraduate students, as well as to serve as the liaison to the First Year Composition Program (CO 150), the library credit course (LI 301), campus groups (such as Preview CSU—a freshman orientation program for incoming students and their parents given in the summer), and the local K-12 population. Other subject-specialist reference librarians provide bibliographic instruction to faculty and graduate students and also teach classes for most of the subject-specific undergraduate courses.

After a disaster, instruction to your users will become more critical. If your library's materials were lost or damaged, then locating or determining the status of materials can be a big challenge. Additionally, the number of formal classroom instruction sessions may decline during the months after the disaster. You will find that informal instructional sessions at service points will increase, requiring you to make the appropriate adjustments (e.g., staffing, handouts, document delivery options). Library staff at all levels (including shelvers) will have more questions asked of them about locating items than before a disaster.

Our experiences after the disaster were fraught with hazards. Explanations about how to circumvent the lack of materials in the building for many subject areas took up class time which previously was used for describing research strategies. Handouts were created for almost any imaginable purpose. New pages were added to the Libraries' Website. Keeping up-to-date with changes in locations and availability was very important, lest untruths be told to students in instructional sessions. What or where something was one morning or day might very well be different that afternoon or the next day. It was certainly a challenging time!

This chapter covers the elements in library instruction that could be affected by a disaster, such as revising user-oriented materials, adjusting instruction lectures, and providing instructional data. We also have included overall recommendations.

REVISING IN-HOUSE INFORMATIONAL / INSTRUCTIONAL MATERIALS

Using Your World Wide Web (WWW) Pages to Your Advantage

The Web is a good way to transmit information to users and others interested in finding out about the impact of a disaster. Place updated information of your library's status on the Web so users do not need to enter the building or even go to its location in order to find out what they need to know about your disaster situation. Your library's homepage can be used as a jumping-off point to information. However, if items that are of immediate interest are hidden, then people will not find them. Be sure to place important information up-front and center.

If you have a "News & Update" category on your homepage (or its equivalent), a list or separate lists of damaged journals and broad categories of damaged books can be posted. You might also want to include photographs that show the extent of the damage and other disaster-related information, such as available services. Anyone who visits your library's or university's Web pages will then see a link to the list of journals and subject areas of books that need replacement because they were damaged or destroyed in the disaster. Having the lists of journals and books readily visible to potential donors can be a boon for replacement gifts.

Place handouts with links to other Websites—this makes good use of the technology by enabling your users to continue to access resources from remote sites. After a disaster, although users may have no access to the printed library collection, they can make use of sources previously identified on the Web.

For example, at Colorado State University Libraries, "Business Resources" (*http://manta.library.colostate.edu/research/busines*) pages have direct Web links to topical and full-text resources, such as company information. Affiliated users with access to the Web can identify and quickly link to recommended sources. Additionally, our "How to Do Library Research" pages (*http://manta.library. colostate.edu/howto/*) give strategies and suggestions for researchers. These pages, serving as a major component of the library's liaison with the First Year Composition Program, remained available on the Web throughout the crisis.

Because so many bound volumes of journals were damaged (journal articles are heavily used at our university) and other libraries generously agreed to give fast delivery of journal articles, the *FastFlood* Interlibrary Loan (ILL) project was developed. It was promoted on the Libraries' homepage with a specially linked graphic box to the *FastFlood* document delivery service of articles from damaged journals. The red box used to link the *FastFlood* page was deliberately designed to stand out so that it would be noticed. By its being noticeable, users were alerted to this extraordinary service. See Chapter 8 for additional information about post-disaster Interlibrary Loan. Web pages serve as a way to promote special services widely. These pages can be mentioned and/or displayed in instructional sessions.

Using Handouts

Library handouts and guides need to present accurate and up-to-date information, and many need to parallel the research process. Update your handouts as quickly as possible after a disaster has occurred so that users will not be referred to materials that are no longer available because they were damaged or destroyed.

As part of the reference service, orientation, and instruction provided to Colorado State University Libraries' users, subject librarians create handouts of recommended resources (print, electronic, and Web). These handouts are available at major service points. Most of the subject librarians use the summer session to update these. The handouts consist of the most relevant, recent, and useful materials available.

Our reference collection is located on the first floor, but some of the old reference materials were housed in the lower level where the library received extensive water damage. When the disaster occurred, most of the handouts were already updated. A selected number of these subject handouts were available on the Libraries' Web page. Some handouts included reference to those materials in the lower level. The subject librarians who created handouts, which included citations to those damaged materials, had to update them again for the fall semester. After the disaster, we were involved in many unexpected tasks, and updating handouts was one of them. One of the librarians had written a welcome to students on one of her handouts explaining that the construction was near completion. All of a sudden, this was no longer true.

During disaster recovery, it is imperative that users be kept informed about the status of damaged and/or lost materials. This is particularly important if, during your recovery process, you have resumed services and access to your library.

In addition to the subject handouts, we also provide information sheets: one, entitled the *Library Locator,* indicates the location of the collection's materials. During 1996, the library was in the process of remodeling. Throughout the remodeling, the *Library Locator* sheets were updated often. The materials were moved so frequently during the remodeling that it was necessary to update the locator sheets sometimes as much as twice a week to assist library users in finding materials with as little difficulty as possible. These *Library Locators* were enormously helpful during disaster recovery (see Appendix 9-A).

After the disaster, this process continued and included materials lost as "flood damaged." In this way, we kept library users informed on a regular basis. The front page of a typical locator sheet includes the location of the materials by call number and by major stack areas in the Morgan Library: Books, Bound Journals, and Oversize. The back side of the locator sheet gives the location of other library collections: Documents, Journal Room, Microtext, etc. Each time the *Library Locator* is revised, the color of its paper is changed and it gets a new date to make a distinction between the previous and the current sheet. We continued to update the location of the materials for over 17 months after the disaster because the collection was constantly being moved until the recovery process was complete.

Other handouts were created to inform our users of new services or to emphasize the availability of nearby research collections. For example, handouts with information on the shuttle service that transported affiliated library users from Colorado State University to other libraries in the region and on how to make an ILL request were quickly designed once the services were implemented or expanded. Library hours and information on how to borrow materials from these other libraries were provided on a detailed *Regional Libraries* handout.

Revising In-House Library Instruction—Textbooks

If your instructional program (such as a library research skills credit course) has an in-house textbook, then:

- Make sure you keep it updated and make changes immediately, because you don't know when a disaster will occur.
- Make sure that you have a copy of the disk necessary to make updates kept somewhere outside your library.
- If you don't have access to your library and its personal computers, then you must find a location and compatible equipment to do your updates.

A week after the disaster, Morgan Library reference staff were allowed into the building for a few minutes so that they could take things home with them. I took with me the disk and the current drafts of the textbook, as well as the completed pages I had printed out. Once one of the computing labs on campus opened, I went there to continue updating the textbook. Having a current copy of the textbook on disk (or whatever the current available technology) makes updating from another site possible.

ADJUSTING YOUR ONE-TIME LECTURE SESSIONS

If you are able to occupy some, or all, of your library during disaster recovery, then you need to focus your post-disaster instruction sessions on emphasizing how the library is functioning and on how materials can be retrieved despite the disaster. Many users will think that most or all of your collection was destroyed (even if this is not true), and they will not have any expectation of finding any of the materials that they need.

After a disaster, depending on your situation, there are some things to keep in mind about the classroom facilities for your library instruction sessions:

- Equipment may not be available (computers, overhead projectors, tables, etc).
- Noise from reconstruction can be a distraction.
- Air quality, lighting, and temperature may vary.
- You will be using class time to describe new or changed services. This will reduce the amount of time you have to cover other topics in the session.

Acknowledge to your students that you are aware of their probable discomfort. If the classroom facilities are really dreadful, you might find out if there is another location nearby where you can teach.

It is necessary to reassure users that, yes, it is still possible to do research at the library. Explain to them any limitations and what the library is doing to provide alternative services and/or access. For example, during each session, we made it clear that most of our bound journals were damaged, but that there were ways to retrieve copies of these items: via ILL's *FastFlood* project or by visiting other libraries.

Users have to be reminded that they need to plan ahead in order to be relatively certain that they can acquire services and/or their materials in time to write their papers or do other projects. The need to plan ahead is always valid, but after a disaster it will be necessary to remind users to make good use of their time.

During disaster recovery, when access to materials is critical, you may find that you have an increase in the number of full-text databases available at your library. They may be purchased or donated. This access is crucial. At the same time, the addition of databases with full-text articles online will probably raise the level of expectation for some users who will want everything online. We experienced this at CSU.

At CSU Libraries, the following topics were also emphasized during the post-disaster instruction sessions:

- ILL services.
- Full-text articles available on the online databases.
- Free trial databases (many companies were generous with contributions).
- The importance of requesting directions and asking for assistance.

Your emphases may be different. Nevertheless, it is important to let users know what is still available and what is being done, if anything, to augment services.

TEACHING ALTERNATIVE SOLUTIONS

During library instruction sessions, you will find it necessary to focus your teaching on alternative methods for dealing with services affected by your disaster. Whatever the topic, alternative methods of doing research may have been just briefly mentioned in previous class sessions. However, after a disaster it will be necessary to be flexible in how and what you teach to reflect modifications of existing services and/or alternatives to services for your users.

After our disaster, ILL/Document Delivery and alternative services became important topics in our presentations. Information we needed to explain to students included:

- The service is free.
- Books and articles that we don't own (i.e., never owned) can be requested from other libraries.
- Books we owned that were damaged can be requested through the same service.
- Articles found in bound journals that were damaged can be requested through an expedited ILL/Document Delivery service.

PROMOTING THE USE OF OTHER LIBRARIES

In the aftermath of a disaster, it is important to let your users know about accessing alternative libraries (as available). You must keep information about surrounding libraries as up-to-date as possible. We were able to tell our users that regional libraries were more than willing to give them extra assistance under the circumstances.

Visiting other libraries in the region should be promoted as a way for users to acquire or browse through materials. Wise use of the online catalogs that are accessible from remote sites means that when researchers visit the other libraries, they can have a pretty good idea of what is available in advance (or find out that they might want to go to a different library instead).

By showing up prepared, users can make better use of their time in a location where they might be paying for parking or have time constraints in their schedule that limit the amount of time they have to spend in the other library. Mentioning that libraries have similar arrangements will, with any good luck, demystify the other libraries in the students' eyes. Also, let them know they can ask for help at the other libraries.

At CSU, our library information system has an option for users to access other library catalogs from the main screens—on the telnet/ASCII version and on the Libraries' Home Web page. In the online catalog itself, users can repeat their searches in gateway libraries without having to retype them. (Once in the other libraries' catalogs, they can conduct regular searches.) This capability is a time saver, especially when almost entire subject areas (for example, chemistry) were inaccessible because they were damaged. If your system has a similar capacity, make sure to explain it to your users.

Your library's administration will need to be creative and utilitarian in devising ways to provide alternative services previously unimaginable. Be prepared for these different options. Once they are in place, make them known in your instructional and/or informational programs.

The availability of the shuttles to other libraries that were provided for Colorado State University faculty, students, and staff was mentioned in instructional sessions, on the Website, and at service points around the library. Handouts describing the service were available at the service points so users could take the information with them. The shuttles only left at certain times and on certain days of the week, so planning ahead was essential (see Appendix 9-B).

If there is a local public library (or another local academic library), the staff will know about your situation and should be willing to help out. In our city, users with a state drivers' license or documented local address are allowed to check out materials from the local public library. In addition, our library has a link to the public library's catalog so specific sources can be easily identified along with their availability status. Showing this capability in instructional sessions lets students know that they can find out ahead of time if they want to visit the local library.

Other libraries in our area also helped out. For example, the University of Colorado at Boulder Libraries created a special Web page and handout for Colorado State University affiliates. These sources assured students that they were welcome to use the libraries at the other university and provided useful information about accessing materials, hours, where they could get help, and other tips. This welcoming Web page came up when users selected the University of Colorado library catalog from the "Other Libraries' Catalogs" page on the Colorado State University Libraries' Web page.

USING POST-DISASTER DATA

You may find that administrators will be asking for various data comparisons of your operation pre-disaster and post-disaster. Figure 9-1 demonstrates that during the peak month, September 1996, the number of class sessions taught was 48. For September 1997 (post-disaster), we taught only 21 class sessions. This is a difference of 27 classes, showing a 56 percent drop during 1997. This type of information may be requested, so you should be prepared by keeping the appropriate data.

It is interesting to speculate how the disaster impacted the number of instructional sessions taught. For example, one librarian mentioned that a teaching faculty member indicated that arranging for instruction under disaster recovery was "too much of a hassle." You may need to get the word out if your facilities are not as badly damaged as is generally believed. Do not miss opportunities to describe the availability of materials, equipment, and classroom instruction.

FIGURE 9-1
Classes Taught by Month

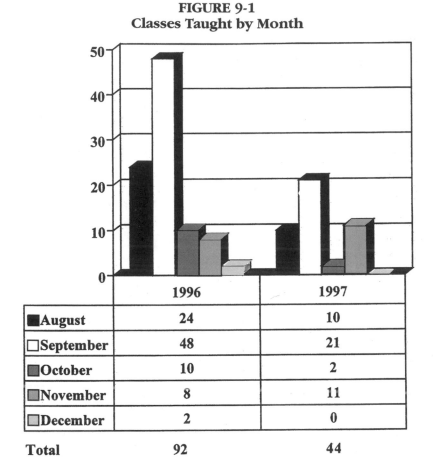

	1996	1997
■August	24	10
□September	48	21
■October	10	2
■November	8	11
□December	2	0
Total	**92**	**44**

REVIEW OF THE LITERATURE

A survey of the literature was conducted. There were no articles identified that related to this topic of library instruction offered during disaster recovery.

CONCLUSION

In 1997, we were already coping with the difficulties related to the construction and renovation projects that had started in 1995. One challenge for the instruction program was keeping up with the ongoing movement of the collection. Procedural changes were constant. After the disaster, the number of online databases from vendors whose software we were not familiar with increased dramatically (tripled). As a consequence, we had to familiarize ourselves with the new software in order to provide enhanced instruction to students in the classroom and users at service desks. The enhanced instruction enabled users to make good use of the additional resources. Flexibility and a sense of humor in the classroom became more important than ever before; and we survived.

Fortunately for us, when this disaster struck, CSU Libraries already had an ILL/Document Delivery department that was subsequently recognized as top-notch in 1998 by the Association of Research Libraries. Thus, in our instructional sessions we could assure our students, faculty, and staff that they would be able to request and acquire materials relatively quickly and efficiently.

Keeping on the cutting edge of available technologies allows you some leeway in informing your users about what is going on and how a disaster impacts them. Having a strong instructional program to begin with helped us weather the aftermath of the disaster. You also can survive.

Library Disaster Planning and Recovery Handbook

KEY RECOMMENDATIONS

Library Instruction

- Keep Web pages as current as possible at all times.

- Have key information directly accessible from your library's home Web page.

- Essential information needs to be reliable.

- Have current copies of materials on disks (or the current available technology) and keep spare print copies.

- Make sure someone is responsible for keeping a copy of important disks off-site.

- Spend extra class time explaining about ILL and reminding students to order their articles and books as soon as they are identified as being damaged or not owned.

- Keep the handouts to a minimum.

- Because you probably won't need as many handouts as you might think, carefully choose the topics for which you prepare handouts.

- Keep handouts up-to-date.

- Emphasize one-on-one instruction and assistance to help users cope with the loss of on-site materials.

- Be prepared to provide data on post-disaster effects on library instruction.

- Stay flexible.

APPENDIX 9-A
LIBRARY LOCATOR

MORGAN LIBRARY
Library of Congress Call Numbers

Be sure to check the location and availability of materials on SAGE.

BOOKS

A, B-BD	3rd Floor, South
BF-BX	3rd Floor, West
C-DS 135.R6G44	3rd Floor, West
DS135.R9G46-DX,E,F,G	3rd Floor, West
H-HG4905	2nd Floor, West
*Hg4905-HZ	**FLOOD – SEE ILL**
*J,K,L,M	**FLOOD – SEE ILL**
N	2nd Floor, West
P-PZ	Lower Level, West
*Q,R,S,T,U,V	**FLOOD – SEE ILL**
*Z	**FLOOD – SEE ILL**

BOUND JOURNALS

*A-Z	**FLOOD – SEE ILL**

OVERSIZE

*A-V	**FLOOD – SEE ILL**

*Collections damaged by flood. Be sure to check if specific volume is listed as being "AVAILABLE" on SAGE.

APPENDIX 9-A *(Continued)*

OTHER LOCATIONS

ARCHIVES	In Special Collections	2nd Floor, South
ATMOS	Atmospheric Sciences Branch Library	Atmospheric Science, 302A (Foothills Camps)
COLORADO DOCS	Colorado Documents	2nd Floor, South
*CURRENT AWARE	Current Awareness Coll.	**FLOOD – SEE ILL** 2nd Floor, West
*CURRICULUM	Curriculum Collection	**FLOOD – SEE ILL** 2nd Floor, West
DOCUMENTS	Government Documents A1 to I 1.98/2:81-22 I 1.98/2:81-23 to Z	4th Floor, South 3rd Floor, South
DOCS OVERSZ	Documents Oversized	3rd Floor, South
DOCS POSTER	Documents Poster	1st Floor, South
DOCS REF	Documents Reference	1st Floor, West
ELEC MEDIA	CD-ROM in the EIC	1st Floor, West
ELECTRONIC REF	Electronic Information Center (EIC)	1st Floor, West
ENGINEER	Engineering Sciences Branch Library	Engineering Research Center, B-209 (Foothills Campus)
INFO DESK	Information Desk	1st Floor, East
JOURNAL ROOM	Current Periodicals	2nd Floor, West
LAW/TAX	Law/Tax Collection	1st Floor, West
LOAN DESK	Protected Collection	Loan/Reserve Desk, 1st Floor, Lobby
MAPS	Map Collection Government Documents	1st Floor, South
MICROTEXT (FICHE, FILM CARD)	Microform Collection	Journal Room 2nd Floor, West
MORGAN	Bookshelves of	See reverse side for location of materials in Morgan
*MOVEABLE SHELVES	Bound Journals	**FLOOD – SEE ILL** Lower Level, South
NEWSPAPERS	Current Newspapers	Journal Rm, 2nd Floor, West
*OVERSZ	Oversized Materials	**FLOOD – SEE ILL** 2nd Floor, West
REFERENCE	General Reference	1st Floor, West
SPECIAL	Special Collections	2nd Floor, South
STORAGE	Storage	Ask at Loan Desk
VET	Vet Hospital	Vet. Teaching Hospital Branch Library A-236
WESTERN	Western American Literature	1st Floor, South

APPENDIX 9-B
FREE SHUTTLE SERVICE TO LIBRARIES
STARTING AUGUST 25, 1997

How to ride:
Check the schedule (subject to change).
Reserve a seat in advance (both ways); call 491-0016.
Show your Colorado State University ID to ride.

University of Wyoming Coe Library and Science Library

Every Monday:
Departs from CSU: 7:30 am, 11:30 am, 3:30 pm
Departs from Laramie: 9:30 am, 1:30 pm, 5:30 pm

UNC Greeley Michener Library

Departs from CSU: 7:30 am, 11:30 am, 3:30 pm, 5:30 pm*
Departs from Greeley: 9:30 am, 1:30 pm, 5:30 pm, 10 pm*
(*from 9/4)
Friday:
Departs from CSU: 7:30 am, 11:30 am
Departs from Greeley: 9:30 am, 1:30 pm

Colorado State University
All shuttles leave from CSU
TransFort station

CU Health Sciences Library
Only faculty and grad students
may check out materials

University of Denver Penrose Library

CU Boulder Norlin Library and branch libraries

Sunday:
Departs from CSU: 11:30 am, 3:30 pm, 5:30 pm
Departs from Boulder: 1:30 pm, 5:30 pm, 10 pm
Monday-Thursday:
Departs from CSU: 7:30 am, 11:30 am, 3:30 pm, 5:30 pm
Departs from Boulder: 9:30 am, 1:30 pm, 5:30 pm, 10 pm*
(*8 pm 8/25-8/27)
Friday:
Departs from CSU: 7:30 am, 11:30 am
Departs from Boulder: 9:30 am, 1:30 pm

Tuesday and Wednesday:
Departs from CSU: 7 am, 12 noon, 5:00 pm
Departs from Denver: 9:30 am, 2:30 pm, 10 pm

Students and faculty can:
use collections and databases;
borrow library materials as allowed.

10 Providing Reference Services When You're Under the Weather

Joan Beam, Lindsey Wess, and Tom Moothart

INTRODUCTION

Summers at Colorado State University Libraries are typically calm and relaxed times with relatively few students enrolled in the eight week mid-summer session and many of the library faculty and staff taking the opportunity to indulge in some much-needed vacation time. Service desks are single-staffed, and evenings especially are times when librarians and paraprofessionals are infrequently called upon to assist students or faculty. Sometimes the only exciting thing happening is the weather. Certainly, the night of July 28, 1997, fit that category with little to entertain the persons on duty except the driving rain visible through the new two-story tall windows to the west of the general reference desk and the Electronic Information Center (EIC). Around 8:00 p.m., things livened up a bit when water started to leak down through a seam in the ceiling in the area between the reference desk and the EIC. At that point, it had been raining hard outside for several hours. A new west wing had been recently added to the entire length of the building, and the connecting seam had not been thoroughly sealed as the renovation was not complete. A few strategically placed wastebaskets seemed to deal with the problem adequately. Rain water had leaked down this building seam before during heavy rains that spring and summer. Users, student employees, and staff shifted book cases and moved government document reference materials to avoid dampness, and university facilities workers investigated the source of the leak.

As acting coordinator of the Social Sciences and Humanities Reference Unit, I (Beam) was the librarian on duty at the reference desk that evening. I closed and left the desk at the usual 9:00 p.m., assuming that the not untypical rainstorm would eventually abate. Colorado is known for its short heavy rainfalls, and most streets and buildings have been engineered to deal with intensive runoffs. Meanwhile, a member of the EIC staff was exploring various other parts of the building and discovered that water was collecting in the lower level. Facilities were aware of the leaks but powerless to deal with them. On my way home, 45 minutes later, I noticed the rainstorm was not widespread, as it was not raining even a few blocks east of the campus, although to the west and over the campus the storm continued. By the time I arrived home, three miles southeast of campus, the rain storm had ended. Or so I thought. The next contact came at 5:00 a.m. with a telephone call from the assistant dean of Public Services. Overnight, the entire campus, including Morgan Library, had sustained severe water damage, and the campus was closed. No one had any access to Morgan Library, which was closed for safety reasons. That night, students and staff had been scheduled to work until 10:00. Those that had parked their cars west of the library found them completely submerged.

The reference department at Morgan Library at that time was composed of three units—Social Sciences and Humanities, Sciences and Technology, and Government Documents—with approximately 35 classified staff and librarians. The three unit coordinators worked closely with the assistant dean for Public Services to set policy and procedures for reference activities. I (Moothart) was acting coordinator for the Science and Technology Unit and had been since the departure of the former coordinator for another position out of state one month earlier. There was also our veteran coordinator of the Government Documents Unit. We had only recently begun our supervisory roles over the large service areas. To begin new responsibilities in the face of such a disaster was not a comforting situation. With access to the library and library offices, computers and files restricted, and little experience to fall back upon, the acting coordinators approached the situation with trepidation. This chapter covers aspects of disaster recovery relative to reference services. It should prepare the reader for challenges and events that could occur should a disaster happen in your library.

BEGIN COMMUNICATING WITH STAFF IMMEDIATELY

Set up a telephone tree immediately to inform other members of your staff about the situation. Even though news reports may confirm the closure of your facilities, it is very important to notify individual staff members personally and to let them hear from their supervisors the latest information regarding the disaster and how it will affect them and their employment. Each supervisor should have a list of their employees and their home telephone numbers at a location other than their office. Many of your employees may not live close by or have unlisted telephone numbers. Contacting them will be delayed if accurate telephone numbers have to be tracked down. It is important for supervisors to agree on what to inform staff and to stick with the known facts of the situation. Half-truths and rumors can quickly spread among the staff if the message is not controlled.

With much of the CSU campus damaged, news reports were not entirely accurate; and it was often necessary to tell staff about inaccuracies. A rumor started among the staff the day after the disaster that the building was structurally damaged and the entire building would need to be demolished.

Be Prepared for Communications Systems to be Dysfunctional

Problems communicating with staff may be compounded by the inability to get working telephone lines after a disaster. Depending on the type of disaster, communication systems may not be operational for several weeks or longer. Your disaster plan needs to address this possibility.

We were fortunate. The city's telephone system was working to some extent. Staff became frustrated over the slowness of the telephone tree. Since Fort Collins, not just the campus, had experienced the worst flooding in the city's history, it was extremely difficult to get a reliable telephone connection. Contacting ten employees could take more than an hour because of the overloaded telephone system. The frustration of the staff dealing with personal disaster, work disasters, and a shortage of accurate information from their supervisors and the news media was telling.

Find an Alternative Site for Emergency Response Meetings

The first order of business when a workplace has been closed due to an emergency is to find an alternative site for meetings to plan emergency public-services operations. It will be necessary for the members of the Library Disaster Recovery Team (LDRT) to have separate meetings with their individual supervisors and/or staff. If your library or organization has branches or offices in an area unaffected by the disaster, you are in luck. If not, then you may need to meet at someone's undamaged house or in some other undamaged space.

It was necessary for the coordinators to meet with the assistant dean of Public Services to develop a contingency plan for providing public services. Although Morgan Library was the major library facility on campus, there also existed several small remote branches. The Veterinary Teaching Hospital Branch Library (Vet Library), a mile south of campus, was the largest and closest branch. The smaller Engineering and Atmospheric Sciences branches were each a few miles northwest from campus. None of the branch libraries suffered any damage from the heavy rains. Initially, it was decided to use the Vet Library as a base of operations for reference, and that is where the first post-disaster meeting between the coordinators of all the public service units and the assistant dean was held on Thursday, July 31.

ASSESS THE DAMAGE TO THE PUBLIC SERVICE AREAS

The Public Services division at Morgan Library includes Interlibrary Loan, Circulation and Reserve, and the Reference and Information desks. An initial priority is to determine the extent of damage to the library's public service areas. Through representatives of your LDRT, an initial assessment of the damage should be made service area by service area. Based upon this assessment, you will be better able to determine what temporary action needs to be taken in each area in order to restore service. The lower level seemed to be a total loss, the collections soaked. The print collection in the reference area had suffered minimally. The microtext collection of fiche and film were intact, along with their readers and printers. The electronic reference tools, the CD-ROMs, the computer workstations, and printers had also escaped damage; as did most of the offices, equipment, and other collections on the first (above ground) floor. The Interlibrary Loan and Circulation areas were free of water damage. Unfortunately the telecommunications system was severely affected; and all power to the building had been cut, thus restricting access to the internal library e-mail system, the CD-ROM network, the Internet, remote electronic resources, and even our own innovative online catalog, SAGE. The teaching laboratory in the lower level, which contained the multiple workstations used for group demonstrations and instruction, had been completely inundated; and the workstations were unusable. Electronic reference service would not be restored in Morgan Library for quite some time due to damage to the telecommunications lines in the building and sodden wiring all over the campus.

In addition, health concerns, water, molds and mildews, and large pieces of dehumidifying and drying equipment all made a return to Morgan Library unlikely for an undetermined amount of time. Reference service would have to be provided from temporary sites. Alternative telecommunication routes to our online catalog, e-mail, and remote databases would have to be established. The Reference coordinators came up with both short-term and long-term plans.

TRANSFER ACCESS TO ELECTRONIC REFERENCE SERVICES AND TELECOMMUNICATIONS SYSTEMS TO A REMOTE SITE

The goal is to get as much of your services as up-and-running as possible. If that means moving hardware, so be it.

Reference service was set up in the Vet Library for the first week of August, with staff volunteering to work shifts for a few hours from 8:00 a.m. to 6:00 p.m. The reference and general number for the library were transferred to the Vet Library. Fortunately, our online catalog, SAGE, was available as it had been literally moved to a site on campus which still had functional wiring. The Academic Computing and Networking Services (ACNS) on campus had not sustained damage and allowed library technology staff to transfer SAGE to their location. The entire DEC computer used to run SAGE was loaded into a pickup truck and physically moved to the ACNS server room in the Engineering Building.

The Vet Library had a small ready-reference collection in place, and a few workstations to access the online system. Additional workstations and general reference works not held at the Vet Library were taken from Morgan Library during a brief, designated entry period to retrieve priority items.

For easy location by users, an alternative site for service should be as nearby the original site as possible. For this reason, a site on the campus itself was sought out because the Vet Library was one mile away from the main campus. Fortunately, several buildings, including the main computer labs on campus, had not been damaged. The Reference coordinators negotiated with the coordinator of computer support for the campus to utilize the public computer labs. By the second week of August, in the brief quiet period between summer and fall semesters, Reference was allowed to use the Weber Building Macintosh Lab to set up public services. Interlibrary Loan and Access Services used a second Weber computerized classroom.

BE WILLING TO UTILIZE ALTERNATIVES TO TRADITIONAL PRINT REFERENCE MATERIALS AND AREA LIBRARY COLLECTIONS

Since the print collections in the building were either inaccessible or water damaged, the only resources accessible by users were the Libraries' e-journals and full-text collections. We felt it was imperative that reference be located in a computer lab on the main campus with multiple Internet workstations to effectively utilize these resources. You may be surprised to learn, on close examination, as we were that the core reference collection had become electronic rather than print based. On August 11th, library reference staff moved into the Weber Building, to a laboratory of Macintosh computers which had primarily been used by students for Internet access and e-mail. Since no telephone was available in the Mac Lab, a telephone line was strung through the ceiling from a nearby office and the reference number was then transferred to this lab.

All of the public workstations in the library are PC compatible and very few staff had used the Macintosh operating system. Reference staff with Mac skills volunteered to assist those who might need help in transferring their ability from the PC operating system to the Macintosh environment. The Netscape browser on each of the Mac Lab computers was set up to default to our online catalog, as well as other Web-based electronic databases and reference resources. The staff could also access their e-mail accounts through Pine (the campus-wide, UNIX-based e-mail program). The Mac Lab became an important nerve center for impromptu staff meetings and a place where everyone became informed of recent developments through their e-mail accounts.

Having close relationships with a consortium and/or area libraries is advantageous when you need to provide alternative access to your print collections. Fortunately the library belongs to an alliance of area research libraries. The staff of the various research libraries have worked cooperatively on many projects over the years. It might seem obvious that good working relationships with other libraries in the geographic area should be maintained, but ours was an example of how these relationships can be put to good use in an emergency. With access to the Mac Lab, the catalogs of the area libraries were searched to find the most appropriate library to which to refer users. Users were encouraged to verify that the material they needed was available at another library or to call the library directly if they needed specialized assistance. We even had a plan to place our reference librarians at the other libraries in the area or to place them on the vans that were traveling to the libraries if the staff in those libraries became overwhelmed assisting our students. Fortunately, we did not need to implement this plan. The reference staff and their respective libraries in the area were extremely cooperative and provided materials and outstanding assistance for our users during the disaster. We can't imagine what the situation would have been without them. In retrospect, the area libraries could have been better served if we had communicated regularly with their reference supervisors.

PREPARE A LIST OF READY-REFERENCE TOOLS AS AN APPENDIX TO YOUR DISASTER PLAN

In order to provide a minimal level of service, a basic ready-reference collection is needed for your remote-reference site. It would be most useful to have that list prepared in advance which would include ready-reference tools from not only the general reference collection, but also in the fields of science and technology and from the government documents reference collection. Such a list would make a quick collection of these critical works possible.

Because of health concerns, anyone entering the Morgan Library building was required to wear face masks. The inside of the building was crisscrossed with three-foot-wide yellow tubes that controlled the temperature and humidity in the building. Power lines connected to external generators snaked through the building powering fans that distributed air in the building. The standard works—almanacs, statistical sources, directories, and two encyclopedia sets—were loaded up on a book truck and trundled across campus by the coordinators, who were given face masks and permission to enter the library and retrieve the books. Since few of the buildings on campus had working elevators, the books were carried up to the second floor of the Mac Lab. Because of the limited space, no more than a standard three-shelf bookcase was filled with this collection, but it frequently came in handy in the next few weeks. With a telephone line, computers to access the catalog and databases, and a small ready-reference collection, we were able to handle calls and simple reference queries from the alternative reference desk in the Weber Mac Lab.

TAKE THE NECESSARY TIME FOR STAFF RELATIONS AND COMMUNICATIONS DURING DISASTER RECOVERY

A far greater concern than computer equipment, telecommunications, or site location should be the effect on the library staff of the disaster and the closing of your facilities. Reference services staff are geared to interact with the public. Most reference staff are scheduled to spend 25–50 percent of their day at one or more service points. When the disaster occurs, all your service points become off-limits with the closure of the library. Offices will be inaccessible and most of your reference staff have a great deal of work which centers on access to their work spaces. Your reference staff will feel uneasy, ineffective, and frustrated by their inability to do their routine work. Although you may establish shifts at alternative reference services sites, you may only require one or two staff members for each shift. A large number of people may simply have nothing to do. Files cannot be updated, mail can be sorted and read but not acted upon, and frustration will mount. Your reference staff will feel that they have lost control of their individual jobs; work will be piling up untended; and a second disaster in work backlogs becomes their only prospect for the immediate future.

Keeping people informed helps them feel a part of the recovery effort. Large, all-library-staff meetings should be held regularly, perhaps once a week, or more often if needed. Most libraries closed for an emergency or disaster will have to locate a large meeting room or area for their staff to collect. After the main meeting, smaller groups should take advantage of the collected staff to conduct unit or department meetings.

Reference coordinators at Morgan Library held quick group meetings after all-library-staff meetings. In these small group meetings, volunteers signed up for desk shifts and collected information on the damages to, or the recovery efforts of, their particular service areas. Although most staff then went home, at least they had some contact with their place of employment and felt involved in the effort to reestablish order.

If your main communication system within your library system or organization is e-mail, you may find yourself without that communication system for some time. As mentioned earlier, set up a telephone tree for reference services immediately after the disaster for maintaining contact. Your reference managers may need to spend a great deal of time on the telephone every day talking to their supervisors, to their staff, and to each other. Managers should plan to incorporate this time for maintaining communication with their staff into their day, as it is extremely time consuming. An e-mail can be sent to an entire department, but telephone calls are on an individual basis. It is a rare person who is content with a brief update. Most want to talk for at least a few minutes or longer. Decisions made between your managers may have to be shared, revised, and shared again with supervisors, other non-reference service managers, and staff. Telephone communication is time consuming and inefficient, but in an emergency, it is often the only means by which to be linked together.

As soon as possible, e-mail should be reestablished. This is a much quicker and more efficient method to maintain contact with staff. When the university's Weber lab was established as the reference site, staff e-mail accounts were set up to allow individuals the ability to check their e-mail. Regular postal-mail delivery was restored and delivered to this same lab, and individuals could sort and check their paper mail. Staff regularly stopped by the Weber lab to check their mail even if they did not have scheduled desk duty, just as a way of staying in touch with the situation and with each other. Do not underestimate the importance of work as a social outlet for some employees. Investigate opportunities for after-work social functions to help relieve the stress of some staff.

One cannot stress often enough the importance of communication. As tired as a supervisor is at the end of the day, he or she must be aware that their employees are eager for updates and information. Every attempt should be made to send e-mail out daily, even if it is only a brief message of highlighted items. Frequent meetings between the administrators, service heads, and the coordinators/managers were held in another building on campus to organize the recovery effort. Long meetings were held daily because insurance estimates had to be created, lists of core journals compiled, and contacts to surrounding area libraries established to redirect our students and faculty for research and reference assistance.

While the majority of the reference staff felt out of the loop and underutilized, the Reference coordinators felt overwhelmed. When the coordinators did delegate responsibilities to the librarians and classified staff, it was usually with very little notice and changing duty requirements. Communication between the two groups sometimes suffered, as coordinators felt too busy to compose e-mail messages, while staff constantly checked this same e-mail for updated information. Coordinators learned to be more sensitive to the frustration of their staff and began a regular informational e-mail letter to the reference personnel.

DO NOT IGNORE THE EFFECTS OF THE DISASTER ON YOUR PROFESSIONAL STAFF IN REFERENCE SERVICES

Some of your reference librarians will have spent much of their professional careers building a collection that may be damaged. Providing access to information resources that are no longer available within the building will require a mental shift for many of your reference librarians. For example, you may need to provide referrals to other libraries in the state without a first-hand knowledge of the libraries' policies and arrangements. They may need to assist graduate students and faculty by explaining how to order huge numbers of research journal articles through interlibrary loan rather than walking them to the bound-journal collection.

At Morgan Library, many staff saw the completion of a badly needed building expansion and renovation as an opportunity to bring students and faculty into the building and re-establish the library as the focal point of the campus. With the loss of approximately 50 percent of the collection and an extension of the building project for at least another year, this was seen as a lost opportunity.

The quiet weeks in August gave the staff time to focus on both short-term and long-term goals for recovery of library reference services. The cooperative spirit of staff was evident and, in many ways, inspirational. Everyone attended all of the general library meetings and most were anxious to begin working at the various makeshift service points as soon as it was feasible. Though intense concern over the immediate future was apparent, overall staff morale was high and characterized by an eagerness to help in any way possible.

COMMUNICATE WITH THE REST OF YOUR CAMPUS/ SYSTEM WITH A STANDARD MESSAGE AS SOON AS POSSIBLE

Communication is important, not only between the layers of the library administration and staff but also between the library faculty and the university faculty. Devise a coordinated message so all librarians have the same information to convey to their university departmental liaisons. All librarians should be urged to contact their academic liaisons and inform them of the scope of the damage to the facility and collection and to explain the alternative services.

Library faculty on the reference staff had another responsibility in addition to their reference duties. Many faculty members are also collection development librarians responsible for purchasing the monographs and journals in the subject areas assigned to them. Many members of the library reference faculty have several academic departments on campus for which they act as a liaison between the library and the academic unit. Close associations with faculty liaisons in each academic department mean better communication in the building of subject areas in the library collections. Library faculty teach research classes within different disciplines for their areas of collection-development responsibility as well; often working closely with other academic faculty to do so. Many of these classes are taught at the onset of fall semester to acquaint students with the literature in their field of research. Obviously, the disaster and the loss of the collection was going to negatively impact the relationship between each library faculty liaison and their academic departments. An appropriate message had to be sent out explaining the situation so that returning departmental faculty were officially informed of disaster recovery status.

The plan to re-open Morgan Library for the public in late August presented some technical difficulties for the reference services staff. Though the building was drying out, there were few working telephones and no local computer network had been reestablished. The fiber optics line to the library required a complete re-installation, and that wasn't scheduled for several weeks. When the library opened, there would be a need for at least three public service points to have access to the SAGE electronic catalog as well as the Internet. To accomplish this goal, it was decided to target the front-foyer Information Desk, the Reference Desk, and the Electronic Information Center (EIC) Assistance Desk. These areas definitely would need active telephone jacks for telephone and modem access. Arrangements were made with the campus telecommunications department to ensure that connection and activation was a priority for these service locations. In one instance, at the EIC, it was necessary to string the telephone line from an adjacent room through the suspended ceiling because the required number of jacks could not be activated at the Assistance Desk. When the modems were purchased and installed in the personal computers, the reference staff was instructed on modem access and troubleshooting procedures. Though this arrangement was less than optimal for the users, there were at least key service points on the main floor of the library where reference staff could accommodate inquiries about the collection.

PLAN ON MAJOR TECHNICAL DIFFICULTIES HAPPENING BEFORE RESUMING REFERENCE SERVICES

Depending on the extent of your disaster, your technical difficulties may need to be prioritized in terms of resolution. That is, to restore reference services upon entering your facilities may mean you will not have the technical capabilities to offer all services immediately.

Plan on Special Gifts Causing Special Challenges

Understand that special gifts, offered during disaster recovery, may mean special challenges for Reference Services. If your library receives gifts like free access to electronic resources to help with your damaged collection, be prepared for challenges. Some of the challenges could include the following:

- Your reference staff will have to find the time to evaluate each electronic database donation for its usefulness to the university's/organization's users.
- Your reference staff will have to determine the full-text content, the search interface, and the software applications that need to be loaded to make these resources available.
- As the donated databases are added to your library's electronic resources, there will be concern over the library's ability to purchase the resources once the period of the donation expires.
- You will need to anticipate the amount of training that will be required for your staff to master the software interfaces even during disaster recovery.
- Some database products require additional software to be

loaded on each workstation in order to view image files.
- The amount of printing taking place will increase at an alarming rate due to the expansion of electronic resources made available.

We received over $250,000 of free access to various electronic databases including full-text ones. Although we were most appreciative and delighted for this alternative access to our damaged materials, the unanticipated challenges required time and human resources already taxed in disaster recovery. However, the benefits of these gifts for our university community far outweighed their challenges.

RETHINK YOUR CURRENT LIBRARY-DISASTER PLAN RELATIVE TO REFERENCE SERVICES

Kahn (1994) suggests that libraries draft a plan where the library staff are physically separated from the users without access to telephones or e-mail. She advises that the disaster plan includes keeping rolodexes, manuals, documentation, and passwords at a home. Morgan Library had a disaster plan, but Reference Services had not considered the possibility of providing assistance outside of the building. Reference Services was lucky that two viable alternative locations were identified and the campus telecommunications department was able to transfer telephones to the remote locations.

PLAN TO COOPERATE WITH OTHER STAFF, INTERNALLY AND EXTERNALLY, TO IMPROVE REFERENCE SERVICES DURING DISASTER RECOVERY

The technical expertise of other non-reference staff can be another essential component of your reference services recovery effort. Staff from your technology/automation services can be crucial to the recovery of reference services depending on the extent of the disaster damage. For example, both staffs together can move quickly to relocate and re-establish connection to your library's online public access catalog. Aptitude for technical troubleshooting and personal flexibility are staff attributes that can contribute to meeting important short-term goals such as moving telephone lines and setting up temporary modem access to public service desks. Also, for training purposes, it can be fortuitous to have non-reference personnel familiar with an array of systems other than those strictly in place at your library before any disaster.

In our case, it was commendable of the public service reference staff for their willingness to learn a different computer system in order to stay operational. The change in reference service venue required staff to switch from Windows PC-based operating system to a Macintosh environment for all their on-site computing needs. It was also fortunate that many of the electronic reference resources were already Web-based, so the specificity of computer platforms made less of a difference. Without question, a staff willing and able to adapt is a great boon to any organization, especially during times of crisis and stress.

The timely resumption of reference service to campus constituents would have been impossible without the generosity the university's Academic Computer and Networking Services (ACNS) staff extended to the library. The donation of the Mac Lab and the assistance that was given with telephone lines, e-mail accounts, and copy services permitted a rapid return of public reference service.

CONCLUSION

No matter the complexity and/or the organizational make-up of your library's reference services, when a disaster strikes, much of those services will be affected. How well you are prepared to handle disaster challenges ahead of time can lessen major frustrations.

Library Disaster Planning and Recovery Handbook

KEY RECOMMENDATIONS

Reference Services

- Work and communicate with your staff affected by a disaster on a continuous basis (this cannot be overstated).

- Do whatever is necessary to establish temporary reference services as soon as possible no matter what site or equipment is used.

- Accept the premise that your core reference collection may be electronic rather than print.

- If additional resources are added to your collection, do not neglect to train your staff on the content and use of these resources.

- Cooperate closely with other library units and university/organizational units as necessary to restore reference services.

- Know the strengths and weaknesses of area library collections.

- Communicate regularly with area libraries.

REFERENCE

Kahn, Miriam. 1994. "Fires, Earthquakes, and Floods: How to Prepare Your Library Staff." *Online* 18, No. 3: 18–24.

PART THREE

Technical Services
in Disaster Recovery

11 It Was A Dark And Stormy Night: A Technical Services Overview

Carmel Bush

INTRODUCTION TO TECHNICAL SERVICES IN DISASTER RESPONSE AND RECOVERY

The strategic plan for technical services in 1997 included revision of the Disaster Quick Reference Guide and training on disaster recovery. Per previous disaster training, an exercise would be conducted in which we would pack-out and perform initial salvage efforts. Several construction-related disasters had given staff experience with small numbers of water-damaged materials. In fact, preservation staff had become quite adept as a team in responding and assisting in these occurrences. Although we had considered the worst disaster that could happen in a table-top exercise in a disaster recovery team meeting, no one really thought that it could happen. One rainy night in July proved otherwise.

This chapter provides an overview of the key involvement by technical services in disaster-recovery efforts with examples from the Colorado State University (CSU) staff experience. Included is a discussion of contingency planning for regular operations which must be reassessed for disaster preparedness.

REVIEW OF THE LITERATURE

The literature of disaster reflects an ownership of responsibility and involvement that does not focus on a particular division of library responsibility but rather on the leadership and skills that staff contribute to response and recovery. Although libraries or-

255

ganize technical services differently, Godden's (1991) definition, which builds on Tauber's (1954), defines technical services as "those services involved in the acquisitions or collection, preservation, and organization of information in any form or medium for the purpose of eventual dissemination" (1991: 7). What is foremost discussed in the literature are the processes of salvaging and treating materials, with little mention given to the process that reintegrates treated materials or adds replacement materials. Outside of the library literature, the business literature provides guidance on contingency planning for disaster that can aid in library disaster planning.

PUTTING THE PLAN TO WORK

The disaster-recovery plan identifies the initial steps to take in responding to disaster. With prior testing and training, the response will be guided by skilled members of the organization well prepared to put into practice the appropriate recovery measures. Within Technical Services, Preservation Services has major responsibilities defined for recovery of collections; Acquisitions and Cataloging Services share in the processing and replacement of the collections. All have ongoing responsibilities for physical and bibliographic access for information in many forms. How these services are continued and their efforts coordinated for recovery are the challenges in administering the plan.

Invoking the Team

A telephone tree to notify staff is one of the steps recommended for disaster-recovery plans. For those outside the center of the disaster, hearing about it may come as a surprise; for those who have been contending with the disaster personally, it adds to the magnitude of the situation. Key points to share with staff members in relating the disaster include what happened, how future notifications will be delivered, and what actions staff are to take. In the CSU disaster, supervisors let staff know that the campus was closed and not to come to work the next day. Staff would receive notification of when to report to work.

Involving the Managers

Several calls to supervisors were placed to discuss contingencies and maintenance of technical services operations and contemplate the additional recovery operations. Those who direct the regular operations have the expertise and knowledge of the existing state of business to reliably inform the maintenance of operations. Making sure that the basic services continue requires first a recap of what these services are in order to align everyone's thinking about their maintenance. With information on the type and extent of disaster, it is possible to begin a plan for regular operations that takes into account expectations for recovery operations and existing conditions.

Reviewing Roles in Disaster Response and Recovery

Recovery involves both the actions for restoring service and the continuation of service. For technical services operations, it is likely that there will be members who have prominent roles in the restoration of collections as well as continuing services that provide organized resources to users. It is immediately important to begin considering how major responsibilities in both of these areas will be handled. In large-scale disaster recovery, these individuals will be immersed with the initial restoration of collections. How are these individuals normally supported? What other options exist to provide temporary conduct of their duties considered to be basic? Are there other staff who can take on all or part of the role? Can temporary staff or vendors fill in a gap? If other staff assist, what support will they need to perform duties temporarily? According to studies, organizational strategies that involve individuals who have expertise allied with conduct of duties work best.

Assessing the Situation

The initial walk-through called for in the disaster-recovery plan will assess the condition of collections, facilities, and environment. The details from this assessment will determine if the building can be occupied and if collections and staff will be relocated. For a library that has had a large-scale disaster, it is likely, as CSU found, that the conditions dictate relocation of staffing and the damaged materials. For technical services operations with heavy materials-handling operations, relocation sites ideally have several features besides being available: proximity, loading docks, elevators, computer networking and telecommunications, sufficient workstations, and storage space with shelving. Staff members require access to the building, bathrooms, and other amenities associated when there are numbers of staff. The ideal and what is available may not be a perfect match. For CSU, the off-site Depository provided available space and had some of the features to support operations: limited networking and telecommunications, a loading dock, and shelving. There was little space for workstations.

Maintaining Communications with Staff in a Major Disaster

In addition to telephones, the public media, the Internet, and/ or arrangements with an auxiliary communications network can facilitate communications with staff in a major disaster. Disruptions may affect any of these methods, so multiple measures are best. If possible, daily contact keeps staff aware of developments related to the disaster. Major questions will include: When do they return to work? Will they be able to resume regular work? Where will they be doing this work? Where to park can also be a significant consideration. Damage can affect what's available so temporary measures may need to be arranged with other departments for parking. Staff will look for assurances about their jobs and the safety of conditions. For staff whose home lives have been affected by disaster, they will be concerned about the flexibility to deal with their situations. Listening and being mindful of the ability to digest information in stressful situations will abet communications.

RETHINKING SERVICES AND ORGANIZATION

Failure to provide continuity of service will cost the library support in the long term. Users, who expect to be served and whose sense of crisis will be very different if not personally affected by the disaster, will experience frustration. The library action plan must assure that interruption of service is minimized.

Developing a Plan to Fit the Situation

While the disaster-recovery plan provides a preview for actions, the particular complexities of the disaster will imprint the plan's refinement. Clarke (1999) advises recognizing the limits of formal planning and the need to develop realistic solutions. Using the information collected in the assessment stage, staff can answer the questions of place of work, operations, and conditions. The first step is to determine priorities for operations, identify resources to support operations, assign staff to these operations, and set communications systems for both technical operations and restoration operations and relocations. At CSU, Technical Services supervisors developed the plan for technical operation within a couple of days while staff worked on plans detailing restoration operations simultaneously. For technical operations, the limitations of the facility to which staff were relocated resulted in the development of a special project that would capitalize on a previously identified need to complete the inventory and barcoding of the serials collection. Other conditions affecting the plan included available resources, materials at-hand, and the site.

Holding on to Basic Services

The particular units of technical services vary from one library to another. At CSU, the units include acquisitions (monographs, serials, and depository documents), cataloging (copy, original, database, and projects), and preservation (marking, preservation lab, and stacks management). The process of determining what services to offer in time of disaster will take into account the planning by the library as a whole, the particular contingencies associated with the disaster that affect delivery of services, and the demands for recovery. Consideration of service offerings is not a one-time event but must be repeated as developments change and more information is available to redirect efforts.

WHAT WILL YOU CONTINUE TO DO?

The adoption of the business-as-usual approach may require modification for disaster. Most libraries have defined priorities for work that should be reviewed with respect to what must be done or delayed. If the delivery infrastructure is in place, incoming materials must be handled and are linked to processes for mail handling, library materials, storage, and access for users. Orders for materials may remain important, but can shipments be received? Arrangements with vendors can provide temporary hiatus in deliveries if materials are not immediately needed for users. For the latter, new processes must be in place to handle them. If you can't shelve in the library, other storage space will be required for new materials and those returned from circulation. For technical services, operations have interdependence with other units in the library, offices of the parent organization, vendors, or networks in accomplishing its aims. Assessing these connections is a necessary step in planning and deciding what services to perform.

WHAT NOTIFICATIONS ARE NEEDED?

Once the priorities are determined, sharing them with other library staff and users will assure them that basic services are underway and by what means they will be available. Despite the damage to many departments at CSU, there were a number of departments undamaged whose work proceeded with little relation to the disaster. Graduate students still had dissertations to deposit, researchers had their journals to read, and other users had borrowed books to return. CSU Technical Services staff published a fact sheet on the arrangements to handle these situations so that all library staff could respond to queries.

Determining Changes in Operations

WHAT'S STOPPED?

A disaster may destroy in-process operations or curtail regular activities. The impact may directly occur in the library or another office of the organization upon which the library is dependent for follow-through. Destruction to a library unit may require a startup from scratch at temporary locations or may necessitate a service break until there is a return to permanent conditions. Determining what is possible based upon related units of the organization is one step. For example, an accounting office may pay bills received by the library; and if it is destroyed, there will be a hiatus until work can be resumed. Binding and Gifts Units were destroyed at Morgan Library. Whatever was in-process was destroyed. Rather than continue with the regular activities of these units, staff were initially involved in other efforts.

WHAT'S DONE DIFFERENTLY OR IS NEW?

New routines can be a function of setting, resources, or different priorities. What are the limitations or exceptions that must be made? What new ways of doing things are possible? Necessity as the mother of invention can create new and better ways of doing work. With the availability of electronic resources, staff in some specializations could work more effectively by telecommuting rather than actually being on-site. At CSU, temporary shelving arrangements were made and locations were established on the local system so that users would know what is available.

Sharing the Plan

With the plan in hand and reviewed by supervisors, the next step is to introduce and review the plan with staff. If supervisors have been communicating with staff in the interim, then this step will not be a surprise but a formalization of what staff are expecting. New activities will require more time and effort to explain. Underestimating the emotional response to a plan which involves changes will protract the time of reception. It is crucial to spend the time up-front on introducing and supporting the rationale for the change. Providing multiple avenues for sharing the plan reinforces the message.

Reassigning Staff

Assignments should be made on the basis of expertise according to the work to be performed. Staff who have major roles in restoration will need their backups to step in and assume duties. Whether duties are additive or supplanting, there will need to be clear discussion about responsibilities. Reassignments normally involve concerns, but these concerns are heightened in a disaster situation. Instructions should be supplied verbally and in writing to reinforce requirements of associated assignments. Staff under the stress of the disaster will need more of their supervisor's time; and these supervisors will find themselves more devoted to listening and understanding their concerns.

Providing Continuity of Management

The recovery response includes restoring the library to normal operations as rapidly and smoothly as possible. The continuity of operations is essential to institutional survival and the perception of ability to anticipate and respond to disaster. Providing management through the regular supervisory chain, team, or through alternates assures basic service during the recovery period. These managers or staffing from other structures for management must be well-versed in the authority they have to act, the services that are to be performed, and the impact of the disaster and the consequences for services. They will need to communicate expectations clearly and to be attentive to and acknowledge the communication needs of staff under stress.

Relocating Staff

Assessment of the alternate work site will have identified conditions of the facility that will have an impact on staff: the telecommunications, computing, electrical service, bathrooms, environmental controls, control of access, equipment, and space layout. Deficits of the site may create discomfort for staff, so improving the conditions and making available insofar as possible the files, equipment, and materials to approximate normal conditions will have overall benefits for operations and for the well-being of staff.

Establishing Workflows

Without a normal setting and resources, every process continued during the period should undergo re-examination. Staff members and their supervisors will have to consider adjustments for space, equipment, and a host of other factors that influence operations.

"Work arounds" are inevitable. With staff temporarily assigned to projects, training may also be implemented. Scheduling can become confining with limitations of resources. Flexibility in scheduling work should be considered. Staff efforts for establishing new routines and making adjustments should be recognized and contributions acknowledged.

Contacting Partners

The library's bibliographic utility, its vendors, and consortial partners may play a role in establishing business-as-usual and in the restoration process. With relocation, it may be necessary to establish alternate telecommunications or Internet access to use bibliographic systems or vendor files. The library may need to establish different services or arrangements with its partners. File transmission, payment schedules, or adjustments to local system parameters or programming are examples of what may be reviewed. Shipments of materials may be curtailed for a time by book jobbers. Staff involved in shipping and receiving may want to follow up with delivery services and U.S. Postal Services about temporary arrangements.

RESTORING COLLECTIONS

Reprocessing treated materials and identifying materials that are not salvageable are complex processes in a large-scale disaster. The planning and development of procedures involve making assumptions about outcomes, testing these assumptions, and extensive dialog with staff, decision makers, and other organizations and individuals that may assist in the recovery process.

Gathering Data on the Collection

WHAT DO YOU KNOW ABOUT THE COLLECTION?

Knowing the collection and the priorities for collecting inform the restoration process. What is the nature and size of the collections? Are they rare or working collections? What collections are in high demand? What formats are in the collection? How has the collection been housed? What is the condition of the collection pre-disaster? Information about the distribution of collections according to discipline helps characterize the collection. If total loss is known then it can be factored into the over-all plan for restoration.

WHAT DO YOU NEED TO FIND OUT ABOUT THE COLLECTION?

Administrators and insurers are most eager to learn cost estimates, ability to restore and rebuild collections, and the timetable for recovery. National average cost data is available for general monograph replacement but not for general serials volumes. Computed costs can be developed and attention should be given to special collections that are among the damaged materials. Defining what are high-use materials is based, however, upon an understanding of library services and data-keeping practices. The library's ability to perform collection analysis relies on data about the collection usually supplied via an integrated library system (ILS). Knowing this system and its capabilities to generate data will enable staff to create reports appropriate to questions that are being explored.

Interacting with Vendors, Consultants, and Colleagues

With integrated library systems (ILS), the process of documenting restoration can be immeasurably assisted if the system has the flexibility to record information that is needed for insurance and administrative purposes. It can also be used to track the repatriation of materials and the replacement processes associated with restoration. Because functionality may need to be extended, it is important to engage the ILS vendor in discussing what is possible. If the system cannot accommodate what is needed, a vendor may be able to assist in the output of information to an external database. Such an external database may meet special requirements for the project and be designed to interface with the ILS where updates are required. Record retention for audit purposes needs to be defined.

Vendors and jobbers can provide assistance in identifying costs of materials and options in the marketplace for replacement. With potentially large insurance settlements, this data may also be used to develop projections for replacement that may be used in negotiation. Furthermore, the vendors and jobbers may cooperate in the design of strategies for replacement that are streamlined and maximize shelf-ready status.

Large-scale disasters are complex and well suited for contracting with consultants for particular aspects of recovery. These aspects may include treatments of materials, organization for large processing operations, supplemental systems that facilitate the flow of materials, repair techniques, among others. FEMA-supplied consultants, and consultants experienced in the type and scale of the library's disaster, can offer valuable advice.

Colleagues whose libraries have recovered from a disaster can be a great help to planning and organizing for recovery. Some consortia specialize in regional assistance for recovery. Emergency assistance teams can provide direct help in recovery (e.g., temporary locations for services or expert advice on planning).

Creating and Implementing a Plan to Process Treated Materials or Substituted Gift Materials

WHAT PROCESSES ARE REQUIRED?

Collections may be rebuilt through salvage of damaged materials, gifts, and purchases of exact titles or other replacement materials. If a library receives gifts, a number of elements must be contemplated in their processing:

- Does the library want gifts to substitute for damaged materials?
- Will only exact matches to damaged materials be processed?
- What are the funding provisions and tradeoffs of processing accepted as part of the insurance settlement?
- What is the impact on the rebuilding of the collection?

At CSU, an enormously successful gifts program netted thousands of donations. To meet the insurance requirement of replacing with exact copy, first it was necessary to sort these gift materials to determine which matched damaged materials. The record was then changed to reflect that the gift substituted for the damaged item. For example, some gifts of journal volumes may be bound differently than those originally held by the library. More often, binding and full physical processing was necessary for journal issues. Returning these materials to the shelves and updating the status in the database after processing completed the basic functions. Quality control was applied against all functions. Problems arose associated with incompletely received items and holdings that had not been entered into the database prior to the disaster. Materials not matching damaged materials were entered into an inventory for possible use in enhancing the collection at a later stage. Duplicated materials will be offered to other libraries or will be disposed.

Treated materials differ from gifts in that inspection for repair or declaration of loss lead to other functions. The repairs may involve cleaning, paper mending, or page replacement; otherwise, the functions are similar to those for gifts in reprocessing these materials back to the shelves.

WHAT ARE THE SPECIFICATIONS FOR PERFORMING WORK?

The involvement of contracted assistance reinforces requirements for detailed procedures. Each function must be spelled out in cookbook fashion along with its purpose. In addition, outcomes of procedures, the quality control measures that are pertinent to each, and their reporting should be incorporated. It is not reasonable to think that specifications can distill every situation that may be encountered in processing; hence, it is advisable to include the contact for the inevitable questions that will arise. The compliance with these specifications is a key term in establishing an agreement with the contractor. Acceptance criteria must be in place as part of contract administration and strategies in place to remedy problems.

WHO WILL PERFORM THE WORK?

There is no readily available experienced work force for large-scale restoration of collections. Training is necessary to develop the necessary skills for working with library materials and systems. The design of training accounts for the acquisition of general knowledge and vocabulary regarding library materials and their organization. Specific skills are taught for the staff assigned to each function. There should be a two-phase training program with supervisors trained in advance of staff. Because of the scale of operations in large-scale disaster recovery, a cookie-cutter style of training should be used for staff below the supervisor level. The timing of training with respect to staging of each function is recommended. For the CSU contractor, a more effective training schedule would have been based on a phase-in of functions based upon flow of materials to the function.

How long will it take to perform the work?

Starting with the specifications, the work is broken down into tasks and then grouped into similar functions to create the most efficient flow of materials. Inspection of materials, page cleaning, page repair, page replacement, binding or other housing structures, database maintenance, and quality control are processes that may apply to recovery. Coupled with the breakdown of task definitions is the need to match skills and the knowledge required to perform each group of tasks. In this process, having internal time and motion data in performing a group of tasks by staff is invaluable in determining how much time the recovery process will take. Lacking such data, estimates can be made by quick trials of processes. Once there is timing data, the numbers of volumes to be recovered can be factored against the processing times for tasks. Not all materials will require the full array of processing; however, allowing for that possibility may be necessary if there is no data available to refine further the estimate. Studies based upon random sampling can provide more accurate projection of the work to be done. It is also clear that, in any estimate involving large numbers of volumes, it is necessary to allow time for the inevitable delays.

What system and interfaces are required?

Tracking volumes that are processed back into the collection after treatment and identification of materials that are a loss may be supported in the ILS and/or specially-developed databases. In determining to use an ILS or deciding which database software to use, staff will need to identify the data to be collected; the method of creating, storing, and archiving this data; and requirements for record retention. A local ILS has advantages in complete records for damaged materials, provision of one place to track, and the potential to study further restored materials over time in relationship to their circulation and future repair. An independently-developed database may allow for handling by less-trained staff and may have the ability to be tailored to the types of data and functions to be output, such as statistics and reports. However, independently-developed databases may also have disadvantages associated with start-up databases. For CSU, our ILS and specially-developed databases by the Colorado Alliance for Research Libraries with specifications from library technical services staff supported gift and damaged materials. Design of new databases requires understanding of data and functions. Systems and database staff can contribute greatly to the design, and, when local systems are involved, the ILS vendor will be an important partner in planning and perhaps programming. If multiple systems and databases are used, then the ability to transfer and update data may be appropriate for bringing information into synch across the databases through updating processes. Use of an ILS and databases should incorporate security provisions.

WHAT DATA IS NEEDED FOR REPORTS AND AUDITING?

Insurance companies, FEMA, and local or state emergency management offices may fund all or part of recovery. Requirements for data, its retention, and reports on the recovery process will depend on the mode of funding and agencies that are involved. There may also be requirements for data on the part of the parent institution or other organizations to which the library reports on the status of its collections. The number of damaged volumes and the portion of them that are total loss volumes are certain to be among the data that a library will need to maintain and report. Intermediate processes of repair and any replacement of materials by gifts will be other possible categories to record. How data is identified and retrieved in records should be documented and shared with representatives of funding agencies so that they will be able to audit and verify what has happened with any individual volume or item in the claim. When processes begin before settlements are made, which is par for a disaster-recovery operation, the rule of thumb should be the ability to substantiate any action that has a cost associated with it. The plan should have a provision for keeping and categorizing this data to confirm payments.

WHAT OUTCOMES MUST BE TRACKED?

Besides corroboration of expenditures, the accounting for the damage must be completed in order to have coherent status of the collections, that is, to document salvage or loss of holdings as the recovery process proceeds. Large-scale disaster recovery covers a period of years. During that time, it is necessary to provide interim progress reports. How many volumes are restored? What parts of the collection are restored? What volumes are in process? What volumes are replaced with gifts? What volumes must be replaced by purchases or topical replacements?

In addition to status of the collections, contractual arrangements may dictate tracking other outcomes. What types of errors are found in the database or materials returned to the library after processing? What is the rate of acceptance of work? Have specifications been followed in the completion of work? If there are approved change orders and other contract modifications in work, are these changes documented? Is there a record of general contract administration? Through the tracking of this data, the library will be in position to report and discuss performance for recovery.

WHERE CAN WORK BE DONE?

In a large-scale disaster, the recovery operations and post-initial treatments require space to handle the numbers of items that will be processed back into the collection. Finding an appropriate space may be easy in locales with organizational or commercial space readily available. In locales where space is at a premium and costs high, options may be few; and there will be an impact on the structuring of the recovery process. Essential features are a loading dock and adequate space for storage, workstations, interim shelving of in-process materials, telecommunications, and utilities. Regulations for occupancy will also govern what spaces are suitable.

In Fort Collins, there were two commercial spaces identified as appropriate in size. Each had problems with their use, so the university initially opted not to complete the restoration of the north wing of the lower level of the library where the disaster originally occurred and locate the processing center temporarily in that space. It lacked sufficient storage, so commercial storage space also was rented, requiring transportation to and from the library. Later the center was moved to a building that had been vacated on campus in anticipation of its reconstruction.

WHAT ADDITIONAL RESOURCES ARE NEEDED TO PROCESS MATERIALS FOR RETURN TO THE COLLECTION?

There are several services that are likely to be part of processing materials back to the collection that may benefit from supplementary arrangements or contract. Page replacement can be contracted to vendors who can supply missing or damaged papers. With nearly all covers of the working collection damaged, binding service has proven to be a high demand for the CSU recovery. In large-scale disaster recovery, it may be necessary to have multiple contracts in order to supply binding at a pace to match the over-all processing goals. Gift journals are also likely to add to the binding demand since few come bound.

Aside from the service contracts, it is prudent to involve consultants in training and evaluation of operations. There are intensive needs for training with large numbers of staff, including support for delivery of instruction, follow-up to monitor development of skill, ongoing advising in response to the many questions that will be asked in the start-up of operations, and evaluation of the work that is performed through audits. Having experts who are familiar with work and can corroborate that it is done correctly can reduce the burden on staff. At CSU, the latter was not supportable under insurance provisions, although it was possible to recover a portion of the salary of the preservation librarian for the time spent on recovery activities.

Developing Cost Models for Processing

Negotiation of settlement in large-scale claims requires a solid basis of data upon which all parties agree. Data that the cost model will need to supply include:

- What are the numbers of items that will be processed?
- What processes will they undergo?
- What are the costs of labor, materials and subcontracts for repair, binding, database maintenance, physical processing, transport, and shelving, among other cost elements, that can apply in recovery?
- What customized developments, such as databases, or services add to the cost picture?
- What inflation is applied to costs over the years of the project?

As in the planning stage when trying to establish the rate of processing, the studies that supply time and effort in regard to tasks of recovery serve double duty. The experience itself of processing recovery materials will inform earlier data. Data will be further refined by studies to categorize the type of damage and loss so that a projection can be made against the total number of damaged volumes or items. The formulation of such data is only as good as the sample. Having outside statistical assistance in developing such a study serves not only the purpose of validity of study but also the independent view that is favored by negotiators of settlements. The methodology for the sample should be documented and reviewed by all parties so that there is agreement from the onset. After studies are completed, a forecast may be made of costs using the time and motion or other data that is available and the input of potential vendors that may be involved in processing.

Communicating Progress

Communication about recovery must occur in multiple venues. Contracts for processing include reporting and statistical provisions that provide weekly data. In large-scale recovery, too long a period of reporting may lead to problems given the volume of materials that will be handled in that period. There should also be audits and other evaluative processes such as acceptance reviews that verify that work is performed as required in specifications. Problems have to be identified for remedy. Regularly scheduled administrative meetings with contractor staff to discuss progress and issues will help contain technical problems and address the conflict that inevitably arises between organizations with demanding timelines. Periodic formal progress meetings can also be useful to demonstrate progress and to allow parent organization administrators, insurers, and other partners to ask questions, provide assessment of progress in the recovery process, and to discuss developments.

REBUILDING THE COLLECTIONS

As processing proceeds on the salvageable collection and as total loss of volumes or items becomes known, the library is faced with making decision about the total loss in order to rebuild the collection. This rebuilding, however, will not produce the collection that existed before. This may not be undesirable depending on the nature of the collection that is damaged. Having the opportunity to fit the collection better to current needs in the university is a distinct advantage. Collections developed over the years serve purposes that may no longer be in demand for curriculum or research. Yet, the destruction of materials is not selective; materials will also be lost that may be essential but not replaceable through other resources. It is important at this stage of recovery to include selectors and faculty in decision making about how the collection will be rebuilt.

Understanding Insurance Provisions for Restoring the Collection

The ideal insurance policy provides for restoration of the complete collection. Coverage not only includes the salvaged material as determined by the library but also acquisitions and processing that integrates items physically and bibliographically into the collection when items are not salvaged. Once it's known what items are not going to be salvaged, the library will need to describe and justify the methodology for pricing the replacements.

It is to the library's advantage to share its plan early on with insurers so that they will know the steps that are involved in the replacement process. The settlement will determine the extent to which rebuilding is supported by insurance and will be a major factor in determining the time-frame for rebuilding the collection.

Knowing the Vendor Marketplace

Replacement may include acquisitions of materials that exactly match what was lost by vendors through their inventories or out-of-print services. It may also include archival reproductions, alternative formats such as microform or electronic, and topical replacements—that is, replacement that may be in the same subject field or may be redirected to materials supporting other subject disciplines. An analysis of loss will determine what types of assistance is needed. Depending on the formats and titles that are involved, the library can determine the array of vendors that can possibly help with recovery. A large number of unsalvageable materials will require careful thinking of how to engage vendors. It is to the library's benefit to identify those vendors that can push the envelope of service; that is, marry a number of services—even those not only normally delivered but special services—in order to save time and money. These additional services include technical processing and subcontracting with other vendors for service.

Developing Contracts for Vendor Services

Knowing what services are needed is the first step. What are the library's requirements for building a collection in terms of types of acquisitions, fiscal management of acquisitions, additional services such as binding, processing, cataloging, reproduction, and database maintenance support? Identifying the potential sources of the services and those vendors that can maximize service is a key consideration. The fully-developed solicitation approach will include a statement of specifications, evaluation criteria, method for weighing the criteria, pricing analysis, past performance analysis, and dispassionate analysis of vendors' ability to perform requirements. In a disaster with large numbers of items to replace or add, the library and the vendor(s) will have to negotiate an agreement. The requirements may involve developments on the part of the vendor that have no basis in past performance. Providing flexibility in the contracting process is essential to effective management in the complex process of rebuilding the collection. Institutional policy will dictate the actual form of contracting and the approval process. It is preferable for the library or its parent institution to draft the agreement. As part of this agreement, a clear administration plan needs to be put into place at the start of the contract.

Designing and Managing Multiple Strategies to Replace and Enhance the Collection

Rebuilding the collection takes into account availability of materials, format of materials, nature of collections, current mission served by the collections, and resources available to build the collection. When replacements will be made of damaged materials, integrated library systems can be used to output files of records for the damaged "wanted" materials. This is essential to streamlining the acquisitions processes. By using report-generation capabilities, files can be created according to library-defined parameters of bibliographic and holdings data and then transmitted in MARC or ASCII to vendors whose systems have the capability to translate these files into orders in their systems. The library can code these records via local MARC tags so that the disposition of the orders is known. If several vendors are used, each can be reflected as appropriate by coding. For those items filled by the vendor that are exact, they can be treated as though they are an added copy.

If materials are replaced topically, then the library is faced with identifying what to order. Vendors with the capability to search a library's database and familiar with its collecting profile through an approval plan or other service can be in a good position to support this identification. Using the parameters for collecting, the vendor can identify materials for selecting that can be reviewed and turned into bona fide orders with online processes. This can be supplemented by library selector designation of materials that can close gaps in the collection. The combination of these approaches streamlines the rebuilding and takes advantage of selector expertise.

Ideally, it is to the library's advantage to have the vendor perform as many functions associated with the orders as possible so that materials can be received in shelf-ready status. Developments associated with outsourcing of technical processes have created an improved environment for maximizing services. In designing strategies, a library should be exploring what the vendor will provide for cataloging, maintaining the database, physical processing, out-of-print searching, reproducing archival copies, binding, suggesting topical replacements, and interfacing transactions with local systems. The vendor may achieve the ability to perform more functions by establishing articulating agreements with other vendors for the range of services that are desired.

When large-scale rebuilding of the collection is required, the library will have to phase the strategies according to priorities. Phases may be structured according to breakdowns of the collections by various parameters. These may include high-priority titles; early-known, total-loss titles; titles for high-demand subject areas; titles that have already been identified as not being replaced; or acquisitions associated with special projects. An example of the latter at CSU was the project to replace personal collections of faculty. The library staff became involved because state funding required deposit of the titles in the library collection (see Chapter 20).

The strategies that are developed must recognize that their context is fluid. What is available now may not be available by the time orders are actually placed. Permission to borrow essential texts not otherwise available for copying may not be granted. Format choices may support microform or electronic access but may not be favored by the faculty who are served by them. In rebuilding the collection, library selectors have the opportunity to collect in ways different from the past and to reshape the collections.

WHAT TITLES SHOULD BE REPLACED?

In a large-scale disaster recovery, it will not be immediately known what all is lost. Priorities defined in the library's disaster plan are on a collection-level basis. For these collections, decisions can readily be made. For those collections that are declared a loss in the initial recovery, response review and request for repurchase can proceed apace depending upon provisions of insurance. High-priority titles based upon the circulation statistics or demands for curriculum may not be a loss. In the evolving work of recovery, these will be identified. However, there must be decisions made initially about what must be replaced to serve critical curricular and research needs and how expenses for these will be covered when settlements are pending. As recovery proceeds and losses are identified, subsequent important items can be determined at certain points such as decisions to replace out-of-print items or to reproduce them. It is impractical to expect to have hundreds of thousands of titles reviewed by collection development prospectively. Deciding ahead where decision points will be for replacing titles should be made in the plan. Technical services should aid the identification of options for replacement.

WHAT TITLES DON'T YOU WANT TO REPLACE?

Any titles already identified for weeding but unprocessed before disaster are an obvious choice not to replace. When weeding decisions have not been made in advance, it can be daunting to review entire collections. The deselection policy of the library will come into play. Because of the size of disaster, deselection efforts should be assigned priorities. These will reflect the current mission and type of use of library materials.

WHAT FORMATS ARE ACCEPTABLE FOR REPLACEMENT?

Microform is a common alternative for print journal volumes; electronic versions are becoming more available but are not as plentiful at this time in considering them as an alternate format for replacements. Unless books are for reference or representing specialized collections, alternative formats are not available in electronic form. Archival photocopying may be a choice if funding permits. The marketplace will determine what many options are, but it is the library's users who will determine what is truly acceptable. In determining the strategies, consultation with faculty about format is key.

WHAT ARE THE TOTAL-LOSS ITEMS IN THE COLLECTION?

Total loss is known with certainty at the end of the recovery process. In order to have a workable plan for replacement, it will be necessary to estimate the size of total loss. Sampling can be done, and a study constructed to determine total loss. With this data, it is then possible to project, over the total damaged items, what will be total loss and what their characteristics may be regarding date, classification, format, and other characteristics available for these items.

WHAT ARE THE COSTS ASSOCIATED WITH LOSS?

With no appropriate recovery cost models to follow, a library will have to decide what elements to include for an insurance claim. There are several factors to consider in the replacement model for total loss:

- the loss of value on the materials that are salvaged
- the selection of materials
- their purchase and processing, administrative and overhead costs
- the inflationary costs that apply for the duration of the project

Since no average costs for purchasing backruns of serials titles or out-of-print materials exist, construct of costs for replacing serials and monographs requires study. Knowledge of the damaged collection, statistical sampling methods, pricing sources, and costs of processing are necessary to develop these costs. The assistance of a qualified statistical consultant is important to guide and validate the process. Vendors that supply pricing for materials and their processing are integral to developing a model. The library should contact several vendors who, through their services, have the capability to serve large-scale replacement.

HOW DOES THE STRATEGY INVOLVE COLLECTION MANAGEMENT STAFF?

If items are not salvaged, there is opportunity to replace with the exact or alternative or to buy something different. For collections that undergo continuous weeding review, are collected at comprehensive levels, or are of special significance because of institutional aims, the library may be positioned to commit to a repurchase plan. If neither approach applies, then the library is certainly in a position to shape the collection differently in the replacement process.

Technical services and collection development librarians need to be engaged in the planning of a review. In a large-scale disaster recovery, the volume-by-volume decision making over the whole of the loss is impossible. Designing a filtering process in much the same way as one sets up an approval plan allows replacement to proceed in a more effective manner. These filters can be established by publisher, date, format, genre, subject, and the like. Items can be considered in categories and only exceptions may require further decision making. Depending upon the library's model for collection development, this approach can also involve consultation with subject faculty.

WHAT ARE THE OPPORTUNITIES TO ENHANCE THE COLLECTION?

An outpouring of gifts and cash gifts in the aftermath of a disaster may augment the collection. New titles can be selected from gift items or donations may be available to purchase for segments of the collection. Plans that identify gift items to keep and designate new purchases will need to incorporate the same elements that are found in library gift or development programs.

As an outgrowth of the use of gift items to match for the collection, CSU Technical Services has been able to use the database created in recovery to analyze gifts and propose an approach to enhancing the collection that helps screen receipts for addition to the collection. It is also wise to consider what materials to dispose of at the onset of a gifts project, a belated decision on CSU's part that added to the size of the inventory. Vendor services for making selected gift materials shelf ready can also be considered. Determining what initial organization will be given to gifts with potential to enhance the collection will facilitate future selecting and processing.

WHAT ARE AUDIT REQUIREMENTS?

Technical services librarians often provide the institutional record keeping for the purchase of library materials. As a result, it is important to review with insurers how collection rebuilding accounts and the categories should be indicated. What tracking will be needed to document total loss and acquired materials?

Re-Establishing Operations

In a large-scale disaster, a technical services operation will not be the same as it was during the entire period of recovery. Heightened activity with contractors, database integrity issues, and demands placed on staffing specialists with regard to the processes are inherent in the advising and monitoring of such a project.

RETURNING TO THE LIBRARY

As in the process to relocate staff and operations from the library, there must be planning for return. What will be the order of return? What equipment and resources will be moved? What new contingencies exist at the time of the move? What tasks will be resumed? What tasks will remain in hiatus? What vendors need to be contacted and what will you be doing differently? All of these are questions you will need to be prepared to address. At CSU, the conditions were not perfect upon return. Utilities and telecommunications were not fully in place when the first group of staff returned. The lack of working elevators posed a special challenge to moving materials from one floor to another. There should be a concrete plan shared with staff that includes the contingencies and how they will be addressed.

RECONCILING WITH NEW DEMANDS

The long-term nature of large-scale disaster recovery requires stamina and creativity. Technical services expertise lent to the disaster in salvaging, replacing, database managing, training, and monitoring allow improved integration of recovery with ongoing library processes but can take a toll. The continuing operations for acquisitions, cataloging, and preservation can not be ignored. Materials must be acquired, processed, shelved, and maintained. It is imperative in large-scale disaster recovery to provide staffing relief to those staff specialists who must be engaged for the term of the recovery project. Equally important is the demand to re-evaluate work processes in order to streamline ongoing operations.

CONCLUSION

Recovery from a disaster is not solely a preservation staff concern or even a technical services concern but engages the entire library staff. Technical services staff do have, however, key roles to play in recovery of collections. To engage successfully in recovery, knowledge of an array of physical and bibliographic processes—repair, binding, microfilming, material conservation, acquisitions, cataloging and classification, database management, marking, and stacks management—and the vendor marketplace are key. Technical services staff possess this knowledge and hence abet the design and management of recovery of the collections. While it is advisable to engage experts to advise on recovery and to hire specialists who can help manage large-scale projects, technical services staff are needed to coordinate the project vis a vis internal operations. At the same time, the impact of a disaster will require assessment of technical services operations for those functions that are a priority within the context of the conditions of the disaster. Technical services staff are caught between revamping operations and workflow to accommodate these conditions and achieving efficiency and accuracy in other services upon which other library departments and users depend. Chapters 11–15 and 20–25 provide detail on the contributions of technical services to recovery efforts at CSU. From the experience of our disaster to date, technical services staff have made changes that have the potential for incorporation into practice beyond the completion of recovery.

Library Disaster Planning and Recovery Handbook

KEY RECOMMENDATIONS

Technical Services

- Assess ability to deliver basic technical services; then develop a plan for continuity of services that identifies accommodations that will be made in service and share this plan with users, vendors, utilities, and consortial partners as appropriate.
- Review staffing vis a vis their expertise in disaster recovery and arrange back-ups or additional staffing to help cover those regular job duties that must be continued in recovery.
- Realize that, inevitably, your staff experienced in technical services and systems will need to participate at some level in response and recovery, even if consultants and contractor(s) are hired.
- Select staff to participate in designing response and recovery measures specific to the disaster who have excellent skills and knowledge in preservation and disaster-recovery measures, project management, contract development, vendor marketplace, collection history, training, and communications.
- Keep staff informed of how their jobs and work setting will be impacted throughout disaster response and recovery.
- Prepare for disaster by maintaining up-to-date information about the collections and the priorities for them.
- Understand that a collection completely cataloged and inventoried in an integrated library system abets decision making and provides support needed to conduct work in disaster response and recovery and to audit the outcomes.
- Consider multiple strategies for restoring and rebuilding collections.
- Learn the limitations and requirements imposed by insurance carriers.
- Become knowledgeable about what approvals will be required by your institution.
- Talk to vendors about ways they may be able to help in collection recovery.
- Plan on testing in new-strategy development.
- Know that, in large-scale disaster, recovery time may involve years.
- Determine a plan for recovering the collection based upon the nature of damage and the priority of the collection.
- For collections that are not special or are no longer a priority, use this opportunity to reshape the collection to meet current institutional demands for resources.
- Recognize that a disaster provides opportunities to review routines and introduce new practices whose benefits warrant retention post recovery.

REFERENCES

Clarke, Lee Ben. 1999. *Mission Improbable: Using Fantasy Documents to Tame Disaster.* Chicago: University of Chicago Press.

Godden, Irene P. 1991. *Library Technical Services: Operations and Management.* New York: Academic Press.

Tauber, Maurice Falculm. 1954. *Technical Services in Libraries.* New York: Columbia University Press.

12 Data, Data, They Want the Data

Donnice Cochenour, Nora Copeland,
and James Farmer

INTRODUCTION

The final pages of our report listing all of our bound journal titles were just coming off the printer at 4:45 p.m. on Monday afternoon. Serials and bindery staff had a quick meeting to finalize our plans. The next morning we would begin the project to inventory the journal titles which had recently been moved into the lower level. The entire journal collection had been moved from an integrated shelving arrangement used prior to the building expansion into a segregated arrangement in the lower-level compact shelving area without completing the normal paperwork for transfers. Now we had the arduous task of identifying the titles and updating the location information in our integrated library system (ILS).

The report loomed before us—several inches thick and listing thousands of titles—and the serials and bindery staff discussed the procedures we would follow. Each of us would take a section of the report and begin checking the shelves Tuesday morning. We were feeling both anxious and optimistic about the prospect of getting the locations corrected in our ILS for this large collection. None of us were happy about the situation which had required these materials to be moved so quickly without following the normal transfer procedures, but the use of contract labor to relocate large sections of the collection following the building expansion had required an expeditious process to minimize moving costs.

Of course, we did not complete the inventory of the compact-shelving area. Later that night, the entire lower level filled with water, and the disaster was upon us. This seemingly minor lapse in procedures demonstrated the importance of accurate information in the ILS when a disaster occurs. The water disaster impacted all materials in the library's lower level, and an item's location in the ILS would become one of the crucial pieces of information we would use when attempting to compile the needed reports, statistics, and estimates in the following weeks of disaster recovery.

IMPACT OF THE DISASTER ON BASIC SERVICES

In one month, students would be returning to classes and would expect library materials to be here to support their studies. There was considerable pressure to identify key materials for immediate replacement, but we couldn't enter the library building due to health and safety factors. We couldn't get into our offices to retrieve paper files which held annual reports, unit-cost statistics, collection summaries, and other types of aggregate data. Our ILS computer system was safely dry on the library's first floor; however, all network cabling was damaged making remote access to the online catalog impossible. These barriers made attempts to determine cost estimates for proposed strategies (which seemed to change daily) to cope with the enormous damage to the collection a real guessing game.

In the first few days, while the disaster-recovery service was still removing damaged items from the lower level, campus administrators were beginning to question how to quickly provide materials needed at the beginning of fall semester. One possible strategy was to declare all journal titles a complete loss and replace them with microforms. What would this cost? Was this a feasible alternative? Without access to any collection information, we quickly queried UMI's[1] Website to check prices for backfiles of journal titles, relying on memory and knowledge of the collection to sample representative titles. Assumptions were made about length of backfiles to replace, and extrapolations were made to estimate costs for replacement of the entire journal collection. When the estimate ran into millions of dollars, the strategy was abandoned as quickly as it was raised. An immediate response to this question was critical since the answer determined whether these materials would be packed-out along with everything else or simply discarded.

Within a few days, the Library Technology Services (LTS) staff quickly took action to physically relocate the ILS computer system where it could be connected to the campus network and to relocate computer workstations at various satellite offices where staff could work. This, coupled with personal offices in our homes, allowed us to access the ILS with collection data necessary to begin to answer the plethora of administrative questions about what exactly had been damaged.

REVIEW OF THE LITERATURE

Many articles, books, and manuals exist which describe how to create a disaster plan, how to restore materials after a disaster, and case studies of disasters at other libraries. None address the need to manipulate system data about the damaged collection for the purposes of making management decisions. The disaster plan implies that the library's shelf list, whether online or a card file, will act as an inventory to provide the list of damaged materials. However, in a major disaster where a large portion, but not all of the collection, is damaged, there are many other questions besides what titles were damaged? These include:

- How many volumes were damaged?
- What types of materials were damaged?
- How many were monographs?
- How many were journal volumes?
- What, if any, will be declared an immediate loss?
- If all of the journal volumes should be discarded and replaced with microforms, what would this cost?
- If damaged titles included newspapers, loose-leaf binder sets, and other materials on low-grade paper, could these be identified since restoration is unlikely?

The ability to manipulate the data in the ILS using a variety of standard bibliographic codes together with locally-defined codes will determine how many of these questions can be answered and the quality and reliability of the data gathered.

THE ILS MAKES ALL THE DIFFERENCE

"An important criteria for measuring the effectiveness of library automation systems is their ability to manipulate and generate information for management use" (Cortez, 1983: 22). Key is the ability "to provide multiple access points to data stored in the database and cross tabulate the data in a manner which yields information for the purpose of management decision making" (Cortez, 1983: 28). Nancy Sanders described the ideal ILS as "including the capability to provide routine and unique reports; ability to capture and store transitory data; and ability to operate on a real-time basis," as quoted by Casserly and Ciliberti (Gorman and Miller, 1997).

The ability to create customized reports on-demand in real time is crucial when beginning the disaster-recovery process. The standard reports designed by the ILS vendor may not provide the required information. The system needs the flexibility to provide statistics and customized reports about the collection based on multiple attributes across the various modules (cataloging, circulation, acquisitions, serials) to reflect holdings, location within the building, current circulation status of each item (including items sent to be bound), accumulated use, and cost of materials. If the online system is incapable of producing customized reports across modules, then ways to work around this system deficiency must be found.

If a disaster occurs which impacts only one floor or one wing of a building, the library will immediately need the ability to identify exactly what volumes in the collection have been damaged. Besides the obvious need to inform users of volumes now unavailable, the insurance company will likely require proof of loss (Ungarelli, 1990). Also, administrators within the institution will want to know exact numbers, not estimates, when requesting damage analysis of the collection. Knowledge of what materials were assigned to the affected sections of the building and the ability to identify the corresponding item records[2] in the online catalog are essential.

Because we were just completing a major building renovation which required extensive analysis of the shelving arrangement, detailed in-house documents existed which identified the call number ranges for materials located in the lower level. Since our online system was able to produce customized reports, the information in these shelving documents, coupled with the ILS's circulation status of volumes, allowed us to create a report identifying the damaged titles and to flag the associated item records in the online catalog. With the ILS's capability to perform a *rapid update*[3] of coded fields such as the circulation status, we were able to create and quickly implement a new circulation status for the damaged materials. Within a few weeks time, the item records for approximately 400,000 volumes in the water-logged lower level had their circulation status changed to reflect their unavailability. The new status was displayed in the OPAC as *"Flood: See ILL"* so that patrons would know immediately to request the damaged volumes through the interlibrary loan department.

As was intimated in the introduction, there was a significant problem with this process that had to be worked around. All of the journal volumes (over 200,000 volumes) had recently been moved from an integrated arrangement throughout the building into new compact shelving in the lower level. A unique location code had been established in the ILS for the compact-shelving area; however, the codes in the item records for these volumes still reflected their previous locations. This meant the location codes in the system could not be used to identify these damaged journal volumes. The database maintenance and serials staff collaborated to identify various methods to create a report listing just these titles. Using a variety of bibliographic codes and locally-defined codes, plus knowledge of the customized indexing of our system, we were able to identify the majority of these volumes and include them when updating the status of damaged materials. This collaboration was the first of many such problem-solving sessions.

HISTORICAL KNOWLEDGE OF YOUR DATABASE

Following a major disaster, expect immediate requests from administrators for collection-analysis information to make action decisions quickly. To meet these demands, it is imperative to know the history of the library's online database, such as:

- Have all of the volumes in the collection been barcoded and item records created in the ILS?

- Which fixed field codes in the bibliographic and item records have been maintained?
- Are all of the location codes in the item records correct?
- Is the circulation status accessible for all checked-out volumes?
- Does the system include historical circulation data?
- Is this data stored as a cumulative figure or is it only available for the current year?

As with any library, there are always ongoing clean-up projects associated with the online catalog. We recommend that any project which will improve the accuracy and completeness of the database should be a priority. Do not wait for a disaster to happen to complete such a project. Otherwise, getting data demanded by library and university administrators will be either difficult and/or incomplete.

We had begun a project to barcode and create item records in the ILS for all serials volumes that did not already have records in the system. Even though bibliographic records existed for all serials titles, item records had only systematically been created for new volumes added to the collection since 1989. Serials volumes received prior to that date were included on a scattered basis. High-use titles had been identified and converted as a special project. Other individual volumes had been barcoded, and item records were created if/when the volume was brought to the circulation desk to be checked out. This left a significant number of volumes without item records in the online system[4]. The official record of these volumes was a manual serials holdings file on 3" × 5" index cards. Because of this, the lists, statistics, and reports we created using the ILS did not accurately reflect the exact numbers the administration continued to demand. Consequently, we had to repeatedly include caveats with all the reports stating that the data was incomplete and that we could only provide exact numbers to the extent that the records existed in the online system. In a disaster, the demands are great. Make sure your database records are accurate, complete, and timely. Be prepared to retrieve data at a moment's notice.

MATERIALS REPLACEMENT OR TOTAL LOSS?

The disaster literature does not offer criteria for the selection of materials for immediate replacement. In some cases, you may decide that selected materials need to be replaced immediately, rather than waiting for the disaster-recovery process. A disaster plan usually includes a section describing the salvage priorities in the event of a disaster. Our disaster plan included this information in the form of statements such as "salvage the monographs first, then the journals in the Library of Congress call number ranges Q–T (sciences and technology)." However, when confronted with the magnitude of the damage to the library's collection and with materials strewn by the force of the water far from their original locations, our salvage plans were of little value. With materials tossed around and covers gone, it was impossible to tell exactly what was being removed for salvage. To deal with such a situation, you need to answer questions such as:

- Should high-cost titles be selected for immediate replacement?
- Should high-use titles be chosen instead?
- Should particular subject areas be given priority?

Inventory Data is Critical

On Monday, August 11th, two of us—heads of Database Maintenance and of Access Services—were paged to come to an emergency Library Disaster Team meeting to discuss our roles in preparing data to identify high-use monographs. The university administration was requesting cost figures for immediate replacement of the most frequently-used monographic materials so they could be ordered and made available to users as soon as possible. The first day of classes was starting in two weeks, and time was of the essence.

In our case, we were given the specific task to identify the number of damaged monograph titles with high-use. However, no definition of *high-use* existed. We were unaware of any universal standard for high-use and were left with the challenge of determining this value within the context of our own situation.

With a six-hour deadline, we set out to define the different measures we would use to determine these most heavily-used materials for immediate re-order. Because our circulation data was zeroed out when we moved to the new ILS a year earlier, it quickly became apparent that only titles which had been on course reserve would show generous circulation statistics. Since our system parameters had been set to alert the collection management staff when a book had four simultaneous patron holds on it (to aid in making second-copy purchase decisions), we determined that this was the best figure to use as a starting point.

Having determined the circulation level for which we were looking, the next step was to derive the logic for our list-creation process. Our ILS had no simple location parameter for the lower level; therefore, we had to use call numbers to eliminate those materials untouched by the disaster. This was the single, most difficult part of the entire process, exacerbated by the fact that, prior to the disaster, books were being shifted daily to accommodate our building renovation. We had to check with the stacks maintenance staff to determine what the cutoffs were for the call numbers shelved in the lower level. Monographs in the Library of Congress call number ranges HG5000 through M were in the lower level, as were books in the Q–Z ranges. Based on the quick instructions received that morning, we also pinpointed that any list we created had to exclude materials in circulation at the time of the disaster, Reserve materials, journals (being handled on another report by the serials librarian), and volumes at the bindery. Care had to be taken to include oversize materials in all the Library of Congress classification call numbers since this collection was housed entirely in the lower level.

Our initial iteration through the circulation data yielded a surprisingly low number of titles. Four circulations in a relatively young database did not produce a robust number. Our goal was to minimize research frustrations for users by replacing the items most in demand, so we revised our high-use value down to three circulations. From this we obtained a replacement total of 6,136 monographs. (See Chapter 20 for more on the replacement.)

Although this request was library-specific, you must be prepared to have access and some sort of inventory of materials, preferably database accessible. Should a disaster occur in your library, you will receive some type of request that requires such information. We recommend keeping inventories of materials by building (or branch) location. For example, if there are five floors in your building, keep the inventory by floor. If each floor is divided into wings, consider an inventory by wing. In some cases there may be justification for mapping the collection by specific ranges within an area. This type of online stamping of data can be invisible from the public. If the ILS is capable of handling locally-defined fields, use a special field in the item record to indicate where a specific volume is housed. This does increase database maintenance—the stacks maintenance/shelving staff will have to be careful to notify the database maintenance department whenever there are any shifts of materials from one wing or floor to another.

If your system does not support the methodology we described, then it may be worthwhile to maintain a paper inventory by range, floor, or building wing. It is wise to keep a copy of this inventory off-site. Careful upkeep of this data will allow for the isolation of the information needed following a disaster which may affect only part of a collection.

What Constitutes a High-Use Journal?

When a disaster occurs which drastically affects your collection, you will receive data requests relative to that collection. If your journal collection is damaged, you will be required to answer questions about which titles to replace and their replacement costs. You must address several issues when estimating the cost to replace journal titles based on high-use. First, determine whether your ILS is capable of generating circulation data at the title level, or at all, for journals. Most systems maintain circulation statistics in the item record for each volume, not at the title level. Also, many libraries do not allow journals to circulate; and, even when circulation is allowed, most journal use still occurs in-house. Realize that even if the library maintains statistics on in-house use, use data will be skewed by user behaviors such as reshelving materials before they have been counted, by cubbyholing personal favorites, and by unrecorded borrowing.

Secondly, decide what constitutes high-use for a journal and provide supporting rationale for this number. Finally, decide how many years of backfiles to replace and determine a figure for the average cost of a replacement volume for the journal collection. The next section of this chapter describes some methodology for doing this.

While two of us worked on the monograph high-use study, only one of us began to work on replacement costs for high-use bound journals. Knowing that we only had circulation statistics for one year, we decided that the interlibrary loan restriction on borrowing more than five articles from a journal without paying copyright fees was a reasonable criteria for high-use. Drawing on the report created earlier to identify the journal volumes moved to the compact shelving, we were able to create a report of the titles with five or more circulations during the previous year.

We next set out to discover what volume/years of these titles had the most use in order to determine how far back to repurchase volumes to meet the majority of our users needs. We elected to do a random sampling of the 1,384 journal titles with five or more circulations to identify which volumes/years had been checked out. Figure 12-1 shows the results of that sampling. For each title in the random sample, we examined every item record and manually tallied the volume/years with any circulations. The number of volumes circulated were cumulated into five-year groupings and the percentage of total circulations was computed for each group. Our figures indicated that 78 percent of our use could be supported by volumes published in the last twenty years.

Arriving at a cost per volume for our journals was controversial. There is no national average cost for journal replacement volumes such as those available for monographs. We have several different in-house statistics which could be used. The university maintains an annual inventory for purposes of self-insurance which calculates the library's per-volume cost across the entire collection. The library also maintains annual unit-cost statistics which separate monographs from journals. As one can imagine, there is a significant difference between these two figures. Although we felt that the figure was too low, we were directed to use the university's annual inventory figure for this report.

Volumes and years are not synonymous for journal titles. Some titles produce multiple volumes a year, and some volumes are large enough to require binding in several parts. Replacement volumes

FIGURE 12-1
Distribution of Circulation Across Volume-Years
Based on a Random Sampling of
51 Journal Titles with 5+ Circulations

Years Covered	No. of volumes circulated	Percent of circulation	Cum. Percent of circulation
1991–1995 (5-year backfile)	137	34.08%	34.08%
1986–1990 (10-year backfile)	86	21.39%	55.47%
1981–1985 (15-year backfile)	54	13.43%	68.90%
1976–1980 (20-year backfile)	38	9.45%	78.35%
1971–1975 (25-year backfile)	25	6.22%	84.57%
1966–1970 (30-year backfile)	18	4.48%	89.05%
1961–1965 (35-year backfile)	11	2.74%	91.79%
1956–1960 (40-year backfile)	19	4.73%	96.52%
1951–1955 (45-year backfile)	5	1.24%	97.76%
1950 and earlier	9	2.24%	100.00%
Total circulations in sample	402	100%	100%

are generally priced by the bibliographic or intellectual volume, but our loss was counted by physical pieces. This irregularity also skews the cost analysis for replacement volumes.

Using data from our bindery practices, we determined that in our collection for science titles we currently bind two and one-half volumes per title per year, and for liberal arts titles we bind two volumes per title per year. Computation of the average cost to replace volumes for the journal titles with five or more circulations (1,384) was based on this binding information times the number of titles times the university's annual inventory cost/volume[5]. Rather than present a proposal to the university administration with a single recommendation, we decided to reflect the cost of backfiles for several different periods (see Figure 12-2) and allow them to select from the various options.

After several days of number crunching, report generating, and analysis of the data, the university administration ultimately decided to wait to repurchase journals until after the damaged materials were processed and exact needs were known. During the interim, journal articles would be provided through an elaborate interlibrary loan operation. (See Chapter 8 for more on the interlibrary loan activities.)

FIGURE 12-2
Estimated Cost to Repurchase Journal
Backfiles for High-Use Titles

Years of backfiles	Sci/Tech titles	Liberal Arts titles	Total
5 years (34% of use)	$1,023,285	$546,410	$1,569,695
10 years (55% of use)	$2,046,570	$1,092,820	$3,139,390
20 years (78% of use)	$4,093,140	$2,185,640	$6,278,780
30 years (89% of use)	$6,139,710	$3,278,460	$9,418,170

DISTINCTIVE COLLECTIONS: SPECIAL DECISIONS

In a disaster, you may find some specific subject areas or sub-collections that may be appropriate to declare as an immediate total loss. These collections will need to be selected, titles identified, and justifications made with the insurance adjustor to declare these materials a total loss and therefore eligible for repurchase. Specific titles in these collections must be identified in the online system in order to flag the records to indicate their disposition.

In our situation, included in our damaged materials were a teacher-education curriculum collection and a current-awareness collection. These collections could easily be identified in our ILS by their special location codes. Because the curriculum collection included multimedia teaching materials, workbooks, and textbooks, most of the materials would either be in-print or available in newer editions. The current-awareness collection contained materials on topics of current interest and was primarily in paperback format. This collection was weeded regularly and most titles could be purchased from the local bookstore. For these reasons, the subject specialists and preservation librarian determined that these collections would be easier to replace than to restore and sought approval from the insurance adjustor to discard them. Permission was granted, and these materials were not systematically packed-out by the disaster recovery service (unless their location in the lower level or their condition made it impossible to identify them as part of these collections). In the ILS, the item record for each piece was flagged with a disposition note "Not packed-out" to reflect this decision.

Two other subject areas were identified for special consideration: computer science and library science. Even though materials in these subject areas were packed-out by the disaster-recovery service, they were later identified as areas to review for replacement rather than restoration. The selectors reviewed and selected titles for special handling based on lists created from Library of Congress classification call number ranges. Approximately 400 computer science books (QA76) were determined to be either out-of-date or cheaper to replace than restore. Over 500 library science monographs and ceased journal titles were selected based on format and timeliness (i.e., newsletters, catalogs of publications, and directories) and retention policies (i.e., keep latest two years only). Once titles were identified, their records were flagged in the ILS so that the materials could be disposed of when they were returned from the freeze-drying process rather than attempting to restore them (see Chapter 22 for more on the repurchase of these materials).

Be prepared to have your subject specialists/collection management staff work on identifying certain collections you may not want to salvage. You will have to present a sound rationale with supporting documentation to library administrators and to insurance personnel.

REUSABLE DATA FOR LATER RECOVERY PROJECTS

Be aware that data generated from one project (i.e., the data set created to update statuses for damaged materials) may be useful for later projects (the identification of high-use journal titles). Throughout your disaster-recovery process, you will find yourselves referring back to data sets created for one project or study to support later projects. During disaster recovery, time is of the essence. You won't have the luxury of time to keep reinventing the wheel. Make every attempt to use data collected pre-disaster and to modify pre-disaster projects or programs to help in disaster recovery.

One way to accelerate implementation of recovery efforts is to look for existing programs or projects which can be modified to deliver needed services. Using the ability to communicate globally via files mounted on the World Wide Web can easily augment the more traditional communication methods following a disaster. With

FIGURE 12-3
Sample Monograph Record

Author: Sharky, Bruce
Title: Ready, set, practice: elements of landscape architecture
                 professional practice/ Bruce G. Sharky
Publisher: New York: Wiley, c1994.
                 Landscape architecture – Vocational guidance.
Call number: SB469.37.S48 1994

Make a donation

---

the Web's ability to deliver searchable files and interactive online forms, the information is easier to use and gift offers are easier to make. If expertise already exists within your library to develop Web-based files, this expertise can be used to advertise your losses/ needs to the community at-large.

In our case, when telephone calls and e-mail offers of assistance began to pour in after the disaster, we discussed ways to communicate our replacement needs to others around the world. As a member of the Colorado Alliance of Research Libraries (the Alliance), we had recently participated in a grant project to mount an electronic journal database on the Web. Our knowledge of the construction and indexing methods used with the Alliance database quickly came to mind as a model to follow. We contacted the Alliance to see if the existing programming used for the Alliance E-Journal Access database[6] could be ported over to create a new database of damaged monograph and journal titles. Knowledge and experience with exporting selected fields in the ILS records gained from earlier projects made the planning and implementation of this project a simple matter. With an affirmative response in-hand, plans were quickly laid out to export files listing damaged titles to the Alliance computer.

No matter how your database is created for presenting damaged monographs and journal titles, we recommend the following for your consideration. Use the lists generated by your high-use studies to determine the content for these files. Decide whether you wish to emphasize some needs as a higher priority (first priority) by creating separate lists of first-priority and second-priority materials, and decide whether you wish to create separate lists

Figure 12-4
Sample Journal Record

Title:	Harvard Business Review
Publisher:	Boston [etc.] Graduate School of Business Administration, Harvard University.
	v. 1-Oct. 1922-
	Business—Periodicals
	Economic history—Periodicals
	0017-8012
Call Number:	HF 5001 H3

Make a donation

for monographs and journals. Creating separate files for priority materials and by material types can serve to keep the file sizes smaller and may assist users to identify which of your specific needs they may be able to fill.

When designing the Website, the appropriate bibliographic data to include for both monograph and journal titles must be selected. See Figures 12-3 and 12-4 for sample monograph and journal records.

Screen layouts will need to be determined, and the desired indexing will need to be identified. You may also want to develop an online form for users to offer gift replacement materials. (See Appendix 12-A for a sample online form.) An introductory page describing the criteria used to create your site, including instructions to would-be donors, and providing links to the various searchable indices will present a useful entry point for the site. (See Appendix 12-B as a sample.) Each screen should include a link to the online form whereby gifts can be offered immediately. When all this is complete, it is important to test all features of the Website before announcing it to the world.

It was our experience that between August, 1997, and April, 1998, when our Website was closed, over 1,500 donor contacts constituting approximately 40 percent of the gifts offers came from this online Web form.

CONCLUSION

Following a disaster, data will be a hot commodity. How well one is able to provide data will depend not only on pre-disaster planning but also on how well the ILS allows the information to be assembled into meaningful reports. Another critical component is the staff's knowledge of the capabilities of the ILS and of the history and codes used in the database. Additionally important is the staff's ability to combine these features to generate precise data sets. This is also where those expensive retrospective conversion projects pay off by providing complete, consistent holdings information about the collection.

The nature of the requests for data from university and library administrators is reflective of their understanding of the intricacies of library operations. Initial requests for information from the administration may have wide-open interpretations; thus, a clear communication process is doubly stressed during times of disaster. This can lead to frustrations when pressures mount to produce data within limited time frames.

Lists of damaged items and, more importantly, their associated costs will be the bottom line of many requests, but there are infinite ways to produce and deliver these figures. The new awareness of library operations derived from the first reports will likely generate requests for more and different information. There may be times when the report being compiled is not completed before requests for a different set of data are received. For the staff who must take volumes of data and whittle it down into a readable report, the pressure can be enormous.

Library Disaster Planning and Recovery Handbook

KEY RECOMMENDATIONS

Data Collection

- Take whatever time is necessary:
  - * to ask detailed questions about the use or intent of the data being requested to fully understand what is needed;
  - * to consult with cohorts and carefully construct the strategies to derive the needed data;
  - * to review the data generated to be sure the results are as expected; and
  - * to enumerate any caveats necessary about the limitations and reliability of the data generated.
- Be sure every title is cataloged and each physical piece in your collection is represented by an item record in the ILS.
- Keep the data in your ILS as accurate and up-to-date as possible; don't take shortcuts thinking you'll clean it up later. Consistent and complete data for holdings is vital following a disaster.
- Know the history of your ILS database, the use of locally defined codes, local cataloging practices, and your system's capabilities to combine these to identify various subsets of your collection.
- Know how circulation data impacts item record information in your ILS and whether this data includes in-house use.
- Collaborate to combine the talents of those who know the most about the various components of the ILS; no one knows everything.
- Consider maintaining an off-site inventory of the collection by location within the building(s) realizing that this will require continuous updates.
- Be sure you understand the purpose/use of disaster data being requested and verify that the search strategy being used is accurately producing the desired information.
- Keep a list of vendor services' technical support phone numbers with passwords and logon protocols for vendor database services at home, and test access to these using home or off-site equipment.
- Look for ways to piggy-back on existing programs/projects to accelerate implementation of recovery plans; use the Web to communicate replacement needs to the world.
- Ask for help from your system vendor, consortium, campus information system staff, and other associates.

APPENDIX 12-A
SAMPLE OF WEB-BASED FORM FOR GIFT OFFER

Colorado State University Libraries' Gift/Donor Offer

For gift offerings to the Colorado State University Libraries Flood Relief efforts, please complete the following information. Complete only those items which pertain to the particular title you wish to donate. When complete, click on the "Submit" button to automatically send the offering to the libraries. You will be contacted regarding shipping arrangements. CSU would like to thank you for your offers and assistance.

Publication Information

Type of Offer: | Offer of Journal Title |

Author:

Title:

Publisher:

Volumes, Numbers, Parts:

Years:

Donor Information

Name:

Address:

City:

State:

ZIP:

Phone:

Email Address:

Institution Affiliation:

[Submit] [Reset]

PLEASE DO NOT WRITE BELOW THIS LINE

APPENDIX 12-A *(Continued)*
SAMPLE OF WEB-BASED FORM FOR GIFT OFFER

Follow-UP: [   ]

Results: [   ]

Thank You: [   ]

Donor Type: [   ]

CSU Library Assistance Center
Colorado Alliance of Research Libraries
webmaster@coalliance.org
Backgrounds courtesy of Greg Schorno (who generously gives them away)

APPENDIX 12-B
SAMPLE OF WEB-BASED FORM FOR DAMAGED TITLES

Search for Flood Damaged Titles

This site contains lists of the Libraries' titles that were damaged in the flood of July 28th. There are two parts to the lists. One part contains the bound journals. Current issues of active subscriptions (mostly 1995/96 -) were not affected. The second list includes damaged book titles. These books have been separated into **first priority** (materials most heavily used) and **second priority**.

When you are interested in contributing specific titles, this list may be used to determine if it is an item we own and need to replace. A form is available if you wish to submit your offer automatically. Otherwise, please send a list of authors, titles, years, and volumes (if appropriate) that we can check. Please do not send any materials. We will get back to you after receiving your offer. If possible, we would prefer complete sets of journals, or at least significant coverage of a particular title.

Contacts for Donations		
Insert Name	Insert Telephone Number	Insert e-mail address

Search for needed titles by:

Top Priority Books	**Other Books**	**Journals**
Call number	Call number	Call number
Title	Title	Title

Keywords

Match: [All]   Format: [Long]

Section: [All]

Search: [   ]   [Search]

Please be advised that this site is not only under construction, it's also still under development. Some of the index files for this information are rather large, and it may take your browser a while to download them. Please be patient with this process, particularly if you're on a low-speed internet connection.

We will continue to work on improving the performance of the search engine and the indexing program to minimize the file sizes. However, due to the nature of this site, we didn't want to delay the release of this page any longer than we had to. We hope you'll be as understanding of slowness at this site as you have been of CSU's current situation.

Once again, we'd like to thank you for your assistance.

CSU Flood Page	CSU Student Svcs	Gifts Received

CSU Library Assistance Center
Colorado Alliance of Research Libraries
webmaster@coalliance.org
Backgrounds courtesy of Greg Schorno (who generously gives them away)

ENDNOTES

1. The UMI *Serials in Microform* catalog is available on the Web at *wwwlib.umi.com*
2. The item record contains the barcode, location, circulation history, and other copy- or volume-specific information, and is linked to its associated bibliographic record.
3. Rapid update is an ILS feature which allows selected records to have fixed fields automatically changed without having to touch each record.
4. Later analysis calculated approximately 29,000 damaged volumes with no item records.
5. These figures were later determined to be unreliable and an extensive cost study is being completed to obtain an average cost per volume for the damaged volumes.
6. The Alliance's Electronic Journal Access database is available on the Web at *www.coalliance.org/ejournal.*

REFERENCES

Cortez, Edwin M. 1983. "Library Automation and Management Information Systems." *Journal of Library Administration* 4, No. 3: (Fall): 22, 28.

Sanders, Nancy P. "The Automation of Academic Library Collection Management: From Fragmentation to Integration." Quoted by Mary F. Casserly and Anne C. Ciliberti "Collection Management and Integrated Library Systems" in *Collection Management for the 21st Century: A Handbook for Librarians*, edited by G. E. Gorman and Ruth H. Miller. Westport, CT: Greenwood Press, 1997. Originally published in *Collection Management for the 1990s*, edited by Joseph Branin. Chicago: American Library Association, 1993.

Ungarelli, Donald L. 1990. "Insurance, Protection and Prevention: Are our libraries safe from losses?" *Library and Archival Security* 10, No. 1: 56.

13 Technology Tales

Karen Weedman

INTRODUCTION

The skies were overcast in Loveland, Colorado, during the evening of July 28, 1997, but no rain had fallen. Loveland is located about 15 miles south of Fort Collins. Our network manager at the Colorado State University Libraries had been home watching television, and the 10 p.m. regional news had not mentioned floods or disasters. He had just crawled into bed around 11 p.m. when the telephone rang. A disaster team member was on the line with bad news: there was water in the Morgan Library lower level and there was no electricity! He was asked to come in and turn off the critical computers in the library's secured computer room to protect them from power surges that can occur when power is restored.

He quickly grabbed a flashlight and fishing waders, thinking he might be able to rescue the network switch in the lower level. About a mile from the main campus, he was stopped by a police blockade. All bridges over Spring Creek had been closed or washed out, and he was told there was no way that he could get to campus. After pressing the issue and explaining that he was on the Library Disaster Recovery Team, he was told of a possible alternate route. This involved driving 15 miles east to the interstate, driving several miles north, and then driving west back to town. He made it back into town via this route with only minutes to spare before the road was closed. Along the way, he drove by a traffic safety crew who were unloading road blockades from a truck.

As he approached campus, he discovered a derailed train blocking access to the east side of campus. He drove to the west side of campus and found a new, large lake that was too deep to wade. Cars were floating in the water. Morgan Library and several other buildings were standing in the water on the far side of the lake. He drove back to the derailed train, parked his truck, put on his waders, and walked around the train. After walking through several knee-deep pools of water, he finally made it to Morgan Library.

Accompanied by a campus security officer and a facilities staff member, he entered the dark building with the sole purpose of protecting the library's critical computers. Using his flashlight, he proceeded to the main floor computer room where he turned off and unplugged the centralized computer servers. He also unplugged the uninterruptible power supplies (UPS), which are used to protect computers and other types of electrical equipment from power surges and power outages for a specified period of time that usually ranges from minutes to hours. On the way out of the building, he checked the stairwells and saw that the water level was only a few steps down from the main floor. Everything in the lower level was underwater. He left the building and gave a status report to the assistant dean for Technical Services who was waiting outside. She was also one of the Disaster Team leaders.

Our network manager also notified the staff in Library Technology Services (LTS). This unit analyzes, develops, implements, supports, and maintains the automation projects, equipment, and network throughout the Libraries. The unit, consisting of four full-time information technology specialists and two students, were working for LTS during the summer. These six people would become instrumental in the disaster-recovery efforts related to technology.

A major water disaster had occurred. Computers and networks had been affected. In the hours, days, and weeks that followed, strategic questions had to be faced and resolved: Where do you start? What should be done? How do you recover? These are the topics that will be covered in this chapter as related to automation technology.

There are many types of disasters that impact information technology. Disasters may include losing an essential server, network or telecommunication problems, loss of data, loss of power, heat or air conditioning problems or other environmental factors, damage to automation equipment, and damage to the facility. For large disasters, many of these factors may be present.

REVIEW OF THE LITERATURE

There are a proliferation of articles which cover various aspects of disaster planning and recovery related to computer technology. Computers, networking, and automation equipment are used by most businesses and organizations to support their operations and to provide services. There are also computers in many homes. Studies have shown that one out of every hundred corporate data-processing centers will be affected by some type of computer related disaster (Murphy, 1991), so this is a topic of interest and concern to many people. The literature describes many types of disasters that have affected technology. The disasters can be caused by a wide variety of circumstances such as floods, fires, earthquakes, stolen equipment or data, corrupted disks, software bugs, hardware errors, computer viruses, human mistakes, computer hackers, power outages, inappropriate environmental conditions, or even loss of a key employee.

The majority of the journal articles cover disaster planning and/ or recovery affecting centralized computers or servers. Some articles include networking. Several publications mention the need to provide technology support for the various areas within an organization that require access to computers and data. Interestingly, no articles were found which discuss new, substantial, automation projects or increased technology demands that emerge during the recovery process. While most of the articles were useful, only a few were comprehensive or covered the effects of wide-area disasters.

There are several excellent publications with information on disaster and recovery topics pertinent to libraries. Miriam Kahn (1998) in her book *Disaster Response and Planning for Libraries* covers disaster prevention, planning, response, and recovery issues applicable to libraries. There were several places where computer technology is discussed along with insurance implications. George Cunha (1992) has information on library disaster planning and recovery and includes issues related to technology. This article also contains many references to resources that provide information in developing disaster plans as well as sources that can help with recovery efforts.

There are books that specifically cover disaster planning and recovery for computers, networks, and related technology equipment. For example, Jon William Toigo (1996) covers disaster planning and recovery of automation equipment from the perspective of the impacts on companies. The World Wide Web is also a source for finding information on disaster/recovery companies that provide services for computer technology recovery and planning.

Overall, the literature details various options and areas related to disaster planning and recovery of computer technology equipment, software, and data. However, the literature cannot assess your environment or determine the risks or impacts of potential disasters on your organization. This must be done by the organization. The approaches used to handle disasters and to prepare disaster plans are also dependent upon the costs, the time intervals acceptable for recovery, and the resources available to the organization.

INITIAL STEPS FOR TECHNOLOGY RECOVERY

Disaster Plan

A disaster plan that addresses computer equipment, software, data, and automation services will be extremely helpful if a disaster occurs. One of the purposes of a disaster plan is to identify all automation equipment, software, and data within your organization and to determine how each part can be recovered after a disaster. One of the most critical items to recover in information technology disasters is the data. Data can be unique, irreplaceable, and crucial to the mission of your organization. The recovery of data is usually accomplished with some type of backup. Software will also be needed for a recovery. Software includes operating systems as well as applications and must be accessible from an off-site source or reside on backups. It is critical that backups are stored in a safe, external site. A disaster plan that addresses data and software recovery will help assure that the appropriate backups exist in a secure location so that recovery is possible.

A disaster plan should specify how quickly computer services, software, and data must be available after a disaster. Often, selected automation services and data will be needed immediately. If it will take considerable time to restore or replace the associated facility or equipment, then temporary facilities and equipment may be used while the initial facility or equipment is being repaired or replaced. In these cases, the disaster plan should identify how these situations should be handled. The disaster plan may specify a "hot" site where backups of data and software can be loaded onto prearranged computer equipment. The plan may list a "cold" site where computers may be moved if they are still functional. Many cold sites have appropriate power, network access, temperature controls, and other environmental factors, but some cold sites need modifications before they would be fully functional. Some organizations implement and maintain similar computers at their own remote sites. These computers are either updated in tandem with the primary site or updated nightly with data from the primary site. The disaster plan may also list potential temporary locations that could be used if needed, or the plan may specify other recovery arrangements, such as an agreement with your library system vendor. If advance arrangements are needed to support a disaster recovery, then these arrangements should be made when the plan is developed. There are varying costs associated with these various options of disaster recovery.

Another important area in a disaster plan involves insurance policies and having adequate technology coverage for the needs of your organization. For example, insurance policies may cover the value of your computer equipment using current costs. It may be more appropriate to obtain functional replacement coverage which would assure that a replacement computer would be able to perform the same functions as your damaged computer. If damaged equipment is recovered instead of replaced, current warranties or maintenance contracts may not be valid, depending upon the type of damage. You may want to consider insurance where damaged computers would always be replaced instead of repaired. Business interruption coverage supports the implementation of alternate sites and services while the primary site or service is unavailable. The insurance company will oversee the recovery process and will review or authorize expenditures that are covered by insurance. Your policy defines the parameters of the recovery operation.

Disaster plans should also include names of the disaster team and how they may be contacted. Plans usually include priorities, such as which services should be restored first. Many parts of an existing disaster plan will apply to your current disaster. However, each disaster brings unique circumstances that may not be covered in your plan.

Initial Notification

Whenever a disaster involving automation technology occurs, the starting point for recovery is to notify the staff responsible for the automation equipment, services, and data. The initial contact person should be indicated in the disaster recovery plan. Usually this will be someone in the information technology section within your immediate organization. Since automation is involved with many activities throughout the organization, this person must be aware of all these different activities and the various information technology staff that have helped implement and maintain them. These additional people will be needed to help support the recovery if the disaster impacted areas in which they worked. These people may be within your library, or they may be from centralized automation support units for the campus or organization.

For many disasters, the technology staff may discover the problem. For other types of disasters, people in other areas of the building—facilities support staff or security personnel—may be the first to be aware of the situation. For large disasters, the telephone numbers of staff may be inaccessible, or the telephones may not be working. Often the first priority of large disasters is to assure the safety of the people at the site and minimize the destruction. When a disaster occurs, it is important to notify an information technology staff member as quickly as possible because they may be able to implement plans or procedures to mitigate some of the potential damage.

Damage Assessment

One of the first steps in disaster recovery is to assess the scope of the damage and to determine what needs to be done. This can be a complicated process full of frustrating delays and inaccurate information. The disaster may involve just the technology section or a small area. Other disasters may involve the whole building, several buildings, or a larger geographic area. Staff may not be able to physically get to the disaster area, or the disaster area may be declared off limits so you cannot determine the damages. There could be damages in external areas that will have an impact on computer equipment and networking. It may be impossible to contact the appropriate people for information; or when you reach them, they do not have the information you need.

One of the early assessments concerns the status of the building and the computer room. Is the room or building still usable? Are the utilities such as power, air conditioning, networking, humidity controls, etc. still available? Can information technology operations continue in some sort of degraded but sufficient mode in the current location? Is there a time estimate for repairs? Should you wait for repairs? Will the computer operations need to be moved? What are the costs for moving and for using remote locations? Will staff throughout the organization be relocated to external sites? If people or computers are to be moved, will it be a temporary or permanent move? For a temporary situation, will it be short term or long term? Where are the locations of these external sites, and what are the automation needs for each location? Do the sites have the appropriate utilities to support the needed automation? What will insurance cover?

Another area of assessment concerns the status of the automation equipment, the software, the data, and the telecommunications network. What equipment has been damaged or destroyed? What needs to be done to fix the equipment? Is alternate equipment available? What is the status of the data? If data backups are needed, can they be obtained? Is the network, or part of the network, operational? Are inventories available that list the serial numbers for all automation equipment?

The Colorado State University Libraries' disaster was part of a larger main campus and city-wide disaster. Many homes and businesses were flooded. There were problems in the city with electrical power, telephones, and closed streets. The main campus was closed the following day. People throughout the city were told to stay home so that emergencies could be handled. It took multiple attempts to contact staff by telephone. For this first day after the disaster, all knowledge of the status of the technology equipment in Morgan Library was based upon our network manager's hurried inspection the night of the disaster.

The second day after the disaster, the full Library Disaster Recovery Team met. The team had been expanded to include additional LTS staff, as well as other selected library staff. At the meeting, we learned that there was no electricity, no network, no heating, no air conditioning, and no working telephones in Morgan Library. The extent of the damage to the utilities equipment was unknown, but there was some discussion that certain types of equipment might be recoverable, such as the power switches. There were no time lines for getting further information on the equipment or infrastructure or for having repairs made. We also learned that access to the building, and particularly the lower level, would be restricted due to health concerns. Only limited access for a short amount of time would be permitted to retrieve needed equipment and files.

On campus, there were 34 buildings affected by excess water, with 15 of these having significant problems. There was also damage to the telephone and network lines between buildings, as well as to heating and cooling components in the steam tunnels. On a positive note, the campus Computer Center escaped damage by a few inches.

During the assessment process, it is important to identify where help may be obtained. For large disasters, there may be many areas that need the same type of help that you do. This will impact the recovery time. Companies or resources that you had previously identified may not be available at the time of your disaster. Additional sources of help include partners, colleges and universities, disaster vendors, and volunteers.

Communication

Communication and coordination are important factors throughout the disaster and recovery process. The information technology staff will need to communicate among themselves, as well as with all other areas within the library or organization that were impacted by the disaster. The technology staff will need to be aware of the status of the disaster, the technology needs of each area, and the recovery priorities for the library or organization as a whole. During a disaster, this will be an evolving process. Urgent requests for technology support may occur every day or even several times a day.

Coordination meetings of the disaster team are usually held on a frequent basis after a disaster. This provides a forum to learn the latest status and to coordinate with people who are working on the various projects. The status of the different parts of the recovery process such as power or the building environment often have an impact on the recovery of technology. Plans for alternate services or temporary projects also may have a technology component that will need to be implemented.

Technology staff may also need to communicate with many external resources, such as recovery sites, facilities, vendors, contractors, telecommunication centers, and other sources of computer support. These resources can be sources of help and information. They may also be contacted to provide price quotes, to coordinate activities, and/or to obtain time estimates. In addition, any external computer site that either sends or receives files from your organization may need to be informed of your situation.

The normal modes of communication may not be available immediately following a disaster. There may be no offices, no telephones, no meeting rooms, and no e-mail. In this environment, it is hard to find people and it is also hard for them to find you during unscheduled times. If you leave a message, they cannot get back in touch with you. In this situation, obtaining cellular telephones and pagers can help significantly with communications.

The Morgan Library staff worked in an environment with no offices, no telephones, and no e-mail for several days following the disaster. Coordination meetings with the Disaster Team were held in an outdoor courtyard once or twice a day. There was a library command center with one telephone that was staffed during normal work hours. Our working space was wherever we sat down. Our supplies were whatever we carried. After a few days, we obtained cellular telephones which helped immensely with communications and with coordinating activities.

During the recovery process following large disasters, there will be much confusion on the extent of the damages, on what is needed to restore services, and on time estimates concerning when different events will occur. As work progresses on each project, the assessments and estimates will be more accurate. Often the time for an event to occur is much longer than the initial estimates. Do not wait for something to be done if there are other reasonable alternatives that can be implemented on a temporary basis.

Priorities

The decisions and actions taken during disaster recovery will be based upon the needs of your organization, the damages, the costs, the estimated time lines for recovery, your insurance coverage, and the resources available to help.

The highest priority for the library was to rescue library materials and prevent further damage. Initial priorities involving technology were to arrange and set up the technology support for a command center for the entire building, to provide access to the critical data and computers such as the library online catalog, and to provide technology support to staff members who had been relocated to temporary sites.

IMPLEMENT OFF-SITE TECHNOLOGY ACCESS AND SERVICES, IF APPROPRIATE

After a disaster, selected automation services, applications, data, and equipment are often implemented at alternate locations if they cannot be accessed or used from their normal site for a period of time. Determining what should move and when it should be moved is dependent upon:

- the data and applications,
- the services that need to be provided,
- impacts if the data or application is not available,
- time estimates for recovery,
- the availability of needed equipment and resources,
- the costs to move associated equipment,
- the costs to set up replacement equipment,
- the insurance coverage, and
- adequate data and software backups.

Some computers are dedicated to a particular application or function, and these applications must remain on a dedicated computer. Other applications need to reside on similar automation equipment. It is also possible to implement some centralized functions using different applications or systems. If library staff are relocated to temporary locations, then appropriate automation equipment and software must be obtained to support their assignments at the temporary sites.

Relocate Critical Computers, Applications, and Data

The circumstances of your disaster and the needs of your organization will determine if the computer applications and data files need to be implemented at a temporary location. Relocating equipment, data, and applications to an alternate site usually occurs when high-priority computer applications or data files cannot be accessed within a reasonable time frame. For some disasters, the automation equipment may be functional and can be moved to a new site. In other situations, alternate or new equipment must be obtained. Often, several computer applications and data systems will be classified as critical and will need to be relocated and restored immediately. Other items will be needed within days instead of hours. If you have a disaster plan, the plan should specify the urgent applications and data. The plan should also indicate any hot or cold site arrangements or other remote site options that should be used, and the procedures to follow.

If arrangements for off-site locations or alternate equipment have not been made in advance, then it may take significant time for arrangements to be made after a disaster. It may be possible to borrow or rent a similar computer. Computer recovery centers could be contacted to see if they can provide services. You may be able to buy "off the shelf" equipment, or rush-order equipment.

It cannot be overemphasized that data and software must be on some type of backup that is reasonably current and accessible. A disaster can not only destroy computers, but it can also damage both the buildings that house them and the surrounding area. A recent version of the backups must also be located off-site.

Once the computer is moved, or the data and software are

One of 30 PCs ruined by water damage.

loaded on comparable equipment, adjustments will probably need to be made for accessing the data. For example, the computer will probably have a different Internet address. Staff procedures will need to be changed to access the new address.

All the centralized computer servers in Morgan Library escaped damage from the disaster, but they were inaccessible in a closed building with no power. Our disaster plan covered the loss of a server or using a cold site with minimal utilities. A new plan was developed to provide access based upon the circumstances of our disaster. The first day that the main campus was opened, LTS staff talked to the managers of the campus Computer Center. Since their site was intact, we checked on the possibilities of moving our criti-

The computer lab after the water disaster.

cal servers to their location. For the Libraries, this included the server that contained the library catalog, and a statewide Interlibrary Loan server. In addition, we asked if it was possible to wire a subnet with the same IP address as the subnet in our building. The campus computer staff were able to support us, and they made the space and wiring configurations in a day. As soon as the wiring was in place, we moved the servers ourselves.

A site that was five miles from the main library building was used to store weekly backup tapes. However, the disaster also encompassed areas immediately next to this remote backup site. The backups were intact, but we were naive in thinking that five miles away was perfectly safe. Monthly backup tapes are now sent to a site that is 65 miles away, and these tapes would be retrieved in the case of a large, regional disaster.

Implement Central Functions Using Other Applications or Systems

It may be possible to implement some of the essential computer applications or data systems with substitutes or similar applications that provide the needed functionality. These alternatives may already exist on computers available to your organization, or the alternatives may be easier to implement and support at remote sites. Similar sites, affiliates, or organizations may be able to support various parts of your needed functionality with existing applications and equipment.

At the Colorado State University Libraries the e-mail system was on a large UNIX server that was not moved. Moving this large server would have required outside assistance which was not easily available with the other urgent tasks of disaster recovery. The Campus Computer Center was able to create an alternate e-mail system on a small UNIX computer. The alternate computer was given the same Internet name and address as our large server which allowed all staff in the Libraries to retain their original e-mail addresses. It was extremely helpful for our staff to use e-mail during the recovery process. With limited telephone service, e-mail became a heavily used method of communication.

An older version of the Libraries' Web pages existed on one of the central campus servers. Over two days, this older version was brought up-to-date and reactivated. The Web pages allowed the library to continue to provide library services to remote databases and other electronic resources while the main building was closed. The Libraries' Web pages also provided a means to communicate information related to the disaster.

Support Automation Activities for Staff at Temporary Locations

Staff will have multiple activities during disaster recovery. Many will be involved with recovery operations. Others may need to keep up with normal activities so that a large backlog does not occur. When various staff from the organization need to be relocated, this will usually involve technology support. The first step is determining where they will be located, and what functions and activities will be done at each site. It is very helpful if these external locations have been identified in a disaster-recovery plan and confirmed that they can support the needed activities and equipment. However, depending upon the extent of the disaster, these sites may not be available. Finding external sites immediately after a disaster has occurred can take considerable time. Also, if there has been a large disaster, many other areas may be competing for the available spaces.

Several issues need to be quickly addressed when implementing automation for staff at temporary locations. What technology equipment and software will be needed? Where can the equipment and software be obtained? What tools and materials are needed to implement the equipment? What are the electrical capabilities of the area? What networking options are available and what type of connections can be used? What is the size of the area? What are the environmental and ergonomic conditions such as air quality, heat, light, and air conditioning? Will the workstations be shared?

The Morgan Library staff were relocated to many alternate sites during the initial phases of our disaster recovery. The major site for processing on-going materials had been identified in our disaster plan. All other sites were obtained after the disaster occurred. Fortunately, it was summer, and some rooms on campus were available until the fall semester started. The site for the command center was identified rather quickly in a building next to Morgan Library. A week later, several additional offices in this same building were obtained. One of these rooms was designated for LTS. This greatly helped with technology-related communications, plus it allowed for a central location to keep technology supplies.

Every temporary site required at least one personal computer (PC) and a nearby printer. Most sites had some type of network wiring. PCs were selected and moved from the closed library building based upon the type of connection supported by their ethernet card. Morgan Library had recently completed an upgrade from COAX to Cat 5 wiring, so we had several PCs with network cards that could connect to multiple types of wiring. Internet access had to be coordinated with the network manager of each building or area. Software previously located on different PCs or accessed from the Libraries' servers had to be loaded on the relocated PCs. Fortunately, the Libraries already had sufficient software licenses to cover the PCs at the alternate sites. Telephone service also had to be arranged.

The Libraries has a depository for the storage of books and journals which is located several blocks from Morgan Library and which houses many items beyond the capacity of our main building. The Depository required special attention as it became the base for our technical services operations with over 40 staff members temporarily relocated there. Initially, there was one COAX ethernet drop at the facility. Over three days, LTS staff wired and implemented a network that supported 14 PCs. This was done with existing supplies such as an old COAX hub, wiring, and connectors that we had in our work area. Existing PCs from the closed building that could connect to COAX wiring were carried to this site. These PCs were then configured with a common operating system and loaded with the software that was previously accessible from the Libraries' servers. A locally-shared printer network was created using Windows for Workgroups. This also allowed for the sharing of files. Two printers dedicated to the library catalog were also transferred, which required configuration changes to the online catalog server. Label printers and barcode scanners were moved. Access to OCLC was switched from dedicated access to Internet access. Most of the equipment was shared among the staff reassigned to this facility. This setup allowed the technical staff to continue to receive materials, update the catalog, and perform other related functions.

Two classrooms were obtained on a temporary basis to provide services to users while the Morgan Library was closed. These rooms were in a central campus building with several computer labs. One room was an existing computer lab which was used to provide reference services and access to electronic databases and resources. The other room was empty and subsequently set up with 14 PCs. This room supported ILL services for users, as well as supporting Reserve processing so materials could be entered and ready when the semester started. LTS staff made the arrangements and set up the equipment and network connections in these rooms.

In addition to alternate locations, some library staff worked on projects that allowed them to telecommute from home. In many cases, these staff members already had PCs and modems at home. However, a few library PCs were reconfigured with modems and loaned to several library staff members for telecommuting while the main building was closed.

RECOVER OR REPLACE DAMAGED AUTOMATION EQUIPMENT, NETWORK WIRING, AND INFRASTRUCTURE

Recover Automation Equipment

Immediately after a disaster, one of the first tasks is to determine what automation equipment was involved in the disaster and the status of the equipment. Often you can obtain this information by inspecting the equipment. However, you may not have immediate access to the area. In some situations, you may never see the damaged area or equipment. An existing inventory can help with the identification of equipment involved in the disaster. An inventory can also be generated from purchase records or from other resources. You may need to prove that any lost or unaccounted for equipment was involved in the disaster. You may also have to provide serial numbers, hardware configurations, and initial costs. The ability to trace damaged or lost equipment to official records can be helpful.

Equipment damaged in a natural disaster is usually excluded from existing warranties and maintenance contracts. The recovery and replacement of equipment is often determined, directed, and managed by the insurance company. Your insurance policy determines what type of coverage is in effect, such as functional replacement or current value coverage. The insurance company will have the damaged equipment assessed. They will determine what equipment should be repaired and what can be replaced. They may select the vendors that can be used. All orders and repairs may need to be reviewed by the insurance company, which will impact the recovery time. You may also find that your definition of equipment that is beyond repair may be different than the opinion of your insurance company.

In many situations, insurance companies will try to have automation and electronic equipment cleaned rather than replace the equipment. This has been successful under some circumstances. Be sure to check the equipment carefully if it has been restored. You will also need to confirm if existing maintenance agreements will accept the refurbished equipment. Often new maintenance arrangements must be made. The vendors or maintenance companies will usually require that the restored equipment be recertified by their own technicians or by an independent company to document that the equipment is fully recovered and working properly before maintenance will start or resume.

The automation equipment damaged or destroyed by the water in Morgan Library included the main network switch for the building, three hubs, 30 PCs, two LaserJet printers, six dot-matrix printers, five barcode scanners, a VCR, and a color TV. All the equipment was under water for over 24 hours; then it remained untouched in the lower level for over a week. Library staff were not allowed to remove or recover the equipment.

The insurance company initially arranged for most computer equipment to be recovered through a cleaning process by a computer disaster-recovery company that specialized in these procedures. The initial exceptions were monitors, power supplies, and dot matrix printers, which would all be replaced. Although the director of Academic Computing on campus had recommended that most automation equipment be replaced, insurance required that attempts to recover the equipment occur first. The library network manager also had previous experience with trying to salvage water-damaged PCs, and he had observed that most recovered PCs failed within six months, but his comments were ignored.

The recovery company attempted to refurbish several network switches and hubs from various areas across campus. None of the switches and hubs worked after the cleaning. Only when this process was proven ineffective on hubs and switches, could orders be submitted to replace them.

The disaster-recovery company was assigned to retrieve and clean the damaged PCs and other computer-related equipment. When staff from this company came to the library building, they entered the lower level, took the computers and other damaged automation equipment that they could find, and then left. They did not confer with any library staff. They did not have a list of the equipment in the lower level, so they missed five PCs, five barcode scanners, and six printers. It took months to reconcile the counts from the disaster-recovery company with the library's list of equipment that was involved in the disaster.

The disaster-recovery company opened each damaged PC and cleaned each part separately. The company did not keep track of which disk, ethernet card, or CD-ROM drive was associated with what PC. Weeks later, the PCs were returned to us and purported to be fully functional. Many problems were immediately found. Some of the PCs would not power on. Many had the wrong ethernet card, so the PCs could not be used with our wiring. Several had small disks which would not support the needed applications. Almost all PCs had corroded batteries on the motherboard, and several PCs stopped working within a few days of testing. Dirt could be seen on most of the motherboards. Many of the cases showed signs of rust. Several LTS staff spent days testing and documenting the problems with these refurbished PCs. Because of the documentation, we were finally allowed to purchase replacements for all our damaged PCs.

There were no guarantees on the quality of the refurbished equipment or on how long the equipment would last. Once the equipment was cleaned and restored, the company left town to work on recovering equipment from a new disaster. All previous warranties on the equipment were no longer valid since the equipment had been involved in the disaster.

Recover Software and Data

The best plan for recovering data and software from a damaged computer is to have a copy of the data and software available at a remote location. Making frequent backups of all critical data and software should be part of standard computer operations. A reasonably recent backup should always be available at a safe, remote site.

Information on central computer servers should be backed up on a regular basis, preferably daily. Data on individual PCs should also be backed up in a timely manner. In a networked environment, it may be possible for individuals at PCs or workstations to have their file services located on a central computer. This would allow the central server to include individual user data and programs on the central computer backups.

It is sometimes possible to recover data from damaged hard drives, diskettes, and tapes. Often, this is best handled by companies with experience in this area. Insurance often includes attempts to recover the files from damaged storage media. Insurance usually does not cover the value of any lost data, or the costs to reconstruct the data.

All the damaged PCs in the Morgan Library lower level were networked, and they were configured so that the primary user files were actually stored on one of our main UNIX servers. All data files stored in this manner were untouched by the water. However, there was one file that a staff member stored on a local drive instead of the networked drives. The backups of this file were on diskettes in her desk in the lower level, so this one file was lost.

Restore Wiring for Networking and Telecommunications

After a disaster, network and telephone wiring such as fiber, Cat 5 utp, Cat 3 utp, or COAX will need to be checked. Any wire that is damaged or broken will need to be replaced. Any part of the wire that was wet will need to be cut off. If wire sits in water, the water can wick up to three feet beyond the high water mark. This will also need to be removed. Any wiring patch panels that were wet or damaged should be replaced. After cutting off the damaged ends of the wiring, if the wire becomes too short, it should be replaced. If possible, lines should not be spliced since this contributes to the degradation of the line. All lines should be tested and certified after they are repaired or replaced. The wiring closets themselves should be checked to be sure they are still usable and secure. If there is physical damage to the closet, it will need to be repaired or rebuilt.

At Colorado State University Libraries, all fiber and Cat 5 utp wiring, and all telephone lines are the responsibility of the campus Telecommunications Department. There were many campus buildings affected by the disaster, and this unit was responsible for restoring services to all the buildings. They were also responsible for the wiring in the steam tunnels that ran between buildings. The steam tunnels filled with water during the disaster. In addition, staff from many buildings were relocated to temporary locations, and new telephone service was needed in many of these temporary locations.

In the lower level of Morgan Library, all wiring up to the ceiling was wet and had to be cut. All patch panels in the lower level were wet and had to be replaced. The wiring closets themselves had to be demolished, and then reconstructed before the wiring could be replaced or re-terminated. The lower-level cable trays were above the ceiling panels, and the wiring in them remained dry.

After all the salvageable materials in the lower level were removed, the insurance company arranged for the removal of the debris and a thorough cleaning of the damaged areas. This included taking down all existing walls, removing all ceiling panels, removing floor tiling, and tossing any materials that were not salvageable. Any wiring in the walls was cut above the ceiling level. What remained were the cement pillars, the outside walls, and some equipment in the machine room. The five missing PCs from Morgan Library were probably tossed in this process, as the PCs were in an area that had been blocked by debris. Library staff were not allowed to help with this process, nor were they consulted during the debris removal. Better communications would have prevented several things from being tossed without being evaluated or counted.

After the damaged areas were extensively cleaned, the telecommunications closets were one of the first areas to be rebuilt in the library lower level. However, telecommunications staff would not enter the new closets because of environmental concerns. Mold, bacteria, and yeast had appeared shortly after the disaster, but they were controlled through treatments, the removal of the debris, and the cleaning process. The campus Environmental Health Safety unit had tested the lower-level environment, and the tests indicated that the air was fine. However, one of the contractors consulted with an off-site expert. The expert advised caution without running any tests, reviewing any data, or inspecting the area. So some of the contractors wore Tyvak clean room suits, while other contractors wore no protection at all. This caused confusion among the workers as to the status of the environment. With deadlines approaching, telecommunications staff decided to wear face masks while they worked. They installed the new switches and hubs. They re-terminated the fiber connections, and other wires to support services on the floors above the lower level. Restoring the wiring in the lower level came later, as it was rebuilt.

Restore Power and Other Utilities

Computer equipment will not work unless there is power available. Restoring power to the building is covered in another section of this book (see Chapter 4). Arrangements can be made to use power generators for computer equipment when the primary source of power is unavailable. Before pursuing this option, the warranties and maintenance contracts for any automation equipment should be checked to be sure the use of power generators is acceptable. For one of the primary servers in Morgan Library, the warranty would have been invalidated if a power generator had been used.

Most automation equipment must operate within specified temperature and humidity ranges. Sometimes the environment is controlled by the building HVAC systems. In other situations, special air conditioners or dehumidifiers may be used. If the environment is not acceptable for the automation equipment, then alternatives may be investigated. This includes implementing portable air conditioners, heaters, or humidifiers.

Communicate with Contractors

Throughout the recovery process, it is helpful to have good working relations with the many contractors involved with the automation recovery. There are so many things they will be doing that some details will be missed. With good communications, problems can be caught and addressed quickly. Contractors can give you up-to-date status reports; these will help you coordinate and plan activities. Reports that go through many people often do not give you the details that you may need. It is also advisable to follow up with contractors by reviewing time lines and priorities. The workers may not know which projects within the building should be done first. With large disasters, they may not know which buildings come first.

Automation Equipment Security

During a large disaster, it may be hard to maintain security for both the building and the computer equipment. There are many curious people and news crews who will want to see the damages. People will walk in through broken windows, holes in the wall, or open doors. Later in the recovery, there will be many contractors, and additional people who can walk in and not be noticed. The contractors usually have identification, but it is often not checked. The contractors may leave doors open or take a break and leave a secure area fully accessible to anyone.

LTS staff moved many PCs and other automation equipment to various locations on campus. Only on the very last equipment move was any LTS staff member questioned about moving or taking computers. The front door to Morgan Library was monitored by library staff, but other entrances to the building and many other places on campus had no security.

The damaged automation equipment in the Morgan Library lower level was removed without the knowledge of any library staff. Initially, we thought that the equipment had been stolen. Later, the PC refurbishing center was telephoned to see if they had the equipment—which they did. The computer room in Morgan Library had special locks on the doors that did not operate with any of the building or campus master keys. There were no problems with unauthorized entry in this area. In spite of these security problems, no automation equipment was stolen from Morgan Library. We were lucky. However, library staff should not rely on good fortune. Security of automation equipment should be a primary concern during disaster recovery.

Resume Services

If a building has been damaged and closed for repairs, at some point the building will be reopened. This may occur before networks or computers have been fully recovered. The utilities or the environmental controls may also not be fully functional.

Morgan Library was closed for three weeks. The building was initially reopened only for staff access. Several days later, the building was opened to the public, which was three days before the beginning of the fall semester. There was electrical power, but no networking, no heat, no air conditioning, and high humidity. The telephone lines had yet to be re-terminated, but somehow a few telephone lines still worked in the building. Modems were put in a few PCs and connected to the working telephone lines. This allowed users to search the catalog from the PCs, obtain call numbers, and find materials that were not damaged.

Networking was restored to the building one week after the building was reopened. The Campus Computer Center made some wiring modifications so that the Libraries' computer servers at the temporary site could continue to be accessed on the same subnet as the one in Morgan Library. Since the computer room environment in Morgan Library was not ideal for large computer servers, it was necessary to keep the critical servers at their temporary location for several months. Moving automation equipment back to Morgan Library was relatively quick and easy, compared to setting up and implementing temporary locations.

It took three to four more months before the Morgan Library had heat. Air conditioning was not restored until the following summer. Several portable air conditioners were used to keep the temperature at acceptable levels in the computer room during this time.

The successful handling of a disaster-recovery operation requires staff to be adaptable, to see the impacts and repercussions of each step within the recovery process, to address new needs as they emerge, and to do whatever needs to be done. For example, moving equipment or changing software applications may require that staff be trained in new procedures. A new system of communicating may also need to be developed. Working in crowded areas with minimal equipment and supplies can create stress and frustration.

NEW AUTOMATION ACTIVITIES RELATED TO DISASTER RECOVERY

Previous sections of this chapter discussed recovering and restoring the technology infrastructure and providing technology services at temporary locations during disaster recovery. For large disasters, the recovery of library materials takes a significantly longer time than the recovery of automation equipment or the recovery of the building itself. There will be many new projects related to the recovery of library materials. There may also be additional projects to provide services to users during the recovery period. The projects often have information technology components that need to be addressed.

For the recovery of materials in large disasters, additional library staffing will be required unless this process will be handled by an outside contractor. The work may be done either within the building or at an off-site location. Automation equipment and networking will be required to support the recovery activities. Information technology staff will be involved at many different levels. Technology staff should be involved with the identification of the site where the recovery will take place to assure that the site can accommodate the needed automation equipment by having adequate power and telecommunications lines. If the site needs to be modified to support automation activities, technology staff will investigate the options to determine if the modifications can be done within the needed time frame. Technology staff will need to identify or review automation equipment specifications to confirm that the equipment has the capabilities to perform the needed functions. Examples of equipment include PCs, printers, and barcode scanners. Arrangements, such as obtaining additional hubs and switches as well as adding wiring, may be made so that networking can be provided. The new equipment will need to be configured and installed. Additional technology staff may be hired either by the library or contractor to help with the setup, installations, and providing automation support for troubleshooting or training.

For the disaster recovery at the library, a Processing Center, operated by an outside contractor, was established to process all items received as gifts, as well as to process the damaged books and periodicals that were salvageable. This center was initially located in the gutted lower level of Morgan Library. This operation required 78 PCs, plus a number of barcode scanners and printers. Although Processing Center staff were responsible for obtaining, implementing, and maintaining their own equipment, LTS helped with the equipment specifications, helped obtain the hubs, coordinated the network wiring, and configured all the barcode scanners. The building network also supported their telecommunications needs.

The processing of damaged materials will require some type of data system to identify and account for the materials, as well as to document what was done. It will require interfacing with existing data systems, such as the library online catalog. Your technology staff will be involved in this process. The "Tools for Tracking" chapter in this book gives further details on this topic (see Chapter 23).

There may be increased staffing in existing areas, and the new staff will need automation equipment and networking capabilities. Additional equipment will need to be obtained and installed for the new staff. For example, the Interlibrary Loan Department was quickly increased to more than double the original size because there would be a much greater need to borrow materials while the damaged materials were unavailable.

New projects may be implemented to provide alternative resources and new services during the recovery period. Electronic databases with full-text may serve as reasonable substitutes for damaged journals while they are unavailable. A gift solicitation project may be undertaken to obtain gifts to replace damaged materials. New Web pages on the disaster-recovery process may be implemented along with Web pages that list the titles of the damaged periodicals and have forms that can be used to offer donations. Library staff will be involved with the setup and implementation of automation equipment to support these projects. They may also write Web pages, generate special reports, and arrange access to additional electronic databases.

Large recovery projects may generate a significant increase of activities on existing computer systems and networks. The computers and associated software may need to be upgraded, enhanced, or scheduled so that response times remain reasonable with the increased activities. Additional disks or CPUs may be obtained for the servers to help disperse the load. Some activities such as generating large reports may be scheduled during non-peak hours. Software may need new functionality, or it may need to be modified to handle new limits.

At the Colorado State University Libraries, the computer server that supported the library online catalog needed some adjustments. There was a greater demand to run reports requiring additional report files to be purchased. Several software modifications were needed to the system, such as supporting the transfer of a list of barcodes from the Processing Center. After the vendor of our system was contacted, the adjustments were quickly made. The computer started experiencing significantly slower response times. One of the causes was the simultaneous generation of many reports for the gift solicitation project. Another cause was many Processing Center staff adding information to the data item records. To help with these problems, the computer files were rebalanced, and certain functions were scheduled during lower-use periods.

One of the Interlibrary Loan software packages generated a tremendous amount of network traffic that caused a congestion problem. The technology staff identified the source, balanced the loads on the hubs, and then implemented a network switch to better handle the traffic in the Interlibrary Loan area.

A disaster recovery database was implemented on one of our large servers. When the database started approaching 40,000 records, the entire computer slowed down. LTS staff worked with the software developers to change the code to minimize the impacts on the server. An additional disk and two CPUs were also added to this server as the database grew even larger.

ANECDOTAL RECOVERY TALES

During a large disaster-recovery project, surprises often occur. For us, the predominant ones were related to construction workers who turned off power circuits to functioning areas instead of to the locations where they were working. The power outages always seemed to involve several PCs. Some workmen would power-off circuits when they left at the end of their shifts. LTS staff actually placed signs by some of the circuit switches to prevent them from being turned off inadvertently.

After the large, built-in air conditioner in the computer room was back in service, the cooling loop for the air conditioner was turned off on several occasions causing the computer room temperatures to rise to higher than acceptable limits. Two portable air conditioners were used to stabilize the temperature.

Another tale concerns the electrician who accidentally sent a 220-volt current down a 110-volt circuit. This circuit went to the newly replaced, main network switch for Morgan Library. Suddenly, all networking died in the building. When LTS staff checked the wiring closet, there was a strong, electrical burning smell by the new network switch. The electrician, chagrined by what had transpired, fixed the electrical problem while a spare network switch was quickly requested from another campus unit. During the process of unplugging the original switch, a surge protector was found hidden under the equipment. The surge protector was opened to reveal melted wiring inside. The original network switch was fine, and the surge protector was replaced with a UPS.

It took several months before heat was available in the library. There were some cold days in the fall where the building was rather chilly. Campus Facilities supplied small heaters for the staff work areas. The heaters would trigger the circuit breakers bringing down several computers.

A few days after the disaster, library administrators plus several staff worked late into the evening gathering budget figures for disaster-recovery estimates. The report was due early the next day, but there were no working computers available that had the needed software and printers. The head of the Campus Computer Training Center was telephoned at home and asked if our administrators could use the campus computer facilities. She met us on campus late at night and heard tales of no offices, no rooms, and no working computers. She offered to check the availability of rooms in her building that were in the final stages of renovation. Within a few days, library staff were providing library services to users using two of these rooms. We imposed on someone late at night, and we were offered additional help. This was typical of the wonderful support we received from our campus.

CONCLUSION

Reflections on What Worked Well

For the disaster at the Morgan Library, there were several factors that contributed to the quick response and fairly smooth recovery of technology-related equipment and services. At the top of the list was our versatile staff. These people knew the Libraries' services, applications, computer configurations, data, and networking infrastructure. They could come up with new solutions based upon the circumstances. They could install and reconfigure computers, wire networks, set up servers, move equipment, talk to vendors and contractors, and help in any way that was needed. They also tested the refurbished PCs and documented the problems which eventually led to their full replacement.

The Campus Computer Center was another great source of help. They quickly accommodated our Libraries' requests for help by giving space to relocate the critical servers and by wiring their computer room so our servers could be accessed using their normal Internet addresses. They also implemented a temporary e-mail system using the current e-mail addresses for our library.

Another aspect that worked well was that alternative sites were quickly set up rather than waiting for things to be fixed. It took weeks instead of the initial estimates of days for many things to be repaired or replaced. Since staff could work at these alternate sites, they could get needed reports and other projects done. A very important part of providing quick responses for technology support was the availability of automation-related equipment, supplies, and tools.

Summary of Problematic Areas During the Recovery

There were several automation-related recovery activities that did not work well. At the top of the list was attempting to recover automation equipment that had been under water for over 24 hours. Significant time was wasted on the refurbishing process, testing and documenting the problems with the returned equipment, and convincing the insurance company that the process did not work. We were eventually able to order replacement PCs, but the delays impacted staff productivity.

Another problematic area was that two central university units, Telecommunications and Facilities, were responsible for the recovery of all damages related to telecommunications, network wiring, power, heat, and other utilities that occurred on campus. These two units had to coordinate repairs and replacements for over 34 buildings. They were not adequately staffed to handle a wide-area disaster of this magnitude. There were delays in assessments and in getting the work done. There were also delays in bringing in subcontractors, especially since the disaster also impacted the city and there was high demand for extra help.

During the first week after the disaster, the technology staff had no offices or telephones. The first week involved coordinating, moving servers and other automation equipment, and setting up equipment for temporary areas. It was hard to contact anyone, to leave a message, and to get messages. The ability to communicate was actually more important than having an office.

Library Disaster Planning and Recovery Handbook

KEY RECOMMENDATIONS

Technology

- Have a plan to restore access to the critical data and applications from your computer servers within the time frames needed by your organization. This includes providing access to data such as the library online catalog so the damage can be assessed, documented, and reported. Other examples of data or programs include Web pages, accounting information, electronic access to remote resources, and e-mail systems.
- Store equipment inventories, telephone numbers, the disaster plan, computer hardware configurations, copies of computer purchase orders, software license copies, diagrams of the network topography, and especially data backups in a safe, remote place that is easily accessible. Telephone numbers should also be given to building facilities and security staff.
- Have access to technology staff who can restore data on servers from backups, configure and implement computers, set up and wire networks, move equipment, and troubleshoot automation problems. The better the staff know your data, applications, and environment, the faster the recovery will occur and with fewer errors.
- Provide a plan to obtain supplies, software, PCs, and printers to provide the technology needs for staff to work at remote locations. Supplies include wiring, tools, ethernet cards, etc.
- Have a list of software, functionality, and various configurations that may need to be implemented.
- Have alternate sites pre-selected and checked for adequate power, network, and telephone support. Critical servers and data will also need to be well-secured in appropriate environments.
- Design a communications plan that includes cellular telephones to communicate if you are displaced from your normal base of operations.
- Obtain help, if possible and appropriate, from your vendors, central campus computer services, peers, partners, and affiliates.

REFERENCES

Cunha, George Martin. 1992. "Disaster Planning and a Guide to Recovery Resources." *Library Technology Reports* 28: 533–624.

Kahn, Miriam B. 1998. *Disaster Response and Planning for Libraries*. Chicago: American Library Association.

Murphy, Joan H. 1991. "Taking the Disaster Out of Recovery." *Security Management* 35, No. 8: 60–66.

Toigo, Jon William. 1996. *Disaster Recovery Planning for Computers and Communication Resources*. New York: John Wiley.

14 Technical Services: Business-As-Usual Under Unusual Circumstances[1]

Holley R. Lange

INTRODUCTION AND PERSONAL ACCOUNT

Even as the water rose in the lower level of the Colorado State University's Morgan Library on the night of July 28, 1997, dozens of daily newspapers, hundreds of weekly and monthly journals, books purchased (perhaps for fall reserve), volumes sent for binding, many federal and state documents, and countless individual pieces of mail headed toward the library. Work left on desks, in boxes, and on shelves sat waiting for action. Dealing with business-as-usual aspects of a disaster experience is important for any organization or business, particularly one that directly serves the public. So, as much of the disaster team struggled in the early hours, days, and weeks to deal with the direct impact of the water on materials and the building, it was clear that plans also must be made to deal with this continuing flow of materials and mail into the library, with the maintenance of daily work to meet future needs, and with the library staff[2] responsible for these tasks. This chapter will summarize relevant disaster literature; examine issues involved in carrying on business-as-usual in technical services operations following a disaster, with examples taken from the weeks immediately following the disaster; and examine what is needed to provide continuity for technical services staff in libraries faced with equally major disasters.

Rain fell for hours on the west side of Fort Collins. Yards filled and streets ran full with water, taking over the concrete and running free, pouring through window wells and filling basements.

When the telephone calls began, it became clear that not only some of our lives and homes were affected, but our work, and perhaps our livelihood, as well. When the sun dawned on the 29th, the world, or at least the world that was the west side of town, was gravely changed. People, houses, and property were gone forever. Colorado State University, standing broadly in the path of the waters, was deeply impacted as well, with Morgan Library suffering a major blow.

The phone calls came in the middle of an otherwise sleepless night for some, in the early hours of the morning for others, or in the midst of preparations for a new work day. The telephone tree proposed in the disaster plan worked and was the first step toward recovery. And as the sun shone, the water stood deep around the library, filling the lower level, and making clear this was a disaster of enormous proportions. The library would be inaccessible for some time and some areas in the lower level housing technical services staff had been totally destroyed, but already plans for adapting to the new reality were underway.

REVIEW OF THE LITERATURE: DISASTER PLANS, CONTINGENCY PLANNING, AND CONTINUITY

No articles or books were expected to exist dealing with disaster activities of technical services units in situations paralleling that at Colorado State University. However, some literature provided background information on disaster recovery, business-as-usual efforts following a disaster, and personnel issues in disaster situations.

The library literature on disaster planning focuses more on remediation and recovery of materials. The business disaster literature focuses primarily on contingency plans, identification of core activities and the individuals needed to carry them out, alternate site location, and accessibility of computer data. In his analysis of disaster planning in museums and libraries, McCracken (1995) explains this basic difference in disaster responses of libraries or museums and businesses: a business can be moved with little interruption, and in this way contingency planning is more easily effected with backup computer systems and backup data at hand. However, museums and libraries are in large part their contents, so collections and service cannot be moved in a similar fashion following a disaster; and museum and library personnel also have an on-site obligation to protect the collection from further damage.

Since libraries are largely the material held within the walls, the online systems, and access to both, it is not surprising that the focus of library disaster literature is on those items, and generally on mitigation of damage and restoration, rather than on maintenance of existing operations (Fortson, 1992; George, 1994; Kahn, 1998). While in lesser disasters continuity may not be a problem, in larger events it is vital and must take place simultaneously with restoration, often under difficult circumstances. Little mention is made in the literature of continuing service or is brief, as presented by Nelms (1984), who notes its importance to their library in North Carolina following their 1984 water leak. No literature was identified specifically dealing with continuation of technical services operations during a major disaster nor with how that might have been carried out.

Disaster literature from the business world often addresses the importance of the basic disaster plan, contingency planning, and continuity. These plans recommend inclusion of a proposed alternate work site, off-site access to necessary computer and paper data, a pre-disaster agreement of work priorities and staffing plans, and the goal to resume operations quickly (Records Management, 1997; Duitch and Oppelt, 1997; Nemzow, 1997). If a business cannot continue its work in a timely and nearly seamless manner following a disaster, that in itself will assure a total disaster—complete business failure. Menkus (1994), while focusing on a data-processing disaster, emphasizes the importance of business continuity as part of the planning process and identification of essential activities so these can be restored quickly. Levitt (1997) discusses contingency management for an out-of-course event, stressing that planning may mitigate the resulting level of disaster. He includes information on recovery including re-establishing delivery of services. Nemzow (1997: 131) cautions that recovery planning not be specifically related to a particular type of disaster, but rather basic plans should be established that are not dependent on a particular type of misfortune. He further notes that "disaster recovery is not just equipment, hot sites, and materials. It also represents communications, people interaction, knowledge bases, workflows, strategy, and backup."

People are key in any emergency, and both library and business literature touch on the human or personnel aspects of disasters. Kahn (1998) includes emotional issues as part of the response and recovery phases to a disaster; Solomon (1994) discusses human resources against a variety of emergency situations; and Graham (1998) stresses the need for care and nurturing of employees in the adjustment of a business to the Grand Forks disaster in 1997. Ruyle and Schobernd (1997) comment on the emotional impact of a disaster and the importance of training as preparation for these human responses to disasters. Nemzow (1997) notes the frequent and simultaneous personal impacts on employees during times when businesses are hit by disasters. Higginbotham (1996) includes staffing issues as part of her recommended post-emergency steps needed following a disaster.

While it is nearly impossible to imagine the unknown, and equally difficult to plan for the unexpected, that is just what those writing disaster plans are asked to do. Drafting a disaster plan is itself a mitigating activity as it provides not only a plan but also a preview to problems. The Libraries' primary work of reference on disasters is the in-house disaster plan, which contains a partial page on the Services Recovery Coordinator that served as a pre-disaster basis for business-as-usual efforts should a major disaster occur (Colorado State University Libraries, 1996).

ONGOING WORK VERSUS THE DISASTER: ORGANIZATIONAL AND HUMAN DIMENSIONS

Technical services[3] units are generally computer and material dependent, so any continuation or resumption of operations following a disaster will require undamaged space, furniture, computers, online connections, materials, and appropriate staff. If this construct of needs cannot be met, or met quickly, then alternate activities might be needed or the implications of having inactive staff must be addressed. This section summarizes technical services actions and operations supporting business-as-usual activities following the disaster.

The Libraries' plan for services recovery suggests that, following a major disaster, options be developed for continuing or re-suming service; that departmental operations be continued based on a priority list of critical functions, noting high-priority activities, temporary operating procedures, facilities requirements, requirements for equipment, forms, and supplies; and that minimum staff be identified (Colorado State University Libraries, 1996). Following the disaster, a plan was quickly formulated that identified space, activities, required notifications, supervision, and reassignments. Although the time period was not then known, these activities would be ongoing until the return to Morgan Library one month after the disaster. In brief:

- The Libraries' Depository was selected for ongoing technical services operations.
- Priorities were set for work and communicated to the rest of the library.
- Based on proposed operations, equipment, furniture, supplies, and computer connections were identified and moved to or set up in the depository.
- A special project was developed based on utility, availability, staff, and material at hand to employ technical services staff at least in part until more complete operations could be resumed.
- Staff were identified to carry out necessary work.
- A communication system was set in place.
- Later, as possible, staff planned and effected a return to Morgan Library.

Even though Morgan Library would be inaccessible until electric and telecommunications systems could be repaired or replaced and the building cleaned and inspected, computers were in working condition and the online catalog was not damaged. For most of technical services located on the upper floors of the library, work remained as it had been left at the end of the day before the disaster; a bit more damp, perhaps, but untouched. However, the areas housing the Bindery, and Gifts and Exchange Units were in the lower level and were entirely submerged. The result was that files, equipment, computers, materials, and personal belongings in those areas, as well as some shipments ready for binding and some incoming books also temporarily housed in the lower level, were destroyed.

Since much of technical services work arrives regularly by mail, it was clear that any interruption in regular processing would rapidly result in a tremendous backlog which would impact our ability to meet the ongoing needs of students and faculty. While the disaster damage was overwhelming, any ongoing work would effect progress in the library and provide some normalcy for staff through routine processing of incoming materials. Making decisions that allowed this work was a beginning, but the details and implementation of the follow-through were at times complex and surprising. Some of these added complexities are addressed below.

CRITICAL OVERVIEW AND ASSESSMENT OF OPERATIONS

While operations may be thought of in terms of a physical place, material, equipment, and/or procedures, any overview of operations must include the more human aspects as well. Even though the work of technical services is important to your institution, staff, and users following any disaster, it is the human dimension of post-disaster activities that may prove to be most interesting and instructive.

Several issues are important when dealing with people in an emergency or post-emergency situation. These include communication, individual assignments, work conditions, extent of personal impact, and the natural variation people exhibit in adjusting to sudden changes. However, in many ways, people will rise to the occasion, applying themselves through hard work, ideas, flexibility, and good humor as they approach a drastically-changed work life. This section will examine technical services post-disaster operations, as well as underlying personnel issues that can arise as a result of these decisions.

Select a Work Site for Ongoing Technical Services Operations

Work environment impacts people, and as such the choice of work location brings with it the potential for greater human impact than most other decisions. Selection of an alternative work site should be based on finding a place where staff can approximate their work environment outside of the damaged facility. Proximity, size, services, and availability are all important.

Choice of work location brings with it a multitude of other issues that must be met from the basic setup to the more complex human issues. Clearly, in choosing an alternative location, the details of the choice can impact staff and the choice in itself may present complications and implications for work. A visit can help identify and envision setup and note any possible weaknesses. Things as simple but necessary as electrical outlets, location of phone jacks, potential safety problems, unfamiliar equipment, ventilation, available furniture, or parking space can quickly be seen.

The Libraries' off-site storage facility, or Depository, was selected for use by technical services staff and in part by Interlibrary Loan and Circulation. It was undamaged and only two blocks away from Morgan Library; had telephone and computer lines, a loading dock, book stacks, at least some work space; and was under the purview of the library.

The Depository was superficially familiar to many, but few knew it well, so a walk through in advance of occupancy was vital. There were no electrical outlets on one side of the building. While there were two telephone jacks, one was located near a noisy ventilation fan. Exits were noted as were location of fire alarms, condition of stairs, level of lighting, mechanics of the moveable shelves, and potential hazards. It seemed clear that a past emphasis on work-space ergonomics could no longer be a focus in this new situation. Because of the noisy fans, it would be difficult to communicate in parts of the building and difficult to know if people remained in the back areas of the building. There was only one bathroom, no drinking fountain, no separate area for lunch or breaks, and the amenities of candy and soft drink machines were no longer at hand.

Once your staff begin reporting to the temporary work site, they will be faced with new routines and new rules, such as uncomfortable and unfamiliar surroundings, a wider variety of fellow workers, no individual work space, less space overall, and constant changes in decisions related to their work. In almost every aspect of their work, the simple may become more complex.

Some examples of the challenges of working at a temporary work site come from our experience at the Depository. The area, although clean enough for its usual purposes, was too dirty to allow work without first cleaning shelves and other work surfaces. Shelves and other space were allotted and organized, only to have decisions changed again and again. A cellular telephone installed at the front of the building was answered with people summoned if possible or messages taken and posted on the wall (later another was put in place for outgoing calls, and the Depository's telephone also made available for use). Regular cleaning took some time to set up; concerns over safety demanded that a sign-in/out sheet be used to know if people remained in the building; staff were identified to open and close the building and keys assigned. Lockers stored in the building were cleaned and made available for personal belongings; and eventually bottled water was ordered for the building. Meetings were held outside, pausing as trains passed, their whistles drowning out all possibility of discussion, and frequent fire alarms caused by dust or spider webs in the alarms themselves caused even more outdoor gatherings.

Working in unusual surroundings can cause stress. While some may enjoy a variety of co-workers, when there is a new mixture of people working together under stressful conditions, initially there may be some jockeying for space, territory, and computers. But along with this, there will be a show of caring. In our case, food was brought in and shared, ice chests and a small refrigerator made available, and coffee prepared daily to help get the day started. Staff suggested and organized a pot-luck, labeled the "Ark in the Park," and a pizza party was given for everyone by the assistant dean for Technical Services.

Set Priorities For Work and Communicate Them to the Rest of the Organization

As an alternate work site is being identified, staff should begin to prioritize activities to assure, as much as possible, a business-as-usual approach to the work of technical services. Priorities largely will be common-sense, but their identification formalizes what must be done, what could be done even if of a lower priority, and

A welcomed break—pizza party at the Depository.

what could not be done. All this effort aids in identifying necessary equipment, staff, and time frame. It is critical to consider what must be done and what might be delayed; to examine work for possible temporary exceptions to procedures that might be needed for work in unaccustomed surroundings, limited staff, or limited equipment; to consider space and equipment issues; to explore the direct impact of the disaster on needed files, equipment and materials; and to consider the personnel implications of any decision. Once determined, the priorities must be shared across the library, and as necessary with faculty and students, since this will help provide the assurance that ongoing operations will soon be underway.

Priorities in the Technical Services units at Morgan Library were established as follows, and communicated via a fact sheet compiled by staff in Technical Services soon after the disaster. These were quickly distributed in print as well as verbally.

ACQUISITIONS SERVICES (ACQUISITIONS, SERIALS, AND GIFTS AND
EXCHANGE)

Since placing and receiving orders and payment for same is the
key work of Acquisitions Services, staff rapidly established rush
orders as a clear priority. One staff member, then telecommuting,
had the resources at hand to make any such orders from home.
Acquisitions staff also rapidly placed calls to vendors to halt all
incoming orders, although one shipment of approval books already on its way to the library was eventually received. Exceptions to normal processing were made for this order. As selectors
could not easily review the shipment, all items were accepted,
altering, at least momentarily, the usual procedures that included
subject selector overview. Vendors were immediately cooperative,
held shipments, and responded with special consideration, offering assistance, kind words and encouragement, and accepted the
reality of delayed billing. There were some problems, however,
when incoming calls from vendors were unavailable, captured in
voicemail messages but not accessible from the outside. Vendor
relations are all important, even in ordinary times, but good vendor relations built up over years are invaluable during unusual
times, and these relationships were key to Acquisitions Services'
ability to adjust work following the disaster. Like many other technical services units, Acquisitions required computers with OCLC
connections, access to the online catalog, and some of their own
files for work to continue in the new setting.

In the Serials Unit, receipt of incoming journals must be immediate and ongoing. This required early decisions on mail handling,
serials check-in, interim storage of materials, and potential for stu-
dent/faculty access to these materials. As soon as the Depository
was available for use, space for incoming journals was allotted;
and when computers were set up, staff began to receive incoming materials. The unit required computers, specialized label and
claims printers, and considerable work space for the serial check-
in process. Just getting computers and needed printers working
was complex and time consuming. Certain portions of the normal workflow had to be worked around, as in stacks checking
usually done before claiming missing journals. To further complicate work of the Serials Unit, they were at a transition period moving the Periodicals Room from their supervision to Public Services.

The Gifts and Exchange offices, located in the lower level, were totally destroyed, eliminating files, materials in process, and personal belongings. However, the staff member involved in that work was quickly called upon in two ways: first, to act, as needed, as supervisor for Acquisitions staff in the Depository, and second, to begin initial processing of promised disaster replacement gifts as offers began to come in from around the country.

CATALOGING (COPY CATALOGING, DATABASE MAINTENANCE, ORIGINAL CATALOGING)

Copy Cataloging established rush cataloging as a priority, and computers, tables, printers, and connections were soon available for that and continued work on priority items in process before the disaster. Additional materials were received and cataloged at the Depository, including new books, as well as a shipment of dissertations and theses returned from the bindery. Work was continued as possible, since any decrease in cataloging could impact number of titles added, and so might well result in a decrease for the year.

Database Maintenance staff were involved in the special project identified and described below and in the related linking project as they had this expertise. Supervisors in the unit were heavily involved in broader recovery activities, but also trained other staff in barcode linking. Several staff from Database Maintenance assisted in receiving documents shipments.

Original cataloging continued with rush materials received set as a priority. Other items were not processed as quickly as possible because of a lack of available materials and cataloging tools, although some were available online. Again, there were concerns about maintaining statistics, and especially, the related cataloging credits for original cataloging on OCLC. Portable items, such as several slim government documents volumes in series, were selected for cataloging as they could be easily carried out of the library for work off-site.

DOCUMENTS PROCESSING

The aim of the Documents Processing unit was to continue to receive and process shipments from the Government Printing Office which involved opening, marking and re-boxing as possible. Non-depository items were to be accumulated for the interim. Since the shelflist remained in Morgan Library, some work was not possible, such as the manual check-in. Work with the microtext collection was also postponed until the return to Morgan. The staff needed a telephone if ordering from the *Federal Register* was to continue, but finding one in a quiet area proved impossible in the Depository, and an alternate site was not found for several weeks.

PRESERVATION SERVICES (BINDERY, STACKS, MARKING AND REPAIR, SHIPPING AND RECEIVING)

The Bindery Unit was directly impacted by the disaster with offices, files, and personal belongings all lost; so the possibility for regular work by this group was greatly impacted. A bindery shipment received just prior to the disaster was lost, as were other materials being processed to send out. Bindery staff processed a bindery delivery while in the Depository which included dissertations and theses, as well as other materials. Not being able to set up the business-as-usual aspects of the Bindery Unit was difficult from an organizational, and more importantly, from a personal view. And a later decision not to bind journals would further impact work in the unit for the coming year. Since the Bindery Unit receives completed dissertations and theses from Colorado State University students, temporary arrangements were made for students to bring these directly to the Graduate School Office in the weeks immediately following the disaster.

The Shipping and Receiving Unit quickly resumed processing mail as an early priority with newspapers important because of their numbers, currency, and the dependence, particularly among international students, on them. Staff in this unit were among the longest displaced from Morgan Library, only returning when the new loading dock was completed.

Staff in the Marking and Repair Unit also assisted with the mail, and some also were called on initially to help professors with damaged books. Eventually, staff in this unit were able to set up their equipment to process/mark books through the unit.

Staff working in the Stacks Unit also assisted with the barcoding project and with the mail. An attempt was made to employ students from the Stacks Unit where possible, and while some worked on the barcoding project others found jobs elsewhere.

Identify, Move, and Set Up Equipment, Furniture, Supplies, and Computer Connections at the Temporary Work Site

Although establishing priorities will provide the basis for what materials and equipment are needed, clearly needing and getting are not necessarily related in a disaster situation; and, even if and when needs are met, the setup will likely be markedly different from what had been available pre-disaster. However, setting priorities for work in each of the units helps define what staff and equipment will be needed in your temporary site. At Morgan Library, within days of the disaster, some staff were allowed to enter the library, grab supplies, work in process, needed forms and files, ergonomic chairs, book trucks, and reference materials, and hand carry these down unlit stairways so they could be transported or rolled over to the Depository.

While efforts are made to bring needed equipment and supplies to your temporary work site, certain things will be lacking. In our case, tables were regular height, rather than the lower computer workstation height, resulting in potential ergonomic problems. The tables faced the windows, sometimes sunny and sometimes open, making control of glare and air difficult, and lighting problematic. There was barely space to move behind chairs at the workstations, and certainly not if someone had a book truck in close proximity. Simple supplies, such as pencils, staplers, foot rests, work holders were often in limited supply, while other supplies were quickly ordered and abundant.

Make sure computers are available, and connections made early in the transition to the temporary work site since they are key in allowing a return to necessary routines. The lack of full equipment and space may necessitate intensive scheduling of computers, rather than allowing staff to work according to accustomed patterns. However, with equipment at hand and priorities set, at least some of the time, staff could shift back into the more com-

Business-as-usual under unusual circumstances—at work in the Depository.

fortable routines of usual work. At the Depository, because of limited seating, staff often stood to do non-computer work or sat outside, on steps, or in their cars parked nearby.

Redeploy Staff for Special Projects as Needed

Business-as-usual is the goal following a disaster; but when faced with a disaster of broad impact, this may not be possible to the extent necessary to employ all staff. Developing special projects based on utility, availability, staff, and materials at hand may be necessary to employ staff at least in part until more complete operations can be resumed. While some will be involved in the recovery effort, and some with certain aspects of usual operations, what will others do?

Within Technical Services, the barcoding project, as it became known, quickly became the subject of discussion and controversy for staff. It was clear from the beginning that if all technical services staff were to be employed, at least initially, some alterna-

Special projects—barcoding in the Depository.

tive activities would be needed. For years there had been discussion about the possibility of a barcoding project at the Depository. Many of the materials housed there, particularly journal volumes, had been transferred to the facility without barcodes, and item records for these materials were lacking in the online catalog. With the sudden loss of a major portion of the collection, it became even more important to have a precise inventory of the exact volumes held in the storage facility so that it would be clear what had been located in Morgan Library and what was in the Depository, and so that all materials still held by the library could be available to faculty and students. Staff assigned to the Depository could examine volumes, adding barcodes as needed, then later add item records linked to the title in the online catalog as time and equipment allowed.

While the intent of any special project may be positive, and the project itself is useful, it may raise some complex emotions. Many of your staff will be glad to be at work, but there could be considerable discussion as to whether or not the special project is make work or necessary work. When explanations are given about the task, early and ongoing communication can help to assure staff that the project is real and necessary.

Identify Staff to Carry Out Necessary Work

Just identifying necessary staff and finding a place for them to work will not guarantee a seamless or stress-free operation. Following a disaster, some staff will be pulled off of usual tasks to address the recovery process which, by necessity, will demand more from others working in the business-as-usual operations; for example, supervisory staff may be substitutes, and everyone will be under additional pressures. Hold early meetings for discussions on who will be involved in the core recovery effort, who is and will be scheduled to be away from the library, and who might be available to take over the work, particularly supervisory responsibilities. These meetings will offer an opportunity to discuss the longer-term implications of the disaster. Staff from many units could suddenly find themselves assigned to the temporary work site. What may seem a straightforward assignment of similar staff to similar tasks could cause additional stress. The propensity for conflict can be great, so be prepared for possible initial competition for space and equipment that might be compounded by unfamiliar supervisors directing work and many decisions and revisions in setting up schedules and work spaces.

It may be necessary to be flexible in enforcing rules and procedures and/or to establish new but temporary ones. For example, the use of the Depository introduced new safety issues with requisite rule-setting, from things as simple as suggestions not to wear sandals because of the wooden stairs, to the requirement to sign in and out on a daily basis, to dealing with differing supervisory styles, to adapting to poor ergonomics, poor lighting, and difficult working conditions. Some found a different environment an interesting experience, and others welcomed the informality of working in the Depository. While stress at times occasioned harsh words, these were frequently balanced by humor and caring.

Set a Communication System in Place Immediately

Communication, always important, becomes even more so following a disaster. People are under stress, away from usual routines, and perhaps coping with personal disasters as well. Plans will undoubtedly change quickly as efforts are made to deal with the disaster. Communication can be enhanced at the temporary work site by having one person assigned to receive and relay telephone messages, to greet and direct visitors, and work as a liaison with the administration. Make sure supervisors meet frequently with staff, and that supervisors meet together as well. However, even frequent meetings and discussions cannot assuage all concerns. Distance from the administrative center of disaster operations and from usual colleagues can be isolating. If you have e-mail, make it available quickly. Consider issuing a temporary newsletter designed specifically for staff communications during disaster recovery.

The need for communication during and after a disaster cannot be over emphasized, although perhaps it is impossible to fully meet this need. It is difficult to understand and digest information in stressful situations, and sometimes basic explanations can be overlooked when much needs to be done. Communication must also involve more than talking, but listening as well, with time for staff to talk and express concerns and to be acknowledged and heard clearly. Make counseling available as soon as possible after the disaster. This is extremely important and allows a different type of communication necessary following a disaster when difficult situations cannot be changed, but still must be faced (see Chapter 2).

Plan for Your Staff to Return to the Library

Following all but the most terrible disasters, eventually there will be a return to normalcy—to familiar or at least more permanent routines and facilities. Ultimately, the goal for all staff working at the temporary site is to return to your library and back to business-as-usual. This process, by necessity and design, can be much more gradual than the initial temporary move and will involve people, equipment, and materials.

It was our experience that on one level staff looked forward to a return to Morgan Library, but on another level they were anxious and had many mixed emotions. And, as the return move was only one part in the ongoing disaster recovery activity that included the need to begin classes on schedule and simultaneously reopen the library, there was neither opportunity nor thought of formally recognizing this return.

Staff may express concerns about safety, air quality, and possible contamination of materials in your library. Will the air be breathable? Can the water in the drinking fountains cause problems? Is the building truly safe? Anxiety may appear again, since by the time of the return to the original site the temporary site will have become the more familiar place providing a sense of security and safety which can be difficult to relinquish. This could be a second loss of place and another loss of familiar routines. A gradual return to your library may be helpful in producing a smooth transition.

At Morgan Library, having had previous problems with air quality in past years, many Technical Services staff were unsure that assurances actually meant the building would be safe. "Clean to the walls" appeared to mean one thing to those overseeing environmental safety, and another to staff as they observed mud still visible on the lower-level floor.

The move back into Morgan Library itself was hard, just as the outward move had been. The materials and equipment moved to the Depository had to be returned, books, journals, supplies and furniture, all had to make the return trip; and for a time, some staff worked at the Depository while others worked in the library, splitting some units. The barcoding project continued long after most other activities had ceased in the Depository, and the mail operation was ongoing there for many months.

Conditions in Morgan Library were not without problems. Elevators did not work so everything had to be hand carried back up the stairs, air systems were not working well with temperatures either very high or very low, depending on the part of the building; and in part of the Technical Services area, the air was extremely humid. For the return to the library, journals were sorted by call number and boxed, loaded into a car, and then hand carried up the stairs to the Periodical Room. The Bindery and Gifts and Exchange Units, having lost everything in their offices, had to begin again with temporary furniture and temporary space, and different tasks.

THE HUMAN DIMENSION

As previously noted, people are critical to the entire post-disaster operation—the successes will come from everyone involved in the work. But it is through and from these individuals that the hardest lessons will come to light. It is vital to remember that people react and adjust at different levels and over different periods of time. Any way that can be used to remind all staff of this, particularly supervisors, will help in the overall adjustment process, although understanding this disparity is needed at all levels. It is unrealistic to believe that people can move from disaster to a new situation seamlessly; problems are inevitable, but leaders will emerge to take over when needed and staff will employ ingenuity, humor, and caring to face each new situation. Relationships which develop over time are invaluable in disaster situations since a foundation of trust and respect can ease disaster-created difficulties. Acknowledge that your staff will experience different emotions based on how the disaster affects them at work and/or at home. Arrange counseling sessions for individuals and/or work units. Be prepared for these sessions to be emotionally charged.

Although a part of Technical Services, some Morgan Library staff assigned to the Depository felt more like outsiders than others. Technical Services was treated as an integrated unit, but each part continued to have disparate needs and was accustomed to their own staffing; and certainly, the disaster may have driven units to focus more inward.

There was also a disparity in the immediacy of disaster impact. Two units, the Gifts and Exchange Unit and the Bindery Unit, lost all equipment, files, work, and personal materials in their offices, and they were not officially allowed to retrieve items—even those of special personal importance. The extent of this loss, although widely known, was not always publicly acknowledged; and those staff members often felt isolated from others because of this difference and perceived lack of empathy about their situation.

At the Depository, the amount and variety of work accomplished was impressive, and people assumed unfamiliar roles, stepping in as needed. Business-as-usual was effected quite quickly, and many felt that the work was worthwhile. They were glad to be working, but most would have liked to be involved more directly with overall recovery efforts. Lack of control of the situation, lack of routine, lack of familiar place, and lack of simple comforts challenged everyone.

CONCLUSION

Identifying the ongoing work to be done is perhaps the most straightforward of post-disaster activities. But when determining how the work can be done, where, with what staff, and with what equipment, problems rapidly become apparent. Added to that are the natural differences in human nature and the disaster that impact people in many real and ongoing ways.

Consider all the possible ways to get the necessary work done with the materials, equipment, space, and staff available; but in the drive to accomplish a great deal in a very short time, be sure to remember the most important resources at hand—the people, their skills, their needs, and their own difficulties.

In summary, what follows in the next section are some recommendations to consider when faced with a disaster such at that at Colorado State University, in terms of the work itself, and the individuals carrying out that work.

Library Disaster Planning and Recovery Handbook

KEY RECOMMENDATIONS

Staffing in Technical Services

- Plan and prioritize ongoing work, but expect that these decisions will be fluid and change as work progresses.
- Understand that people are key in successfully weathering any disaster, and their experience, expertise, flexibility, and ingenuity in facing the disaster will go beyond all expectations.
- Expect that the previous levels of trust developed over time be magnified and returned during a disaster.
- Realize that actions and decisions that show interest in and caring for staff during a disaster are extremely important, particularly for those dealing with personal disasters in addition to the work-related disaster.
- Understand that human response to a disaster may vary enormously, since individuals bring a variety of personalities and experiences to the disaster.
- Develop an effective communication process. Communication is vital, but during a disaster messages may get lost, even those communicated directly and repeated often. Therefore, patience, listening, and understanding should be the goal—some prefer written communication, others a personal touch.
- Because in a disaster counseling is important, offer these services quickly with a variety of approaches. Early in the disaster some may not realize the need for and importance of this type of assistance; some may resist counseling initially, but might respond later. Some may prefer individual meetings, while others appreciate the support of a group session.
- Understand that life will not stand still during a disaster. The good and bad of everyday life will carry on—some people or their families will be seriously ill, some will take vacations, others will quit, and others will experience any measure of personal problems. Even during a disaster, all these ordinary difficulties, stressful in the best of times, also must be faced and resolved.
- Acknowledge what is being done, but remember that verbal thanks may not be enough nor be immediately appreciated.
- Realize that, in choosing an alternate work location, there may be hidden challenges in setup, space, availability of ordinary amenities, or equipment that may drastically impact staff.
- Expect that staff whose job assignments may change during a disaster situation will want to have input into these changes.
- Be aware that people will want to help directly with the disaster, and any other work may seem much less important. Be prepared to deal with this since your disaster-recovery situation may not allow all staff to be involved in disaster recovery.

ENDNOTES

1. Thanks go to the following individuals who shared their recollections of the time spent in the Depository so that I could more nearly present an accurate picture of the work there: Donnice Cochenour, Nora Copeland, Mary Gray, Eleanor Millis, Bonnie Mueller, Patricia Smith, Maryann Snyder, and Cheryl Wells. I only wish I could have included the stories I heard in talking with everyone. Any errors in the chapter are mine alone.

2. "Staff" here is defined to be faculty and/or classified staff.

3. While the work of technical services departments is generally known, each library has its own way to divide responsibilities. At the Colorado State University Libraries, Technical Services includes: Acquisitions Services (Monographs, Serials, Gifts and Exchange); Cataloging Services (Copy Cataloging, Database Maintenance, and Original Cataloging); Preservation Services (Bindery, Shelving, Shipping and Receiving, Marking, and Repair); and Documents, which at the time of the disaster was in transition from a separate department to one that would be absorbed in part by Acquisitions and Cataloging Services. Staff included seven librarians, more than 30 classified staff, and numerous students, especially those involved in shelving.

REFERENCES

Colorado State University Libraries. 1996. *Disaster Recovery Manual.*

Duitch, Dennis, and Terri Oppelt. 1997. "Disaster and Contingency Planning: A Practical Approach." *Law Practice Management* (January/February): 36–39.

Fortson, Judith. 1992. *Disaster Planning and Recovery: A How-To-Do-It Manual for Librarians and Archivists.* New York: Neal-Schuman.

George, Susan C. 1994. *Emergency Planning and Management in College Libraries.* ACRL CLIP Note #17. Chicago, IL: Association of College and Research Libraries.

Graham, Alan. 1998. "When the River Ran Wild." *Security Management* (March):46–51.

Higginbotham, Barbara Buckner. 1996. "'It Ain't Over 'Til It's Over': The Process of Disaster Recovery." *Technicalities* 16 (May): 12–13.

Kahn, Miriam B. 1998. *Disaster Response and Planning for Libraries.* Chicago: American Library Association.

Levitt, Alan M. 1997. *Disaster Planning and Recovery: A Guide for Facility Professionals*. New York: Wiley.

McCracken, Peter. 1995. *The Crucial Inadequacy: Disaster Planning in Libraries and Museums*. Master's paper. University of North Carolina at Chapel Hill. (April): 7.

Menkus, Belden. 1994. "New Importance of Business Continuity in Data Processing." *Computers & Security* 13, No.2: 115–118.

Nelms, Willie. 1984. "One Library's Response to Disaster." *North Carolina Libraries* 42 (Fall): 140–142.

Nemzow, Martin. 1997. "Business Continuity Planning." *International Journal of Network Management* 7:127–136.

Records Management. 1997. "Part C—Disaster Recovery—A Planned Approach." *www.system.missouri.edu/records/partc.html*.

Ruyle, Carol J., and Elizabeth M. Schobernd. 1997. "Disaster Recovery Without the Disaster." *Technical Services Quarterly* 14, No. 4:13–24.

Solomon, Charlene. 1994. "Bracing for Emergencies." *Personnel Journal* 73, No. 4: 74–83.

15 Upstairs/Downstairs: Implementing a Processing Center for Restoring the Collection

Patricia Smith

INTRODUCTION

"It's going to be UGLY!" Those words from our consultant proved to be prophetic as the Library Disaster Recovery Team (LDRT) began discussions for processing gifts, now over 900,000 items, and some 462,500 water-damaged volumes. Under pressure from the university and desiring to provide users with a restored collection as soon as possible, the LDRT—the assistant director for Technical Services, the coordinator for Preservation, the coordinator for Acquisitions, and the head of Database Maintenance—joined the university's consultant for damage recovery to plan and operate a local processing center designed to process over 1,000,000 volumes and pieces in two years' time.

BACKGROUND

The July 28, 1997, disaster that scattered chaos throughout the campus brought to the university a damage-recovery consultant with experience in coping with physical cleanup and restoration. Because State Civil Service regulations require that temporary employees on the job for six months become permanent, the university decided to hire this same damage-recovery consultant to implement and manage a local processing facility to process gifts and to reintroduce to the collection the freeze-dried materials soon to be returning from treatment in Texas. When the first test materials from Texas arrived, library staff immediately saw that any gift in good condition would look and smell better than a book that

361

had been water-damaged, and our insurance representatives agreed that gifts would be cheaper to process than restoring or repurchasing damaged materials. Given certain problems and delays in preparing the database for disaster-damaged materials, moreover, the LDRT decided that gifts should be processed during the first year of operation while water-damaged materials would be dealt with in the second year.

After examining potential sites to house the Processing Center, the university concluded that using a portion of the water-damaged lower-level of the library was the cheapest option. Locating the Center in the library would also make the inevitable consultations between upstairs library staff and downstairs Center personnel quick and convenient. The university accordingly built temporary, plywood walls to isolate the Processing Center so that restorations to the remainder of the lower level might proceed. Our contractor, meanwhile, was working with two local employment agencies to find temporary staff quickly.

In October 1997, scarcely more than two months after the disaster, we brought over 200 temporary workers into the gutted lower level of the library for their first orientation session. On that day we became acutely aware of the magnitude of what we were facing and just how ugly things could be.

IMPLEMENTATION ISSUES

Other libraries might find the following issues as helpful considerations when setting up similar operations:

Selecting the Management of a Local Out-Processing Facility

Our most important advice to others, of course, is to write a contract that gives librarians control over legitimate professional concerns and provides for resolution by knowledgeable experts when short-term profitability conflicts with long-term usability. More importantly, the contract should stipulate that the contractor should report directly to the library.

The university's decision to hire the same consultant who helped with the general disaster-cleanup effort on campus to manage the Processing Center meant that an individual with largely physical cleanup experience, such as that resulting from the World Trade Center bombing, faced a steep learning curve regarding library technical services operations. University librarians, similarly, unaccustomed to the manners and modes of a for-profit organization had just as much to learn. These professional differences did not always make our relationship an easy alliance and led to many interesting departures of opinion.

For example, early in the project, we learned that personnel in the Processing Center downstairs had been told that they had been restricted to the downstairs. Upstairs was strictly off-limits unless they had official business upstairs. We recognized, of course, that Processing staff assigned to the graveyard shift should not be upstairs late at night when the library was closed, but were unprepared for the contractor's quick approach to security and supervision. We eventually clarified that Center staff, as Colorado citizens, could have access to library public service areas when their breaks or lunch hours occurred during the library's regular hours.

Not all differences were as amicably resolved. As librarians and supervisors of staff, we are used to investing in staff as long-term resources; a for-profit, temporary agency, on the other hand, makes no long-term commitment. When the center's staff were discontented about a personnel policy, as a result, it was difficult for us to step aside and let the contractor rule. While we were successful in insisting on certain adjustments, we compiled a losing record on such concerns. When system downtime occurred or when one area ran out of work of a particular kind, for example, the center's policy was to send staff home without pay. As a result, some staff summarily quit, and our arguments, especially when we were responsible for much of the training of new staff, went unheeded. Similarly, having become accustomed to new hires through the temporary employment agencies, we were surprised when the contractor dropped one agency and asked staff to move to the other agency. Then, a year into the project, we learned that the contractor—upon learning that the State of Colorado required that a contractor supervise staff directly rather than letting hiring agencies handle supervision—had formed his own hiring agency for temporary staff and required that all center staff transfer to his agency. But would new hires be of the same quality as those from established agencies? And whose business was it if they weren't?

Unfortunately, not ours, or not ours directly. Not only does Colorado law forbid state agencies from hiring temporary employees for more than six months, it also prohibits state employees from supervising employees from outside agencies. Although library staff had written the procedures, did the majority of the training, and reviewed work for quality control, our changes or suggestions had to be routed through a hierarchy of supervisors in the Center. This complicated personnel scheme was perhaps the most frustrating part of the operation. Roles were never clear. The contractor had the right to establish rules that could lead to resignations, but when they occurred, library staff were faced with extensive retraining. Rightly or wrongly, we felt that policies leading to frequent turnover were our concern. We also argued that restrictive policies in the Center reflected badly on the university and could generate poor public relations. The library and the university, not the contractor, we felt, would live with the aftermath of an operation that might leave disgruntled employees.

Another interconnected responsibility similarly led to continuing disagreement: the proper balance between quality and quantity. As service-oriented librarians, we are committed to the long-term quality of our collections, and we readily accept the often complex procedures required to maintain quality. A short-term contractor, on the other hand, may be given incentive to speed the project and adopt any procedure that results in cost-savings. Each contract may have different provisions that might affect the nature of the work. As an expert in physical cleanup operations, our contractor was used to simplifying processes to get the job done quickly. Processing gifts, he often implied, should be no more complicated than replacing a damaged copy of *Catcher in the Rye* with a gift copy—one book, same title, add the call number and throw it on the shelf to replace the damaged copy. But, as librarians know, even adding a book as clear cut as this Salinger novel is not always a simple step and may raise questions: What edition did the library own? Was the gift copy the same edition? Was it a true different edition or just a different printing? Such oversimplification, as assuming all materials are single-edition novels, hardly spoke to a multiple-part gift that was bound differently from the original item we lost or a journal record for volumes damaged in the disaster that had incomplete item records. Even some of our own university officials often were attracted to such simplified, *Catcher-in-the-Rye* solutions while we librarians had nightmares of being saddled with massive cleanup projects after the Processing Center was dissolved.

Care in selecting a manager, obviously, is important, and flexibility on both sides is necessary. Our contractor succeeded in making it clear to us that he was in control of the daily operation of the Center and would run his operation as he thought best, and we more consistently focused our efforts on the level of accuracy necessary with a good deal less regard for how he achieved it.

Sizing the Operation and Setting Time Frames

Setting up an operation to reprocess materials and handle gifts after a disaster has elements basic to setting up any new operation. What chiefly distinguishes a disaster recovery is the speed at which everything must go forward. In-depth analysis is rarely possible, especially when a parent institution or other factors intervene, and acting without strong data is common (we referred to our method for moving ahead as "throwing mud at a wall and seeing what stuck"). Such a method, of course, means that you have to be prepared for deadlines that could not be met, major shifts in how and when to process material, and the like.

Nevertheless, decisions and implementation deadlines are necessary even if alterations must occur later. At the library, we knew we had over 460,000 damaged volumes to return to the library shelves and an indeterminate number of gifts to process. Library staff and university administrators agreed that 18 to 24 months from the July disaster was a crucial time frame for doing so. That meant we needed an operation large enough to deal with no fewer than 7,000 items per week or 26,000 per month.

Once you have determined, through whatever means, your production requirement, you need to estimate the staff, equipment, and space needed. Not knowing how much individual attention certain materials might require, you nonetheless must attempt to break down as many anticipated activities as possible into measurable units of work to arrive at the time required to carry out each task.

In our case, how we wished that we had done all those time/motion studies and statistics for hourly production that we had been postponing until some better time! Library literature, we found, offered little useful data, probably because library operations differ greatly from institution to institution. As a result, we often found ourselves quickly timing an activity or relying on knowledge of statistics for similar activities, such as searching in online catalogs, to produce rough estimates.

Breaking each activity down in this way was useful for another important reason as well: generally, the key to the success of a temporary operation with high productivity as one of its primary goals is to break the work into simple tasks so that even unskilled staff can learn it quickly and perform it without extensive supervision. Thus, after you have defined the activities, you need to group them into plausible positions so that you would know what skills are required.

For example, receiving gift materials and sorting them into journal piles and book piles are two activities that the same position could perform. Both activities require no computer skills, minimal training, and the same general space and equipment, namely shelving or a book truck. On the other hand, matching a volume to the record in the library's database requires basic typing and sufficient computer skill to know how to move around in a system and to manipulate its data. These activities, obviously, required network connections, a workstation, certain supplies, and appropriate space. Defining the jobs in this way will also help you to prepare job descriptions as well as to determine the space, equipment, and supplies required by each position.

Next, you need to estimate the number of positions, pieces of equipment, and square feet of space required. Our initial figures projected over 200 staff. Since we did not have a facility large enough to house that many staff, we considered multiple shifts up to a continuous operation running 24 hours a day, 7 days a week. Multiple shifts, however, bring added complications: would library staff be paid extra to conduct training sessions at 1:00 a.m. or to be available at 5:00 a.m. when unforeseen complications arose? What about security and supervision? For a variety of causes, we later moved to just one shift for the gifts operation, but we opted initially for two shifts, overlapping, at least in part, normal work hours of key members of the library staff. When document recovery begins, we expect to resume two shifts. Two shifts, of course, cut certain needs in half—number of workstations, for example—but not all: the supervisor of the early shift, for example, requires filing space separate from that of the supervisor of the second shift. Properly sizing an operation also requires attention to other spaces as well, for example, conference space when library staff consult with the project staff.

Finding and Designing a Facility

Again, like all new operations, finding an appropriate facility for a recovery operation is a major consideration. An on-site production facility will require significant space for processing and storage. Finding an appropriate facility for a large, even temporary, operation requires a footprint describing the operation as a physical layout. Such a design is most helpful not only in selecting a facility but also in picturing and planning the way that the materials will flow through it. Since loading docks for receiving materials are necessary, for example, a building with no dock won't work; and buildings with docks will work best if materials flow naturally from the dock to the appropriate in-plant process. Attention to local, state, and federal building codes is also important. Many institutions already have standards covering square-foot listings for workstations, aisles, shelving, restrooms, and the like. Light and power needs must be established along with the location of telephones, fax machines, copiers, power outlets, and data lines.

Networking connections are also essential for restoration work. Automated databases for tracking data pertinent to the restoration process allow assessment of progress and analysis of results. Support of communications with partners, such as your binderies, in the restoration process is critical in high-volume operations. The production and transmission of electronic files speed the processes and provide up-to-date information for users about availability of materials that have been restored.

Planning for adequate resources should include an assessment of the demands for computing memory, storage, and backup and what computing facilities will be used. If the library's current computers host a network operation for the processing center, the im-

A view of the Processing Center in the lower level of the library, showing the long processing tables quickly constructed by university Facilities staff.

pact on regular operations must be identified. In our case, the Processing Center had up to 75 workstations with network connections operating at one time.

Resources will most likely have to be assembled immediately; so finding available stores of supplies and equipment will need to be done quickly. It may be possible to develop a local alternative for customized needs. The university's Facilities Department constructed book trucks and tables for Processing Center activities. The tables, in particular, were exactly suited to the performance of specific restorative functions.

As you work on these details, you will soon realize that work spaces for temporary workers need not match the same expectation for comfortable surroundings as for full-time workers. For example, long tables with power strips down the middle could serve as computer stations for eight people, four on each side. Workers did not need privacy walls. Floors could be concrete. Break areas could be Spartan. One librarian observed that the local arrangement was comparable to a sweatshop operation.

Armed with a footprint prepared with the help of staff from

your facilities department, you will need to survey your internal and external environments for an appropriate facility. You may turn to other options, from local realtors helping to find community resources to consideration of prefabricated buildings that could be placed near your library. In our case, to save on space requirements, we considered splitting our operations into those that house staff and those that house materials so that truck trailers might be used for storage of materials while staff worked in safer places. Our choices were limited by the lack of commercially available space in the community. Even if we had opted for a warehouse on the edge of town, we faced fixing the space to code and dealing with additional transportation issues since bus lines did not extend that far. Commercial space has another disadvantage as it may not be available long term and is not likely to be cheap. Library and university personnel, after exploring these and other options, determined, finally, that the gutted lower level would be the best place for the first year of operation. Even that option was not ideal as there were implications for service to our users by delaying the remodeling of the damaged area. In the second year of operation, as renovations in the lower level proceeded and books began to be introduced there, the university and the contractor moved the operation to a condemned dormitory on campus.

You may need to be concerned about providing transportation and access to the facility for workers and delivery vans as part of other considerations for providing an adequate facility. Does the facility have parking spaces nearby? Is there a bus line nearby? Can delivery trucks get to the loading dock? Parking on the Colorado State campus is limited so our contractor arranged for center staff to park in a nearby hotel's large lot and provided buses to transport them to and from the Processing Center.

Finding a Work Force

When disasters strike, public institutions often find volunteers in the community willing to help in the recovery effort. When floods inundated Florence, Italy, in 1966, hundreds of students volunteered for various restoration projects in the aftermath of the disaster. The city of Fort Collins and Colorado State University similarly benefited from volunteers who helped in the early days after the disaster; but, as the Florentines discovered, volunteers rarely sign-on for more than a few days or weeks, and training costs soon exceed the value gained, especially when long hours of dull work are required (Bennon, 1967).

Given the magnitude of your project and the exacting but unexciting work required, you should seriously consider not appealing to volunteers. Although options for staffing can include your current staff, a large-scale disaster will exceed the capability of library staff. There will, however, be positions of oversight and monitoring that can be assigned to experienced library staff. Hiring additional staff will require major personnel and administrative resources to recruit, interview, and provide human resource support to these staff. Contracting out this activity will alleviate strain on your library and may be required by state regulations.

One of the several roles of our contractor for restoration services was to supply a labor force. Without interfering in the legal sense with the contractor's relationship as employer of personnel, we were careful to specify in the contract what skills were required for the jobs. Our contractor also subcontracted with other agencies, such as the binderies, for part of the work.

Geographic location and city size, of course, determine how fast a large work force of temporary staff can be assembled. You may find that you have hiring restrictions like those we experienced. If that is the case, look to temporary employment agencies to assist you with finding and managing your labor pool. In some areas of the country, a library or contractor wishing to hire staff might have turned to agencies listed on the Internet with library-skilled staff. Most such agencies, however, are located near heavily populated areas on the coasts.

Located in a university town of about 100,000 in an attractive part of the country, our contractor, despite the era of full-employment we enjoyed nationwide, was able to find two hundred qualified employees in a remarkably short few weeks. Like many others in college towns, he might have turned to the campus employment office or hired large numbers of those many students willing to do temporary work, but he wanted only full-time employees and did not want to use part-time workers because of the additional bookkeeping and scheduling required. Still, he found

Processing Center staff check library online catalog to match gifts to records.

everyone needed, some of whom, it turned out, were students attracted to the hours of the late shift, which ran from 3:30 p.m. to 1:00 a.m.

What the contractor did initially was to turn to two local temporary employment agencies. Like such agencies generally do, these two companies advertise in the local newspapers and greatly simplify employment, supervision, and payment. Because of the large number of such employees, our contractor required the agencies to send supervisors for such matters as attendance, notifications of changes in schedule, firing, and the like. But, as mentioned previously, state regulations later required the contractor to assume the full role of employer to the Processing Center employees; and the temporary agencies were dismissed.

In general, we were pleased with the staff who worked in the Processing Center. Despite the temporary nature of their jobs, many displayed genuine commitment to the process. And the Center became a good training ground for several staff who were later hired as permanent support staff in the library.

Determining Training Needs

Training will be another feature common to your start-up operations. To determine your training needs, you need to answer three essential questions: Who will do the training? What must be taught? How will you train such a large and varied staff?

If, like us, you have a contractor who knows little about library operations, the answer to your first question is easy: your librarians must do it. Turning next to "what must be taught," we recommend you divide the training required into two parts: first, the general skills or knowledge included in all or significant segments of the job descriptions and, second, the specific skills or knowledge required by particular job descriptions. With respect to the first, here are general training topics to consider which cut across all or significant groups of the job descriptions:

- Overview of the project.
- General operations and policies for center employees.
- Safety and ergonomics for employees.
- Structure of Library of Congress call numbers.
- Reading a bibliographic record and item record.
- How to distinguish a book from a serial.
- Tour of the area.

Prepare a matrix showing which functions require what parts of the general training. This matrix will enable you to schedule the training sessions and to make sure no one requiring any part of the general training is overlooked. (See Appendix 15-A; see also Chapter 24, Appendix 24-A.)

To cover the training specific to particular job descriptions, we recommend assigning a library liaison to each job description and give that librarian the task of writing procedures and preparing the proper training materials. This simple technique will greatly reduce the magnitude of the undertaking and intimately involve librarians in your technical services division directly and meaningfully in your recovery processes.

You may have minimal time to prepare and test your training materials. If that is the case, train your processing-center supervisors first. Doing this will serve a number of functions: the supervisors become acquainted with the processing center as a whole; they learn or are exposed to the skills soon to be required of their staff; they can assist with the staff training once it begins; and, perhaps, they can help you evaluate and perfect your training methods and materials.

In our experience, our contractor was putting together his work force and had fixed the same starting date for all employees. Fearing that he might lose employees over the pending holiday period if they did not start on the announced date, he wanted to bring in his labor pool for initial training on the same day to give employees something to do and to start their pay. So that our librarians didn't have to put in a 16-hour day that first day, we brought in both shifts of workers for training at the same time. To accommodate those few who could not be available at any time other than their normal shift, we scheduled the initial training session so that it overlapped both shifts.

The upside of training all the employees at once was that those members of the library staff required to adjust their normal working schedules did so, for the most part, only once. The downside, however, was more serious: in a start-up operation, not every stage of the operation begins at the same time. Staff members trained to prepare journals for the bindery cannot do so until the journals have been unpacked and matched with the records, and staff members trained to mark books returning from the bindery cannot do so until the books return from the bindery. In the preliminary stages, as a result, some weeks passed before sufficient quantities of materials were steadily fed to each station. In addition, the receipt pattern of gifts initially posed a workflow problem because more journals were received that involved stoppage in marking operations while materials were at the bindery. For the sake of simple efficiency, it would have been wiser to have built a backlog of materials at various stations before fixing a starting date there; and for the sake of effective training, no gap between initial training and beginning the job would have prevented retraining for certain of the more complex operations. Beginning in stages and training in stages, in short, would have been more efficient and effective. Despite the uneven start, however, the intense training and review by library staff was effective as center staff began almost immediately to process large numbers of gift materials to return to the shelves.

In summary, since there are not large pools of trained staff on hand to hire for large-scale disasters in libraries, the majority of a labor pool will need training from experienced library staff. Such training must be "cookie cutter" in delivery since time will not permit mastery of different skills.

Maintaining Open Communication

Communication can cause any project, disaster-related or otherwise, to go awry. We experienced a variety of problems related to communication that simple, basic principles of good communication followed by all parties might have alleviated, but much the same might be said, of course, for almost all relationships. Most of our unexpected problems stemmed from those aspects of our project that fell outside our general experience as academic librarians. While the chief sources of difficulty have a certain intrinsic interest, they may offer illustrations of potential sources of conflict for other efforts at disaster recovery.

COMMUNICATION BETWEEN LIBRARY AND PROJECT PERSONNEL

Managing a processing center requires clear supervisory and reporting channels and regular use of these channels to communicate both up and down the chain as well as to all external parties interested in the operation.

The CSU Libraries' team of liaisons (headed by the coordinator of Preservation) was responsible for specifying procedures and for confirming that quality was maintained in each job category. As librarians, we felt a strong ownership of the operation and connection with the staff whom we had trained—an emotional tie that was difficult to break. After initial training was over, both the library staff and the contractor expected the role of library staff to lessen. In reality, heavy turnover necessitated continued training by library staff of center staff, and we saw a need for a continuing presence in the plant to participate in the ever-evolving development of procedures. Even though we had a role as advisors specified in the contract, interpretation between what the contractor thought this meant and what we felt we were entitled to do differed. Sometimes, we felt we were not receiving information about changes to procedures that we needed.

In a normal business operation, libraries would not question the role of the vendor/contractor to handle the vendor operation, but the uniqueness of our situation often meant that library staff were the only ones with expertise to answer a question or provide guidelines. Compounding the difficulty, especially at the beginning, was the complexity of various levels of supervision within the project. Along with three management levels (center manager for each shift, lead supervisor for each shift, and unit supervisors for each shift) were four different employers: the university who hired the contractor, the contractor who hired the two center managers and two temporary agencies, and the two temporary agencies who hired all the remaining employees. In addition, the supervisors were not *working supervisors*, which meant they might not have the daily familiarity with the work to allow them to understand the issues as clearly as needed.

To resolve the many difficulties, we set up weekly meetings between the center supervisors and the library team with the expectation that both sides would inform subordinates of decisions. We also demanded to be present at meetings with university officials and representatives of the Center. In addition, during the early stages of the project we found that weekly meetings between the supervisor of the work unit and the librarian assigned to devise procedures and review the quality of the work for that unit were important to review understanding of procedures and determine solutions to new problems. Given the premium on speed in the project and the complexity of library procedures, we found it to be essential to write up and distribute copies of all decisions, both formal and informal. Unfortunately, the burden of documenting fell largely on library staff during our project. Although the library staff could have insisted through channels that the center staff provide the documentation, sometimes it was easier to do it ourselves rather than risk incorrect information or explain to someone how to do it.

COMMUNICATION BETWEEN SHIFTS

Using two or more shifts of workers can bring special problems. Shifts need to let each other know about problems and solutions worked out during one shift so procedures are consistently updated. If they are sharing the same work, they need to know at what stage the prior shift left the task. At the very least, it is necessary to insist that managers and supervisors be scheduled together for training and ongoing instruction so that everyone hears the same message, and the more that existing personnel can modify their normal schedules so as to balance the training and advising given different shifts the better. We partly solved these problems by overlapping supervisors' shifts so that they could meet several times a week. Keeping a notebook at each station so that the supervisors could pass information back and forth also helped.

We found, too, that we had to take care to avoid apparent favoritism for one shift over another. Because we had two shifts initially and because the morning shift corresponded most closely with the hours that the library staff worked, we tended to spend more time working out problems with the first shift and gave them more training, which we expected, somewhat unrealistically, would be carefully passed on to the second shift. In some units, the second shift also felt the first shift was receiving special assignments that kept them busier during down times when there was not enough work for everyone and a shift had to be sent home without compensation. Shifts also became defensive about mistakes, claiming that the other shift had caused the difficulty or being quick to point out mistakes by the other shift. And worst, we realized that information was being passed incorrectly from shift to shift. Balanced, hands-on attention by library staff is definitely needed for unskilled employees dealing with the ambiguities of library records.

Some of the inter-shift problems evaporated when the contractor appointed one center manager to replace the two previous center managers. We could then pass essential information and procedures through this single source. When the manager then rotated her shifts so that she might maintain communication with both shifts—two weeks on one shift and two weeks on the other— more problems disappeared. But new problems surfaced as the manager became a bottle neck in the communication flow when she was overwhelmed with work. Anyone contemplating shifts in an operation such as ours must be prepared for similar difficulties.

COMMUNICATION WITHIN STAFF AND BETWEEN STAFF AND THE OUTSIDE WORLD

Some attention must also be given to how temporary staff will communicate with each other. Will temporary staff be permitted to use e-mail and telephone, and if so, how and when? Our contractor did not want staff members to have e-mail access since the bulk of jobs required only that the staff member perform specific, uniform tasks. As a result, only managers and supervisors had access to e-mail and phones. A central receptionist was hired to screen messages and handle phones for the operation.

COMMUNICATION BETWEEN SITES

When the Processing Center operation was in the lower level of the library, it was easy to run upstairs or downstairs to communicate. When the operation moved two blocks away to a condemned dormitory, however, communication became more difficult and transporting materials back and forth for quality checks became inefficient. We requested that the contractor provide library liaisons with office space in the new facility and access to phones, photocopiers, and faxes as needed. Later in the project, the burden on library staff trying to work out of two offices led us to consider the possibility of hiring staff independent of our contractor who would serve as auditor of the contractor's performance of the contract specifications.

COMMUNICATION UPSTAIRS, DOWNSTAIRS, AND ELSEWHERE

Different languages will always be a barrier to good communication with any outside group. Without careful attention, misunderstandings can arise from the use of a term that means something very specific in a library operation but something else to others. Make sure you define terms carefully in order to educate your university administration and your contractor.

For example, *volume* became the standard term to describe our loss to insurance and to calculate statistics for the Center operation. The basis of our definition of volume was our online item record as it matched the way a piece was bound. It did not matter if the item consisted of two physical volumes bound together or only part of a year bound in one volume. But it was important not only to have a reliable way to measure the work in the plant but also to communicate clearly with everyone involved.

PROVIDING ADEQUATE SECURITY

Allowing outside parties to work inside the library and with library databases brings certain risks. Managers of any such project will want to consider ways to reduce that risk. Here are some steps to consider taking:

a) Safety of temporary staff: Adherence to building and institutional codes goes a considerable distance in assuring the safety of temporary staff, but before new staff are onsite, the facility itself should be carefully reviewed for safety and security, and security checks should include all those places used by the staff. Is there, for example, adequate lighting for late-night staff as they leave the facility and go to their cars?

b) Security of library materials: Make sure you have this type of security in place, especially if you have a shift working after library hours. In our case, one of the shifts worked after the library was closed so staff were not allowed to go upstairs during that time. Our campus police were called in to review security with the center staff, particularly since center staff used doors not available to other staff. Consider having staff wear badges as a quick way to identify personnel authorized to be in restricted areas.

c) Security of databases: The first step to data security is password control. Centralizing the authorization and assignment of passwords and deleting passwords when an employee leaves is sound practice. Staff should also be required to change passwords periodically. You may want your library staff to maintain control of password assignment.

A second way to make data more secure is restricting workstations to only those functions needed to do the job. After an incident with an angry employee who was fired, we realized that our entire inventory file of unmatched gifts was vulnerable since anyone with an Internet account could access certain Web pages that interfaced with the database. We immediately did what we should have done at the outset: specified the IP address of each computer that could access the database. Perhaps the most important way to ensure the integrity of the data is to build accuracy into quality control and make supervisors responsible for reviewing work done by staff members who may enter incorrect, humorous, or malicious data.

d) Security of documentation: You should consider all procedures relating to the use of your integrated library system as confidential since your system vendor is a proprietary system and probably requires that its documentation be confidential. Thus, employees should be expected to not share information about their procedures and should be required to turn in their procedure manuals if they leave your project.

CONCLUSION

Generally speaking, were we to do the project again, we would have written as many of the above concerns into the contract as possible. If working with external staffing, we would have asked for library skills for key positions of supervision and management. An inescapable aspect of our situation was that several parties demanded a say and control over the process—the university administration, the broker, and the insurance companies—since the magnitude of the disaster enfolded the entire institution. Thus, the library did not have the autonomy it might have had were we the only building on the campus damaged and the cost had not been in the millions. But even so, in retrospect, we should have insisted more in the beginning on the importance of librarians in controlling the design of the procedures and in auditing the quality of the process.

Library Disaster Planning and Recovery Handbook

KEY RECOMMENDATIONS

Processing Center

- Make sure that your librarians have control over the design of the project and the auditing of the quality-control process.

- Include in your contract as many of the concerns mentioned in this chapter as possible.

- If external staff are required for a disaster-recovery technical-services operations, like a processing center, make sure that library skills are a requirement for key supervisors and managers.

- Demand that the recovery operation is under the control of the library and not some other institutional unit.

- Realize that the involvement of other parties may be required (insurance and institutional officials); try to maintain as much autonomy in the process.

- Remember that with autonomy and control comes severe accountability. Be prepared for those demands to be made.

APPENDIX 15-A
GIFTS TRAINING

SUBJECT	WHO TRAINED	#STAFF/ SHIFT	WHO TRAINS	TIME NEEDED	SESSION TYPE
Overview of processing plant — aims of the gift processing	All staff		Contractor	15 min.	General
General operations (information on transportation, parking, time records, badging system, phone policy, where to put personal possessions, where to eat lunch, etc.), logistics	All staff		Contractor	30 min.	General
Security/safety/emergency procedures/responsibilities	All staff		Library & Contractor	30 min.	General
Ergonomics	All staff		Library	30 min.	General
Computer operations	Supervisors	12	Contractor	1 hr.	Group
LC call numbers	Staff/Supervisors in SAGE Station, Binding, Marking, Shelving, QC		Library	1 hr.	General
Books vs. serials/periodicals	Staff/Supervisors in SAGE Station, Unpacking, QC Barcoding, Binding, Inventory		Library	1 hr.	General
General operations of SAGE passwords/security	Staff/Supervisors in SAGE Station, Quality Control		Library	1 hr.	Group
How to tead a SAGE printout	Staff/supervisors SAGE station, Barcode, Binding, Marking, Quality Control		Library		General
Shipping & receiving procedures: general	Staff /Supervisors in Station	6	Contractor	1 hr.	General
Shipping & receiving procedures: binding	Staff/Supervisors in Station		Contractor	1 hr.	General
Unpacking procedures	Staff/Supervisors in Station	10	Library	1 hr.	General
SAGE procedures	Staff/Supervisors in Station	20	Library	8 hrs.	Group
Barcode operations	Staff/Supervisors in Station	8	Library	1 hr.	Group
Binding procedures/LARS	Staff/Supervisors in Station	32	Library	8 hrs.	Group
Marking procedures	Staff/Supervisors in Station	4	Library	2 hrs.	Group
Reshelving procedures	Staff/Supervisors in Station	6	Library	2 hrs.	Group
Quality control	Staff/Supervisors in Station	8	Library	4 hrs.	Group
CIRC/DBM	Staff/Supervisors in Station	4	Library	3 hrs.	Group
Suspend operations	Staff/Supervisors in Station	2	Contractor		General
IMS training: gifts	Staff/Supervisors in Station		Library	1 hr.	Group
Inexact matches inventory	Staff/Supervisors in Station	10	Library	2 hrs	Group
IMS training: binding	Staff/Supervisors in Station	32	Library	1 hrs.	Group

REFERENCES

Bennon, Barbara A. 1967. "Book Restoration in Florence." *Publisher's Weekly* 192 (November 6): 27–28.

PART FOUR

Gifts and Donations

16 The Fine Art of Gift Raising: An Overview

Joel Rutstein

INTRODUCTION

This and the next three chapters discuss the efforts by the Colorado State University Libraries to rebuild and replace the damaged collections, primarily through *gifts of kind*. Although gifts of money and service were welcomed, no formal fund-raising program was instituted.

The literature relating to library recoveries from natural disasters is almost non-existent regarding alternative sources for replacing damaged material. Sally Buchanan (1988: 17), a recognized expert in preservation of materials and disaster recovery, noted that:

> . . . alternatives to available funds for replacing damaged library materials can include the following, which include gifts from donors, grant or foundation assistance, fund-raising efforts, loans, and consolidation of collections from several libraries or archives (Buchanan, 1988).

While this is an appropriate listing of potential sources, an explanation of how this is to be accomplished is not discussed. The concept of disaster planning/response committees is important, however, it is not a model for the operations and mission of a gift-raising program. The only comparable disaster of magnitude was the Los Angeles County Library fire of 1986. The fire, combined with subsequent water damage incurred by the firefighters, remains the single worst event in the annals of American library calamities. But there are significant differences between the CSU disaster and the Los Angeles fire:

- A large portion of the collection was unsalvageable.
- Most of the damaged materials were books, not journals, and most were in non-science fields.
- Journals that were lost could be replaced with microfilm.
- Fund-raising was allowed to replace many of the damaged books through a highly publicized "Save the Books Campaign."
- The library was closed for three years.

Now compared to the Morgan Library disaster:

- Preservation experts believed that most of the damaged material was salvageable (80 percent).
- At least half the damaged materials were journal runs, and most were in the sciences and technology.
- Until declared a *total loss* by the insurance companies, no money was available to purchase replacements.
- The university president vetoed any plans for disaster-related fund-raising.
- The president also declared that the campus would be open and functioning as normally as possible by the start of fall semester, just one month after the July 28th disaster.

These four chapters follow a sequential process, beginning with the first early efforts to develop a gifts program with existing resources, followed by a formalized structure with the capacity to accept hundreds of thousands of donated volumes, arrange and cover all costs of shipping, and track all donations throughout the entire process. See Chapter 25 for the technical services perspective of processing gifts.

EARLY EFFORTS NEED COORDINATION

Expect Large Numbers of Gift Offers

The enormity of the calamity truly took shape when the impact on the university's 13 designated Programs of Excellence was determined. Eleven of these areas were impaired by the disaster, including world-class programs in chemistry, biochemistry, natural resources, and water research. While measures were introduced to ameliorate conditions, such as enhanced interlibrary-loan operations, computerized database access, document-delivery services, and direct shuttles to nearby research collections, restoring the traditional print collections to their former eminence remained the library's overarching goal.

Following a disaster of this scope, plans are necessary to develop for returning damaged material to the shelves. A large processing center eventually would be located in the same space where the disaster occurred, the Morgan Library lower level. But while these plans were evolving, another activity soon attracted attention. Individuals, corporations, other libraries, publishers and book dealers from around the country began offering "gifts of kind," cash, and services to augment and replace our battered collections.

At first these offers were assigned second priority behind the recovery of the original materials. Since no precedent existed for rebuilding mainstream collections with gifts, the initial response was understandable. Gift programs in most libraries, research or otherwise, have always been supplemental operations. *Gift raising,* the appellation we ascribed to this activity, is an amorphous function when compared to the highly sophisticated and structured framework utilized for the routine process of selection and acquisition of books and journals. Gift programs lack formal access to publishers, vendors, dealers, and other established production and distribution centers within the knowledge industry.

At the time of the disaster, I was head of Collection Development and in this position accepted the task of fielding offers. But what began as an ad hoc mission quickly took on a life of its own. Here is part of a memo I sent to our dean of Libraries, barely a month after the disaster:

> I know we're a bit sensitive about water-related metaphors, but the donations/gifts side of our recovery efforts has gone from a trickle to a tidal wave. Besides the phone calls, letters, faxes, and e-mail (I currently have 171 messages on my screen, not counting 80 that were printed out yesterday), we are now getting many responses from our Alliance Website electronic form. My assistant started working yesterday and will be a great help on the phone. But it's like putting a finger in the dike. It's become a big business operation! Some

of the things that need to be done include: record keeping of contacts, following up on offers, re-contacting people about shipping procedures and where to ship, sorting journal offers, checking against our holdings, keeping a master file of both contacts and titles offered, preparing acknowledgments, tracking shipments, etc. . . . (e-mail to the dean of Libraries, 9/27/97).

Control and Exploit the Message

Why was all this happening? Obviously, no gifts program of large magnitude can be promulgated without a certain degree of publicity. In our case, it began rather auspiciously with a natural disaster capturing national attention.

I was in Mexico City where my wife and I were visiting friends in the United States Information Service (USIS) when the first news came across embassy wires. Fort Collins made the front page of Mexico City dailies the next day. Five people had been killed. The news media reported this event across the continent. It became readily apparent if we were to receive support, the message would have to be exploited. Utilize channels like the following:

- Official pronouncements from campus media relations.
- Information placed on the Internet, especially as a header on the university home page.
- Library networks, both online and in print, including the Association of Research Libraries (ARL) and other national/ regional sources.
- Faculty contacts with their respective professional associations, networks, and colleagues.

Expect to Modify Plans as the Crisis Shifts

Natural disasters occur without warning, and no matter how extensive a library may plan for such eventualities, each crisis takes on its own persona, and the initial phases of recovery can easily turn into a process of reaction. For a two-month period, from the middle of August to the middle of October, as gift offers mounted, I was actively engaged in developing a structure addressing the issue of gifts as a feature of the library-recovery effort. It can be expected that the university administration will require restoration schemes, but such schemes will undergo close scrutiny. In my plan, a fund-raising category was included. This was turned down by the president, who raised concerns about interference with ongoing development activities, which would confuse or even hamper the work of the university Advancement Office. The Provost's Office also explored an option for subsidizing donor appraisal requests, but this was quickly dropped after the average hourly expense was calculated for appraiser fees.

The four-phase plan below delineates tasks and ensures that every facet is covered. If confronted with the need to develop a gift-donation plan, these steps may be incorporated:

PHASE I: INVENTORY

- Prepare a list of damaged titles to be replaced.
- Sort lists by defined subject category and distribute to appropriate faculty and constituents.
- Place lists on Websites. Mount the entire list of damaged titles on a Website and utilize consortial Websites as appropriate. Organize the site by author, title, book, journal, and call-number sequence. Anyone with a book or journal offer could query the system, and if a match is found, it would be electronically forwarded to gift managers.

PHASE II: INDIVIDUAL CONTACTS; LETTERS PREPARED BY PRESIDENT OR PROVOST AS APPROPRIATE

- Emeritus/retired faculty for journal back runs. Have provost request deans to identify emeritus faculty.
- Work with provost and deans to name department liaisons and build lists of professional contacts and contributors.
- Include a letter from your president to the alumni for inclusion in the campus alumni magazine.
- Follow up on messages of support from unsolicited individuals.

PHASE III: INSTITUTIONAL AND CORPORATE CONTACTS

- Identify library groups such as Big 12, ARL, land-grant universities, other state libraries, and corporate libraries for assistance. Send out letters as appropriate from the president, provost, or dean.
- Publishers, bookstores, learned societies, and professional associations who can help. Letters sent out as appropriate by president, provost, or dean.

PHASE IV: FOUNDATIONS

- Identify grant opportunities utilizing lists of educational foundations.
- Write and submit grant proposals in cooperation with your university development office.

In addition to this four-phase plan, it is imperative to enlist the actual involvement of the university administration. Here are some ideas to consider:

- Under the auspices of the provost, form an umbrella campus donations committee to monitor and advise on the ongoing gift-program efforts, initially based upon the above plan. The committee should include faculty representing each college, as well as the library-development officer, collection manager, and representatives from university media relations.
- Develop a second tier of faculty flood-gift liaisons, each member representing the academic departments.
- Write guidelines which explain faculty liaison involvement, as well as library needs. (See Appendix 16-A.)
- Request all faculty to list journal titles considered important to their work, and submit to the umbrella donations committee.
- Place faculty journal list prominently on the institution's Web page. See Appendix 16-B for an example of a partial listing.

Once a four-phase plan of this type is in place, manpower needs may be determined, and the process flowcharted. It may be necessary to step back and review the plans. Are tasks on target? What can or should be handled differently? If anything looks awry or needs tweaking, don't despair. Instead, take the time to review and redesign.

In our case, our president was convinced that donations could be a significant factor in the replacement of disaster-damaged material. Librarians were more skeptical, being accustomed to the ancillary role always assumed for gift operations. Second, the initial gifts program was set up to augment, not supplant the return of damaged material. Changes had to take place in order to enlarge the gifts program and assign it the highest priority.

CONCLUSION

The art of raising gifts of kind after a major disaster is less an act of fundraising than it is an act of desperation. Several weeks were consumed before reaching the conclusion in official circles that the many offers of material donations should be harnessed and incorporated into a highly structured programmatic effort. Key people had to be identified immediately and reassigned to an operation requiring enormous amounts of time and energy, as well as the capacity to formulate goals and procedures practically overnight.

A gifts program on this scale may not be for everyone. In our case, the primary research tools for the campus—our core journals—were all damaged. This made access to pristine gift materials critical because, if identified, they could be brought in, accessioned, bound (when necessary), and placed on the shelves far faster than the long, laborious process of treating and processing the damaged material. By early 1999, nearly 100,000 exact matches of gifts had been placed in circulation, equating to almost one quarter of all items damaged. This statistic alone is a confirmation of the decision to proceed with donations as a major priority and attests to the skill and dedication of the members of the Gifts Team who made it happen.

CSU library staff shelving the first gift volume processed.

Library Disaster Planning and Recovery Handbook

KEY RECOMMENDATIONS

Gift Raising

- Consider alternative means for replacing disaster-damaged materials other than seeking insurance claims which may take an inordinate amount of time to be negotiated and finalized.
- Collections may be rebuilt/replaced through *gifts of kind*, grant monies, loans, fund-raising, etc.
- If restoring the traditional print collections to their former eminence remains your library's overarching goal, then measures introduced to ameliorate conditions, such as enhanced interlibrary-loan operations, computerized-database access, document-delivery services, and direct shuttles to nearby research collections should be perceived as only temporary fixes.
- Plans are necessary to develop for returning damaged material to the shelves.
- Gift-raising programs of a large magnitude promulgate a certain degree of publicity; you need to control the message of what materials your recovering library really needs.
- Utilize channels like the following: official pronouncements from campus/ community media relations; information placed on the Internet via the library/university/community homepage; library networks, both online and in print, including national/regional sources; and faculty contacts with their respective professional associations, networks, and colleagues.
- Modify plans as the crisis shifts; the powers that be may lend their suggestions before you get a chance to implement your ideas on how to proceed.
- Design and implement a multi-phase restoration plan.
- Place the entire list of damaged titles on a Website.
- Utilize consortial Websites as appropriate.
- Explore individual contacts; follow up on messages of support from unsolicited individuals.
- Identify institutional and corporate contacts.
- Identify funding opportunities from educational foundations.
- Write and submit grant proposals in cooperation with your university development office.
- Enlist the actual involvement of the university/community administration.
- Develop contingency augmentation plans should your original efforts fall short of their desired goals.

APPENDIX 16-A
LIBRARIES GIFT ACCEPTANCE PROGRAM—GUIDELINES

Role of Liaisons

Academic department liaisons can aid in the gift-acceptance program by both serving as contacts for gifts within their departments
and getting the message out to their professional colleagues and
associations, both in and outside of the university. Liaisons may
collect donor information to forward to the Gifts Team, or refer
contacts directly. The following guidelines should also help liaisons control the message, answer questions, and help with the
flow of donor contacts.

Guidelines for Receiving Journals

1. Desire complete runs of journals to 1995.

2. Will accept journals dating from the most recent ten or
   twenty years.

3. Broken runs (many missing issues) are not acceptable.

4. Current titles from 1995–present are not needed.

5. If donor offers more than a few titles, the list should be
   sent to the Gifts Team head.

6. Do not send any materials; donor will be contacted regarding where to drop off or ship materials.

7. Lists of damaged journal titles may be found on the Web at
   www.coalliance.org. The lists may be searched by title or
   call number. Electronic form included for prospective donors.

Guidelines for Receiving Books

1. It is unnecessary to list donated books by title.

2. Books should be described by subject areas covered.

3. Hard copy titles are preferred.

4. Recently published books (since 1985) are preferred.

5. Do not send books. Donor will be contacted regarding where to drop off or ship materials.

6. Lists of damaged book titles may be found on the Web at *www.coalliance.org.* Lists may be searched by author, title, or call number. Electronic form included for prospective donors.

University Policies

1. If necessary, the university will pay for shipping costs.

2. Donated material becomes the property of Colorado State University.

3. The university does not conduct appraisals for tax purposes. Donors may supply an estimate of value if the gift is thought to be worth less than $5,000. For a value $5,000 and higher, for tax purposes the donor should have the collection appraised: Fill out IRS form 8283 and send a copy to the Colorado State University Foundation, P.O. Box 1870, Fort Collins, CO 80522-1870.

4. Letters of acknowledgement will be sent to each donor after the material has been received. This form may be used as an official receipt for tax purposes.

Satellite Department Collections

Faculty may wish to donate journals and books to their respective department reading rooms. Such an act may be especially pertinent if the donor wishes to "reclaim" his or her material at a later time. Such activity is not necessarily linked to library operations. Remember, however, that department reading rooms and/ or collections are not organized for use by the general public, and access hours are often limited.

Receiving Local Gifts

Gifts from faculty, staff, and other individuals in the community may be dropped off at the rear of the library depository on Lake

Street. This service will begin Monday, Sept. 15, and will be staffed during the hours of 10:00 a.m.–1:00 p.m. Monday–Wednesday; 3:00–6:00 p.m. Thursday; and 2:00–5:00 p.m. Friday. It would greatly help if local gifts (boxed) could be taken to the site by the donor. If this is physically impossible, arrangements will be made on a case-by-case basis.

Subject Areas NOT Impacted (Books)

These areas of the collection were mostly undamaged by the flood:

Anthropology
Art
Fiction
Foreign Language
History
Literature
Philosophy
Psychology
Religion
Sports
(Textbooks are not necessary in all subject areas, except Curriculum Collection)

APPENDIX 16-B
WEB-BASED FACULTY JOURNAL LIST

In an August survey conducted by the provost, Colorado State University faculty identified the following journals as critical. If you can donate any of these titles, please list your name, address, phone number, the name of the title(s), years, and volumes you have to donate. Please contact [name] at [phone] or [e-mail address]. The Libraries greatly appreciates your generosity.

Critical Flood-Damaged Journals Identified by CSU Faculty
[Complete List of Journal Titles]

Subject Area Impacted (Books)
[Complete List of Subject Areas] (example)

Business (Finance)	HG, HJ
Sociology	HM, HN, HQ
Music	M

Subject Area Impacted (Bound Journals)

ALL Bound Journals	A–Z
(Humanities, Social Sciences, Science)	

Areas/Programs of Excellence Impacted by Damaged Materials (11 of 13 Programs)

[Complete List of Programs] (example)
Animal Reproduction & Biotechnology Laboratory
Department of Chemistry
Radiological Sciences & Cancer Research

Other

All current awareness browse material
All curriculum materials collection
All oversize materials

REFERENCE

Buchanan, Sally. 1988. *Disaster Planning, Preparedness and Recovery for Libraries and Archives: A RAMP Study.* Paris: UNESCO.

17 The Fine Art of Gift Raising: Redesigning the Gifts Program

Cathy Tweedie

INTRODUCTION

Since the disaster at Colorado State University Libraries in July 1997, developments occurred that made it essential to rethink where the university was heading in dealing with donated library materials. The volume of offers was overwhelming, and it seemed that there was a distinct possibility of replacing a significant percentage of our damaged collections through gifts.

For this kind of disaster, this is not an obvious strategy. Insurance should cover the repair or replacement of the damaged books and journals, so the question arises: Why should we need donations? For us, there were two reasons. One was that the offers were there—we needed a decision quickly on whether to accept them or announce that we didn't want these materials. The second reason was that we really had no idea how much of the damage to our collection was repairable. There was a working assumption that perhaps 80 percent of the collection could be repaired, but there were no real data to support the assumption. No one had yet thought of doing a scientific random sample and evaluating the results. Because of the nature of the materials, we knew that the damaged books and journals would not be easy to replace. Even at the most optimistic, it would take several years to purchase replacements for the lost materials. And it was also highly likely that many titles, possibly those that were unique and valuable, might not be replaceable.

This is a decision that must not be put off for long. It must be all or nothing. Considered rationally, the decision to accept donations releases a chain of consequences. It means committing significant resources to managing a full-fledged gift program: soliciting, evaluating and accepting, receiving, storing, and processing the gifts. Starting the process without carrying it through to the end is pointless. Yet it is by no means apparent where these resources will come from; this is not the way insurance usually works. The program will require a significant amount of space, at a time when space may be the scarcest resource within the organization. It may also affect the recovery process. It will not only complicate the processes but will also have the potential to divert resources from the recovery program.

The positive consequences of soliciting donations are that the goodwill pouring out from well-wishers will be productively harnessed. It will also be feasible to replace at least some of the damaged materials with relatively clean and undamaged copies. On the face of it, the costs of replacing with donations seem intuitively to be less than the costs of either repairing the damaged materials or replacing them.

While there are also substantial, rational reasons for avoiding accepting gifts, for us the consequences of not accepting gift donations would have been significant. It would mean declining many generous offers from individuals and organizations, many of them within the local community. Some offers had already been accepted, and people had been told we would get back to them before long, as soon as we had a shipping address. Each donor would not see the enormity of the overall situation, and there would be a danger that they would see only the rejection of their own generosity. Goodwill towards the university could be jeopardized. Further, because of the uncertain prospects of the recovery process, there was a risk of missing out on good quality replacements of material we would later be unable to restore or re-purchase.

Rational reasoning aside, there may be overwhelming political reasons to accept donations. Decisions that in normal times would require at least a task force and months of meetings are made in an instant, for better or worse. This proved to be the case at Colorado State University (CSU). The university president cut the

Gordian knot, if a knot there was, by deciding that the library would go all out to replace damaged materials with gifts.

It is not uncommon for the charitable response to a disaster to become overwhelming, and it is something that your disaster team should be prepared to handle. You need the ability to assess the situation in the light of the overall needs of the disaster recovery and reallocate resources if necessary. It's something of a paradox: you cannot do anything successfully without a plan, and yet you must keep the flexibility to change your plan in response to a fluctuating situation. So it proved for our fledgling gift program.

THE NEED FOR PROGRAM REDESIGN

By the end of September, the gifts operation had grown to three or four people, operating very much still in reactive mode. We were running as fast as we could just to keep pace; we had never really had time to plan. The dean of Libraries recognized that there was a crisis and asked key members of the disaster team to drop everything for two days to hold a planning retreat and assess the situation. I cannot stress too strongly how important this proved to be. Taking two days of time from up to ten people, when everyone was hard-pressed, might seem like a dubious use of resources, but it was critically necessary. It took the concentrated focus of the entire team to break an apparently insurmountable problem into pieces that could be dealt with one at a time, to carry the planning process through, and create an operation that could move ahead and reach its goals when it was in danger of bogging down and spinning its wheels ineffectually.

In redesigning the gifts program we employed a fairly standard planning process, using the following eight steps:

1. Identify your objectives and your focus.

2. Develop reasonable planning assumptions.

3. Establish a realistic yet acceptable time frame.

4. Chart the necessary processes.

5. Develop a schedule and set milestones to chart your progress.

6. Obtain all the resources you will need.

7. Set up mechanisms for reporting and evaluating progress.

8. Make it happen!

In the next sections I shall outline how we worked through each step in the hope that our process can serve as a model for anyone faced with a similar undertaking in disaster recovery.

Step 1: Identify Your Objectives and Your Focus

You need to identify the aim and objectives of the donations program; for example, to solicit, accept, and receive donated books and journals in an expeditious manner in order to achieve the following:

- Maximize acceptability to library users of items returned to the library collections.
- Maximize the number of gift volumes used in restoring the collections.
- Reduce the number of total losses.
- Reduce the resources spent on reprocessing damaged materials.

In our case, our overarching goal was to restore as many materials to our collection as possible in a condition that would be not only readable and usable but would also be highly acceptable to our users: clean to the eye, the touch, and the nose. If we could assume that most donated materials would be in good condition, similar to the state of our materials before the disaster, then the more donated materials that could exactly replace the damaged volumes, the better. Secondly, since we did not know what percentage of the damaged books was salvageable, we hoped that at least some of the donations would replace materials that would otherwise be written off as non-repairable. Lastly, it seemed a reasonable assumption that accepting and processing donations should be less costly overall than the repair and restoration process that had been developed (but not yet implemented). This last factor would be important in making a case to the university's insurers that it would be within their scope, and in their interest, to agree to pay the costs of handling and processing the donations.

Throughout the planning process, we recognized that we would inevitably receive a proportion of donations of items we had never previously owned; we assumed that a percentage of these would be items we would want if possible to add to our collections. This possible augmentation of our collections through the gifts program was recognized as a beneficial side effect of the program, but was not one of the program objectives.

Step 2: Develop Reasonable Planning Assumptions

In a standard planning process, the next step is to gather and review relevant data about the environment, the client group, the market, and so on, depending on the nature of the project. Past experience and results are also used to set the parameters. This step is just as important in planning for disaster recovery; however, the probability of finding a wealth of useful experience to draw upon is not high.

In our case, we found there was no precedent to which we could refer. Like most libraries, we had a modest gift department which accepted mostly unsolicited donations and added one or two thousand volumes a year. No library had ever attempted a gifts program on the scale we were contemplating and there wasn't a prior example of soliciting donations of such a highly specific nature.

The real data we had at this point were few: we knew the rate at which unsolicited offers were coming in and the amount that had been promised to date; we knew exactly which journals and books were needed. Another important piece of data was our knowledge that if insurance was to pay the costs of the gift program, then only exact replacements of damaged volumes could be processed and placed on the shelves.

In order to proceed, then, it was essential to come to a reasonable estimate of the number of donations we would have to handle, and the number of volumes we were likely to be offered. By pooling the ideas, experience, and intuitions of the planning group, we developed projections for various types of donors and an estimated number of donations for each accordingly.

- Individual donors, including our own Colorado State University faculty: we estimated that 200 members of our own faculty, and 800 other individuals, would donate personal collections, and we projected an average of 80 volumes from each donor (80,000 volumes).
- Societies/Associations: We projected that, of the societies whose journals were part of our collections, 200 would offer on average five journal titles, in 20-year runs, and that these would average two bound volumes per year (48,000 volumes).
- Publishers: We estimated that we could expect 100 large monograph and journal publishers each to donate seven journal titles or 40 monographs, for a projected total of 48,000 volumes.
- Academic libraries: We projected that 50 academic libraries would each offer 10 journal titles and 50 monographs, for a total of 15,000 volumes.
- Other organizations, such as government or corporate special libraries: We projected that fifty organizations would each donate twenty journal titles and ten monographs, for a total of 25,000 volumes.
- Offers already on hand totaled about 73,000 volumes.

Planning went forward on the basis of these projections. We would accept and receive around 291,500 volumes from offers and solicitations, and 80 percent of them would be journals. It was further established that the program would focus on journal replacement for several reasons. First, the loss of the journals was most important to our user population, especially in the sciences. Second, while journals in all subjects had been damaged, most social science and humanities monographs were intact. Finally, the handling of long journal runs appeared far more manageable than individual monographs. Focusing on journals promised a better return for the resources invested.

We also had to make the reasonable assumption that our projected numbers would include a proportion of items that we had never owned, of duplicates, and of items that were not in an acceptable condition. We found it impossible to project what this proportion would be. In our standard gift operation, only ten to twenty percent of donated materials is processed and added to the collection; we could not draw a definite analogy with the new program because solicitation would uniquely be targeted to a specific list of items, which would also be available through the World Wide Web to potential donors.

Step 3: Establish a Realistic Yet Acceptable Time Frame

For your donations program to succeed, immediate implementation is essential. The planning assumptions will clarify just how large a project you will be getting into. The pressures to get the gift material in and processed will be strong from a number of directions.

At Morgan Library, we already knew that offers of donations were backed up, and there was some detectable donor dissatisfaction. There was pressure from the university administration to deal with the issue immediately and defuse any possible embarrassment. There was pressure not to delay the reprocessing of the damaged, freeze-dried materials.

The feeling of the university administration was that two months would be ample time to bring in and deal with all the potential donations. However, we had established that in order to meet our projections, we would need to accept and receive an average of 50,000 volumes per month—2,500 volumes per day—for six months. This was a huge undertaking—50,000 volumes is more than the size of many libraries and is the same quantity Colorado State University Libraries usually adds to its collections in a year. While politically we needed to emphasize the receipt and handling of existing offers in the following two months, in reality we knew that the process would have to continue over several more months to reach the projected figures. We also knew that the turnaround time from offer to receipt, even in a streamlined operation, could stretch out considerably. By adopting a working assumption that the project would continue for six months, we could begin to plan labor, space and other resource needs.

Step 4: Chart the Necessary Processes

At this point in the planning process, it becomes necessary to identify the tasks and analyze the processes that you will use to accomplish the objectives. First, get a clear picture of the system you are creating. What are the steps by which the initial input—an offer to donate books—flows through the system and becomes output as books shelved in the library? What needs to be done, by whom, how often, how soon? Are there tasks that are critically urgent or bottlenecks that must be cleared before the program can function effectively? What outside forces and constraints will affect the processes? What time delays must be expected and planned for? What aspects of the operation are most critical—speed of turnaround, throughput, accuracy of output—and are these the same in all areas? The results of this part of the planning processes will be flow charts, step-by-step descriptions of processes, and descriptions of the various tasks and type of staffing required for each.

In our experience, in this part of the planning process we identified several distinct parts of the operation. The front end consisted of a team of library staff and temporary employees whose job was to find the donations and bring them in. Their task stopped at the delivery dock; at that point the material would become the responsibility of a separate processing operation to be managed by the contractor who had already been engaged by the university to manage the reprocessing of the damaged materials.

We also determined how we would deal with the two critical bottlenecks that had precipitated the gifts program review and that had to be resolved immediately to prevent embarrassment for the university. One was the large backlog of offers that, because the existing staff was overwhelmed, had not yet received an appropriate response; the second was the backlog of donations that could not be delivered because there was no space available to store them. On these, we had to practice crisis management.

The expanded and revamped front end of the gifts program comprised two main units: the Gift Solicitation Unit and the Gift Receipt Unit. A description of the units follows.

GIFT SOLICITATION/ACCEPTANCE UNIT

The Gift Solicitation/Acceptance Unit had staffing requirements of 1.5 FTE library professionals, .5 FTE development professionals, .5 FTE paraprofessionals, and 2 FTE clerical. This unit had responsibility for bringing in donations to meet the targets we had set. The members would work closely as a team. The professional tasks involved initiating and managing the solicitation program; negotiating donations with individuals and organizations; serving as liaison with donors; coordinating solicitations with CSU faculty and others, as well as evaluating offers and making decisions on acceptance based on expert knowledge of our collections. For these tasks, we had no alternative but to assign our own collection-development experts and to try to cover their normal jobs with temporary replacements. At the time of writing, the library has received no reimbursement for these salary costs.

Paraprofessional aspects included maintaining and checking records of items accepted and making routine acceptance decisions. Clerical aspects included contacting donors, making shipping arrangements, maintaining donor database and documentation, and acknowledging donations.

Key factors were timely handling of offers, accurate documentation of decisions, rapid responses to donors, and efficient problem solving. Performance would be measured by volume of offers processed against the time schedule and accuracy of records leading to a minimum of mix ups with donors.

When we considered in detail the tasks facing this unit, it became clear that attempting to do exhaustive duplicate checking at the acceptance phase would bog the process down and would never be reliable. We discussed seriously whether any duplicate checking at all should be done. The plan that emerged was to maintain a "quick and dirty" file of journal titles accepted and to do a rough check on titles and holdings at the discretion of the content reviewer. For monographs, there was consensus in the planning group that we should not attempt to record offers or screen for duplication.

First priority for this unit was to resolve the donor response crisis by sending out a blanket message to all the pending donors for whom we had records.

GIFT RECEIPT UNIT

The Gift Receipt Unit had staffing requirements of .5 FTE professionals and .5 FTE students. This smaller unit was responsible for keeping track of donations after acceptance, documenting receipts, helping donors with shipping and delivery arrangements, following up on delayed receipts, and resolving problems. It worked closely with the main Solicitation/Acceptance unit and with the Processing Center keeping track of each donation as it went through the full process. Because of the complexity of the operation and the potential for confusion, professional input into the management of the operation was needed.

Key factors were meeting targets for receipts, sorting out problems, and forwarding accurate information on receipts to Donor Control for acknowledgment of donations. First priority for this unit was to resolve the delivery and storage problem.

Because the gift project was so critical for the disaster recovery, we agreed on the necessity to appoint myself as project manager. This role required an experienced administrator who could make sure each unit had the staff, equipment, and resources they needed to meet their targets and who could monitor progress closely, take action to resolve bottlenecks and delays if they should occur, and make sure the lines of communication stayed open. I would also act as the official contact between the Gifts Team and the Processing Center, and would be responsible for compiling management information and reporting to the library and university administration. My first priority was to get both critical problems resolved without delay and next to make sure that the necessary steps to get the program set up and running were accomplished.

The Gifts Processing Center was to be operated by a contractor hired by the university as described above. Its first function would be to take delivery of all incoming shipments, unpack and check them, and forward shipping documentation to the Gifts Receipt Unit. Next, each item would be checked to determine if it was an exact match. If so, the item would be processed for adding to the collection. Duplicates would simply be repacked and stored, and items the library had never owned would be inventoried before re-packing and storing. The actual operations of the Processing Center are treated in detail in Chapter 15. At this point, their first priority was to provide both storage space and provision to receive deliveries.

Step 5: Develop a Schedule and Set Milestones to Chart your Progress.

Once you understand the process, the volume of production you are aiming for, and the rate of throughput required, you can begin to develop your schedule. First, though, you need to take account of the preliminary setup tasks that have to be completed before the system can operate smoothly, to estimate turnaround time, and to allow for other inevitable delays. Once you do this, you can create a week-by-week schedule showing specific tasks to be accomplished and a cumulative target for volumes accepted and volumes received. In our case, after the first month, we predicted that the system would be running smoothly, and the schedule dropped from weekly to monthly. We projected we would meet the goal of 300,000 volumes by March 31, 1998. An example of the project management schedule is shown as Appendix 17-A.

Step 6: Obtain All the Resources You will Need

Based on your assumptions and your program design, you can project costs for staffing, space, equipment, supplies, and miscellaneous expenses. You can proceed to recruit staff, find space, and obtain other resources that money can buy.

In our experience, total projected costs—for the front end only—came to $396,000, a unit cost of approximately $1.32 per volume received. These estimates were approved when the new plan was presented to the university administration. To obtain office space, we were able to use some marginally satisfactory space in Morgan Library that was temporarily unoccupied because of the building renovation. The responsibility for setting up storage and processing space lay with the contractor.

Step 7: Set Up Mechanisms for Reporting and Evaluating Progress.

Most likely, the key performance measure for the project will be meeting the schedule in terms of total estimated volumes accepted and actual volumes received. There must be an estimate, so it is probably best to use, as we did, a very conservative rule of thumb and count one year of journal issues as the equivalent of one bound volume.

For actual volumes received, you will have to rely on reports from your processing center, and these may also have to be estimated because of the difficulty in translating loose pieces into volumes. The head of your acceptance unit should be responsible for maintaining these statistics and reporting weekly. Understand that, from the start, these two counts can never be reconciled, so do not build this requirement into your performance measures. You should also consider keeping statistics on the sources of offers and types of donors so that you can measure actuality against your assumptions. In our case, we were required to make a weekly progress report to the university Donations Committee, consisting of the associate provost, other administrative officials, and faculty representatives, as well as to the dean of Libraries.

Step 8: Make it Happen!

Your planning process sets the scene and gives you a structure to work within. Reality, of course, will probably prove somewhat different from the plan. The details of how this all worked out for Morgan Library are treated fully in other parts of following chapters.

Here, I should like to give a brief analysis of how the plan shaped up in relation to the reality—where it helped us, where it fell short, and what factors proved most influential on the success of the program. We did succeed. By the end of March, our target date, we had accepted more than 375,000 volumes from more than 3,700 donors and had actually received more than 330,000 volumes, some 30,000 more than our target. By the end of May, when we stopped soliciting donations, we were at 425,000 volumes received, and the final total was well over 500,000.

YOU HAVE A TIGER BY THE TAIL, DON'T LET GO!—OR, STAND BY YOUR PLAN

You will be dealing with a process you cannot fully control and with forces that could easily pull you off course. At times, you will be tempted to react reflexively to an immediate crisis and forget the broader picture. And, as with any team composed of individuals, your perceptions and assumptions will not always be uniform. However, because you know your objectives and your priorities, you will be able to keep focused. Keep your operational structure as simple as possible, with a small, flexible, close-knit team. Set up standard procedures which you have worked out together and then documented. When complications arise, as they will every day, solve them with the same combination: respond to the problem with flexibility and creativity, reach a team consensus on how to proceed, then document the solution and turn it into yet another standard procedure.

THE IMPORTANCE OF PEOPLE—TEAMWORK AND COMMUNICATION

For the project to succeed, good communication is absolutely essential among members of the gifts team, between the gifts team and the processing plant contractor, and between the gifts team and other groups in your library who are working with processing plant operations. Most of the problems and mix ups that inevitably arise will be the result of miscommunication or mistaken assumptions. Establish a weekly team meeting where you take the time as a group to share problems and issues and come to a common understanding of any changes you will be making. These meetings will help you to determine when and where more resources are needed and when to add or reallocate people and equipment. For example, we found we needed to add support to the publisher-solicitation program and keep closer control of the content-review process.

Initially, the gifts team assumed that communication with other key library staff, who were working on setting up the Processing Center and liaising with its staff, would be automatic. However, when everyone is working under great pressure, this just does not happen. We found it necessary to hold formal meetings to communicate on important issues with colleagues we saw every day. No project of this type should ever take any level of communication for granted.

CONTROL THAT FOR WHICH YOU ARE ACCOUNTABLE

If you are accountable for any part of the process, then you must maintain control of the process. It will save you a lot of headaches.

The only times we risked missing our targets were when we had to rely on outside contractors and others we could not control. One issue that nagged us for months was the lack of a reliable means of picking up donations within our local area. We had gladly agreed that the Processing Center contractor would handle this part of the operation, but it didn't seem to be working; and it was our front-end team who were receiving calls from impatient donors. It took several interventions to get this process working satisfactorily; in retrospect, since the gifts team was in the end accountable, it might have been better to keep the whole process under our control.

RECOGNIZE THE IMPORTANCE OF RECORDS AND PAPERWORK

You will need accurate records throughout the entire operation because ultimately each donor has to be formally acknowledged, and that is the final step in the long process. In the planning stages, it is important to realize that your whole team needs access to your key files, in our case the Master Donor File and the Master Journal File (see Chapter 19).

Our donor file had started life as a word-processor table, which listed each offer by a personal name and recorded each follow-up action. At first, we had no well-established procedure for updating the file as actions occurred. However, we worked through our procedures systematically to solve this problem and the donor file became our most important information source. It served as a record of actions, an index to the paper document files, and an easily available source for progress reports. For example, by having the program count how many donors had no entry in the "Results/Thank You" column, we discovered how large that particular backlog was and we were able to monitor progress as that particular count went down. At first the list could be printed out and skimmed through; later it became too big. Also, it didn't matter that only one person could work on the file at a time; soon that became a major obstacle. Similar issues arose with the journal file, which had been created by combining two independently maintained lists. Eventually, we took the step of converting both files to Microsoft Access databases on the library network and training key staff in this new software. We knew immediately that we should have done this sooner!

As the following chapters will show, we also found it extremely useful to develop and use a variety of forms and checklists. These provided background and continuity for each transaction; helped to ensure that each person followed the agreed procedures and that no steps were overlooked; reduced the need for follow ups and re-work; and left a very useful paper trail.

EXPECT A HIGH PROPORTION OF DUPLICATION

You will have no way to predict what percentage of gift receipts will be duplicates. In developing criteria for acceptance of journal offers, you must build in a certain level of duplication so that titles you need will not fall through the gap between what was offered and what actually materialized. You will find that many collections have to be accepted on an all-or-nothing basis without the possibility of selecting or even checking for duplication.

In our case, we stuck to the principle that to meet our target our first priority was to bring in the material, and we would let the Processing Center do the sorting as part of their operation. The result was a collection of duplicates larger than we would have liked; their storage and disposal became a more significant undertaking than we had predicted. Fortunately there exists on campus an active volunteer organization, Overseas Development Network, which collects books and ships them to universities in developing countries. Currently, they are working on a massive volunteer project to ship the duplicates to needy libraries overseas with the cooperation of the Processing Plant. It is difficult to see how extensive duplication can be avoided in a gift-raising project; the issue needs to be addressed from the earliest planning stages.

ALL ESTIMATES ARE OPTIMISTIC—EVEN YOURS

The Gifts Team had undertaken to bring in 300,000 volumes, but we had never predicted, even in whispers, what number of these would prove to be exact replacements and go straight to the library shelves. In our heart of hearts, though, we were hoping that we could restore 100,000 volumes this way. In the end, the percentage yield from the gifts program was less than 20 percent of the total donated; but more than 95,000 exact match volumes (out of over 500,000 received) have gone on the shelves. We also thought that 80 percent would be journals, but of the materials on the shelves, only 67 percent are journals.

Figure 17-1 demonstrates the net yield of what was actually placed on the shelves from the gift raising program. It visually shows the difference between the high number of volumes accepted and received up front and what was actually used in the end.

RECOGNIZE WHEN THE END IS NIGH—WIND DOWN THE PROGRAM GRACEFULLY

To wind down such a massive program you will need to proceed systematically, step-by-step to insure that everyone is notified. Clarify the steps with your internal team first, then the rest of your institution and community. Make sure to announce the close down on any Website you used for this program.

Be prepared for all this to take some time. You will find that the hardest task during the wind-down is saying "No" to new offers. However, you will realize that you have reached a point of diminishing returns, and most new offers will probably be duplicates.

At Morgan Library, our original schedule showed that we would be finished by the end of March. By that time, we were ready to end our active solicitation program, even though the shipping and receipt side of the operation was still in full swing with many thousands of volumes awaiting delivery and the Processing Center was busy handling large shipments every day. We wound down the program step by step, consolidating people and resources as we did so, coordinating the wind-down with the end of our temporary appointments.

FIGURE 17–1
Gifts Receipt and Processing

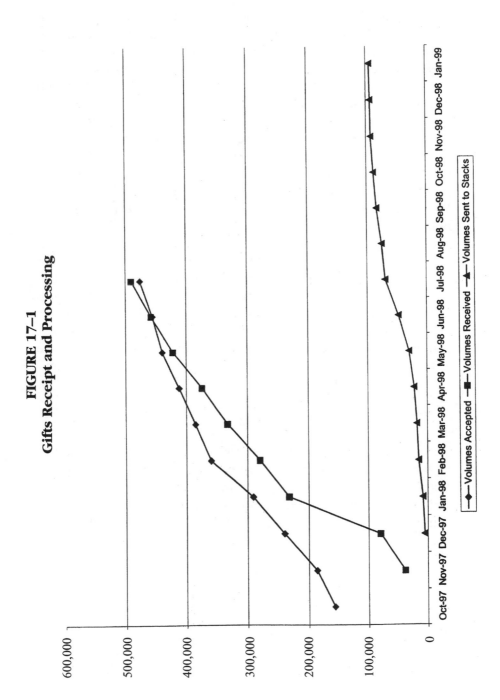

First, we advised the Donations Committee of the wind-down and obtained their approval to end the program. We announced to the campus and to the faculty liaisons that we were no longer seeking donations, and we asked the faculty to stop soliciting as well. We announced it on the Website, and discontinued the Web pages which listed all the damaged material. Of course, none of these measures meant that offers stopped coming in, and it was difficult to switch from the mindset of "if in doubt, accept" to "just say no!" By now, we had not only reached our target in terms of volumes but also had accepted offers for 9,000 unique journal titles, almost half of all the damaged titles, and these included 96 of the 100 journals most often requested through the *FastFlood* Interlibrary-Loan program.

Stopping a juggernaut takes time, however, and a firm application of the brakes. Ironically, the same voices that earlier expected the program to start up in an instant now demanded that it stop on a dime. At the time of writing, almost a year after the wind-down started, we are still not completely done with the processes of matching shipping and receipt documentation, trouble-shooting, and acknowledging donors. A graceful wind-down, we have found, requires careful planning and extremely good communications, no different from a smooth start-up process.

CONCLUSION

How does one evaluate the success of our program, designed to replace damaged and destroyed volumes with exact title/volume matches? Measured by the program's specific goals for quantity and timeliness, we succeeded. Judged financially, the donated non-damaged volumes were placed on the shelves at a cost that compared favorably with the estimated cost of either repairing or replacing them.

Library Disaster Planning and Recovery Handbook

KEY RECOMMENDATIONS

Gift Program Design

- Remember that our experience is not directly translatable to yours. Your disaster and your organizational situation and pressures will be unique.

- Recognize, however, that you will certainly have to deal with offers of donations and build this into your disaster plan.

- Consider carefully before embarking on, or being pressured into, accepting donations to replace your damaged collections.

  * Recognize that once started, you will need to follow through— and that will require significant resources.

  * Be aware of the political consequences, whichever decision you make.

- If you decide to have a donations program, take the time to build a systematic plan. Paradoxically, it will help you be more responsive and flexible to volatile situations if you have that basic structure to guide you.

- Be realistic about the results you promise or expect. Our experience showed that even with a program targeted to very specific needs, the yield of direct matches was not high.

APPENDIX 17-A
PROGRAM MANAGEMENT SCHEDULE

SCHEDULE

Date	Results/Activities		Action
by Oct. 10	▪ Program/process design completed		All
	▪ All contacts have received an initial response		Gift Activity Head
	Est. total volumes accepted	**27-30,000**	
	Est. total received	**16-18,000**	
by Oct. 17	▪ Pick-up or delivery arrangements made for 90% of campus offers		Contractor
	▪ Procedures for acceptance, shipping (merchandise return labels, etc.), receipt finalized		Gift Team
	▪ Hiring completed		Administrator & Personnel
	▪ Office space finalized, equipment ordered		Administrator
	▪ Storage & processing space finalized		Contractor & Administrator
	▪ Volunteers recruited for solicitation program		Gift Team
	▪ Web database created for inventory		Contractor
	▪ Acceptance of pending medium-large offers finalized		Gift Team
	▪ Shipping of medium-large offers starts		Gift Team
	Est. total volumes accepted	**70,000**	
	Est. total received	**23-25,000**	
by Oct. 24	▪ Solicitation program setup, volunteers trained		Gift Team
	▪ Campus receipts finalized, follow-up e-mail sent		Contractor
	▪ Processing plant setup complete		Contractor
	Est. total volumes accepted	**110,000**	
	Est. total received	**26-30,000**	
by Oct. 31	▪ Solicitation program activated		Gift Team
	▪ Shipping arranged for all pending accepted offers		Gift Team
	▪ Gift processing operations start		Contractor
	▪ Medium-large collections begin to be delivered to processing center/storage trailers		Contractor
	Est. total volumes accepted	**123,000**	
	Est. total received	**45,000**	
by Nov. 30	Acceptance, solicitation, receipts ongoing		
	Est. total volumes accepted	**175,000**	
	Est. total received	**95,000**	
by Dec. 31	**Est. total volumes accepted**	**225,000**	
	Est. total received	**195,000**	
by Jan. 31	**Est. total volumes accepted**	**275,000**	
	Est. total received	**145,000**	
by Feb. 28	**Est. total volumes accepted**	**300,000**	
	Est. total received	**245,000**	
by Mar. 31	**Est. total volumes accepted**	**300,000**	
	Est. total received	**300,000**	

18 Gift Acceptance: The Reality and the Results

Joel Rutstein

INTRODUCTION

By the middle of October, 1997, the newly re-designed gifts-so-licitation program was underway. The project manager chaired weekly meetings of the Gifts Team. These meetings were crucial because impediments to the operational flow had to be identified and eliminated. With the operation underway, we were soon work-ing closely with the Processing Center management as well as the librarians (largely Technical Services staff) who designed, trained, and worked with a large, semi-skilled labor force working in the Center. Every so often we would meet with these people as well. To maintain identities, planetary names were assigned. Gifts Team was *Mars*; Processing Center was *Earth*; and the Technical Ser-vices librarians who trained and monitored their work were called *Venus*.

THE ACCEPTANCE PROGRAM IN ACTION

Troubleshooting

Troubleshooting will be a commonplace event. Donor re-contact will be a major headache. Whoever will be processing the do-nated gifts may not be ready to handle the project at the time of gift arrivals. Even though you may maintain a Master Donor File (MDF) to track most of these queries, be prepared for some records simply falling through the cracks because of sheer volume. If this happens and donors are contacted, they may have already dis-posed of their holdings. There will be a litany of other problems, such as impatient donors or individuals needing to act quickly before shipping packets can be mailed. Many donors will request information pertaining to tax deductions or will expect certain results which may be impossible to satisfy. Additionally, anticipate rejecting a donation you find unacceptable even though the donors are insistent about its quality. Shipping problems are another major issue which are discussed elsewhere.

Outline a program of action. See the checklist below to follow a donation from start to finish utilizing the various forms. More detailed explanations of the Master Donor File, Master Journal File, and Shipping List are in Chapter 19.

What To Do When Contacted by a Donor: A Checklist

1. Determine if the item is needed. If the Gift Acceptance Unit determines a certain title is needed, then complete an *Offer of Donation* form providing the necessary information to move this query along. (See Appendix 18-A.)

2. Forward the form, plus any documentation such as e-mail messages, faxed lists, etc., to the Donor Control Unit. Here, the information is entered in two files, the Master Donor File (see Appendix 18-B) and the Master Journal File (see Appendix 18-C). This information is recorded on a *real time* basis. In other words, at any given moment records can be searched as soon as they are entered, although updated printed versions of the two main files should be issued weekly.

3. Donor Control completes a "Shipping/Delivery Checklist," with one copy for the donor's file. A distinct folder should be maintained for every donor. (See Chapter 19, Appendix 19-B.)

4. Prepare a mailing packet and send it to the donor. Include the following documents:

   a) "Information for Donors" documents. (See Appendices 18-D and 18-E.)

   b) "List of Items Donated" triplicate form needs to be filled out by donor. Donor keeps top copy, returns the two other copies in his/her shipment to the library. (See Chapter 19, Appendix 19-A.) When the shipment arrives at the Processing Center, the forms are pulled and sent to the Gifts Receipt Unit. One copy should be forwarded to university advancement, to be used in generating a letter of acknowledgment signed by the library dean. (See Appendix 18-F.) The other copy needs to be used to update the MDF and MJF and close the file. In the normal train of events, the donor would have to wait up to several months to receive his letter after the donation arrived at the Processing Center. These letters are important since they could be used for tax purposes. If needed sooner, compose a similar letter which carries legitimacy for official business until the letter arrives from advancement.

   c) Relevant carrier documents should be included, such as:

      i) U.S. Postal Service *pre-paid merchandise labels* if ten or fewer boxes shipped;

      ii) freight company *bill of lading* if more than ten boxes; and

      iii) moving van line's information if cargo had to be packed and boxed by other than the donor.

5. The "Shipping List" tracks alphabetically by donor and includes information on:

   a) when the packet was mailed;

   b) how many boxes are expected to arrive;

   c) when the material should arrive in your city; and

   d) who the carrier is. (See Appendix 18-G.)

6. All this information is then incorporated in the regular reports for the Gifts Team, the library administration, and the university Provost's Office as appropriate. Entitled the "Diary of Activity/Data Report," it should begin as a weekly

chronicle, and later become monthly when the Gifts Program slows down. (See Appendix 18-H.)

7. The Processing Center should generate its own reports on a weekly basis, recording the number of loaded pallets arriving, how many volumes are sent to *discard*, how many to *inventory*, how many to *bind*, how many to *suspend* (journals held back until volume numbers are completed), and most important, how many gift volumes actually go to the circulating shelves. (See Appendix 18-I.)

LESSONS AND OBSERVATIONS

I offer the following lessons and observations which are covered immediately in greater detail:

- Unsolicited donations will control program activity.
- Control the message.
- Expect to receive large quantities of unwanted materials.
- Target donations on a selective basis.
- Gifts may be free, but logistical support is not.
- The world of gifts has little correlation to the world of acquisitions.

Unsolicited Donations Will Control Program Activity

As discussed above, a natural disaster of great magnitude suffered by any library will generate an overwhelming sense of charity and opportunity for potential donors. By nature, when it comes to aiding others in distress, America is a benevolent country. At the same time, potential donors will see advantages for themselves as well by cleaning out basements of old, unused books and journals and may seek opportunities to claim tax deductions through donations. In the "Instructions to Donors" form, you need to clearly state your role in the appraisal process, and what steps are required by donors when preparing claims for the IRS. Luckily, IRS regulations are clear cut in this regard.

Control the Message

Since the preponderance of gift offers will emanate from unsolicited contacts, it will be paramount on the part of the recipient to control the *needs* message broadcast to the donating public. On this matter we had received advice from one library which experienced a similar, albeit less-threatening disaster. As an example, the University of North Dakota sustained some damage from flooding earlier that year when the Red River overflowed its banks. Their library director warned that people will send all kinds of relief, much of it useless, which could hamper genuine recovery efforts. With this in mind, your messages must be carefully tailored to seek only those materials you desire, and staff must be trained to exercise vigilance about unwanted material.

Expect to Receive Large Quantities of Unwanted Material

Having said that, even with carefully constructed messages, it is nearly impossible to receive only desired material, whether it comes from individuals or libraries. There is the possibility that some large professional society will publish your appeal in their newsletter after being contacted for assistance. If that should happen, you will be receiving daily calls from society members across the country who have sequestered various runs of the society's publications no longer of value to the donor. Working with so many individuals with the same titles will quickly become tedious. However, they cannot be rejected out of hand, since some of these offers could be valid.

Also, from the donors' perspective, they are not disposed to ship to you only what you requested. They will find it burdensome and inefficient to sort through long-hoarded material on basement shelves or in packed cartons. Many of these donors are older people who would have difficulty arranging and transporting heavy boxes to post offices. Even if a contracted shipper came to their houses, they would just as soon be rid of everything, rather than pull out unwanted material that you will eventually have to dump.

These next observations are applicable to libraries and corporate donors. You will receive long lists of disposable items from libraries. Even though you spend the time to scrutinize the selection of journals, including years of coverage you still need, cases will arise where the library will be unable to extract certain years requested from a particular title. This requires the donor library's staff and time, which may be in short supply. In our experience, the final product manifested itself in large quantities of extraneous material: sets we could do without, textbooks we never collected, duplicates of journals already received, and books matching our own that were never damaged or never owned to begin with. By the end of the program, less than 20 percent of all volumes brought in were matches for disaster-damaged items.

Target Donations on a Selective Basis

One component of your gifts program should be a *solicitations unit* which takes on the responsibility for identifying and soliciting damaged material from publishers and societies. This activity will be a valuable complement to the gifts program. If such an operation is contemplated in a recovery effort, the program must be carefully built around available personnel. In our case, there was a lead person responsible for most of the contacts (normally by telephone), and one clerical assistant to handle record keeping. We attempted to recruit retired librarians to volunteer, but this met with only partial success. The Gifts Team certified the existence of damaged materials from our catalog and produced lists of those damaged titles sorted by publisher. The process itself experienced mixed results. Considering the hundreds of publishers needing to be contacted, the effort was simply too limited.

Just finding the appropriate person to speak with on the publishing end will be a time-consuming chore. Further, publishers will rarely be able to provide complete replacements. Because of inventory regulations, most will have small stock holdings. Journal runs in their inventory will most likely be of recent vintage, rarely going back more than five years. In most instances, there will be loose single issues requiring binding.

Many publishers cannot supply materials free of charge, and some will offer titles at cost. Even then, such deals may not be executed since insurance companies may not cover direct replacement costs during the gift-replacement process. Other publishers may not bill you for the titles, but invoice you for sorting and packing. You will need to decide what costs your library and/or insurance companies will cover. We did cover such costs, although sometimes it became nearly as expensive as direct replacement!

The lesson to be learned is that even for limited operations, more staff will be necessary because of the complexities surrounding a solicitation program. Also, publishers must be carefully targeted. It is probably not worth the time to contact a society publishing just one journal, unless critical for your library's collection. It is far better to concentrate on publishers who print a significant number of titles that happened to be damaged in a natural disaster.

Gifts May Be Free, But Logistical Support Is Not

Should part of your disaster recovery include gift solicitation for replacements for damaged materials, there will be related costs from the donor's side. What is important to remember is there will be additional logistical costs, but they are well worth it in the long run. That is, when compared with direct replacement costs, your expenses should be within reason.

For example, in our case, subscription replacement costs for journals alone in one year would easily exceed $2,000,000, disallowing prior-year replacement costs which would add tens of millions of dollars more. One case example is the American Institute of Physics. We received nearly 50 journals published by AIP and affiliated societies. Subscription costs approach $20,000 yearly, but the shipment included several year back runs. Most likely another $100,000 are necessary to replace these. AIP charged us $10,000 for pulling, sorting, and packing this material. Yellow Freight invoiced us $2,000 in shipping charges. So we paid $12,000 for probably $120,000 of equivalent replacement costs. Using this scenario, we paid 10 percent of real costs.

There is another way to calculate costs. Of the 500,000 gift volumes brought in, nearly 20 percent were exact title matches for damaged items. Duplicates went to our *discard* pile for possible shipment overseas. Titles never owned were placed in *inventory* to be later reviewed by selectors for potential enhancement to the collection. If costs are calculated by hit rate, the scenario would look like this: front end, or Gift Team, costs run about a dollar per volume. But if only those titles going back on the shelves are counted, or 20 percent, costs would rise to $5.00 per volume. Processing Center expenses however are higher than the Gifts Team because of labor and operations. Their cost runs to $7.00 per volume, rising to $37.00 per volume for an exact title matching gift. Adding in Gift Team figures, the grand total would be $42.00 for every gift book and journal placed on the shelves. This includes bindery costs as well. Is this economical? Based on our records, $42.00 per title is a less-expensive option than direct replacement costs. Collateral benefits cannot be excluded, such as a) good will from a large population of donors, b) getting materials on the shelves quickly and in better condition, and c) an enrichment of titles to be added that had never been owned before.

The World of Gifts Has Little Correlation to the World of Acquisitions

You will discover a topsy-turvy world when gift raising. In any acquisitions program, as we know it, the truly expensive and sometimes hard to obtain titles are in the sciences and technology. Humanities and social science material comes from more established or mainstream presses and generally are much cheaper. In the gifts world, the reverse will most likely occur in its own fashion. Sci/tech material will be relatively easy to secure. In our case, we were constantly bombarded with offers of the same titles in the sciences. We managed to find donors even for esoteric and expensive journals like *Tetrahedron Letters*. However, *American Scholar* was hard to find. One of our prime distributor contacts would load up pallets of sci/tech journals and automatically ship them our way. However, humanities titles were more difficult to obtain from that company.

Why is this so? Sci/tech networks are mature and robust. People seem to know who owns what, and contacts are easy. Most special libraries focus on science and technology disciplines. For example, many drug companies are closing their libraries as they shift to online databases and Internet sources. Other libraries have switched to microform and are treating their bound journals as surplus. On the other hand, humanities titles often have low print runs, and owners retain them because their intellectual value fails to diminish over time.

In our situation, most materials we received were serial in nature, perhaps up to 85 percent. One donor contributed his entire personal library of constitutional studies amounting to over 10,000 books. But such gifts of book collections were uncommon. Unlike journals, books were not tracked; and many offers came in the form of textbooks, which we never collected in our collection-development process.

Let me end this chapter by providing a bit of flavor extracted from the files of our thousands of donors. One anonymous person wrote:

> Attached are the names of books I have kept since 1974 that hopefully you will say can now reside in the . . . archives of the library. If you do not take them, they are doomed to another 20-plus years in a box in the garage for my relatives to try to figure out what to do with them. Do let me know their fate.

And from another individual:

> I have an almost complete set of PMLA from 1950. Ditto *American Literature.* Also scattered bound volumes of *19^b C. American Review* and *Atlantic,* and publications of the Thoreau Society for fifty years or so. Would you have a use for these periodicals? I am an 82-year-old retired university English professor and doubt that I shall have any use for these materials on the other side of the River Styx. Pro bono, of course.

CONCLUSION: CULTIVATE THE DONOR

As the point person for most donor contacts, which totaled nearly 4,000 individuals, I found it a joy to work with the great majority. For all that is said and done, the average donor truly desired to provide help in some fashion. Although the response was overwhelming, here are some additional recommendations to consider:

- There has to be one contact source for your donors. If there is more than one contact source, confusion will reign. The best approach is probably the way we originally set up the Gifts Acceptance Unit. One person (as head) would receive all messages, which then would be forwarded as necessary to one other support librarian who was assigned half time to the team.

- It is very important to treat each donor in a considerate manner. Infinite patience is required and courtesy must be shown at all times because every donor believes he or she is the only person offering materials. We treated each donor as if this person was a potential friend and booster for the library.

- Acknowledge in a formal fashion all major donors. At the end of the Gifts Program, we held a ceremony to commemorate our recovery on the anniversary year of the disaster. We invited as many donors as possible to attend the event and thank them for their contributions. A special plaque, taking up the space of an entire wall, was commissioned which contained the engraved names of all donors who contributed at least $1,870 (a special figure at CSU because 1870 was the year the university was founded) in gifts of kind, cash, or service.

The inscription above the names reads:

On the Night of July 28, 1997, Waters From an Intensive Storm Damaged 433,000 Books and Journals in Morgan Library. This Plaque Commemorates Those Donors Who Contributed 1,870 Dollars or More as Gifts of Cash, Gifts of Kind, and Gifts of Service. Their Generous Acts Have Greatly Aided Our Recovery. For This the Staff of the University Libraries Are Eternally Grateful.

Library Disaster Planning and Recovery Handbook

KEY RECOMMENDATIONS

Gift Acceptance

- Hold weekly meetings with the project manager and the Gifts Team.
- Be diplomatic in your dealings with all donors and cultivate them in a considerate manner—no matter how impatient, demanding, or lacking in understanding of the donations acceptance process they may be.
- Supply accurate information to donors pertaining to potential tax deductions.
- Outline a program of action that delineates step-by-step what happens with incoming donations.
- Design a checklist of necessary forms.
- Document why a donation was accepted or rejected.
- Implement a Shipping/Delivery/Receiving procedural outline.
- Make sure that your processing center generates weekly activity reports.
- Be forewarned that unsolicited donations—often in great quantities—will still arrive on your doorstep.
- Control the message as to what materials your recovering library really needs.
- Target donations on a selective basis whenever possible by creating a *solicitations unit* within your Gifts Program.
- Realize that gifts may seem to be free, but logistical support to fully handle/process them is not.
- Arrange to pay for shipping costs in order to receive important replacement materials during your library's recovery period; estimate what percentage of real costs you will actually pay by using this technique.
- Consider forwarding discards and duplicates to organizations which forward educational materials to schools or countries in need.
- Expect much duplication in donations; provide a mechanism to keep the best and properly dispose of the rest.
- Acknowledge in a special way all those who contributed to the recovery/restoration of your library collections through their donation of materials, services, or facilities.

APPENDIX 18-A
MORGAN LIBRARY GIFTS PROGRAM

OFFER OF DONATION (LIBRARY MATERIALS)

Donor Name: ....

Address:

....

....

Contact name (if different): ....

Phone................................ Fax:......................... e-mail:..

Date of previous contact (if any):....................................... By whom:..

Description of donation (please provide as much detail as you can)

Approximate size of donation: ☐.................volumes   ☐.................boxes

ACTION TAKEN: Date:.................... Your name: ....
☐   Told them someone will get back to them (give details):...
☐   Accepted offer (give details)..
☐   Declined offer (give details)...
☐   Other (give details):..

SEND THIS FORM TO GIFTS COORDINATOR
GIFTS PROGRAM USE ONLY

Date   Action

....
....
....
....
....

☐   Donor Master List updated Date:.................... Initials....................................

APPENDIX 18-B
MASTER DONOR FILE

Name	Address	Initial Contact	Donation Subject/Title	Follow-Up	Results/Thank You	DNR TY	VLS ACPT	VLS REC'D
Donor 1	Government Office	Website	Journals Jrn Bact, Appl Env Microbio	11/4/97 D1 e-mailed accepting offer 11/14/97 sent shipping packet, 8 mailing labels 2/17/98 Received materials 3/31/98 Acknowledged by Foundation	Accepted offer Packet sent Received materials	1	90	14
Donor 2	Home	Home Telephone	Journals IEEE Transactions On Software, IEEE Computers	9/20/97 Received materials 2/19/98 Acknowledged by Foundation	Received materials Acknowledged -Finished-	LOC	60	60
Donor 3		Publisher Telephone	SEE IG/BR FILES	Will accept, asked for lists. Has many contacts. Waiting for Donor valuation documents 12/12/97 Received materials 2/19/98 Acknowledged by Foundation	SEE IG/BR FILES	P	939	939

APPENDIX 18-C
MASTER JOURNAL FILE

Journal Title	Volumes & Dates of Run	Donor	Accepted ?	Est. Vols	Notes
IEEE Computer	1980-1990 incomplete	Individual	Y	28	
IEEE Computer Graphics & Applications	1-11 1981-91	Publisher	Rec. 12/4	11	
IEEE Computer Graphics & Applications	1976-97	Association	Y	40	
IEEE Computer Magazine	1976-96	Individual	Rec. 2/16/98		5 boxes
IEEE Control Systems	2, 7-11, 1982, 1987-1991 incomplete	Individual	Y	6	
IEEE Control Systems	13-18, 1993-1998	University	Rec. 1/24/98	6	

APPENDIX 18-D
INFORMATION FOR DONORS WHO WILL BE PACKING & SHIPPING

Thank you for your donation to Colorado State University Libraries! While the flood brought destruction, it also brought generosity. We very much appreciate the support of our alumni, community members, and other friends as we rebuild our collections. Here is information we hope will help you get your donation to us with the utmost convenience.

CSU Libraries Gifts Policy

All gifts to the Libraries are made with the understanding that the Libraries becomes the owner of the material upon receipt and as such reserves the right to determine disposition of such gifts. Complimentary or review copies of books received free may be donated to the Libraries, but cannot be used as a tax-deductible gift. Items purchased with state or federal funds cannot be used as a tax-deductible gift.

Gift Valuation

Donors may supply an estimate of value if the gift is valued at less than $5,000. Appraisal of a gift to the Libraries for tax deduction purposes is the responsibility of the donor. The Libraries, and a donee, is disqualified from appraising donations. If a gift is valued at greater than $5,000 and the donor wishes to deduct the gift for tax purposes, the donor should have the collection appraised by a certified appraiser, fill out IRS Form 8283, and send a copy to the Colorado State University Foundation, P.O. Box 1870, Fort Collins, CO 80522-1870. Donors may also wish to consult their attorney or tax consultant.

Packing

Please pack your donation into sturdy cardboard boxes no larger than a copy paper box, and do not exceed 50-lbs. weight in a single box. If the box is not full, use packing material to fill it.

Do not over-fill boxes—leave an inch or so at the top so your books won't be damaged when the box is opened. Recycled boxes are welcome; please make sure the boxes don't have holes in them and remove any old shipping labels.

Complete the enclosed three-part **List of Items Donated** for your entire donation. If your titles will not fit on one form, please attach a list. When you are ready to ship, please remove the top (white) copy of the list as your personal record, and pack the two remaining copies (yellow and pink) and any attached list together **inside** box one of your shipment. Place the form on top of the books, underneath any packing material you have added. Seal the boxes with packing tape and number each box in the shipment, e.g. Box 1 of 1, Box 2 of 5, etc.

SHIPPING INFORMATION

☐ Donor will ship
If you are arranging and paying for shipping, we appreciate your additional generosity. The correct address to use for U.S. Mail is:

Library Rate   Morgan Library—Flood Gifts
Colorado State University
Fort Collins, CO 80523-1019

The correct street address for UPS and other shippers is:
Colorado State University
Morgan Library—Flood Gifts
200 West Lake Street
Fort Collins, CO 80523

Please notify us when you ship by calling or e-mailing [name], [phone], [e-mail address].

If CSU is paying for shipping
☐ Merchandise Return Labels
We have enclosed postage paid USPS Merchandise Return labels for your use in mailing your boxes of books and journals to

CSU. These may be mailed through any post office or collection box or, in the case of a business or organization, through your regular business mail service (please let your carrier know you will be shipping this way). Please attach one label to each box. **Important**: Add your return address in the indicated space on EACH label. It is not necessary to complete any other part of the label. If you need more labels, please call or e-mail [name], [phone], [e-mail address].

☐ Road Freight

To ship by road freight, please call Yellow Freight at 1-800-610-6500 and arrange pickup. Shipping costs will be charged to CSU's account if you request them to charge "Freight Collect". You must complete a Bill of Lading for your shipment. We have attached a preprinted one for your convenience, and they can also be obtained direct from Yellow Freight. The correct description of the freight is "BOOKS Item 161560 Cl.65". When your shipment is picked up, the driver will give you a receipt with a PRO Number. This will be your reference if your shipment needs to be tracked. Please label each box in the shipment with the address:

Colorado State University
Morgan Library—Flood Gifts
200 West Lake St.
Fort Collins, CO 80523-1019

▲ We are sorry, but the university and the Libraries cannot under any circumstances accept C.O.D. deliveries.

If you have questions or need help arranging for shipment, please contact [name], [phone], or [e-mail address].

Thank you again for your donation.

APPENDIX 18-E
INFORMATION FOR DONORS
MORGAN LIBRARY DISASTER RECOVERY GIFTS PROGRAM
(NORTH AMERICAN VAN LINES)

Thank you for your donation to Colorado State University Libraries! While the disaster brought destruction, it also brought generosity. We very much appreciate the support of our alumni, community members, and other friends as we rebuild our collections.

CSU Libraries Gifts Policy
All gifts to the Libraries are made with the understanding that the Libraries becomes the owner of the material upon receipt and as such reserves the right to determine disposition of such gifts. Complimentary or review copies of books received free may be donated to the Libraries, but cannot be used as a tax-deductible gift. Items purchased with state or federal funds cannot be used as a tax-deductible gift.

Gift Valuation
Donors may supply an estimate of value if the gift is valued at less than $5,000. Appraisal of a gift to the Libraries for tax deduction purposes is the responsibility of the donor. The Libraries, as a donee, is disqualified from appraising donations. If a gift is valued at greater than $5,000 and the donor wishes to deduct the gift for tax purposes, the donor should have the collection appraised by a certified appraiser, fill out IRS Form 8283, and send a copy to the Colorado State University Foundation, P.O. Box 1870, Fort Collins CO 80522-1870. Donors may also wish to consult their attorney or tax consultant.

Please complete the enclosed three-part **List of Items Donated** form for your entire donation. If your titles will not fit on one form, please attach a list. When you are ready to ship, remove the top (white) copy of the list as your personal record and pack the two remaining copies (yellow and pink) and any attached list, together **inside** Box one of your shipment.

If you have further questions or need assistance, please contact [name] at [phone] or [e-mail address].

Thank you again for your donation!

APPENDIX 18-F
ACKNOWLEDGMENT LETTER

[Date]

[Name]
[Address 1]
[Address 2]

Dear

On behalf of the students, faculty, and staff of Colorado State University and the University Libraries, thank you so much for your recent contribution to the Morgan Library Flood Relief Fund. All of us at Colorado State University have been moved by your concern and comforted by your generosity and compassion.

The staff of the University Libraries is working hard to restore full service to the students, faculty, and community, and to rebuild the collection. Much of our success in recovery efforts can be attributed to positive support from people like you—our community members, alumni, and friends. We could not do it without your commitment to helping us move forward with rebuilding the library facilities and collection. Thank you for helping us make the Morgan Library whole again!

Sincerely,

Dean of Libraries

APPENDIX 18-G
SHIPPING LIST FOR TRACKING DONORS

Donor Name & Category	Number of Cartons	Expected Receipt Date	Carrier
Doe, Bill	180	12/4	YF
Doe, Jane	17	12/1	USPS
Doe, John	27	pickup	USPS
Company Z	245	12/14	YF
Publisher X	3,010	12/18	YF

APPENDIX 18-H
DIARY OF ACTIVITY / DATA REPORT

★ Solicitation Program Contacts
  Publishers contacted with lists of damaged titles sent.
  23 Associations, Societies, Organizations, Academic Presses contacted this week.
  [List by Name]

★ Gifts Team sets tentative date of April 1 for phasing-out program.

★ Publisher collection accepted. Expect over 30,000 volumes to arrive.

★ Societal publishers now being actively solicited.

★ As of January 31, Gifts Program has accepted 3,685 unique journal title runs.

★ Donor offer contacts reach 3,000.

Progress Data Report

Contact Activity	1/26 – 2/6	Total to Date
Number of e-mail contacts received	22	819
Number of Web responses via electronic form	47	1,346
Number of phone/letter contacts	12	611
Publishers solicited	24	223
Total	**105**	**3,001**

Donated Material Accepted/Received		
Number of shipping packets mailed	104	1,162
Number of volumes accepted	21,225	289,170
Donated materials received (vol. est.)	26,460	245,155

Estimated Amount of Material Offered (by volume)		
Potential Donations of Large/Medium Magnitude		132,000
Corporation	7,300	7,300
Publisher	30,000	30,000
Est. Potential Donations per Contact (excluding above)		
Web response	1,257	18,349
E-mail, phone/letter response	9,991	189,967
Est. Grand Total	**48,548**	**377,616**

APPENDIX 18-I
PROCESSING CENTER ACTIVITY REPORT
GIFTS—TOTAL TO DATE

Report Date: Week Ending October 23, 1998

Activities	This Week	October Total	YTD Total
Volumes Received (est.)[1, 2]	6,169	16,669	863,408
Boxes unpacked	131	568	24,493
Volumes sent to library stacks (match)	1,609	3,609	86,248
Volumes sent to discard[3]	3,367	6,227	195,130
Volumes sent to suspend (match)[4]	249	713	45,982
Volumes sent to inventory[5]	2,686	4,544	83,710
Subtotal volumes processed	*7,911*	*15,093*	*411,070*
Volumes still in process	**-1,742**	**1,576**	**452,338**

Grand Total Volumes sent to Stacks (1997 & 1998)[6]	**88,326**

Definitions:
1. Volumes (estimates) include a) monographs, b) serials volumes received bound, and c) serials volumes received as loose issues.
2. Volumes given in other categories are bound volumes equivalents (1 bound volume = 1 SAGE item record).
3. Discard is defined as volumes not needed by CSU because the CSUL volume was not damaged in the disaster of volumes that are duplicates if volumes already received.
4. Suspend is defined as volumes that are incomplete and will be processed at a later date.
5. Inventory is defined as volumes not owned by CSUL.
6. This total has been adjusted in accordance with CSUL released items.

19 Gift Receipt: What to Do When the Flood Gates Open

Barbara Branstad

INTRODUCTION

Because of my thirty years of experience in collection development, I was brought on board about the middle of September 1997 to assist the collection-development officer with the increasing deluge of disaster gift offers and receipts. Another collection-development specialist was reassigned to aid in answering the vast amount of incoming e-mail messages; but my responsibility was shipping. Did I have any experience with the trucking industry? Absolutely not. But librarians can learn anything, right? So in we plunged.

FINDING A PLACE TO STORE THE MATERIAL

One of the first obstacles you will face will be to locate a physical space for the gifts to be stored before they are processed. Local community members and faculty will be very generous in wanting to give you materials, but it will be difficult to accept them if you have no place to put them, no staff to record them, and no equipment to haul them. Books and journals are heavy!

Luckily for us, our library depository was only two blocks away, but it already contained lesser-used materials in storage. Also, as "orphans" from the disaster, Interlibrary Loan and the mail room were still operating from this facility. Was there room for a small gifts section as well? Our friend from North American Van Lines brought a trailer out and parked it at the Depository. Two students were hired at 20 hours each; supplies were requisitioned including two handtrucks; and suddenly the rudiments of a receipt center was established.

If donors insisted on bringing material to us, they were now able to drop it off at the Depository. While the students' work hours didn't cover an entire 40-hour week, they still were there much of the time to receive items. If they were not available, staff from Interlibrary Loan or the mail room were pressed into service. The students opened each box, filled out a Donor Form, recorded the contents, and moved the box to the trailer. Since they could only lift boxes about waist high, the trailer soon became an inefficiently-packed nightmare, but there was no space anywhere else. We anticipated that this arrangement would last only a few weeks until the contract was signed and the Processing Center opened; in actuality we operated in this make-shift fashion for over two months.

I stopped by the Depository each day to pick up the Donor Forms (see Appendix 19-A). If the contents were books, the general subject area was recorded; if journals, the titles and the volumes and years were captured. I then entered these titles on the Master Journal List so we would have a record not only of what had been offered but of what had actually been received.

Some faculty members were insistent that their materials be picked up *now*. Sometimes they were moving offices and needed to clear materials out; sometimes they were going out of the country; and sometimes they incorrectly assumed that the faster we received the materials, the faster they would be back on the shelves. If a faculty member couldn't wait, the students were sent with a handtruck to their office to pick up the materials. This was a very inefficient system, much of it hard manual labor which the students were ill-prepared to do. As much as possible, the faculty were encouraged to wait, but as the weeks turned into months, they became increasingly, and understandably, impatient. Community donors as well wanted someone to come and get the materials out of their basements, garages, and studies. We were going to lose valuable, needed material if we didn't devise a better system, and soon.

An independent consulting and disaster-recovery firm was still negotiating with the university the contract for the Processing Center and until that was signed no material could begin to go through the system. We could, however, begin to receive and stockpile material in anticipation of the opening of the Processing Center.

CREATING THE RECEIPT PROCESS

The first thing to determine is what information is needed about your donors. Next you need a place to record it. Also needed is the information donors have to get from you in order to facilitate the process at their end.

CREATING AND MAINTAINING FILES

You need to consider an efficient means of tracking and locating gifts materials.

We recommend: the Master Donor File, the Master Journal File, and the Shipping List. Establish the Master Donor File at the beginning to keep track of contacts and offers. This file expands, records, and tracks every piece of information about a donor, the donation, and the dates on which action occurred. Decide whether using the name of the individual making the offer—even if the offer were from another library or a company—as the primary entry will work best for you. Publishers and societies might be the only exceptions; they can be listed under the name of the organization with cross references from the individuals involved. The name of the individual can be perceived to be the most unique tag. You might have several offers from one university, all from different departments, or several individuals in one department. Using personal names allows you the most accuracy in matching up receipts with offers. It won't be a perfect system, however, because some donors perceive themselves to be facilitators and not necessarily donors. In addition, as in our case, the Processing Center didn't always record the name of the individual on the Items Donated Form.

Our Master Donor File (see Chapter 18, Appendix 18-B) was created on WordPerfect, but as it grew it became increasingly cumbersome and access to it for inputting was limited. We finally transferred the Master Donor File from WordPerfect to Microsoft Access, which gave us a much more useable document. It could be searched by any piece of information; frequently the ZIP Code turned out to be the key in reconciling the donor with the donation.

Recommendation: Be sure the donors know that your records and files are kept under their individual names and ask them to put that on the shipping labels.

Establish your Master Journal File as an alphabetical list of journal titles (see Chapter 18, Appendix 18-C). Include the volumes and years of the run, the donor's name, and a "y" for accepted. This "y" changes to "REC" and includes the date as the file is updated to reflect the receipt of the journals. Later on, add a departmental code to all the journal titles in your database; this enables you to print out lists of titles by academic department so faculty in those areas can quickly see what you have received. Continue to build the Master Journal File as offers are accepted, recorded, and eventually received. This will assist you in keeping track of duplicates in order to avoid accepting the same item over and over again. Use a software database such as Microsoft Access to keep track of several hundred pages of data. This worked well for us and allowed us to more efficiently access titles.

Next, we recommend maintaining a third file, the Shipping List (see Appendix 18-G). You need to maintain a list of what material is expected to arrive, by what carrier, and the anticipated date of arrival. As offers are accepted and donor packets sent out, add this information to the Shipping List. Record receipts on this file.

Although it was easy to scan down the list and pick out those items we had anticipated receiving but which had not shown up, I'm not sure the Shipping List was worth the time and labor involved in maintaining it. We maintained this list at the request of the Processing Center contractor. It was printed weekly and given to the Processing Center contractor. If we could have included this information in the Master Donor File and been able to extract reports from that, it would have been preferable. It seems like we ended up recording some of the same information three times.

Recommendation: Although time is of the essence and one does not usually have the luxury of creating and testing a database from scratch, it is preferable to put as much information as possible into one database, capable of being manipulated for many uses.

This will save countless hours of entering the same data in different files and will greatly reduce the error rate.

DELIVERY MECHANISMS

For many donors, having the shipping costs picked up by another party will make the difference as to whether or not they will donate materials to you. In some cases, where huge shipments are involved, you can also pay for the cost of packaging the materials prior to shipment. If speed is of the essence, you must be able to pay for both shipping and packing. If the donor (especially a library) is doing the packing, it is frequently a low-priority for them and takes months for their personnel (often students) to get it completed.

In our case, insurance paid for the cost of having materials shipped to us, whether it was via the U.S. Post Office, Yellow Freight, or North American Van Lines. These were the only carriers by which the university could underwrite the cost of shipping; we could not reimburse a donor if another shipper was selected. We did have donors who were convinced they could get us a better deal with their trucking company, and maybe they could have. However the nightmare of sending these contracts out to bid and maintaining relations with a myriad of shippers made me very glad that we had designated carriers.

HOW DO YOU HANDLE "WALK-INS"?

Although this might seem like the easiest method to receive materials, in reality, it is one of the most difficult. Many of the individuals donating in this way will not have been pre-screened; they just arrive with a bag or a box of materials. Invariably much of it will not be useful because it wasn't lost in the disaster; it is malodorous; it had already been received in a similar donation; or it doesn't fit your collection development criteria regardless of the disaster. We received material like this at the Morgan Library Information Desk which was staffed by students and non-gift staff. Trained to be helpful and responsive, they tried to assist but were often unable to answer questions and were not prepared to deal with angry or frustrated donors. Worse will be the donor who arrives at your Information Desk, announces that he or she has a carload of materials and wants someone to unload it for them *now*. Incidents like these will happen, so be prepared.

In our case, material received from the walk-in donations piled up behind the Information Desk causing an eyesore and space problems. Additionally, these materials needed to be hauled somewhere else. Before the Processing Center opened, two students and I (armed with trusty handcarts) hauled these donations away— usually out to my car where I would then take them to the Depository. When the Processing Center opened, its personnel made regularly scheduled runs up from the lower level to remove the material. Although they frequently had to be prodded, they had the staff and the equipment to do the job. We did not.

DEALING WITH "HIT-AND-RUN," "DROP-OFF" DONORS

Another problem you may experience is keeping track of walk-in donors. Your staff can attempt to give them a List of Items Donated Form (Appendix 19-A) to complete, which is placed with the donation and allows for tracking; however, donors sometimes will just want to leave their materials without filling out a form; don't want to be thanked; or don't want their name(s) in your records. Record these donations as "Unknown." However, it will become difficult to distinguish between those that were truly unknown and those that your Processing Unit records as unknown simply because they fail to keep all boxes of a donation together.

It was our experience that when donations were being accepted at our Depository, prior to the opening of the Processing Center, donors were told they could drop their materials off there and many did. At no time could an individual donor drive a car or truck to the Morgan Library loading dock and off-load a shipment. The loading dock was not a safe place since it was still a staging area for the ongoing building construction. Also, there were no library personnel stationed there to receive donations, and the Processing Center staff received materials only from the scheduled shippers and only at specified times during the day. It was difficult to get donors to understand why they just couldn't drive up and drop things off at the library.

Not having a paper trail is the worst thing about walk-in, drop-off donations. We lost a large drop-off donation for nearly six months; the donor had delivered it himself to the Depository, but there was no record of its receipt and it could not be located anywhere. It was a large donation and contained tax information as well. We believed it had been dropped off and taken to warehouse storage but we simply couldn't verify that we actually had it. Eight months after it was originally delivered, it surfaced from warehouse storage.

Recommendation: Realize from the beginning that people will want to give you material. You need to immediately make plans to both accommodate them and to delay them until you can handle the donation.

In times of disasters, people want to help, and their donations and contacts can be a great source of materials. However, you must be prepared to manage both materials and donors as soon as possible. Valuable donations were forfeited at the beginning of our set-up process because the donor was unable to wait until the Processing Center was in place and either tossed the material out or gave it elsewhere. Anything you can do to persuade donors to both wait until you are ready and to let you pick up their items will be to your benefit. They think they are helping by delivering the materials themselves; and it's difficult to persuade them that it's more cost-effective to go through your standard procedures.

ACCOMMODATING LOCAL PICK-UPS

Very likely, several community and faculty members may offer you materials that have been stored in their homes. Often the material will be too voluminous for the donor to deliver, and, in some cases, it may need to be boxed before delivery. We had thought that the students we hired might be able to do this, but it quickly became apparent that this was beyond their capabilities. Time schedules didn't coordinate; the students didn't have the strength to lift the materials; and the library van designated for this service was frequently in use elsewhere. To our benefit, the Processing Center hired a local pickup and delivery service to handle these donations, but they soon realized this was beyond their capacity as well. There was simply too much material for one person and a mini-van to handle. So, what do you do next?

USING A COURIER SERVICE

If you already have some type of cooperative courier service in place, you would think this would work for pick-up of donated material; I hope it does. However, be prepared for the opposite. In our case, there was an established courier service for the regional library system which handled Interlibrary-Loan requests from the participating libraries. It was thought that this system could be utilized for bringing donations from area libraries as well. But it didn't work as anticipated. The volume of material was too heavy; donations had to be sent in numerous small shipments which made tracking and recording difficult; and the couriers themselves didn't buy into this. We had accepted a generous offer of medical journals from the National Jewish Hospital in Denver, but as they shipped materials to us, they ran out of boxes. We had purchased boxes for this and they were sent via the courier to their librarian. After a long delay, the empty boxes arrived back at my door—the courier had simply refused to deliver them. The librarian and I were going to meet halfway between Ft. Collins and Denver, have lunch, and transfer the materials ourselves, when another solution presented itself.

USING AN ESTABLISHED MOVING COMPANY

Assess your packing and shipping needs for donor convenience and, if at all possible, arrange with a local moving company to work with you. The local company will already be sympathetic to your disaster and your recovery needs, thus will probably be more willing to accommodate those needs than an out-of-state company.

Again, our friend at North American Van Lines saved the day. For local donations, we arranged with North American to have their staff go to the donor's home, box the material, and transport it to us. Since North American is a moving company, as opposed to a shipping company, they are bonded to enter individuals' homes and to pack materials. When a donor needed this service, we completed a Shipping Packet and sent it to the donor. A copy of the instructions was faxed to North American Van Lines who called the donor and arranged for the pickup. (See Appendix 19-C).

A similar operation was established for pickups at area libraries. The contact person at the donor library would be sent the Shipping Packet. North American would be faxed a copy; call the library contact and make arrangements for pickup. Not only did this method work well for local donors and local libraries, it also worked well for donors out-of-state, especially those individuals whose material was in their homes and who needed assistance in boxing as well as transporting. Several of our donors were elderly, retired individuals who were generously donating what had been their personal working collections; if we hadn't been able to offer a packing and shipping service to them, they could not have given us the material we needed. In addition to assisting the donors, we also had a paper trail that enabled us to track these shipments and know where they were in the receiving pipeline.

The invoices for North American's services were part of the contract negotiated between the Processing Center contractor and the university; the library did not have to directly pay or keep track of these invoices.

Recommendation: If at all fiscally possible, use a local moving company to handle the large, more complicated donations that require packing the materials. This will lessen the work and the headaches for your staff.

USING THE U.S. POST OFFICE

For small donations, generally ten boxes or less, we recommend sending the donor pre-paid mailing labels using a U.S. Postal Service Merchandise Return Labels deposit account. Address the labels to reflect your particular circumstances (e.g., "Morgan Library—Flood Gifts") and have the gift account number on them. They are extremely inexpensive to print and the postage was charged at a rate similar to *library rate*. These labels should be used by individuals or for small shipments from other libraries. Your donors should have no difficulty in mailing the materials and will be very appreciative that they did not have to pay for the cost of shipping.

As with many complicated processes, something will go awry. In our case, although the labels clearly said "Flood Gift" on them, some did go astray. The Processing Center also accidentally received materials not designated for them, such as Interlibrary-Loan shipments. Several of these were processed before the error was discovered. After much time and effort, these waylaid shipments were tracked down, removed from the processing routine, and directed to the rightful recipients.

Recommendation: Be sure to set up a deposit account and remember to anticipate having to replenish it as funds run low. Charges should be deducted from the deposit account when the materials arrive on your doorstep. Having pre-printed disaster labels printed in a color other than white will make it easier for all involved to identify parcels of donations, direct them properly, and assist in alerting the Processing Center when mistaken shipments are received.

USING A FREIGHT LINE

The greatest number of our shipments were sent via Yellow Freight, an international trucking company. Colorado State University had already negotiated a favorable contract with Yellow Freight, the designated carrier for the State of Colorado, so the library did not have to go to bid for this contract. However, if you need such a service and do put it out to bid, here are some of the things to consider before awarding the contract:

- Negotiate a discount. In our case, Yellow Freight offered us a 60 percent discount on all shipments on the North American continent.
- Look for pleasant personnel. The sales representative for Yellow Freight could not have been more helpful in guiding me through the intricacies of the trucking industry. Although I never dealt directly with any of the drivers, all the other Yellow Freight personnel were also very helpful; and my contact in the Processing Center reported that the drivers were also courteous and cooperative.

- Expect from the company a toll-free number and the computer capacity to track shipments. Occasionally I had to contact Yellow Freight to try and locate a shipment. If I had the shipment number, they could do it instantly. If all I had was the donor's name and/or the place of origin, it may have taken a little longer, but the problem was usually resolved.
- Expect a national network of local trucking companies which feed into the primary shipper. When donors received the shipping packet and were ready to ship, they called the 800 number and were connected with a local representative who would make arrangements for pickup. Out of all freight transactions in this receiving process, only one problem was encountered: when Yellow Freight simply could not get even their smallest truck up into the Berkeley hills in California to pick up some materials on our behalf. They were willing to arrange for a local service to do this and transfer the material, but since it also needed boxing, we arranged for North American Van Lines (with a very small truck!) to handle it. Flexibility is key.
- Expect and demand speed and efficiency. Once a shipment was on the road it usually took no more than five days for it to arrive in Fort Collins.

Recommendation: If your institution does not have a current, most favorable contract with a shipping company, then you may want to see about requesting a waiver to the bid process because of possible time delays. Also, the use of a shipping company is a time-saver and godsend. Do not hesitate to use them for such a massive project.

WORKING WITH INTERNATIONAL SHIPMENTS

Depending on the emphasis of your damaged collection, you may need to accumulate donors from foreign countries who have valuable materials to donate. If that is the case, you must be prepared to deal with the international shipments. The shipments must clear customs, so you either authorize your carrier to clear it through their customs broker via a Power of Attorney or establish your own customs broker.

We had several donors from Europe and Australia who offered valuable, much-needed material. All we had to do was arrange for the shipping. If I knew little about shipping within the United States, I knew less about international shipping, except that it took forever and things always got lost. Fortunately, Yellow Freight International was just as easy to deal with as Yellow Freight itself; and with a minimum of confusion, we were able to receive shipments from overseas. Since the university is prohibited from giving out Powers of Attorney, we established our own customs broker in Denver. Shipments arrived in either the ports of New York or Los Angeles, were then trucked to Denver where the customs broker cleared them with the necessary paperwork, and then shipped on to us.

We had a separate shipping instructions sheet for overseas shipments which included the telephone number for the Yellow Freight partner in the specific country or city. After being contacted by a donor, I would call the Yellow Freight International toll-free number, get the correct phone number for Yellow Fright, and enter it on the sheet to be sent to the donor. The international shipments proved to be relatively straightforward and trouble-free.

Yellow Freight International deals primarily with Europe and Asia; they were just beginning to establish a South American network and do not conduct business in either Africa or the Middle East. One of our potential donors was a librarian in Israel. It was with great regret that I had to tell her we could not accept her donations since we had no way to pay for them. They arrived anyway; she and her library had generously assumed the cost.

PROCESSING OF GIFT RECEIPTS BEGINS

At some point, obviously, you need to prepare for the processing of all donated materials you receive. If you have something sent to a processing center, expect some of the following challenges:

- Expect boxes of materials to be stockpiled because it will take the processing center time to work out all the bugs.
- Expect storage/space problems; prepare for alternative, short-term storage.

- Prioritize important shipments and get these processed first.
- Don't be deterred because everything doesn't work exactly right immediately!

Nearly four months after the disaster, the Processing Center opened for business in the lower level of Morgan Library. All donations received by mail were immediately delivered there. Although donors could still drop materials off at the Depository, most of them had either done so or could be persuaded to let us arrange to have the material picked up. Shipments from Yellow Freight and North American Van Lines started to come directly to the Processing Center, but the volume soon overwhelmed them. Because there was little room to store shipments in the Center itself, shipments from all carriers were automatically re-directed to the North American Van Lines warehouse and stockpiled. They were then brought in to the Center as they were ready to process them.

At one point there were over 500 pallets of material stored in the warehouse. Since a pallet holds approximately 36 boxes, that meant there were 18,000 boxes of volumes waiting to be processed! We attempted to prioritize the shipments as much as possible, asking the Center staff to do the large ones or the ones we knew would have a high exact-title match rate first. The Center attempted to do this as much as possible, but since the shipments were arranged in the warehouse by order of receipt, it was frequently impossible to unearth an early shipment until later ones—which physically blocked access to them—could be processed.

What happens when things don't work exactly right immediately? Here is an example. The first material to be handled by the Processing Center were all the donations received from August through November which had been brought to the Depository and stored in the trailer. When this trailer was hauled to the parking lot next to the library loading dock, the weight of it broke through the asphalt, the material inside (never packed well to begin with) shifted, many boxes split or opened, and the material was separated from the paperwork accompanying it. This was not an auspicious beginning! Yet, we survived the ordeal and so shall you.

HOW THE GIFTS RECEIPT PROCESS SHOULD WORK

After contacts are made and donations accepted, send the donor a shipping packet of instructions and labels or a bill of lading. Require the donor to: 1) pack two copies of the Donor Form in the first box; 2) complete the labels or bills of lading; and 3) number the boxes 1 of 10, 2 of 10, and so forth. These procedures should finalize the arrangements to ship or deliver. When you receive the donated materials, the unpacking staff must first verify that all boxes in the shipment are present. If they are not, set aside the shipment unopened until all boxes have arrived. Once the shipment is complete, open the boxes and extract the copies of the List of Items Donated Form (Appendix 19-A); compare the contents of the shipment to what was written on the form; and make any additions or corrections. The materials then go through the processing routine and the forms go to Gifts Receipts Unit. If a form is not included in the shipment, the unpacking staff will have to complete one.

Once the forms are received in the Gifts Receipts Unit, they are first used to update the Shipping List (arranged by individual donor) to show that this donation had been received. Next, the Master Journal File is updated, discrepancies noted between what was offered and what was received, and new titles are added. Non-received titles should not be deleted as they frequently turn up later. The forms are then sent to the Donor Control Unit where the Master Donor File is updated, and the form separated. One part should be sent to whatever department recognizes gifts made to your library (e.g., development office) for them to prepare a letter of acknowledgment and thanks; place the other part in the donor's individual file. Because a gifts program is a highly visible donation activity, it is important to have the backing and assistance of the parent organization's development office.

Potential Problems

All in all, the gifts receipt system should work quite smoothly if all parties cooperate and fulfill mutually agreed upon procedures. However, a major potential problem with this system and one which will drive everything else is that the library staff who train the processing-center staff usually will concentrate their training on the library records and not on the donors and the information needed by the Gifts Team.

In our case, planning continued to center on the return and processing of our own damaged materials; no one realized the magnitude of the gifts operation or that it would be our sole source of materials processing for over a year. Our Gifts Team was involved neither in this training nor in its planning, and it quickly became apparent that we were losing ground.

Shipments must be kept together, unpackers must not open more than one shipment at a time, the List of Items Donated Form should not be separated from the shipments. It is important that the unpacking staff understand the importance of identifying a journal run by volume and date. Listings without this information can run the gamut: sometimes you will receive every issue listed or sometimes you may receive no volume and date at all making the information useless in terms of accepting or rejecting other donations.

Even though these forms seem to cause a lot of busy-work, they are extremely necessary. Impress the importance of correctly completed forms on those people who are hired to receive and process the gift materials.

Because of the vast numbers of donated materials, forms from unknown donors piled up, as did our files of "orders out." Some of these probably matched, but who could tell? If a donation had been packed by a commercial, intermediary parcel-handling enterprise, their corporate name often appeared on the donor form instead of the individual's name. Sometimes, the label from the box the original contents were shipped in was used, which made it appear materials had been received from food distributors!

Not all problems will be caused by the processing center, some will be due to the donors themselves. Some of your donors will send forms through the mail, separate from the shipment, because they thought it would be safer. Or they forgot to enclose the form until after the box was sealed. Donors may also send the bulk of their shipment and months later discover a few missing issues, bundle them up, and send them on. Occasionally, shipments may fall apart in the postal system. In those cases, the individual issues will be delivered back to the donor's house since they usually still had the original mailing label on them. Sometimes all you receive will be a torn label from the post office, and you will have no idea of who sent the material or what had happened to it.

Be aware of problems like these. Even though you may not be able to do anything about them, you will be able to offer a plausible explanation to the donors if they contact you.

Recommendation: Make sure the Gifts Team is involved with setting up the procedures and with the training of the staff who are responsible for the initial unpacking and recording of the materials. Do not rely on staff members who are primarily concerned with catalog records to know and understand the needs of the Gifts Team.

Interaction with the Donors

Although phone calls from donors may be time-consuming and may not result in a large number of titles accepted, it is an important part of the gifts process and has to be handled tactfully. Besides, one never knows when the donor with yet another garage full of *National Geographic*s has a relative or a neighbor with a garage full of journals desperately needed.

As the months progressed, some wonderful stories from donors emerged. We had offers from alumni and former faculty members who were now at other institutions. They knew the library and the city and did not have to imagine the devastation. One alum told me, "I used to live in that trailer park." That trailer park was where five people lost their lives the night of the disaster.

Another donor sent an e-mail, "I taught at CSU from 1972-1985, so have fond memories of the library. One of my old cronies sent me photos from last summer, including ones of the library damage. You must have shed quite a few tears! At the time I heard about the flood on the radio, I immediately knew it would have had to hit Johnson M. H. court, where an older couple, friends of mine from church, lived in a teensy old trailer. So I was watching CNN like mad and couldn't believe my eyes when I saw this gray head coming out the front window of a home that was submerged up to the window—my friend Sarah Pieske. I was really glad to hear later that her husband came out the window after her—but he wasn't on the sound byte. Small world, huh!?!"

I think my favorite story is this one. In the 1980s during the Reagan administration, a small federal environmental library was being closed in Kansas. The librarian was given no time nor money to dispose of the collection. It was expected that the materials would be destroyed. Several of the researchers there couldn't bear the idea of destroying the journals, so they took them and kept them at their own expense, waiting and knowing that somewhere someone would need and want them. The donor referred to this as "Operation Livre," based on saving books in World War II. Indeed we did need and want these journals, and after years in storage they are now again available for researchers.

Sadly, not all contacts with donors will be positive. It will be frustrating not to be able to pick up materials immediately, especially at the beginning. You may even grow impatient on the phone listening to donors relate their life histories when there are hundreds more phone calls to return. Some donors may not understand why their gift has not been acknowledged, when it had been sent two months previously. Some will be reassured by being told it had been received at the warehouse and was waiting for processing, others muttered things about inefficiency and lack of appreciation which was hard to hear when we knew how hard we were working, what a monumental task we had undertaken, and how much progress we had made.

Fortunately, the genuinely concerned donors far outnumber the difficult donors. It was a pleasure to talk to the gentleman from New York who was donating his personal collection of IEEE proceedings going back to 1918, or the special librarians who were grateful their collections would have a new home in Colorado, or the widow from Arizona who gave us her late husband's geology collection knowing that in some small way his name and work would be remembered.

In the end, books are like that. Collectively, they're heavy and take up space and have to be processed; individually they represent both the knowledge they contain and the individual who donated them. While a lot was lost to the disaster, a lot was gained as well.

Library Disaster Planning and Recovery Handbook

KEY RECOMMENDATIONS

Gift Receipt

- Make sure you design a gift receipt system that follows a process from recognizing the donor at the beginning to acknowledging them at the end and all things in between.

- Use technology to create and maintain a database of information which should save hours of manual labor.

- Because your delivery system of donated materials is so important in terms of time and expense, make sure to consider all pertinent factors in designing that system.

- If at all possible, strongly discourage any walk-in, drop-off donations. Insist that you pick them up to maintain an adequate tracking system for the donations.

- Use as many established delivery businesses (e.g., postal service, freight companies, etc.) as possible to get the job done.

- Understand that the gift-receipt process will be very complex. Expect problems and frustrations; deal with them and continue the process.

APPENDIX 19-A

LIST OF ITEMS DONATED TO COLORADO STATE UNIVERSITY LIBRARIES

DONOR INFORMATION

Name:_____

Address:_____

City:_____State:_____ZIP:_____

Phone:_____

BOOKS

Please list subject areas and approximate number of books donated:_____

_____

_____

JOURNALS

Please list titles, volumes, and years of items being donated, or attach a list to this form.

1._____

2._____

3._____

4._____

5._____

6._____

7._____

8._____

9._____

10._____

Estimated value of donation $_____.

Please return this form with your shipment.
If there is more than one box with your shipment, please return this form in Box #1.

APPENDIX 19-B
MORGAN LIBRARY GIFTS PROGRAM

SHIPPING/DELIVERY CHECKLIST

DONOR CONTACT   Date:.....................   Initials.........................

Donor Name:

Address: *(verify correct mailing address with donor!)*

Contact name (if different):...

Phone.....................................   Fax:...............................   e-mail:..

Date of last previous contact:..   By whom:...

Brief description of donation:

Approximate size of donation: ❑..........volumes   ❑.........boxes *(figure 15 vols or so to a box)*

SHIPPING DETAILS   Date:.....................   Initials.........................

❑   Donor will pay shipping *(ask donor to let _____ know when they ship)*
      Details:

      (We will mail packet with packing instructions, correct address, List of Items Donated)

❑   CSU will pay

❑   Merchandise return labels *(best for up to 10 boxes) (If asked - no registration, no insurance needed)*
      Number of labels needed...................... *(include a few extra)*

      (We will mail packet with labels, packing instructions, correct address, List of Items Donated)

❑   Yellow Freight   Size of shipment?...

      (We will mail packet with Bill of Lading, packing instructions, correct address, List of Items Donated)

❑   Other arrangements requested   *(if local drop-off, bring to Depository Mon-Fri 10-4)*
      _____ ( ) -   (e-mail: _____ @ _____)

❑   PACKET SENT   Date:.....................   Initials.........................

    _   Information for Donors checked   _   List of Items Donated *(fill out top section)*

    _   Merchandise Return labels - How many?.....................

    _   Yellow Freight Bill of Lading   *(use preprinted forms or fill out consignee part)*

OTHER NOTES:

When completed, send form to _____, Donor Control and copy to _____, Gifts Receipt

❑   Donor Master List updated   Date:.....................   Initials.........................

APPENDIX 19-C
INFORMATION FOR DONORS WHO COULD NOT PACK AND/ OR SHIP OWN MATERIALS

MORGAN LIBRARY DISASTER-RECOVERY GIFTS PROGRAM (NORTH AMERICAN VAN LINES)

Thank you for your donation to Colorado State University Libraries! While the disaster brought destruction, it also brought generosity. We very much appreciate the support of our alumni, community members, and other friends as we rebuild our collections.

CSU Libraries Gifts Policy

All gifts to the Libraries are made with the understanding that the Libraries becomes the owner of the material upon receipt and as such reserves the right to determine disposition of such gifts. Complimentary or review copies of books received free may be donated to the Libraries, but cannot be used as a tax-deductible gift. Items purchased with state or federal funds cannot be used as a tax-deductible gift.

Gift Valuation

Donors may supply an estimate of value if the gift is valued at less than $5,000. Appraisal of a gift to the Libraries for tax deduction purposes is the responsibility of the donor. The Libraries, as a donee, is disqualified from appraising donations. If a gift is valued at greater than $5,000 and the donor wishes to deduct the gift for tax purposes, the donor should have the collection appraised by a certified appraiser, fill out IRS Form 8283, and send a copy to the Colorado State University Foundation, P.O. Box 1870, Fort Collins CO 80522-1870. Donors may also wish to consult their attorney or tax consultant.

Please complete the enclosed three-part **List of Items Donated** form for your entire donation. If your titles will not fit on one form, please attach a list. When you are ready to ship, remove the top (white) copy of the list as your personal record, and pack the two remaining copies (yellow and pink), and any attached list, together **inside** Box one of your shipment.

If you have further questions or need assistance, please contact [name] at [phone] or [e-mail address].

Thank you again for your donation!

PART FIVE

Great Expectations: Restoring the Collection

20 Expecting the Unexpected: Handling Special Projects During Disaster Recovery

Patricia Smith, Evelyn Haynes, and Nora Copeland

INTRODUCTION

Any library experiencing a disaster of considerable magnitude will be faced with urgent demands to replace high-priority material for the users and may need to conduct special projects outside the scope of the regular recovery effort. Such projects are likely to have impossible expectations with unrealistic deadlines and few additional resources. Decisions will need to be immediate with limited time for input from normal channels and with rapid assessment of options. Likewise, normal procedures may need to be shortcut or suspended.

While in the midst of its massive recovery efforts, the library at Colorado State University (CSU) was faced with two special projects dictated by university officials to purchase materials rapidly. One project was to have approximately 6,000 of the most heavily-used monographs reordered and on the shelves for students by fall semester, while the second project took advantage of special funds called "Category 2" funds to offset the impact of the personal losses suffered by faculty on campus by allowing these faculty to order new titles for the library. These two projects will be discussed in detail in the following sections to offer perspectives on how libraries might react in similar situations.

465

HIGH-PRIORITY MONOGRAPH REPLACEMENTS: THE 6,000+ PROJECT

Because the loss at Colorado State University was so great, and in part because the loss occurred just as the fall term was about to begin, the library and university administration were concerned about having essentially no books at all available in major research areas for both faculty and students. Knowing that funds from insurance would be months, even years, away, the university administration provided special monies from its FEMA loans to repurchase 6,136 of the most heavily used—that is, most frequently circulating—monographs. How these frequently circulating books were determined is covered in Chapter 12. Journal volumes were not considered for immediate repurchasing because there are viable short-term options for accessing journal articles including document delivery services or interlibrary loan.

Technical Services staff faced the challenge of having these 6,136 monographs in place as soon as possible. This was particularly daunting since we were not even back in our offices and had to work from borrowed offices elsewhere on campus. Although, thanks to the Internet, we were able to find telephone numbers for our vendors, our system printers required to print purchase orders were not working. In addition, we didn't have order forms or access to sufficient numbers of PCs to generate a large number of orders. Obviously, our regular procedures for ordering and processing would not work for this project. Such are the times for innovation! Following are some options that the library considered that might be of use in similar situations.

Explore Your Options Using Your Online System

When faced with any project that involves producing data quickly, think about what your existing automation can do for you. Most modern integrated library systems (ILS) have report capabilities and the ability to tag and store data that will be of great assistance. We needed to produce a list of orders very quickly, within a week, for the 6,000+ repurchasing project. Even if staff had had access to the PCs in their offices, 6,136 orders is nearly one fourth of our annual normal workload for ordering monographs, so generating the orders needed to be streamlined. The list of heavily used materials was already created in the INNOPAC system. Instead of creating order records for each and every title, as we would have done normally, we sent an electronic list of the titles needed to a book vendor. One problem we encountered was that we could send only the bibliographic records without the attached holdings. This led to confusion about what volume(s) we were ordering when we only needed part of a set. Later on, this problem was resolved (but too late for our project) when our system vendor provided a new capability so that we could export attached holdings with bibliographic records. In the meantime, we absorbed the cost of the extra volumes received.

For the 6,000+ project, we also needed a way to indicate that these items were on order so that they would not be duplicated in the reprocessing or gift replacement efforts. To identify these items, we added a local MARC tag to each item record. These tags also came in handy to keep statistics for auditing and insurance purposes.

One critical decision we made about processing these materials was to make the new copy an added copy and to withdraw the original. This was necessary because the new copy would come with a different barcode. If we received a different edition, we withdrew both the bibliographic record (unless it was the title of a set where only some items were replaced) and the item record for the original copy. Each of these actions was coded in the item record, using specially designated local MARC codes, for tracking purposes.

Find Out What Your Regular Vendors Can Do for You

Book vendors often have automation and services that can be of assistance to libraries faced with special purchasing projects. Many have worked with libraries who receive windfall funds at the end of the year and need to spend money quickly; because of that, they have some procedures in place to deal with special situations. And most are willing to explore some customization of services to help you. Since an emergency is not a time to investigate a variety of vendors, working with a single, reliable vendor is best. You are also in a better bargaining position if you can offer the vendor a certain amount of business in return for extra services or programming you might want them to provide for you. In such a situation, the most likely prospects are the vendors with whom you already have existing automation links and long-standing service commitments.

Once we knew that we had the means to tag and send an electronic file of orders, we identified a vendor that had the electronic capability of working with us. Another criterion for this vendor was that it maintained a large inventory and could readily supply many of our requests from stock. Since we wanted to outsource as many steps as possible to save time for our staff, we also wanted the book vendor to assume as many of the ordering steps as possible and provide the book shelf-ready when possible. Our obvious choice for a vendor to handle our special project to repurchase 6,136 books was the same vendor we used to handle our purchase plans and approval plans. Through our purchase plans, we receive our books tattle taped, marked with call numbers, barcoded, and property stamped. We also had an established electronic loader for invoices with the vendor, which also creates an order record when the record is loaded into our online system. Since our university requires that we have a purchase order for each title we order, we decided to treat the orders for the 6,136 books as if they were received on our purchase plan instead of firm orders, letting our automated loading create the official order record when the book was received. Our vendor was willing to provide special programming and services to help us with this unique problem, saving hours of staff time.

Think Innovatively

In an emergency situation, it is unlikely you will be able to apply your normal procedures to handle a unique demand, but try to think about how these procedures can be adapted. Brainstorm with your vendors as well to find new innovations. One of the most expeditious parts of our plan was to ask the vendor to use our local call numbers rather than the Library of Congress call numbers which they would normally provide on a shelf-ready approval item. Since we were ordering exact replacements of our disaster-damaged materials, the vendor agreed to use a file of our call numbers to match against our orders. This worked only if they supplied an exact match for the library edition lost in the disaster. If the only version of the title to be replaced was a different edition, the vendor did not provide call numbers but supplied the book.

As another way to streamline processes at the library we asked the vendor to ship separately the exact matches from the different editions found so different levels of staff could process the exact matches versus the inexact matches. One of the problems was that what the vendor considered an exact match was not always what we considered an exact match per our cataloging policies. However, since our overall goal was to replace the content of the material for the user, we absorbed many of these as new titles.

A side benefit of the project occurred with the formatting of the call numbers. Although we had long-standing problems with formatting call numbers for our regular materials, one of the staff working on the 6,000+ project pursued the issue and came up with a solution.

To Meet Added Demands on Personnel, Be Creative and Flexible in Staffing and Consider Effects on Morale

Despite the demands for impossible timelines, be careful not to impose impossibility on your staff who have regular duties to perform. Try to outsource as much as possible to vendors, including having the vendor create the orders. Find trained staff from other areas of the library to help process the materials quickly. Remember also that staff are suffering various stresses from the crisis and will continue to feel effects from the disaster, so try to accommodate those feelings in your plans. For example, our bindery staff did not have their normal binding load because we decided not to bind for a year in order to leave as many journal issues as possible in the journal room so patrons could access them. (We had so little journal literature left after the disaster!) Key members of the bindery staff had previous acquisitions experience and all of the staff members were familiar with item records. Thus, they were natural candidates to help with this special project. Our regular staff in Acquisitions, Cataloging, and Database Maintenance supervised the project and performed parts of work where extensive training was required. A major benefit of this approach was that the bindery staff—displaced not only from their regular duties but also from their offices which were destroyed in the disaster—were able to identify with a specific, important project during a difficult time for them. Overall, it increased the camaraderie among all the staff who came to appreciate each other's contributions. In fact, it was one of the bindery staff who came up with the solution to our long-standing call number formatting question in Acquisitions.

Accept Imperfection and Shift Priorities When Necessary

Finally, doing major projects quickly means that you will not have thought of everything, so be prepared to accommodate errors. Realize early in the project that even if you try to meet an impossible goal, you will not reach it. Rather than allowing this to be considered failure by your administrators or your staff, emphasize the positive achievements. Recognize that your university administrators may have limited knowledge of your processes and try to educate them during the project even as you demonstrate willingness to try new procedures or adjust priorities to meet goals. Just be careful to let others know through regular reporting you tried new approaches so that you appear flexible and credible.

At Colorado State University, university administrators believed that because the University Bookstore, which lost all of its fall semester textbooks, was able to get textbook orders rushed within 30 days, they assumed the time frame would apply to the 6,000+ project. Although the library did not meet the university's expectation that we would have the books in the 30 days before school started, we did receive almost all the available materials within eight months—remarkable for the types of materials with which we dealt. Whenever possible, we educated our university administrators on the complexity of library operations, giving them well-documented reports on our plans and results, even as we tried to meet their goals.

When we realized that some of the materials were theses and dissertations from our own collection and our vendor was trying to purchase them from our campus departments, we set up special procedures in Acquisitions to pull these from our Archives and photocopy them. And when post-disaster gifts duplicated some of the items we had on order with the vendor, we adjusted procedures to cancel the vendor titles where possible. If we could not cancel the title, we accepted duplication. Overall, we were pleased with receiving fully 67 percent of all the destroyed titles for the 6,000+ project, while recognizing that our staff had performed another near miracle in a time of high stress.

REPLACING PERSONAL COLLECTIONS THROUGH SPECIAL FUNDING

Although replacing teaching faculty members' personal collections—the Category 2 project—may be unique to Colorado State University's situation, it, too, illustrates the type of emergency response that may be expected of any library experiencing a major disaster. The occasion for this project arose outside of the library, but it ended having extensive implications for library operations. This unanticipated windfall was thrust upon the library with little notification and no opportunity to provide advance input. However, the library was able to take the initiative in developing policies and procedures to deal with this directive, an important right that any library should insist on retaining.

This special project resulted from the university's perception of the need to provide some immediate compensation to faculty members whose offices had been inundated with water and who lost personal books, journals, and other research and teaching materials. The damaging waters which inundated the lower level of Morgan Library also devastated the lower levels of the two buildings immediately to the south, the Eddy and Education buildings. The entire philosophy and foreign languages faculty had their offices in the bottom floor of Eddy; and a number of faculty, graduate teaching assistants, and the computer lab were housed in the lowest level of the Education building. A few faculty in the Department of Social Work and the College of Applied Human Sciences were also located in the basement of Education, and their losses were included in the total.

Many, perhaps most, of the faculty affected had not insured their personal items; and since neither university insurance proceeds nor specially allocated state funds could be used to replace personal losses, they were faced with a dilemma. With just three weeks before the beginning of the fall semester, many of these faculty had lost the accumulated record of their teaching careers. One philosophy professor lost $67,000 worth of research, including video documentaries, slides, tapes, artwork, and files (*Rocky Mountain News*, 21 January 1998). Another, who had taught at CSU for 27 years, reported losses that included his entire teaching collection: 300 videos, 400 books, two VCRs, and a file cabinet full of material (*Rocky Mountain News*, 31 July 1997). A member of the foreign languages faculty reported wooden bookshelves tipped and flattened by the water that rose to within a foot of the ceiling and books and class materials tossed helter-skelter. He also talked about the miraculous survival of an 18th-century Bible that had been in his family for generations (*Rocky Mountain News*, 7 August 1997). Another, a newly appointed foreign languages faculty member, described, with obvious emotion, the loss of her entire Spanish literature collection, a gift of her major advisor who had donated her lifetime collection of books and journals when she retired.

The university, bound by state regulations that prohibited the spending of state money for personal expenses, still felt a strong obligation to find some legal way to compensate faculty for these personal losses. These teaching materials, in addition to being the source materials faculty used in their teaching, were often the direct means of educating their students with whom they shared their resources.

The allocation of $4,500,000 in state emergency funds by the Governor of Colorado on July 31, 1997, gave the university a means of solving this dilemma. Affected faculty members were given an amount, pro-rated to the extent of their losses, to purchase materials to be housed in their offices and for their personal use, but to remain the property of the university (Category 2a purchases). In addition, $125,000 (of Category 2b money) was allocated for faculty in the affected departments to request books for the library to compensate for the loss of the research and teaching value of their personal collections. All of these purchases fell under the accounting definition of Category 2 losses, i.e., those items which, although personal property, were essential for university functions.

The Category 2 fund of $125,000 was more than the total allotted for firm-order book purchases (those requiring a pre-selection decision to order) for these individual departments during the same fiscal year. It more than doubled the normal selection and acquisitions load for these areas for an entire year but was expected to be completed within a few weeks. When faced with a project of this magnitude, what does a library do?

Maintain Control Over Library-Related Projects

This project illustrates very well some of the challenges, as well as problems, in attempting to structure special crisis-mode projects that represent part of a major disaster-recovery effort. First of all, the initial decision to launch the project was done without the library's involvement. The library was notified only after the fact but was able to come up with a response plan within a few days. Initially, there was some talk of retaining the funds in a central campus office with all orders to be submitted to, and placed from, that site.

Libraries confronting a similar loss of control over matters that vitally affect their operation must make a strong case that they remain the repository for the funding as well as the administrator of the programs. The Colorado State University library administrators argued that 1) library faculty and staff have the necessary expertise to acquire and to provide access to these materials, 2) the library has established relationships with vendors, and 3) the library has the system knowledge and experience to streamline this process.

In implementing such a plan, however, libraries should expect a new set of challenges, not the least of which may be caused by university administrators' lack of understanding of what is involved in library operations. Librarians must make sure that the whole process includes a great deal of education about what it takes to select and order books and much negotiation over what is possible within the given deadlines. Neglecting to negotiate before the project is underway may create unrealizable goals and set the affected departments up for failure. For example, by the time the CSU library selector most involved in the affected departments became aware of the project, less than two weeks remained before the first deadline for submitting orders.

Libraries faced with projects of the magnitude and complexity described should expect that most faculty will not be prepared to deal with such an unprecedented volume of requests that must be processed in an unrealistically short amount of time. For one thing, there will probably be a lack of usable information in the departments. With the exception of a few key titles, faculty may not be able to pull out of their heads an adequate list of items needed. Most of the catalogs, bibliographies, and reference books that are the tools-of-the-trade that could help them generate requests probably reside in the library. Departments may not have readily available student workers who can drop everything and be trained to check the lists against the library's holdings.

The original intent of the directive to the departments at Colorado State University was that faculty would submit requests for books not owned by the library but which they and their students would use for research. All of the original lists that they compiled included, or were totally made up of, titles already owned by the library, necessitating repeated requests for additional lists. The library's main conclusion, after becoming involved in the project out of necessity, and its advice to others dealing with similar experiences, is that the library must maintain control over the processes that affect its activities and outcomes.

Adapt the Use of Established Procedures and Channels with Appropriate Shortcuts

It may be tempting for libraries operating in an emergency mode to streamline their processes and bypass some of their usual ways of doing business. The experience of Morgan Library may give other libraries motivation to re-examine such reasoning. For example, the selectors were not involved in the initial decision making or communications with departments. The intent was that faculty would submit orders directly to the Acquisitions Department, which would process them speedily. The Department of Foreign Languages was the first to realize that this procedure would deprive them of much of the usable ordering information that they needed, and their liaison contacted the library selector for help. The selector provided an accelerated and amplified version of the usual kinds of material used to inform faculty about available resources: catalogs used in regular acquisitions processes, bibliographies, copies of book reviews, and other standard sources. The department decided at the same time to submit orders in Chinese and Japanese, although these languages had not been previously taught and the programs had been only recently introduced. This change required considerable help from the faculty in locating publishers and vendors and transcribing non-Roman alphabets.

The Philosophy Department and the School of Education, which delayed beginning their projects, were contacted by the library liaison who offered help in the form of catalogs, order slips, and reviews. The philosophy picture was complicated by the large amount of money allocated (two-thirds of the total) and the selection of numerous foreign language titles. Selectors for some of the other departments were asked to become involved only after repeated submissions of requests for duplicates verified that the faculty needed some additional information with which to work. All of these efforts involved a great deal of added work on the part of the selectors, but they provided requests to the Acquisitions Department in a form that could be processed quickly.

A useful by-product of a project such as the one described could provide a library with a bonus evaluation tool. Frustrating as the repeated duplicates lists were, they nevertheless gave assurance that the library's approval plans and the efforts of its selectors had been highly successful in acquiring those items most needed. However, bypassing the usual selection process for this project in the interest of expediency may have sacrificed some of the value that subject selectors bring to the selection process.

Selectors, who are in touch with the needs of the collection, know of gaps and incomplete works that should be considered; have access to the bibliographical apparatus that identifies what is available and how it can be obtained; regularly review evaluation sources and standard bibliographies for recommended titles; and often provide initial screening of titles already in the collection. It is possible that working through established procedures and channels, though perhaps more time consuming at the outset, could have expedited the process eventually.

Explore the Possibility of Outsourcing Major Projects

As advantageous as working through regular channels may be for the selection process, the same may not be true for every stage and function. During the early stages of its project, the library staff explored the possibility of absorbing these orders into its regular acquisitions, cataloging, and processing functions. The acquisitions part was accomplished using regular library staff and procedures, but the tight deadlines and difficult nature of many of the orders placed considerable strain on the staff already overburdened with their usual routine as well as other disaster-recovery projects. The decision to outsource the cataloging and physical processing was made in order to spare the cataloging and labeling/marking staff this same type of overload. However, libraries faced with the need to negotiate such a contract suddenly should be aware that this option does not offer a speedy way out of their dilemma. They must be prepared to accept delays in acquiring institutional administrative approval, securing insurance company acceptance, and negotiating a contract with a suitable cataloging vendor. In the meantime, the volumes acquired under an expedited schedule in order to meet university objectives of priority collection replacement must wait in storage until the process catches up.

CONCLUSION

In conclusion, these two special projects, mandated by the university, illustrate the nature of the general concern and demand that an institution-wide catastrophe will generate. If struck by major disasters, librarians can anticipate similar demands for speedy replacement.

Library Disaster Planning and Recovery Handbook

KEY RECOMMENDATIONS

Special Projects

- Assert the library's need to control the process that affects its collection.

- Seek innovative ways to streamline the process but refer to established and tested practice.

- Utilize outsourcing and vendors.

- Try to educate institutional administrators on the complexity of library procedures.

- Expect and accept imperfection but try regardless.

21 Great Expectations For Restoring The Collection: An Overview

Carmel Bush

INTRODUCTION AND PERSONAL ACCOUNT

With the initial building assessment complete, removal of debris begun, temporary air handling introduced, and pack-out of volumes underway, several staff members from Technical Services and the contractor crowded around the end of the table in the conference room with eyes peeled on the white board. Work has begun on the restoration plan. The volumes were frozen and would undergo cleaning, freeze-drying, and other treatments yet to be determined for combating the effects of mold, bacteria, and yeast. How the salvaged volumes were going to be handled upon return was the focus of everyone in the room. Staff reviewed the facts on the collection. Assumptions were made and debated: How much would be total loss? What processes would the volumes need to undergo to complete their restoration? What arrangement of processes would create the most effective workflow? What rate of return from treatments could be expected? Where would activities of processing be located? What tracking method would handle the processes and the like? Locating displaced staff to find out answers to questions, running across to the next building for photocopies, and going outside to place cellular phone calls provided the few diversions from the meeting. The pace was relentless to propose a restoration plan to administrators.

Already, the long days of recovery activities were showing. Staff were becoming fanciful in their planning. The processes were dubbed with planetary names—Mars, Venus, and Earth—as a shorthand code for the activities of restoration. In an effort to gain a hold of this cosmos, a map was graphed on flip charts. Staff members gazed at the drawings and questioned one another if this plan was the most effective way to return salvaged volumes or replace volumes to the collection. Revisions were made. There were many alternatives, and no single simple approach would satisfy all the conditions. It would be another long day of planning and many, many long days before the collection was restored.

Initial actions to recover the collection must be followed by planning to restore what can be salvaged and to replace as necessary what is lost. When restoration costs for the collection are projected into the multiple millions, careful review should occur of what you know about the damage and what you know about the requirements of decision makers who will approve your plan for restoration. Knowing the facts about your collection, the processes that are required for restoration, the marketplace for services required in restoration, and the administrative process for review and approval of the plan to restore the collection is essential. This chapter begins with an examination of the conceptual basis for the planning process as well as the organizational issues for developing a plan.

REVIEW OF THE LITERATURE

In comparison to the processes involved in the initial recovery and mass treatments of materials, little is written on the organization and design of large-scale restoration processes for damaged collections after mass treatments have been made. What is in the literature is disaster specific. The flood of Florence in 1966 resulted in wide-spread damage to numerous libraries in the city, with the largest, the Biblioteca Nazionale Centrale (BNC), having a million and a quarter wet books. In the aftermath of salvaging the leaves for the wet books in Florence, Horton decried that "there are not enough binders or restorers in the world to handle a job of this magnitude" (Horton, 1967: 1043). She discussed the needs for training a work force and establishing an international conservation center to teach binding and restoring of water-damaged books. Waters (1970) described the requirements for an international center for training and research to realize the potential in the restoration program started by the BNC. Twenty years later, Lenzuni (1986) described the six workshops specializing in restoration for the BNC whose aim was to treat and keep all books. Her discussion of the continuing restoration issues echoed the need for well-trained personnel to restore books along with the need for materials used in the restoration process, storage for newspapers that have been microfilmed, and capturing information about treatment of books so that data are established allowing conclusions to be drawn. Ogden (1979) ascribed the fast-changing methods in mending techniques—that is, use of Japanese paper and paste and heat-set tissue—to the Florentine flood recovery.

The element of training was no less important in the restoration process of 50,000 books in the flood at Stanford University in 1978 (Buchanan, 1979). Although a much smaller-scale disaster, this well-documented disaster presents basic considerations made in restoration. A qualified library manager was hired for the restoration task, and a small number of staff hired for the project. Staff were trained in repair techniques, recovering pamphlets, and conservation considerations. Books were sorted to return to the library, to hold until sets were complete, and to repair for specific problems such as re-casing, spine repairs, paper repairs, pressing, and fumigation. Some spent time searching for replacements for the small number of discards. The restoration's main goal was to return heavily-used materials to the stacks as fast as possible (*Disasters*, 1981; *Stanford-Lockheed*, 1980).

The fires at the Los Angeles Central Library in 1986 wreaked destruction of 400,000 volumes and 700,000 water-soaked volumes (Kelin, 1986; Moreau, 1987). Inventorying resources to assess losses involved checking undamaged and damaged materials. Returning freeze-dried books to the shelves and acquiring replacements were featured in their restoration plan. In considering the daunting tasks, Wyman Jones, the city librarian at the time, was quoted as saying "it takes a long time and a hell of a lot of money, even with people who know what they're doing, to locate a book and to get it back here and to reprocess it and get it back on the shelves" (Moreau 1987: 36).

The Biblioteka Akademiii Nauk (BAN), in St. Petersburg, Russia, suffered the worst library disaster of the century when fire destroyed 400,000 volumes and left 3.5 million volumes water damaged in 1988 (Sung, Leonov, and Waters, 1990). Early in the process, collaboration was established with the international community to support recovery, with the Library of Congress serving as coordinator of these efforts following disinfection and drying. BAN established a phased preservation program and a replacement program. Waters (1990) described sorting of volumes for further action: chemical stabilization and physical non-adhesive support structures, microfilming of most brittle books, and further conservation for selected items. Archival housing structures, linked to an inventory control database and stored in special recovery stacks and rooms, were incorporated in the plan for the initial three years of the program. Afterwards, the plan anticipated the development of criteria for conservation of the collection over the long term, including the establishment of the infrastructure for technology and training for microforms.

All of these disaster experiences required identifying actions to take following initial mass drying and treatments and developing appropriate strategies for restoration that take into account the use and value of materials and the availability of a labor pool to perform the work and costs. Inescapable to the reader of these accounts are the requirements for conservator expertise and coordinated assistance from multiple organizations and individuals in the restoration process. Each has required training as a component in restoration. A variety of conservation techniques may be used. With the advent of information technology support, later reports also recognized the potential for tracking, and supporting the restoration process. It is not possible to review these experiences without gaining a sense of the difficulty posed to regular library staff involved in monumental restoration activities while simultaneously supporting the regular activities for their organizations. Leighton's (1979) admonition not to become "too discouraged" is good advice.

CONCEPTUALIZING AND DESIGNING A PROCESSING EFFORT

Knowing the Facts About Your Collection

Earlier recovery efforts have implications for restoration. These efforts and the particulars of the disaster shape the assumptions made in planning for restoration. In large-scale water disaster, the sound practice of inventorying everything as it is removed or packed-out may not be done dependent upon conditions. Hundreds of thousands of volumes flung by the force of water in every direction and in conditions favorable to mold growth are not suited to a time-consuming pack-out in which volumes are carefully boxed and recorded. With the exception of whole collections or specially noted works declared a loss at the initial assessment, it will not be apparent what total loss is until a full accounting is made as part of the recovery effort. In determining what will be done to restore the collection library, planners face important considerations, with user demand and institutional mission leading the list.

Knowing the collection and the priorities for the collection provide the foundation for subsequent restoration of the collection following treatments. What are the collections of high demand? In a large-scale disaster, the restoration time table is measured in years not a few months. The needs of the user population served will influence the decisions about order of processing and the urgency of processing for restoration. It may be necessary to go beyond the initial salvage priorities and revise priorities for restoration. The highly circulated materials, the materials directly tied to curriculum, the materials to support high-demand research agendas, and the materials supporting grants in progress are typical areas to examine. Collection managers and others in the library familiar with use patterns of the collection, high-profile users, and data on reference demand should have direct input into planning. A restoration plan for large-scale disaster should not be the isolated task of an individual staff member.

The demographics of the water-damaged collection help inform the process. What are the formats in the collection? What are the numbers of volumes in each of these formats? Processing a working monograph collection will have requirements different from rare or specialized collections. Knowledge about pre-existing conditions of volumes aids planning. What is bound, boxed, or placed in other types of enclosure will also influence the process. Information on the distribution of the collection over time periods of publication will inform replacement strategies. Data on total loss or projected total loss influences the size and number of operations that may be needed.

Knowing the Processes For Restoration

Restoration is not a simple process. When faced with extensive water damage, a library will be considering a number of processes, their intricacies, and their interrelationships. Materials that are wet will first have to go through a drying process and, dependent upon the nature of damage, may also be treated for mold if the determination is made to attempt to salvage the collection. Once the decision to salvage is made, inspection must occur after treatments to determine if they have been effective and what if any further action is required to make materials available to users. Paper volumes may need page repair, page replacement, and/or rebinding. Other formats such as computer disks/drives or filmed materials may have to be sent off-site for restoration.

If purchasing is involved for restoration, the processes can mimic usual acquisitions processes. Purchasing materials, especially in a large-scale disaster, involves multiple steps and a diversity of jobbers, publishers, and vendors. There is opportunity to reconsider format of purchase. For example, is substitution by electronic alternative acceptable? If so, then the library will have to factor identifying these alternatives and contracting for databases as part of the replacement process. Is the material so crucial to the collection that reproduction must be considered if the title is no longer in print? Reproductive processes are expensive and available through contract if on-site facilities are not available. Copyright has to be considered when reproduction of materials is involved. There are different interpretations about rights in this regard, hence, consulting legal counsel will provide clarification of the institutional position if a policy does not already exist concerning copyright and reproduction.

Structuring a process for large-scale disaster takes into account the following: the knowledge of publisher and jobber inventories of materials, the services of back-issue dealers, the reformatting options, and the replacement photocopying that meets preservation photocopy standards. Overall accountability and auditing for replacement should be incorporated in planning, preferably via an automated system. In CSU's experience, the insurance company retained an active role in auditing the expenditures throughout the recovery process.

Regardless of the restoration processes contemplated, the processes are labor intensive. The overall complexity of restoration is compounded by the scale of the disaster. In considering this fact, the likelihood of a library absorbing the work or even having all the skills necessary for restoration are small.

Knowing the Vendor Market

The sequencing of restoration activities, the rate that treated materials can return from freeze-drying for assessment and follow-up processing, the mix of materials that are returned, and schedules with contractors will require systems view of the processes. The capacity of vendors to deliver service meeting standards is a key ingredient in the complex stew that a plan for restoration must address.

Emergency facilitation services provide tailored services to bring about the recovery of organizations, although they have limited expertise with regard to libraries; library vendors provide an array of services geared to a steady supply and demand from libraries for acquiring, processing, and systems work. Understanding the business niches of these groups gives planners a realistic view of what may be possible to structure in the plan. For example, page repair and page replacement are not services offered on large scale by any vendor for conservation services. A contractor may choose to extend service to include these functions, but growth will be necessary. Start-up of service will need to allow for this growth. It can take additional investment of a library's staff time or consultants who can guide development of restoration functions according to standards.

While it may be possible to develop a restoration project with a series of single-service contracts, planners have to consider the control of the project. The complexity of tracking library materials through a series of contractors alone provides incentive to maximize the services any one contractor may provide. Exploring with vendors the possibility of expanding their services is prudent. Preliminary discussions with vendors who have high-volume capacity is recommended. This will prove useful to the creation of a request for a proposal or decisions to contract with particular vendors who exhibit the ability to help you fulfill the requirements for restoration. It is also wise to assess the vendor's stability to continue to deliver services over the period of the project.

Knowing the Administrative Processes

Administrators have multiple concerns with restoration plans. Foremost are concerns for the impact on the organization and the return to normal operations as smoothly and quickly as possible. The library's ability to ensure continuity of service to its users and support the mission of the institution will have an effect on the viability of the organization. Any planning processes must recognize and include the priorities of its administrators in the aims for restoration. To the extent applicable, the plan should also reflect what, if any, improved state the library will attain or what decrease in services will result from restorative activities. The library must also demonstrate the effectiveness of the plan through the processes that are employed and through the implementation outlined for these processes. The library must also demonstrate how these processes will address the institutional mission. For a large-scale disaster in which recovery costs are high, it is to the benefit of the library planners to make sure to bring other decision makers from their institutions or their boards into the picture early to share the options for restoration and their costs. Outside consultants may be helpful in providing input to a plan and reviewing the strategies for restoration. Independent experts can help persuade decision makers of the worthiness of the plan when multiple millions of dollars are at stake. It is advantageous if insurance representatives agree with the library and its parent organization on consultants that are hired.

In a large-scale disaster, administrators will focus on the costs for restoration. Not only will library planners want to outline costs, but they will also want to indicate where it may be beneficial to re-examine the costs and benefits at various stages of the process. The findings at treatment stages may precipitate further decision points. These may include replacing volumes with gifts or priority purchases and/or revisiting what formats are preferable— a disaster may be the window for substituting with electronic access or even microforms for low-use materials. An enterprising collection manager may even seize the disaster as an opportunity to reshape a collection that has not undergone evaluation in recent years. How do the relative costs of these approaches compare? What benefits are derived from them if there are additional costs? There is usually no argument if the process is cheaper and faster for restoration and if quality is maintained.

The fiscal resources available for restoring the collection are a major determinant in planning. As a first check, planners should review insurance coverage for the collection. The best policy supports restoring the collection. Holding discussion with institutional risk managers or other individuals responsible for dealing with insurance will clarify the policy. If full restoration is not provided by insurance, it may be necessary to seek other sources of funding such as may be available through FEMA, state or local government, and/or donations. In a large-scale disaster, the library may be ill-equipped to focus on a campaign to fund restoration. Yet colleagues at other institutions may be able to make the case for help as in the BAN and Los Angeles Central Library examples. It is inevitable that there will be an outpouring of offers of assistance from generous individuals or organizations. During recovery, it is an important time to make sure that *wants* are identified that will help with restoration.

Funding for recovery will determine the extent of restoration and may dictate that the restoration is planned in phases as resources become available. The sources of funding may also prescribe the types of activities that will be supported. With knowledge of funding possibilities, the marketplace, the collection, and the restoration processes, library planners are best positioned to devise a plan that is responsive to the needs of their users and institution. Users and administrators should be involved in establishing measures that show responsiveness as part of the plan. In addition to this stewardship function, the measures can serve as a vital tool for public relations. How will progress be reported? The administrator with a bottom-line approach will want cost breakdowns of processes; and users will want to know when their material will be available. Overall, it is critical that the timetable for restoration be understood. How this information will be reported can involve a mixture of approaches. Statistical reports, status reports, program reviews, and the like should be considered from both the accountability and publicity points of view.

ORGANIZING FOR THE PLANNING EFFORT

There is no lull time between the initial recovery effort and serious planning for restoration. The library's collection is the centerpiece of service programs; and those who rely on it will want to know what comes next. Insurance and other funding agencies will have a position on the alternatives for restoration. For a library to be responsive both to its users and to the fiscal exigencies that relate to disaster, it must place serious attention on planning for restoration and at the same time be aware that the assessment of individual restoration needs of volumes is yet to be determined. A flexible approach to planning is thus essential. Keeping this in mind, there are multiple factors to consider in organizing the planning effort for restoration.

Defining the Goals For Restoration

Foremost in the organizing for the planning effort is gaining a clear understanding of what is required for the restoration plan. The library should review what is being accomplished for initial recovery and use this to frame what it wants to achieve in restoration. Will the nature of the collection dictate an aim to restore all salvaged volumes? Should acquisitions of other formats be considered instead of further restorative efforts for some titles? Is the goal to replace titles by ordering copies when salvage is not possible? Should no action occur for some titles if restorative actions cost too much? The goal for restoring may be debatable, but it is the necessary starting point for planning and one that should have wide input. The plan then will need to address how to reach the goal for restoration.

At CSU's Morgan Library, the initial restoration for salvageable volumes considered that page cleaning, repair, and replacement, plus rebinding or re-casing would be necessary for volumes that were salvageable. It would also be necessary to account for and track these materials so that users would know when these volumes would become available. Additionally, the ability to produce for insurers and auditors a record of the status of these volumes would be critical.

As part of the definition of goals, testing may be useful for projecting the scale of work and the demand for resources and labor. Testing can involve timed studies of processes, sampling of types of damage to repair or costs to replace materials, behavioral studies regarding acceptance of recovered materials, and trials of options to organize functions for optimum recovery. Testing contributes data important for making decisions about scheduling, simplifying, and integrating the recovery project.

In determining the charge for creating the plan, the next step is clarifying who the audience is for the plan that will be presented. In a large-scale disaster with millions of dollars involved, planners should expect institutions, boards, insurance companies, and state and federal disaster agencies to have keen interest in the plan. What is it that they will want to know? Understanding their priorities for the plan will help avoid too many resubmissions of plans for yet one more option. In particular, it is important to be aware of the parameters that decision makers may have in mind for the plan. Is there an upward dollar level? Do they want the plan broken down into phases with attached dollar amounts? When do the decision makers want to see the plan? Finally, planners need to ascertain what the approval process will be for the plan so that timelines for restoration can reflect this period.

In those cases that involve complex negotiations with insurance, testing also allows building models with confidence levels that may address insurance concerns regarding settlement. At CSU's Morgan Library, the plan for restoration involved construction of a large random sample in order to determine loss of volumes and types of repairs required for restoration and to determine the distribution of this data over the collection according to classification, date, and format of materials. This data supported the development of a model for insurance settlement and also informed the planning so that projections could be made of resource requirements for the project.

Identifying Expertise For Planning

After the charge for the plan is outlined, the administrator or disaster-recovery team will need to consider the skills that will be necessary to complete the charge. In a large-scale, water disaster, a diversity of talents is required. Input by conservators, technical services, collections librarians, and systems staff will strengthen the plan. The planning group should involve experienced managers who have evaluation and contracting skills. If an institution has negotiated for insurance, involving that individual or team will prepare for the inevitable negotiation in settlements. The large-scale nature of return also argues for discussion of the plan with those experienced in similar production capacity.

How the skills are supplied for creating the restoration plan relates to the number of people on staff and their skills and the program offerings that are continued during the restoration process. Few libraries will have sufficient staffing resources in a large-scale disaster and will have to engage others in developing plans for restoration. A competent and committed work force will be needed. Help may be available through a local library community, consortia, or network. There may be experts in these groups who can offer assistance for planning, advice on a phase of restoration, or provide training. Hiring staff may be possible, as in the Stanford flood experience (Leighton, 1979). It will undoubtedly be necessary to hire or seek consultation with experts on varying aspects of the plan for restoration.

For the CSU Library, the FEMA consultants from the Library of Congress provided invaluable assistance on the design of operations conducted at high volume. There may be library temporary agencies who will work with a library to develop the plan and supply at least some of the varying talents for planning that might be missing within a library. Networks or consortia may also make available experts for advising. Vendors can also provide valuable information for planning. Although voluntary involvement has its limits, this source of help should not be overlooked in the planning stage.

When seeking a professional conservator as a consultant, there are agencies such as the Foundation of the American Institute for Conservation that offer a referral service. In 1998, the National Task Force on Emergency Response initiated the Cultural Heritage Roster with the support of FEMA and the Getty Conservation Institute. Libraries are well-advised to check out the credentials and experience of individuals under consideration. References should be obtained. The cadre of consultants with experience in large-scale disaster is small. Their assistance is invaluable for assessing plans for restoration, particularly those involving volumes of artifactual value. CSU benefited from review of its restorative process by consultants who had experience in the disasters of Florence, Los Angeles, and St. Petersburg. Their report recommended a revision in the order of processes and shared a few additional concerns such as environmental monitoring.

Assembling the Planning Team

Once the players for planning are identified, the organization of the team proceeds. The leadership of the planning team may come from within the library or may be hired. This individual will need to be aligned to the goal for restoration and be a capable manager. The initial energetic response often found in a disaster may be waning by this stage in recovery and parochial interests may begin to resurrect. Where key issues of collection are concerned, and when there are differences of opinion, the leadership must help the team broker these differences into a workable plan. The planning team will need to review their charge, the approach to planning, and the team's accountability for the plan. Each member must understand his/her role (e.g., outlining training requirements, detailing treatment options, and the like). If consultants are used, everyone on the team should understand why they are there. Wrotenbery (1972) advises that if "persons unknown to the staff assist in the restoration process, care should be taken to assure the staff who these people are, why they are present and how they relate to regular staff" (1972: 227).

At the CSU Libraries, the dual responsibilities of the contractor hired by the university led to confusion. Not only was the contractor hired for library recovery, but he also had other advisory responsibilities with regard to the position for insurance. This was further complicated by the contractor's hiring an outside consultant without vetting by the library. The ambiguity of responsibilities made attaining agreement on course of action difficult at times.

In appointing regular staff to the planning team, the administration of the library will have to reckon with reassignment of responsibilities or decisions to make adjustments in programs. The intensity of planning for restoration on a large scale will command the time of staff who are members of the planning team. Any library that has planned a migration to a new integrated library system has only to amplify that demand by several magnitudes to appreciate the commitment that is required for planning for large-scale restoration process. It requires an intense, concentrated time frame. The supervisors of the staff on the team must understand this commitment and support these staff accordingly.

Establishing Values For Planning

At the onset of assembling the team for planning, developing a shared understanding is paramount. Everyone should be familiar with the aim of restoration and the parameters that the plan must take into account. Data already compiled on the damaged collection should be made available to team members. The scale of disaster and conditions of materials already noted in the recovery process will inform planning. Members will benefit from a review of any treatments of the collection to-date. The availability of other resources such as statistical help or network offices should be shared. While the development of the plan will have the stamp of its members, at the initial organizational meeting the leader and members should discuss their collective values for planning.

CSU's set of values for planning included taking a fresh view of the organization of work for restoration, respecting conservation principles, attending to quantity and quality in the development of processes, observing standards, simplifying processes, providing accountability to users through communications about the progress of restoration, and maintaining business practices. The team not only realized that the plan would need to be flexible over the course of the restoration process, but we also maintained our target of getting materials back on the shelves for our users. This aim was not, however, to be achieved at any cost nor with an expediency that would have resulted in unusable volumes on the shelf. Several factors apply in determining the latter. Not only must the intellectual content be usable, but the shelfability and continuity of the volumes returned to the shelves must also be addressed by planners.

Relating the Plan to Contract(s) for Service

In a large-scale disaster, it must be recognized from the start that the plan that is created will serve as a basis for contractual development for services to support restoration. The planning process should therefore define the types of contracts that will be needed (e.g., binding, page replacement, etc.). Additionally, technical specifications should be defined so that potential contractors can determine what the performance deliverables for restoration are along with the indication of the risks, standards for quality, schedule, and costs that may apply to these arrangements. Effective procedures will need to be defined for coordinating requests, the selection of potential contractors, and communications with them. Identifying the measures and policies for contract administration at the time of planning will ensure that appropriate standards are selected with respect to technical requirements.

CONCLUSION

The development of a plan to restore a library's collection cannot be done in isolation. Chances of success are improved by involving other units and acquiring information from throughout the library. The following chapters (22 through 25) describe the complexities, intricacies, and dilemmas involved in trying to restore a library's collection.

Library Disaster Planning and Recovery Handbook

KEY RECOMMENDATIONS

Restoring the Collection

- Collect data on the damaged collection and its use.

- Employ technical knowledge on the restoration processes.

- Use up-to-date knowledge of the marketplace of emergency and library vendors.

- Determine financial assistance to perform processes for restoration.

- Make sure there is a clear understanding of administrative aims for recovery to support users and institutional mission.

- In organizing the planning, give serious consideration to defining goals and expertise for developing the plan.

- Make sure members of the planning team understand their roles on the planning team and have shared values about their approach to the project.

- Use data from testing to inform the development of plans.

REFERENCES

Buchanan, Sally. 1979. "The Stanford Library Flood Restoration Project." *College & Research Libraries* 40, No. 6 (November): 539–548.

Disasters: Prevention & Coping. 1981. *Proceedings of the Conference, May 21-22, 1980.* Stanford, CA: Stanford University Libraries.

Horton, Carolyn. 1967. "Saving the Libraries of Florence." *Wilson Library Bulletin* 41, No. 10 (June):1034–1043.

Kelin, Norman. 1986. "Counting the Losses." *Communicator* 19, Nos. 11–12 (November/December): 49–52.

Leighton, Philip D. 1979. "The Stanford Flood." *College & Research Libraries* 40, No. 5 (September): 450–459.

Lenzuni, Anna. 1987. "Coping with Disaster." Preservation of Library Materials: Conference held at the National Library of Austria, Vienna, April 7–10, 1986. *ILFA Publications* 2: 98–102.

Moreau, Michael. 1987. "Putting It Back Together: Los Angeles Central Library." *Wilson Library Bulletin* 61, No. 7 (March): 35–39.

Ogden, Sherelyn. 1979. "The Impact of the Florence Flood on Library Conservation in the USA: A Study of the Literature Published 1956-1976." *Restaurator* 3: 1–36.

The Stanford-Lockheed Meyer Library Flood Report. 1980. Stanford University Libraries (May).

Sung, Carolyn Hoover, Valeri Pavlovich Leonov, and Peter Waters. 1990. "Fire Recovery at the Library of the Academy of Sciences of the USSR." *American Archivist* 53 (Spring): 298–312.

Waters, Peter. 1970. "Requirements for An International Center for Preservation of Books and Manuscripts." *Bollettino dell'Istituto di patologia del libro,* 60–84.

Waters, Peter. 1990. "Phased Preservation: A Philosophical Concept and Practical Approach to Preservation." *Special Libraries* (Winter): 35–43.

Wrotenbery, Carl R. 1972. "Recovery from Disaster: The University of Corpus Christi Library Recovers from Hurricane Celia." *Libraries and Archives Conservation.* The Boston Athenaeum's 1971 Seminar on the Application of Chemical and Physical Methods to the Conservation of Library and Archival Materials: 221–227.

22 Shadow Dancing with Insurance: Repurchasing Books Declared a Total Loss

Patricia Smith and Evelyn Haynes

INTRODUCTION

When disaster destroys a library collection, an attractive option for replacement is simply to repurchase. Unlike gifts, replacement offers direct control over what is received without processing mountains of unneeded material. Unlike restoration, replacement offers a volume in pristine condition without laborious, costly, and imperfect preservation efforts. Repurchasing the volume is simple and quick. And besides, the collection is insured, isn't it? Unfortunately, repurchasing is not as easy as it might at first appear.

Library literature does not cover repurchasing collections on the scale of that at Colorado State University Libraries. The American Library Association (ALA) has published guidelines for replacing various types of materials that suggest alternatives that a library might consider when replacing materials (Hamilton, 1993). Recent articles describe how libraries, like Kentucky State University, used vendors to help them replace current periodicals damaged in a disaster (Foster, 1996). Libraries have also done large purchasing projects for monographs using vendors with large inventories and automation to select in-print titles in certain subject categories. However, such projects involve start-up collections for new libraries or sudden windfall funds that need to be spent immediately and not replacement of older collections lost in a disaster. Therefore, these projects have limited relevance.

Settling with insurance companies after a loss is a topic that has been touched on in the literature. Librarians at Dartmouth College describe how they used price indexes and an inflation factor to determine a settlement amount acceptable to insurance (Naslund and George, 1986). Comprehensive cost studies are also scarce on the subject of processing materials in technical services which can be useful for developing a model to project the processing costs of repurchasing. Iowa State University provides a useful analysis of costs to consider in monograph acquisitions (Morris, Rebarcak, and Rowley, 1996). In general, however, librarians are wary of studies from other libraries since libraries vary considerably in practice. Such studies can only point to factors other libraries might want to consider in developing their own cost models.

THE NEED FOR REPURCHASING AND ITS PROCESS

Although insurance policies may cover full replacement, insurance companies will rarely, in a large-scale disaster, agree carte blanche to repurchasing without reviewing other, less-expensive methods of replacement. When the loss is small, as in the periodical room at Western Kentucky University, repurchasing may well be less expensive than a restoration project (Foster, 1996). When the materials lost are current issues, as they were at Western Kentucky, repurchasing again makes economical sense. Generally speaking, however, the greater the loss and the older the materials, the less probable repurchasing as a single option becomes. The age of the collection especially complicates simple repurchasing. Although the copyright laws normally permit making a copy to replace a volume lost in a disaster, few libraries lend books for copying since dismantling and rebinding is usually required. As we discovered in our gift-solicitation program, once a book goes out-of-print, many publishers do not keep even archival copies, let alone an inventory of unsold volumes. Out-of-print dealers, both because of expense and uncertainty of success, are places of last resort only.

At Colorado State University's Morgan Library, where a water disaster inundated hundreds of thousands of volumes and years and years of a working collection, repurchasing an entire damaged collection was unlikely at best. And when the initial unit-cost estimates for restoration came in below those for repurchasing, restoration became so much the rule that, except in special situations (which had to be justified to the university and the insurance companies), repurchasing ended up at the very bottom— the last resort for items declared a total loss. Even defining total loss became an important issue. Because we are a research library for adults, books that might normally be considered unusable became salvageable. For example, mold spots—if they are not active molds—will not affect the content. Even partially blocked books became salvageable if pages could be replaced. Only gooey messes or total bricks were undebatable candidates for total loss.

Nevertheless, because the damage to our collection was so extensive and our total losses were also considerable, repurchasing became a necessary part of recovery at Morgan Library. Librarians facing replacement of mixed losses, as in our situation, may find the following considerations useful as they work with insurance adjusters and others to begin the repurchasing process.

WORKING WITH INSURANCE COMPANIES AND OTHER PARTIES

Don't Expect Clear Guidelines or Firm Commitments Up Front.

This is the first and most important rule of working with insurance companies and other parties when library losses occur. As we dealt with insurance officials and others, we often felt (as they did, too, perhaps) that we were shadow dancing without either dancer knowing the steps. Instead, we found it necessary to work toward guidelines and to negotiate any firm commitment we obtained.

Be Prepared for Input from Local Board or University Administrators.

Insurance settlements that involve millions of dollars will engender major interest from your parent organizations on how the money might be spent. Our university administrators, for example, were committed to the idea of creating a virtual library and urged the library to replace journals in electronic formats. We recognized the value of this approach, but only a small portion of journal runs—our main losses—are available electronically; and many of those available require the user to maintain a current subscription to keep access to the back set.

When ongoing commitments are required, you will need to distinguish which part of the subscription cost will go towards back issues and which part will go toward the current subscription. Remember insurance companies typically handle one-time claims, not claims with ongoing costs. Moreover, digitization projects, still in their infancy, currently focus on unique or rare collections. To set up an operation in-house, on the other hand, would incur considerable expense and require significant numbers of new and retrained staff. Despite the bright future for virtual libraries, they remain some years away. We also discovered that few faculty were willing to accept electronic for paper copies. Instead of processing certain gift copies of damaged titles, we proposed to affected faculty those selected core journals be replaced through JSTOR, a non-profit agency that provides full-text electronic back files of selected standard journal titles. However, strong objections from faculty resulted in processing the gift copies in addition. The lesson we found here was that current electronic solutions still work best for fringe materials or to provide alternate means of access but not to replace core materials.

Be Aware That Insurance Companies Typically Settle in Two Ways: Reimbursement for Costs Actually Incurred or Agreed-Upon, Lump-Sum Settlements Based on Estimates of Damages.

Neither method is ideal for library disasters; and because libraries and losses differ, anyone facing replacement should carefully consider both options. If an insurance company agrees to pay actual costs, then you may be assured of full reimbursement once the collection is restored and actual costs are determined; however, in the interim, the institution must bear at least a portion of the up-front costs of replacement. If the time between loss and replacement is lengthy, be aware that insurance companies may be disinclined to handle claims based on actual costs. Nevertheless, time and materials reimbursement is a good approach when costs can be determined relatively rapidly and your library wants to incur minimal risk.

If the insurance company agrees to or requires a lump-sum settlement on the other hand, both parties benefit by avoiding the paper work required to document actual costs; but both parties, and the library in particular, are at a somewhat greater risk since a just settlement depends on how accurately the costs can be estimated. Some libraries may determine that this method of settlement is preferable also because it offers flexibility in how and when items may be replaced. However, estimating costs, especially when many items are out-of-print, is no simple matter; and the method for estimating costs must be carefully and completely negotiated with the insurance company. When lump sums are awarded, there can also be the danger of having administrators in a library's parent institution decide that part of the money not go to the library for replacement of the collection but be used for other priorities on campus, particularly when there has been an institution-wide disaster.

ESTIMATING REPURCHASING COSTS FOR TOTAL LOSSES

Associated Costs for Total Loss Replacement

Because total losses in mixed collections of materials can rarely be replaced with exact duplicates, the process of replacement will have many associated costs. Librarians must always seek to balance what the insurance company will allow with the replacement policy and the needs of the library and the institution. Our insurance policy, for example, covered the cost of replacement. It was our view, and our insurance company agreed, that *replacement* included the price of the material and the associated costs of ordering and processing. It was our view, and our insurance company again agreed, that anything declared a total loss would be replaced. We also agreed that, if an exact replacement was unavailable, we would purchase alternate formats or versions, that is, paperback instead of hardcover, British printings instead of American, later editions instead of earlier, microfiche and electronic versions instead of paper. When no acceptable format or version is available, we agreed that topically similar works would be purchased; and for certain titles adjudged critical, we agreed that we might pursue such expensive options as commercial facsimile digitization and photocopying or even, occasionally, seeking permission and paying the costs for dismantling, copying, and rebinding a volume from another library.

Model for Estimating Per-Volume Costs

Once the replacement parameters have been agreed upon, a second requirement is an institution-specific and loss-specific model for estimating the per-volume cost of repurchasing lost materials.

Unfortunately, library literature provides few standards to follow. After a loss of 1,217 volumes at Dartmouth College in 1983, Naslund and George (1986) recognized the need to establish guidelines for "the calculation of loss associated with water damage that will be acceptable to both libraries and the insurance industry" (1986: 325). In their model, they used a random sampling technique to develop an estimate of the cost of replacing damaged materials through repurchasing. Although their model was primarily used to calculate the useful life span percentage loss of each volume, their methodology offers an example of one way to use sampling to estimate the cost of replacement.

In our case, because no ready-made model applied to our circumstances, we developed our own methodology and sent it through the appropriate channels for clearance with insurance company officials. It consisted of the following seven parts:

1. Identification of a qualified statistician-consultant is an important step in obtaining valid estimates of costs to settle with insurance.

Valid sampling should not be attempted without the advice and direction of a qualified statistician. Insurance adjusters are likely to challenge estimates lacking clear statistical validity. Given the mutual interest of the insurance company and your library in arriving at a valid sample, the insurance company might well be willing to fund such a study.

We were fortunate to have a highly-regarded statistical department on campus whose staff offers free advice. However, with or without such support, it is, as one statistician noted, a good idea to spend several thousand dollars to get a good sample when the settlement may involve millions of dollars.

2.   Identification of appropriate population and subgroups is the first step in random sampling.

Valid sampling requires careful listings of the subgroups that make up the population to be studied so that random samples can be drawn from each subgroup; and, as far as possible, every item in a given subgroup should be representative of the subgroup list as a whole. If it is not, a new subgroup may be necessary. The care that must go into valid sampling is illustrated in the 1983 disaster at Dartmouth when librarians went so far as to prepare a manual card-file listing of each volume damaged.

The scale and character of the disaster at our library precluded such manual attention, but we were able to rely on the robust report generator in our automated system as we turned to the task of preparing the large lists for each subgroup. The first subgroups we distinguished, of course, were monographs and journal volumes because the ways they are acquired can differ so considerably.

Although we could only list records by title, we had to find a way to calculate the number of bound volumes in each title since no title had the same number of volumes. Even with the marvels of automation, however, obtaining useful lists of representative volumes for even the broadest subgroups was not easy. For instance, because of limited funding, Colorado State University Libraries had never completed its project to convert all serials holdings into online item records. Therefore, after identifying a serials sample, our staff had to check many of the items against records of summary holdings and do a physical check of the shelves and storage facility to determine whether the item had been damaged in the disaster. Once again, we were reminded of the value of retrospective conversion of manual records and the need to tag data correctly.

3.   Statistical validity must be assured through sampling technique, size, and randomness.

Once the population to be sampled has been divided into its subgroups, an appropriate sampling technique must be chosen, and a random sample selected. Because we had identified various subgroups, our statistician-consultant recommended that we do stratified random sampling, that is, over-sampling of the selected groups and then adjusting the final results based on the percentage represented by the various strata. Our journal losses, for example, ranged from items received as gifts to subscriptions that cost thousands of dollars per year.

Stratified random sampling allowed us to make sure that the most expensive titles were adequately sampled. Our subgroups for journals included: a) titles with annual subscriptions over $5,000 a year; b) titles ranging in price from $1,500 to $4,900 per annual subscription; and c) journals in the Library of Congress classifications of Q and T that were not included in subgroups one or two. In addition, we ran a sample of randomly-selected items from the entire population also not included in the other three subgroups.

Appropriate sampling sizes based on the relative size of each list is also an important consideration in assuring statistical validity. Our statistician helped us determine, for each subgroup, the minimum sampling size, but since validity is relative to the percent of the total population sampled, he pointed to the wisdom of increasing the sample size as much as time and money would permit since doing so reduces the risk of under- or overestimating the extent of the loss.

Last, of course, drawing a random sample requires that each item be chosen randomly. If the population is small, random sampling may consist of nothing more than manually choosing every 10th or 20th item, and the dice can be thrown to help find a starting point or to choose numbers. For a large sample, such as ours, we relied on the computers to generate a list of random numbers that we then applied to the numbered lists in each subgroups.

4.   Identification of pricing sources and costs is another step in estimating the cost of materials to be replaced.

Cost models also require establishing the price of randomly-selected titles; and here again, success may well depend on mutual agreement between your library and the insurance company as to the validity of the appraisal source. Little debate is likely to occur over such obvious sources as *Books in Print* or a major book vendor's publishing database, both of which are now automated. However, your out-of-print materials are more problematic and require more careful justification.

In our case, what we proposed and then did was to send our

random samples of monographs to a book vendor to have them searched first in its online publishing database and then against standard out-of-print listings such as are now available on many Websites. If the price for a given monograph did not appear in either search, we had our selectors review the items to decide which were critical materials to be replaced by facsimile photo-copying while the remaining percent would be replaced by buy-ing a topical substitute. To determine the cost of a topical replace-ment, libraries can rely on standard price indexes, such as the *Bowker Annual*, or annual cost studies from major approval-plan vendors which are broken down by Library of Congress classifi-cation.

The strategy we proposed for our list of random journal samples was similar. The cost of back volumes for journals are typically available from dealers specializing in back issues. Major dealers are accustomed to providing such information and have even served as expert witnesses to justify the cost of materials. Since such dealers usually have a search charge for each title, this charge, too, should be included in the final estimate. One problem the library encountered involved the definition of a *volume*. For di-saster accounting purposes, a bound journal volume, not a bib-liographic volume, constituted one damaged volume. Journal ven-dors determine the cost of a volume based on the bibliographic volume as they have no knowledge of how a library binds its volumes. Since our lost volumes were figured in number-bound volumes, not bibliographic volumes, we had to estimate how many bound volumes were represented by the cost of the bibliographic volumes reported by the dealer.

5. The final cost model should also include any special cir-cumstances that may affect prices at time of actual pur-chase.

Since more than a year would pass from the time our price study was completed until all the damaged materials would be unpacked, we also built in two additional factors in our estimate of costs: a) with each passing day, more books would go out of print, thus raising the average cost per volume purchased, and b) normal inflation between the time of our study and actual repur-chasing would similarly add to the average cost.

Appropriately combining all costs for monographs and journal volumes results, finally, in an average price per volume which then can be multiplied by the total number of volumes lost. The percentage of volumes declared total loss at Morgan Library was predetermined by a random sample of 7,000 items damaged in the disaster. If you do something similar, the final report to the insurance company should be accompanied by a statement from your statistician indicating the methodology used and the confidence level of the data—that is, the potential range of error plus and minus from the estimated average price.

6. Establishing purchasing and processing costs is a second major cost to determine in a cost model for an insurance settlement for replacement.

No cost model for repurchasing library losses is complete without including all the associated costs of purchasing and processing the materials. Developing the cost model in this area requires detailed thinking about the procedures that will be required to repurchase material and to carry out those tasks required when materials are out-of-print and unavailable through commercial channels. In addition, the costs of processing the material must take into account whether your library's staff will handle the materials or whether contractors will be employed. Flowcharts that Colorado State University Libraries' staff developed to outline steps in repurchasing and processing monographs and journals are included in the appendices at the end of the chapter (Appendix 22-A and Appendix 22-B).

Basic costs to consider include: a) staffing costs to search, order, unpack and receive, claim, re-catalog, maintain and update system records, re-shelve materials, problem solve, and hire and train staff; b) transportation of materials to the library; c) binding charges; d) bibliographic database charges for searching; e) costs of order forms and records; f) supplies for office and for physical processing; g) workstations and equipment; and h) system support and maintenance. If contractors are used for part or all of the operation, additional costs can include: a) contract negotiation costs; b) contractor's administrative costs; and c) transportation costs for shipping materials to and from contract cataloging centers.

Figuring unit costs for each of these many activities can be a challenge unless your library has developed detailed studies of its costs in prior years. Although data from other institutions can vary greatly and is not plentiful in the literature, some help can be had from experience at other institutions and businesses. We found a useful breakdown of acquisitions activities in the Iowa State study (Morris, Rebarcak, and Rowley, 1996); and because outsourcing of cataloging and physical processing to commercial vendors is common among libraries, costs cited by a vendor for a certain activity is another quick way to estimate a unit cost.

7. Construction of a cost model should consider whether all or part of the work of repurchasing will be outsourced or performed in-house.

As a library considers its purchasing and processing costs, it should also consider, in light of the scale of the disaster and how urgent the need is to replace materials, whether it has the resources to handle the repurchasing operation or whether all or parts of the operation should be outsourced. Major utilities such as the Online Computer Library Center (OCLC) or regional utilities like Bibliographical Center for Research (BCR), AMIGOS, or several smaller cataloging services are set up to handle contract cataloging. However, finding an agency to handle an entire repurchasing operation is more complex. Book or journal vendors traditionally handle in-print and selective out-of-print purchasing for libraries, provide cataloging, and some physical processing within certain limits. Ideally, what is needed to handle a massive repurchasing effort is a contractor who is familiar with library operations and the book and serial industry who would be willing to take on the role of an acquisitions department and update the library records. At the time of this publication, however, none exists; but the library is actively exploring options for repurchasing within a multi-vendor environment.

IDENTIFYING AND PROCESSING EXCEPTIONS TO A MASS-REPURCHASING PROJECT

For certain types of material, it is pointless even to consider attempts at recovery of the damaged, original items. Some obvious examples are materials that depend on their currency to retain their value, paperback collections on cheap paper that will no doubt prove to be beyond repair, or inexpensive types of material that will be cheaper to buy than to restore, even with processing costs included. For such collections, insurance companies may be willing to listen to compelling arguments for not salvaging them but instead repurchasing them immediately.

One Factor in Decision Making Will Be the Physical Condition of Materials

Early plans for disaster recovery at Morgan Library took into account the varying nature of the collection and the assumption that not all items should be scheduled for restoration. Three parts of the collection were identified as materials that could be declared as total losses and thus exempted from preservation efforts: 1) the computer manual section of the QA76 classification; 2) the Current Awareness collection and 3) the Curriculum-Materials collection. Most of the books in these collections consisted of paperbacks, unbound notebooks, or other formats whose binding was unlikely to survive major disaster damage.

The library recommended, and the consultant concurred, that the likelihood that any of these items would be considered cost-effectively restorable was extremely remote. The library asked the reprocessing contractor to declare that these collections were a total loss and to authorize their itemization for replacement in order to obligate the insurance company to pay for them.

Current Relevance of Materials is Another Factor in Decisions to Restore or Replace

A second factor may be of equal concern in the decision not to salvage certain materials. If the emphasis on acquiring and retaining the most current information is paramount in these collections, restoring damaged out-of-date items is not a good collection development policy. The Colorado State University collection provides some pertinent examples. For computer science, the rationale was that the field is a rapidly changing one and that it would be advisable to replace selected out-of-date items with current titles on similar topics.

The Current Awareness collection was described as a fluid one representing the changing patterns of student interest. Purchasing paperbacks for this collection had been the pattern for years in that it allowed the flexibility of buying books as soon as student interest was expressed.

The Curriculum collection had been selected and weeded on the basis of retaining only those items which had been published in the last ten years. It was deemed essential that the collection represent the materials and teaching methods currently being used in the schools. A subset of the Curriculum collection, the Adolescent Literature section, was not subject to the ten-year limitation since the purpose in building it had been to acquire and retain those quality current works that were most highly recommended and that were likely to experience the most demand.

Cooperative Efforts Between External Entities and Library Staff
Are Essential in Launching a Successful Program

The physical disposition of the books in the Morgan Library's collections was the responsibility of teams of workers that were hired by the insurance company to manage the physical recovery efforts. Communication between this team and the library staff was critical to assess the nature of the damage. The record-keeping aspects necessary to identify and replace the materials were shared by cataloging and acquisitions staff and the selectors responsible for the collections. Within a few weeks after the disaster, cataloging staff were able to generate electronic lists of titles in the collections from our automated library system and to communicate those lists to selectors for decision making.

Time, Labor, and Cost Estimates Can Provide Useful Guidelines
For Planning and Decision Making

The time spent in planning and projecting can save valuable time in the actual processing, where each step becomes multiplied by the thousands of times that it must be repeated. Through this process, it may be possible to predict, for example, that replacement on a title-by-title basis with the closest match possible will not be economically feasible. In fact, a trial effort to replace a sampling of titles for the Curriculum collection proved that this method would be unacceptably labor intensive and costly if pursued on a larger scale. A less rigorous method could be to prepare deside- rata lists in advance of the placement of orders, creating a pool of records from which to select the designated numbers of items within broad subject areas (e.g., political science, education, mu- sic, mathematics, or engineering). The result will differ in empha- sis from the original collection but will create one that is more current and more reflective of actual needs.

Automation Can Offer Less Costly Ways to Assist Staff Efforts in Repurchasing

Libraries facing the prospect of collection replacement on a large scale are advised to find ways of streamlining their usual labor- intensive acquisitions process. In retrospect, the Libraries' good luck in having in place a powerful electronic system greatly fa- cilitated the huge amount of record-keeping and generation that the scope of this recovery effort required. For example, the library's acquisitions staff developed a proposal that included the creation of electronic lists of destroyed items to replace the generation of individual order records for exact-title replacement. Early estimates had projected that approximately 60 percent of the titles could be replaced with exact or newer editions. The remaining titles would be dealt with through procedures developed by the indi- vidual selectors. Negotiations with vendors should include the pos- sibility of purchasing access to their computer databases for use in selecting alternate titles for inexact replacements. Exact matches can be processed by the library staff, who can use or modify ex- isting records to catalog and prepare the books for shelving. In- exact matches could be outsourced for contract cataloging, cre- ation of item records, and physical processing.

The advantage of identifying total loss collections at the begin- ning of the recovery process is that they do not have to await decisions on whether to shelve, rebind, or replace after they are returned from treatment. Although these collections constituted a small percentage of the total volumes damaged or lost in the di- saster at CSU, managing their replacement provided the library staff with a test case for restoring or replacing the larger collection after books were returned from freeze-drying treatment. Finding ways of expediting the process on this smaller scale could greatly benefit the eventual restoration or replacement of the entire damaged collection.

CONCLUSION

At the time of this publication, Colorado State University Libraries has not yet finalized plans to repurchase the large number of total losses expected during the restoration. Nonetheless, there are many considerations included in this chapter relative to the repurchasing of a damaged collection of which other libraries would need to be aware. The subject of repurchasing some of your total-loss volumes will be a big bone of contention in the disaster-recovery process, especially with insurance companies.

Library Disaster Planning and Recovery Handbook

KEY RECOMMENDATIONS

Insurance

- Begin discussions with insurance companies early in the process to establish what will be acceptable as total loss and what insurance will cover for repurchase.
- Explore your options for settlements with insurance companies. Different types or scales of disasters may be more appropriate to a certain type of settlement.
- Be prepared to defend the cost of repurchasing materials, including the prices of materials, inflation for delays, and associated costs of acquiring and processing.
- Remember that insurance companies may not have encountered your type of disaster and may not be aware of the various costs associated with your situation.
- Seek professional assistance when preparing cost estimates, even if assistance is expensive.
    * Turn to your book and serial vendors for assistance, as well as campus or government statistical experts.
    * Consider any assessed consulting fees part of the cost of replacing the collection and request funds as part of your settlement.
- Consider using subsets of total loss materials as test cases for developing costs and procedures prior to settling on costs with insurance and embarking on a massive repurchasing effort.
- Systematically design a flowchart about your replacing/rebuilding process, both for journals and monographs. This will detail for your library, external administrators, insurance representatives, et al., how you plan to complete the project and illustrate the systematic process on which costs were determined.
- Do not trust anything to luck. Examine the capabilities of your automation systems to generate information that would be useful to you in restoration of materials and include this thinking in your disaster-recovery plans for an emergency.

APPENDIX 22-A
REBUILDING THE COLLECTION: REPLACING MONOGRAPHS

Scenario (see flowchart on next page) assumes:

1. Repurchase of core and classic monographs for research and learning in latest print version.

2. Topical replacement where appropriate and incorporates opportunities for new directions in collections. Electronic book market in embryo stage.

3. Central contractor/vendor to handle disparate ordering, cataloging, and physical processing.

4. Reasonable effort required by copyright law before critical facsimile replacement.

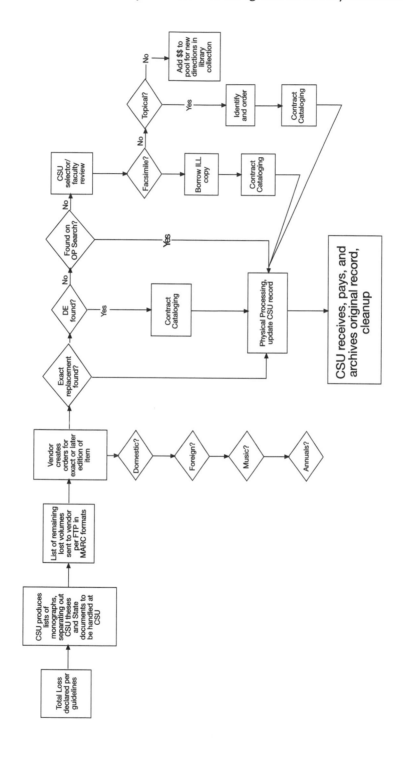

APPENDIX 22-B
REBUILDING THE COLLECTION:
REPLACING JOURNAL VOLUMES

Scenario assumes:

1. Replacement of core and classic titles critical to research and learning at CSU.

2. Recognizes that full back sets in digital form are in infancy stage.

3. Recognizes faculty/student resistance to microtext.

4. Incorporates opportunities for new directions.

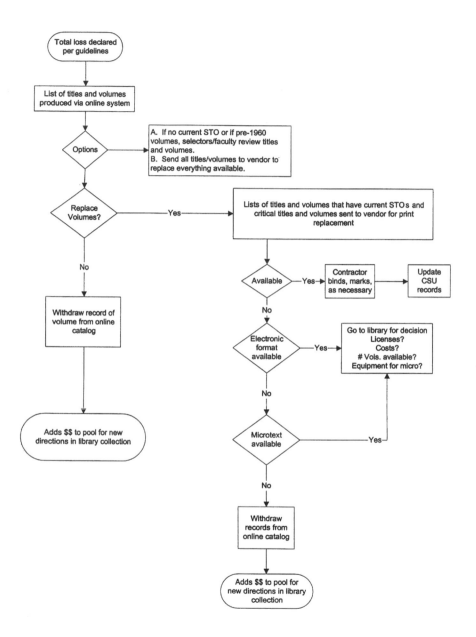

REFERENCES

Foster, Constance L. 1996. "Damaged Periodicals: A Wet Trail Yields Dry Results." *Serials Review* 22, No. 1 (Spring): 33–38.

Hamilton, Marsha J. 1993. *Guide to Preservation in Acquisition Processing*. Chicago: American Library Association (Acquisitions Guidelines, No. 8).

Morris, Dilys E., Pamela Rebarcak, and Gordon Rowley. 1996. "Monographs Acquisitions: Staffing Costs and the Impact of Automation." *Library Resources and Technical Services* 40, No. 4 (October): 301–318.

Naslund, Cheryl T. and Susan C. George. 1986. "Insurance Settlement Negotiation." *C&RL News* 47, No. 5 (May): 325–328.

23 Tools for Tracking: Data for Restoring the Collection

Karen Weedman, Patricia Smith,
and Nora Copeland

INTRODUCTION

Throughout a disaster-recovery process, reports, statistics, and data on each damaged item will be needed. This information may be needed for insurance, institutional administration, and the library's use to determine the status of the recovery process and what remains to be done. Statistics are also useful when making public-relations announcements. Initial decisions will include the type of data needed, how data can be obtained, how it can be stored, and what reports can be produced from it. As recovery projects progress, there is high probability that additional data will be needed, so planning should allow for this expansion.

IDENTIFYING DATA TO TRACK

Insurance Needs

One of the first steps in identifying data is to find out what might be needed to support your insurance claims; so it is important to document the damage as soon as possible. As suggested previously, insurance companies may not be clear on what information they want early in disaster recovery so you may not receive much information from them on the type of data to collect. Also, depending upon what coverage a library may have, there may be multiple insurance companies and/or FEMA involved. For large disasters, the process can take place over a period of years with changing personnel; therefore, providing clear documentation benefits all parties. However, Colorado State University (CSU) Morgan Library did have some direction from the insurance companies. At minimum, the insurance company representatives wanted to know the following: 1) size of the collection damaged and how CSU could prove it; and 2) total loss resulting from the disaster and how the library could justify declaring a volume a total loss.

In addition to the insurance companies themselves, an institution may have in-house experts who can provide advice and guidance on tracking and documentation for the disaster-recovery process. Another source a library might use to identify what insurance companies might want to know is other institutions that have experienced similar disasters and what they needed to provide for insurance companies. Depending on how the settlement is made, insurance companies could settle on a model based on projected costs or on actual costs. In the event of the settling on actual costs, one would be in the position of having to provide an auditable trail. Other considerations will include *value* lost—the devaluation of the longevity or aesthetics of the collection.

Institutional Needs

In the absence of any guidelines, your library needs to determine 1) what information will be needed later and 2) how detailed the information needs to be. For example, do you need to know only the number of items that were repaired or do you need to know what kinds of repairs were done and how many pages were fixed? Do you need to know what was done to a particular item? To be safe, the library opted to be quite detailed at the beginning of the project in case information would be needed later by the insurance companies, the library, and/or the university administration. For each item involved in the disaster, we wanted to know: 1) the identification of each item affected by the disaster; 2) the treatment resolution for each item (was it salvaged, replaced, total loss, etc); and 3) the steps the item went through for recovery.

Another category of statistics was kept on the productivity of the Processing Center; for example, a weekly report on the numbers of items that were returned to the shelves. For quality control in selected areas, we also wanted to track which individuals did the work on each item. We also designed weekly and cumulative reports to indicate totals on what was replaced, what was total loss, and what was salvaged. Some of these reports could be used to show the university community how far along the project was; such as, what percentage of damaged items were back on the shelves. Examples of reports and statistics appear later. (See Appendices 23-A to 23-C.)

Over time, there may be requests for more detailed reports or there may be a preference for more generalized summary reports. As we gained more experience, we learned that reports from the contractor of the Processing Center should cover outcomes of the processing rather than individual productivity. Also, the university placed more emphasis on the final resolution of each piece but not necessarily tracking all the steps involved in reaching the resolution. Finally, given the time and expense associated with collecting data, try to determine which data is critical to your recovery effort.

CREATING AND STORING DATA

Once a library decides what data should be tracked during the recovery process, the next question is where can the data be created and maintained? Choices include your online database, an external database, or manual tracking.

Online Library Databases

The online database already contains the most detailed information available in an automated form about items involved in the disaster. However, some data for older parts of the collection may not be in the online catalog if it has not been converted to an automated format. Even so, it is still the most complete source for data. If your library decides that the damage-related data should be maintained in the online system, you will need to determine first if the system has the capability to store the data to be added. Another consideration is where the data can be stored; that is, in the bibliographic or in the item record. A third consideration is what type of fields—numeric, text, date—can be used for the data. The library needs to confirm whether the system can produce needed reports. If numerical data such as a price must be stored in a text field, for example, then you may not be able to generate a report from your online system that calculates the total of the prices stored in that field. However, you may be able to export this data into a spreadsheet to generate this type of report.

A major disadvantage of maintaining any disaster data in the online catalog is that any temporary staff hired to enter and modify data directly into the catalog will also have the ability to modify or delete far more than disaster data. Temporary staff often will not have the same training and expertise as permanent staff. If a library decides to maintain its disaster records via its catalog and use temporary staff, quality-control criteria and procedures are critical. (See Chapter 24 for coverage of quality control issues.)

External Database

The advantages of external databases are that you can design a system that meets the specific requirements of the project, checks quality of data, confirms that certain conditions are met, stores data in appropriate types of fields, and prevents certain errors. The library will, however, need to provide written specifications that detail what needs to be done. External databases for maintaining disaster records can either be a database system that your library purchases as a package or one that the library designs and has someone develop according to your specifications. It may be difficult to find an existing package, since the most likely prospect would be a database that another library developed during a similar disaster. Designing a database from scratch is more likely to meet your specific needs than purchasing an existing one, but the implementation is fraught with difficulty as well. First, identifying who can create the database and write the programs will take time. Some of the possibilities are bibliographic utilities, automation vendors, institutional computer centers, systems offices within a consortium, or staff within your library. Unfortunately, staff within your own organization are probably already inundated with additional assignments if you are in a disaster situation. Whoever develops the database will also have to provide written documentation on how to use the system.

With an external database system, there will often be a need to interface the external database with the library system. Such interfaces may include initializing the external database by sending data from your online catalog. Another interface could occur when processing has finished on an item and the resolution status needs to be returned to the main catalog.

Manual Databases

Tracking by manual methods might be an option if you have a relatively small number of items to track. Development time and effort of a special database may be more costly than printing the record and manually tracking information on that sheet.

In our case, our first preference was to have an external database for both the tracking of the gift replacements and the recovery processing because we wanted a production-oriented system for the Processing Center staff. Our designed system allowed tracking the status of each item as it moved through the Processing Center, had quality control features, and had program logic that provided instruction for the staff. When processing an item, for example, the software should tell the staff member that a gift replacement had already been received rather than leaving it to the staff member to read codes in the records to see if this had happened. Through our alliance with other libraries, we had a consortial systems office that was extremely talented and able to handle this project. (See Chapter 27 on the Colorado Alliance for Research Libraries.)

When processing of the damaged materials was delayed, we were forced to use the online catalog to document which items were replaced with *matching* gifts. As mentioned previously, our system supported adding disaster data in local MARC fields in item records, so we were able to define a series of MARC fields and associated codes to use to track the status of each volume in the item record. In addition, we displayed in the online catalog the phrase "FLOOD: SEE ILL" as the status for each disaster-damaged volume. (See Appendix 23-D for the list of tags and associated definitions.) We found that we added many new codes as we discovered new situations that needed to be tracked, so using fields that provide for expansion is important.

The integrated library system could not track *non-matching* gifts; therefore, we used an external database designed by library staff and implemented by the Colorado Alliance of Research Libraries to list gifts that did not match our current holdings. Library staff had also designed a binding component as part of the external database system; however, this functionality was subsequently added through the commercial binding system used in the disaster-recovery process, eliminating the need for the library-designed binding component. Since unrecoverable pieces were screened and tossed in Texas, another separate database for entering records for these tossed items was created for the Texas staff to use. Consequently, we used a combination of the various options to track data in our disaster-recovery efforts. As of this writing, we do not know what approach will be used to document the processing of the damaged materials, although the end result will be stored in the online catalog.

RECORD RETENTION

As the recovery process is completed, how long your library needs to retain data for auditors will be determined in part by what kind of insurance settlement is negotiated. If insurance companies settle on a lump sum based on a cost model, there is no need to retain additional data for insurance auditors. If you agree to an ongoing arrangement where claims are paid as costs occur, your library will need to retain records for possible insurance review and audit until the final claim is settled. In addition to insurance claims, libraries will also need to review the retention policies of its parent institution and abide by those requirements for auditing.

In our case, we had no clear guidelines from insurance, but we knew we needed to retain data for internal and state auditors. When the entire disaster-recovery effort is completed and insurance settled, we also plan to have our library system vendor run a program to eliminate all of the local MARC codes related to the disaster.

Because space was limited in the integrated library system and historical records can confuse staff, we did not want to maintain disaster records permanently in the library's online database. Thus, we designed a special database using Microsoft ACCESS software for archiving disaster bibliographic, item, and order records. The export feature of our integrated library system was used to export files of withdrawn disaster records for loading into this AC-CESS database. The database allowed us to retrieve information by the various codes in local MARC fields so we could track how the item was replaced. In addition, we provided the same audit points for tracking ordering data that we expect our regular fiscal auditors to need during a normal audit.

CONCLUSION

Tools for tracking your disaster recovery are crucial no matter how major or minor your recovery effort. Different interested parties— library administration, institutional administration, insurance companies, etc.—will be expecting reports generated by your data. The requests for data will be pervasive throughout the entire disaster-recovery process especially when determination of costs are involved.

Library Disaster Planning and Recovery Handbook

KEY RECOMMENDATIONS

Tracking Tools

- Identify the data needed for tracking the recovery process and for providing reports and statistics.

- Determine where data will be created, stored, and archived.

- Be flexible enough to realize you may need to add more data to track and/or realize that some data you were tracking was not useful.

- Develop written documentation on the storage and usage of the data.

APPENDIX 23-A
GIFT PROCESSING REPORT

(DATE OF WEEK)

FUNCTIONS	WEEK MONO	WEEK SERIAL	WEEK TOTAL	MTD MONOS	MTD SERIALS	MONTH TOTAL	TOTALS 1999	TOTALS 1998	GRAND TOTAL YTD
PALLETS OF GIFT MATERIAL RECEIVED									
BOXES UNPACKED									
VOLUMES UNPACKED									
VOLUMES IN PROCESSING									
VOLUMES SENT TO **INVENTORY**									
VOLUMES SENT TO **DISCARD**									
VOLUMES SENT TO **BARCODE**									
SUBTOTAL									
VOLUMES SENT TO SUSPEND									
TOTAL									
BINDING									
TITLES ADDED TO BINDING MODULE									
VOLUMES PROCESSED FOR BINDING									
BINDING SHIPMENTS SENT OUT (SHIPPED)									
BINDING SHIPMENTS BACK (RECEIVED)									
INVENTORY RECORDS CREATED									
VOLUMES SENT TO LIBRARY STACKS									

APPENDIX 23-B
DAMAGED BOOKS STATISTICAL REPORT

(DATE OF WEEK)

ACTIVITY	CURRENT WEEK Mono Serial Total	MONTH TO DATE Mono Serial Total	ADJUSTMENTS Mono Serial Total	ADJUSTED MONTH TO DATE Mono Serial Total	PROJECT TO DATE Mono Serial Total
ILS PROCESSING					
Item records updated (992)					
Item records created					
Item records with 978 field					
INSPECTION					
Item records with 980, 981, 993 field					
Item records with 995 field					
Volumes sent to Total Loss-Toss					
Volumes sent to Total Loss-Keep					
Volumes sent to Page Repair Only					
Volumes sent to Replace Pages Only					
Volumes sent to Repair & Replace					
Volumes sent to Binding Only					
Volumes Ready to go to shelves					
Replaced by Gift in Process					
TOTAL VOLUMES INSPECTED					
PAGE REPAIR					
Volumes with page repairs completed					
REPLACEMENT PAGES					
Pages photocopied in-house					
No. of volumes					
Pages photocopied at Contractor					
No. of Volumes					
BINDING					
Volumes processed for binding					
Binding shipments sent out					
Binding shipments received back					
MARKING					
Volumes with pamphlet binding					
SHELVING					
Volumes shelved					

Comments:

APPENDIX 23-C
DAMAGED VOLUME INSPECTION STATISTICS

Week of _____

CATEGORY	MONOGRAPHS	JOURNALS	TOTAL	PERCENT
TOTAL LOSS				
PAGE REPAIR				
PAGE DUPLICATION				
REPAIR & DUPLICATION				
BIND ONLY				
READY TO SHELVE				
GIFT IN PROCESS				
WITHDRAWN OR NOT PACKED OUT				
PATRON LOSS				
INCOMPLETE GIFT (JOURNALS ONLY)				
TOTALS				
PERCENTAGE			100%	100%

APPENDIX 23-D

LOCAL MARC TAGS IN BIBLIOGRAPHIC AND ITEM RECORDS FOR FLOOD-RELATED MATERIALS
--------REVISED******JANUARY 28, 1998
MARC TAG FOR ALL FLOOD RELATED ITEMS AT CSU:

       950   FLOOD

SUSPEND:

       955   JSTOR titles

PURCHASES:

      ORDERED
      960   Order - Priority 1 (on the original item record)
      961   Order (after TL) (on the original item record)
      RECEIVED STATUS
      962   Received - Exact (on the item record created)
      962   Received - Inexact (on the item record created)
      964   Received - Inexact (on the item record created) (For contract cataloging)
      NOT AVAILABLE
      965   Order - Priority 1 not available (on the original item record)

GIFT IN PROCESS:

      975   Gift in process
      976   Item record created (for items created from INVENTORY if title exists)
      977   Item record created (for "splitting the more than 2.5" bound items)

INC.   978   (This is a free text field for a journal title that has issues missing to make a complete volume, a book that needs to be compared with the DRS book, etc. It will also be used to alert someone that an item is on the shelf to be compared with the DRS item when the item comes back from DRS)
      979   Item record created - INVENTORY Bound differently
      979   Item record created - SUSPEND Bound differently
      979   Item record created - INVENTORY/SUSPEND Bound differently

TO BE WEEDED (LC classification – Z" collection)
      980   To be weeded (on the original item record)

APPENDIX 23-D *(Continued)*

WITHDRAWALS

      981   Withdrawn (on the original item record)

              (Determined by the CSU library)

              - Exact purchase

              - Inexact purchase

              - Exact gift

              - Inexact gift

              - Cash value

              - Gift split volume

              - SUSPEND bound differently

REPROCESSED MATERIALS FROM THE FLOOD

      990   Barcode (status)

              - Original   (Set in Plant and will be transferred to SAGE)

              - Replicated (Set in Plant and will be transferred to SAGE)

              - TEMP, OCLC, RLIN (Set in SAGE and transferred to Plant)

      991   Item record created

              - No barcode in item (Created in SAGE and transferred to Plant)

              - Barcode in item (Created in SAGE and transferred to Plant)

      992   Return status from Plant (on the original item record)

              - Salvaged

              - Total loss- Kept

              - Total loss- Toss

              - DRS SUSPEND (This is a free text field)

              - Page duplication

              - Page repair

              - DRS 7000

      994   - Reprocess special

PATRON LOSS

      995   - Patron loss

NOT PACKED OUT

      993   -Current Aware

              -Curriculum

24 Who's Minding the Store?: Quality Control in a Contractual Environment

Patricia Smith and Nora Copeland

INTRODUCTION

Libraries traditionally strive to maintain a high degree of accuracy in their records and processes to assure that their users can access the correct records and find needed materials in usable condition. Thus, librarians employ quality-control measures as a matter of course throughout their work and automatically build quality control into the extensive training and supervisory oversight we give our staff. When a disaster, such as the one that struck Colorado State University's Morgan Library, forces a library to initiate a major disaster-recovery effort that involves contractors and large numbers of untrained staff, the library must consider developing a formal system for defining and assuring quality control. Although the concept of floor audits is common in federal contractors and industry—the *American Heritage Dictionary* (3rd edition, 1992: 1,479), defines quality control as "a system for ensuring the maintenance of proper standards in manufactured goods, especially by periodic random inspection of the product"—such a formal definition is not common in libraries.

Although there is nothing in the literature that speaks directly to working with a contractor during library-disaster recovery, outsourcing in general has become a trend in libraries and questions of quality control have risen.

In our case, quality control was a major concern from the moment it was decided that we would contract out a large portion of the collection-restoration effort. Although we did not want untrained staff working on our online catalog, we had to compromise to allow our contractor's staff to update the item record to show that a gift was received or that a repair had been made. We made certain that quality control was mentioned in the contract; however, our first contract, which was hastily assembled by the university after the disaster and based on a generic form the university used, did not give us the protection we found we needed. To safeguard the integrity of our database, we asked the contractor to set up a special quality-control unit for the gifts processing operation that served solely to review the work of the staff who updated an item record in our integrated library system. Library staff were assigned to train and help with questions. By virtue of the original contracts the contractor did not report to the library, which made this working relationship very challenging.

As the processing progressed, however, the contractor objected to the presence of library staff in his operation even though library staff continued to find quality-control problems. The contractor argued that quality control was the role of the contractor, not the library, and that our job was to accept or reject the final product. In a normal outsourcing operation, we might have agreed on these roles but in this situation neither the contractor nor any of his staff were experts in any aspect of library operations. When a revised contract was negotiated at the end of the first year, the library staff saw this as an opportunity to redesign the quality-control system. Surprisingly, several university officials did not support us initially and seemed to think that we, the librarians, were being too demanding and restrictive on the contractor. They even supported the contractor in efforts to exclude library staff from the Processing Center unless our presence was expressly authorized by the contractor.

Serendipitously for the library's case, one of the staff in the Processing Center who had the responsibility to mark the call numbers on the book spines chose this time to begin putting dates erroneously in call numbers on the spine of the book, regardless of whether there was really a date in the call number. If the staff member did not find a date in the call number, he or she used the birth date of the author from the bibliographic record—an error so blatant that even non-library staff understood why library staff were concerned. Concurrently, library staff also discovered that Processing Center staff had begun to use, without permission, one of the fields in the library's item record to place a tracking number for center activities. Faced with these glaring mistakes and library negotiators unwillingness to capitulate on the issue of quality control, university officials finally agreed that the library had the right to confirm the quality of the product at various stages of the process and not just at the end. As we revised our specifications in the original contract, we tried to cover the following points which may be of interest to other libraries recovering from disaster or generally considering an outsourcing contract.

ESTABLISH STANDARDS FOR THE QUALITY YOU EXPECT

One of the first tasks in working with a contractor is to agree on the error rate that is acceptable for the work being performed. Logically, a library should not expect a higher performance standard from a contractor than it would expect of its own staff. Error rates may vary from activity to activity. What you might tolerate in one area might not be tolerable in another. One way of assessing which errors are more serious is to consider activities that will have direct impacts on users and their ability to find material. Another technique is to decide whether work will be reviewed at a later point. You may allow a greater error rate when work has a built-in check later in the process than in a situation where you have only one chance to perform a job correctly and will not be able to find errors later. For example, we allowed a three percent overall error rate in our gifts operation; however, in our recovery-of-materials operation we identified specific activities that we expected to be performed with zero errors. One such activity was recording the barcodes for physical volumes that were going to be declared total loss and discarded. Since the piece, along with its barcode, was tossed, we had to rely on accurate information being logged about the piece. Since the barcode number requires no interpretation, we expected that it be recorded with 100 percent accuracy.

As part of establishing acceptable error rates, consider how you will define an error and supply a way for staff to measure errors. Although certain functions can be easily measured, others will be difficult depending on how much subjectivity in the work occurs.

For example, a call number is either correctly transcribed or it is not. Checking to see whether the item you received as a gift is exactly the same volume as the one you lost is also fairly clearcut. However, inspecting a damaged volume to decide how it can be repaired involves subjective judgment where more room for error or interpretation should be allowed. Despite the number of activities that may be hard to measure in library work, a library should carefully draft written specifications for a contractor to use in performing work that spell out types of errors as well as ways to measure them.

DECIDE WHEN YOU WANT TO PERFORM QUALITY CONTROL

Whether you want to check the quality of the product at various points throughout the process or only check the final product at the end of the process is another decision that needs to be clarified in negotiations with the contractor. Indeed, as we found, contractors may have strong objections to letting representatives from the library review work whenever they choose and may consider outside staff as intruders. Federal contracts, for example, establish when floor audits by the customer can be done. Libraries that have outsourced cataloging to commercial vendors normally check only the final product relying on clear specifications and the established expertise and reputation of the vendor to assure a certain quality.

If a situation like the one at our library should occur, your library staff should be heavily involved in the development of the process and training of the contractor's staff. Appendix 24-A provides forms used for tracking the various staff training for the Processing Center. You will need to establish quality-control guidelines for the contractor as well. If a contractor has not performed the work before, more of the burden for actual review of work will fall on your library. In our case, we reserved the right to perform floor audits of work for a specified period after training by our staff. If error rates exceeded our standards during that period, we retained the right to continue quality-control checks at random until the standards were met. Certifying when the contractor's supervisors are capable of performing the work and training staff properly is another way of minimizing the amount of checking of work that library staff might have to do on an ongoing basis. When there is changeover of supervisors, remember to certify the new supervisor. Such certification should be performed by your library staff.

Your contract should also require the contractor to define when the contractor will perform quality control during the process. However, also expect that your library staff will have to perform quality control on the quality control performed by the contractor—at least in the beginning of the process. During our gift operation, for example, we were most concerned about having the contractor's staff update our item records in our online catalog, so we required that the contractor establish a special work unit called Quality Control that rechecked the work of the staff who updated the online record.

Finally, it is a good idea for you to ask for a chance to review the final product before signing off on the contractor's work. No matter how many quality checkpoints you may have tried to instill throughout the process, unacceptable work can still occur when such a large amount of work is involved. When you sign off on the final product, you lose any rights to have the contractor redo inadequate work.

DETERMINE HOW YOU WANT QUALITY CONTROL PERFORMED

Once agreed that your library staff will perform quality checks of a contractor's work at specified points, you need to consider options for verifying quality of work. Although the ideal is to recheck everything done by a vendor, it is not economically feasible nor practical to repeat every task. Your staff will undoubtedly be already strained by regular work demands as well as the extra demands of coping with a disaster and should not be expected to perform extensive quality control after initial training is complete. Part of the solution is to build quality-control checking into the contractor's procedures as suggested above and to require the contractor to supply the library with regular reports of the error rates found during checking. Remedies for correcting unacceptable error rates should also be made part of the contractor's procedures.

Random sampling is another technique for lowering the cost of quality-control work both for the contractor and the library. Determine the acceptable sampling rates for various quality-control activities and put these rates in the contract. One of our best examples of a carefully conceived quality-control mechanism was the Quality Control Unit within the Processing Center which was utilized during the processing of gift material for Morgan Library. This unit was established to recheck the work of the Processing Center staff who compared gift pieces with the online item record for that volume. If the staff found a match, they updated the item record online and then sent the piece and a printout of the record to the Quality Control Unit where work was rechecked. Although at first 100 percent of the work was rechecked, later percentages were lowered as accuracy improved. Staff compiled weekly reports on the error rates which librarians reviewed (see Appendix 24-B). If errors exceeded three percent, greater percentages of materials were rechecked until the errors were under the acceptable level again. The sampling method was simple: depending on the percentage of pieces that needed to be reviewed according to the error rate, staff calculated how many pieces were on a truck, divided the number by the percent to be sampled, and counted every so many pieces to pull the piece that needed to be sampled.

Random sampling is especially useful when there are large quantities of work to review and a limited amount of time. When we reserved the right to do final acceptance review before signing off on the volumes being returned to the shelf after repair and restoration by the Processing Center, we also agreed to sign off on materials within 72 hours so we would not inhibit the workflow of the contractor. Since the Processing Center expected to process approximately 26,000 damaged volumes a month, we could only handle a certain number of items within each shipment; consequently, we had to do random sampling. To help us establish a valid sampling method, we turned to the Colorado State University Statistics Department for advice. Once the methodology for choosing a valid sample for each shipment returned to the library for shelving was determined, teams of staff hired and supervised by the library reviewed each of the items within the sample to check: 1) if the book matched the online bibliographic and item record; 2) whether the repair work had been done within the specifications; and 3) whether the online record had been updated correctly (see Appendix 24-C). If the material did not pass this inspection, the Processing Center was notified and remedies were applied.

CONCLUSION

Had we our choice whether we could work with a non-library contractor or not, we would have *without a doubt* preferred to do the work ourselves. However, it is a rare library that would have the staff size to handle such a large operation as well as handle regular duties; and it is unlikely that there are library-skilled contractors who are available to move to the site of a disaster and handle a large processing operation. The best a library can do in such a situation is assure that adequate quality control of the contractor takes place.

No matter how much your contractor may balk at certain points or external administrators may think you are being difficult, do not relent. You, your staff, and your future users are the ones who will have to live forever with the recovered collection that you entrusted to a contractor to restore. Remember that someone has *to mind the store.*

Library Disaster Planning and Recovery Handbook

KEY RECOMMENDATIONS

Quality Control

- Determine what quality is expected.

- Decide when you should check the quality of the work.

- Determine how quality will be checked.

- And most critically, ensure that all of your quality-control measures are clearly specified in a signed, enforceable contract before beginning to work with a contractor.

APPENDIX 24-A
TRAINING/REVIEW GUIDELINES FOR SUPERVISOR CERTIFICATION

ACTIVITY	PERIOD NEEDED TO COMPLETE TRAINING	DATES OF TRAINING	END DATE OF TRAINING	END OF 90-DAY REVIEW PERIOD	CERTIFIED PLANT SUPERVISORS
Restoration Vendor					
Inspection					
Total-Loss Checking					
Gifts-Already-Received Checking					
Processing of Damaged Books					
Inspection					
Updating Integrated Library System (ILS)					
Page Repair					
Page Duplication					
Binding					
Marking					
In-House Binding					
File Creation for Uploading ILS					
Shelving					

APPENDIX 24-A (*Continued*)
INITIAL GENERAL STAFF TRAINING NEEDED
BY EACH STATION

STATION	TRAINING NEEDED
Shipping & Receiving	General, Shipping & Receiving
Unpacking	General, Books & Journals, Unpacking
SAGE	General, General SAGE, Books & Journals, LC Call Number, SAGE
Barcode	General, Books & Journals, Read Printout, Barcode
Binding	General, Books & Journals, Read Printout, LC Call Number, Binding, LARS, IMS Binding
Marking	General, LC Call Number, Read Printout, Marking
Reshelving	General, LC Call Number, Shelving
Quality Control	General, General SAGE, Books & Journals, LC Call Number, SAGE, Barcoding, Read Printout
CIRC/DBM	General, CIRC/DBM
Inexact Match Inventory	General, IMS Gift, Inventory, Books & Journals

APPENDIX 24-B
DAMAGED BOOKS ACCEPTANCE REVIEW FORM

Week of: _____   Lot #: _____

Call #: _____
Volume # etc. _____
Title: _____

****
PROBLEM FOUND: (Be as specific as possible)

___ No new SAGE printout

___ Wrong bibliographic record

___ Item record problem: _____

___ Incorrect title on spine/pam label

___ Wrong call number on book
___ Wrong copy number
___ Wrong volume, etc. number
___ White stripe problem
___ Other: _____

Page repair problem
___ Page repair not done:
___ Incorrect page repair _____

Replacement page problem:
___ Page not done:
___ Incorrect repl. page: _____

___ Binding problem: _____

___ Other problem: _____

Inspected by: _____   Date: _____
Date returned to Plant: _____

Date returned to Libraries: _____
Problem Corrected: _____

APPENDIX 24-C
INTEGRATED LIBRARY SYSTEM QUALITY CONTROL
WEEKLY REPORT
ITEM RECORDS FORM

WEEK OF:

ERRORS	MONOGRAPHS AND JOURNALS					PROCESSED
	MONDAY	TUESDAY	WEDNESDAY	THURSDAY	FRIDAY	TOTAL
Wrong Bib						
Coding						
Not Updated						
Barcode						
Volume						
I Type/Loc/Copy						
Item Rec						
Total Errors						
Item Acceptable						
TOTAL						

Error Rate:
("Total Errors" divided by "TOTAL")

ERRORS	DAILY AND WEEKLY PERCENTAGES					
Wrong Bib						
Coding						
Not Updated						
Barcode						
Volume						
I Type/Loc/Copy						
Item Rec						
Total Errors						
Item Acceptable						
TOTAL						

25 Buried Alive: Processing Gifts As An Option

Patricia Smith, Nora Copeland,
and Carmel Bush

INTRODUCTION

As Colorado State University's Morgan Library learned in its gifts solicitation efforts, gifts received from public response to a disaster can be simultaneously gratifying and overwhelming. However, such gifts can offer a viable option to replace your damaged materials. Once accepted, processing these gifts raises many issues and brings additional costs. Libraries need to consider how large a gift operation they want to mount in comparison to other options for replacement. (See Chapter 16 on gift raising.)

Overwhelmed as we were with offers of gifts pouring in from all over the country and given delays in implementing restoration operations for the damaged items, the library decided to process as many gifts as possible prior to reprocessing the original materials damaged in our disaster. We knew most gifts that we added would be in better condition than any book that had been in our disaster—books that had lived underwater for more than 10 hours and then had remained untreated for days. Initially projected to last only a few months, the processing of gifts stretched out over a year from the date of the disaster; and a small operation continued after the reprocessing operation for disaster-damaged materials began. However, as our Library Disaster Recovery Team learned, gifts received in a large gift-solicitation campaign require a major planning and processing operation involving both handling gifts that you are allowed to use as replacements and dealing with the associated costs of gifts that are beyond the definitions of acceptable items for a disaster-recovery project. This chapter encompasses all of the above.

PROCESSING THE GIFTS THAT MATCH DAMAGED VOLUMES

First, a library needs to identify the procedures required to handle gifts it wants to keep. Since many of these procedures are similar to those in a regular gift operation within a library and are not unique to a disaster operation, these steps will only be touched on briefly.

Unpacking and Sorting Materials

One of the initial steps in a massive gift operation is organizing the unpacking. Determine who is going to unpack gifts, how the items are going to be sorted, and who is going to review whether the gifts are in suitable condition. Items should be inspected for mold, insect infestation, torn, brittle, or missing pages, or bindings in poor condition. In any gift situation, donors may occasionally try to get rid of their accumulated books and journals in their basement, attic, or garage and send them to the library regardless of their condition. Generally speaking, you will find it most cost-effective to discard materials in poor condition immediately.

Consider whether you need to record data for donor acknowledgment. We recommend that you request your donors, if possible, to send a completed donor form with each shipment; but if donors do not supply one, instruct your unpacking staff to record the name and address of the shipper and a count of volumes on a form. Staff who unpack should also be instructed to collect all boxes within a shipment, count the number of boxes in a shipment, and list these numbers on the form so missing parts of shipments can be identified.

Since unpacking staff have to touch each piece, they can also be used to sort materials for the next station. In our case, we sorted materials by journal or monographs and had sorters collate journal issues chronologically to make searching them in the online catalog easier.

Piles of boxes of donated gift materials delivered to the Processing Center for unpacking and reviewing.

Matching Gifts to Your Library Item Record and Updating Your Database

Defining what your library will accept as an exact match to an item record in your online catalog is one of the most important issues that must be resolved before entering data in the online catalog to show that a gift has been received as a replacement for a particular damaged volume. In addition to the cataloging policies of your library, you may have to consider the requirements of the insurance company. In our case, our insurance policy allowed payment only for processing gifts that were *exact* matches to the disaster-damaged titles and volumes. This raises questions about different formats. If all the disaster-damaged items are in paper format, do you accept only those formats or do you accept other formats as exact replacements—for instance, microforms? And if you accept them, what will you do with them? Will you add them to your original bibliographic and item record or will you need to create a new record to list them? Since our library's cataloging policy is to treat different formats as different editions, we chose not to accept different formats as exact matches for damaged material during the gift operation. Gift volumes that have the same intellectual content but that are received bound differently are another variation of exact matches to consider. Questions regarding whether to break the volume apart and rebind it to match the original item record or whether to recreate item records to match the pre-bound gift volume need to be resolved. We chose to treat bound-differently gifts by creating new item records as it would have cost more to rebind the volume.

Once you decide what constitutes an exact title match, you have to decide how you want to tag the database to show a gift has been received that replaces the original item. Adding coding to local MARC fields in your item records that can be used to display messages to the staff is an efficient way to handle this need; however, how it is done will depend on the capability of your library system. You may need to discuss this with your system vendor. At Morgan Library, these local codes proved to be extremely important for quality control, for verifying that an item has already been replaced by a gift so another copy would not be processed, and for statistics and for reports to the library and the university. (See Chapter 23, Appendix 23-D for a complete listing of these codes.)

Quality control is an important issue for updating your database, as you probably will need to hire temporary staff to assist with gifts processing. Should temporary staff be allowed to tag items in the library's online database or should they work in a separate database? If data is entered into a separate database, it can be reviewed and sent into the library's online catalog; but designing and maintaining such a database can be more trouble and expense than it is worth. Assuming you decide your online system will be used to track the damaged items and that you must use inexperienced personnel to enter data, quality control should become an important component of your gift operation. At Morgan Library, we established a special work unit in the gift operation that had the sole purpose of checking the work of the staff who updated item records in our online catalog. Quality control is discussed further elsewhere (see Chapter 24).

Physical Processing

In a gift operation the size of the one at Colorado State University Libraries, special work units to create new barcodes, to handle the marking of materials, and to handle any binding that is required may also need to be established. One way to make gifts more cost-effective is not to rebind gifts that come pre-bound even though it means that colors of volumes may vary in the same run of a journal title. Libraries that lose a collection cannot afford to be choosy about aesthetics.

Shelving and Circulation

Prior to sending processed gift volumes to the public shelves, a library needs to update the records to show the user the item is available in the online record. This can be done either while staff are tagging the gift in the online item record or by updating the status globally, if your online system allows this capability.

Statistics and Reports

As you plan, keep in mind statistics and reports that you or your institution may want to know about your gift operation. You will need to incorporate the capability for collecting this data in your automated system or in your staff routines. Our INNOPAC system tallies numbers of records so that we were able to obtain statistics of the number of journal volumes and the number of book volumes returned to the shelf that we could send to the university. Examples of other types of statistics that we gathered for the university for gifts processing are included in Appendix 25-A. There is also further discussion of reports and statistics in Chapter 23.

Problems and Exceptions

Anticipating some of the special exceptions you are likely to encounter will prepare you to handle them. Some examples of exceptions that might be encountered in the gift workflow include the example of the previously-mentioned pre-bound, gift-journal volume that does not exactly match the way the volume was bound according to the library's item records. Another category of exceptions is incomplete issues. Whether to put incomplete issues on suspend shelves and wait on the chance that the rest of the issues will be received as a gift will require a decision on the part of the library.

We decided to put both bound-differently volumes and incomplete issues on suspend shelves until the items could be handled by library staff in a special project. If the library owned all parts within the bound-differently title, staff withdrew the existing item record and created a new item record to match the bound-differently gift. If the library did not own part of the pre-bound gift, the gift copy was disassembled and the part that matched the library's original copy was rebound to match the library's lost item.

Another problem associated with item records occurred when the item records for a particular title were incomplete. We, like many libraries, were in the process of making online records for older holdings. Although we were certain that many of the journal volumes we received as gifts would replace items lost in the disaster, if there was no matching item record in the online database we could not easily prove to insurance we had lost the volume. Even though we could look at the summary holdings statement and guess that we owned the item, we were not able to convince the university that insurance would allow us to do the extensive checking to verify that the item would be likely to match a disaster-damaged item. Most of these gift items went into storage to resurface some day when regular library staff could handle them.

Volumes that matched JSTOR titles—JSTOR is a full-text electronic archive of core journal titles—were another exception to the gifts processing. Faculty donated personal backsets of many core titles hoping they would get on the shelves quickly. In the interim, the library bargained with insurance representatives to allow us to replace JSTOR titles with the electronic access service; thus, JSTOR titles were tagged in the record and sent to storage when they went through processing. A later outcry from faculty reversed this decision and gift backsets were processed. Although we could not anticipate all of the problems we were likely to encounter, thinking ahead helped prevent some problems.

DEALING WITH ASSOCIATED COSTS OF GIFTS

Although a gift program can be the only way to acquire materials to replace certain items in a collection and is generally a less expensive option, the associated costs still need to be absorbed somewhere. While insurance companies generally will pay for the processing costs of a gift operation that relate to replacement, they probably will not pay for processing gifts that enhance collections. Libraries that solicit gifts after a disaster can expect to be deluged with gifts that are not exact title replacements of items that were damaged but that might be desirable candidates to add to the collection.

We, for example, had an amazing public response to our gift solicitation. During the first year, we processed over 92,000 volumes that were exact matches for disaster items; but we also received over 490,000 additional volumes that were not matches for disaster-damaged materials. Encouraged by the university president to seize the opportunity to add potentially valuable items to the collection, we concentrated on defining affordable processes to handle non-matching gifts we might want to use later to augment the collection. Managing such associated costs of gifts should take into account several aspects.

Organization of the Materials

Unless materials are going to be processed immediately, provide some level of organization to allow for tracking of the materials to assist in later screening and to help retrieve materials. To contain costs, however, try to keep it simple so that inexperienced staff can create the records.

Since our library did not have the funds to screen and catalog each gift as it was received, we had to put them into storage for later screening. To easily identify materials that were in boxes, we needed a database that captured basic information regarding these materials. With programming assistance from the systems staff of the Colorado Alliance for Research Libraries' office, we created a database using available software that could handle large numbers of records. The records included the following bibliographic data: Author, Title, Imprint, Edition, ISBN/ISSN, Series, and Enu-

meration/Chronology (if a serial). A special field was also designated to list the first three characters of the Library of Congress
call number from Cataloging in Publication information if it was
present in the piece with the intention of using Library of Congress numbers as broad subject indicators for certain monographs.

In addition to bibliographic information, we provided a field
to list the number of the box where the book was stored. We
also asked the inputter to enter their initials in a field so we could
perform quality control on an individual's work. Inputters indicated the format of the material so we could tell if it was a book
or a journal and whether a journal was bound or in loose issues.
The record could be retrieved within the programmed system by
author, title, series, ISBN/ISSN, or the first three characters of the
Library of Congress number in the Cataloging in Publication. To
retrieve a list of the contents of a particular box, staff could search
by the box number. In addition to pre-defined searches, it was
also possible to enter database commands to generate any other
additional reports we wanted, such as the number of monographs
published within a certain time frame. Although somewhat cumbersome compared to a typical integrated library system, the database was adequate for the simple purposes of providing an inventory of gifts that we wanted to consider for augmenting the
collection when funds might be available.

A library should consider the extra costs of dealing with gifts,
such as keeping an inventory, that do not match damaged items'
legitimate costs of replacement and should be prepared to make
such a case to insurance representatives. Rather surprisingly, the
insurance company agreed with the library and university that creating this inventory of non-matching titles was a legitimate cost
related to replacing items through gifts. Although the insurance
company agreed to fund the staffing operation needed to create
the inventory, the company stopped short of providing funds to
add non-matching gifts to the collection. Part of the logic for funding the creation of this inventory also stemmed from thinking that
this inventory might be of value in identifying gift volumes that
would serve as suitable topical replacements for an item that might
be declared total loss and could not be repurchased.

Managing Storage of Materials

Storing gifts that a library receives in conjunction with a disaster can take an enormous amount of space, so you will need to develop strategies to reduce the space required. First, as mentioned previously, consider eliminating any unneeded gifts as soon as possible by tossing any gift in poor condition. Trying to salvage them adds extra costs. While staff are checking gifts for matches to damaged items, have them identify duplicates of items you already have and route them to the discard pile without further handling, even though in a normal gift operation you may save gifts to compare the physical condition of a gift copy with the matching shelf copy. Use boxes to store acceptable gifts for later processing instead of shelving. We pre-numbered boxes to save time for staff creating records and to avoid mix ups in numbering schemes among different staff creating the records. After boxes were filled, they were stored in sequential order on pallets in a trailer.

Anticipation of Future Processing

In designing processes for listing and storing materials, anticipate how the time of those who will need to select and process materials that a library chooses to add later can be saved, thus, helping cut costs. Good design should include use of an automated database to help store and manipulate data on gifts you want to review. In our case, we decided to add brief Cataloging in Publication call number information to the record in its specially designed database to help sort materials for selectors so that they could see at least a partial list of the monographs in their subject areas without reviewing the entire range of boxes. The reports we were able to obtain from the database also produced information useful in determining policies for screening materials at a later date and in preparing justifications for funding to add materials to the collection.

For example, when we found that only approximately 8,000 monographs had publishing dates of 1987 or later, selectors agreed that these monographs could automatically be added to the collection without individual screening by selectors. By the same token, reports that we drew showing we had received minimal numbers of non-print formats convinced the selectors that we could automatically toss non-print formats.

Establishing screening policies that can be applied by untrained staff can also be a key factor in reducing the impact of processing these materials on staff and in reducing the inventory as soon as possible. Your acquisitions and collection development staff should jointly agree on criteria for pre-screening materials that temporary staff can apply to determine items that can be automatically tossed or automatically added to the collection. To save expensive selection time, only materials that do not meet either criteria for tossing or keeping should be screened by your collection development staff. Reports from a specially designed inventory database, similar to ours, can also be critical to simplifying the pre-screening process. Rather than having staff go through boxes one by one, touching each piece, your staff can print out a report of the record for each title in the box and make decisions based on the printed report. The printed report also serves the dual purpose of a processing and routing form for each title. Thus, decisions made about the database prior to beginning the gifts-enhancement project can be critical to later processing.

Costs of Discarding

Discards result because it is inevitable that the library will receive duplicates or materials unsuited to the library's collection. Normal methods of disposing of discarded items will likely be strained in a large-scale disaster if equally large numbers of materials are donated. Options such as offering an exchange to other libraries or directing the volumes not needed to book sales will have staffing, storage, and other costs that can be considerable when large numbers of volumes are involved. Even costs of sending materials to a landfill can be considerable. Long-term storage can add up. (Storage costs at Colorado State University, for example, cost $8 per pallet, which holds approximately 1,036 volumes, for a month.) Environmental and public relations are additional incentives to reviewing alternatives to storing gifts long term because dumping may not be a feasible solution. Dumping gifts has to be done carefully, because once communities catch wind of this practice there can be a public outcry to save the books from such a fate. For gifts that are valued over the $5,000 limit set by IRS tax requirements, there is also reason to insure that gifts are not disposed of before the required retention period has been met. Hence, exploring options to dispose of gifts to other public agencies or libraries may avoid problems with dumping.

In retrospect, we could have been more proactive in determining collection development policies for gifts augmentation before we began to send any gifts through the Processing Center. Had we decided early in the gift operation that we would not keep any state or federal documents or non-print materials, for example, we would have sorted these out before the item had been entered into the inventory database of non-matching gifts and would never have sent them into storage.

Likewise, we should have been better prepared to handle the public relations of discarding gifts. While nothing extreme occurred, we assumed that we had dumping rights. However, high-ranking university officials offered those discards to city and county officials for consideration for their public libraries. This offer complicated our discard process immensely. Now we have to at least go through the motion of inviting community libraries to a chance to take discards.

CONCLUSION

In conclusion, it is important to recognize that gifts are not free and have many hidden costs. Nonetheless, to accept gifts in a large gift-solicitation project requires major planning and the implementation of a major processing operation. However, there are ways to keep cost factors low and to handle the aftermath of a gift campaign.

Library Disaster Planning and Recovery Handbook

KEY RECOMMENDATIONS

Processing Gifts

- Keep the decisions and processing of gifts as simple as possible. You will not be able to do some of the extra services that you might do in a normal operation, such as comparing shelf copies with gift copies.

- When creating a list of items for a gift inventory, keep the data elements as simple as possible.

- Keep storage costs as low as possible by boxing and storing materials in cheap quarters. Access contents through a database to minimize handling.

- Think ahead about ways to save staff and selection time.

- Remember that all aspects of handling gifts have costs.

- Be sure to request funds to handle the associated costs of gifts.

- Make sure your processing staff communicate frequently with staff soliciting gifts and working with donors.

- Plan your public relations regarding gifts very carefully.

- Be aware that every aspect of handling gifts, from accepting them from donors to discarding the ones you do not need, is potentially a political situation.

APPENDIX 25-A
STATISTICAL REPORTING FORM

FUNCTIONS	WEEK MONO	WEEK SERIAL	WEEK TOTAL	MTD MONOS	MTD SERIALS	MONTH TOTAL	TOTALS 1999	TOTALS 1998	
PALLETS OF GIFT MATERIAL RECEIVED									
BOXES UNPACKED									
VOLUMES UNPACKED									
VOLUMES IN PROCESSING									
VOLUMES SENT TO INVENTORY									
VOLUMES SENT TO DISCARD									
VOLUMES SENT TO BARCODE									
SUBTOTAL									
VOLUMES SENT TO SUSPEND									
TOTAL									
BINDING									
TITLES ADDED TO BINDING MODULE									
VOLUMES PROCESSED FOR BINDING									
BINDING SHIPMENTS SENT OUT (SHIPPED)									
BINDING SHIPMENTS BACK (RECEIVED)									
INVENTORY RECORDS CREATED									
VOLUMES SENT TO LIBRARY STACKS									

PART SIX

Resource Sharing in Disaster Recovery

26 Resource Sharing: A Requirement In Library-Disaster Recovery

Camila Alire

INTRODUCTION

What do you do when you are faced with a debilitating disaster of which the effects are so enormous that you can't recover alone? Most disaster-recovery insurance policies will allow for the various contractual recovery services, but there is always the issue of how to resume services when you are faced with no access to your library facility or library resources. After an initial, preliminary assessment of the damage, how do you prepare for providing resources and services to your users when you have nothing available? How do you enlist the support of other libraries and organizations in your recovery efforts?

This chapter serves a two-fold purpose. It discusses the importance for some mechanism to be in place which could help any library which has experienced a disaster to recover through various aspects of resource-sharing assistance. The extent of and the time frame for that assistance can be affected, to some extent, by whether or not resource-sharing components and/or agreements are already in place.

Secondly, this chapter covers a personal account of working with established resource-sharing connections. It discusses strategic development of disaster preparedness for resource-sharing networks already in place and strategic development if no network/consortium is in place. The chapter ends with top ideas and recommendations for the reader.

PERSONAL ACCOUNT

The second night after the disaster at the Colorado State University (CSU) campus, I received a late-night telephone call at home from Colorado's State Librarian. She offered the assistance of the State Library and its staff. This telephone call was the first step in possible resource-sharing activities. Not knowing the real extent of our disaster, I thanked her for her concern and told her I would let her know how they might be able to help us.

It was only a few days after the disaster that we realized the extent of the damage to the materials housed in the lower level of the library. We also realized that all of our facilities closets— electrical, telecommunications, and computer networking—were eight-and-a-half feet underwater and completely ruined. It did not take a rocket scientist to figure out that we would be without major building services and library resources for awhile. That was the beginning of our realization that we at Morgan Library could not do it alone. There was a need for major resource-sharing with other units on campus and other libraries external to the campus.

Library staff were thinking along the same lines. Our Coordinator of Interlibrary Loan Services (ILL) was in the library the second day after the disaster removing PC equipment from the ILL office—since it was on the yet unaffected upper floor—to set up ILL/document-delivery services elsewhere. He not only had been thinking of sharing someone else's facilities, he was already moving into the library at Front Range Community College! See Chapter 8 for more details.

At the beginning of the second week, the Library Disaster Recovery Team started talking about instituting temporary short-term and long-term services. That was the start of serious brainstorming sessions where issues such as how to provide services and resources to our library community and consideration of possible resource-sharing connections were discussed.

It was at that time that I made a telephone call to the Executive Director of the Colorado Alliance for Research Libraries (the Alliance). Colorado State University was one of eleven institutional members of the Alliance which was established in the mid-1970s primarily for resource-sharing purposes. The Alliance Member Council consists of the dean/directors of the ten Alliance libraries. This group of council members has been a very cohesive and collaborative group for sometime.

At the time of my telephone call to the executive director, people external to campus were still unable to reach us by telephone or e-mail. This call was literally my first official call to the outside world. After letting him know that we were physically fine, I told him about the extent of the known damage to Morgan Library. I asked that he call an emergency meeting of the Alliance Member Council to discuss and develop some resource-sharing strategies to assist us in our disaster-recovery efforts. I also asked him if the Alliance could serve as our communications link/liaison to the rest of Alliance members and the world! He was more than happy to have himself and/or his management staff serve as that link.

Colorado State University Libraries also was a member of the Association of Research Libraries (ARL), and several weeks after the disaster, and after some strategic disaster-recovery planning sessions, I contacted the Executive Director of ARL about some possible assistance from ARL and its member libraries. Colorado State University Libraries was also a member of the Big Twelve Plus Library Consortium at the time of the disaster; and on a more informal basis, I asked that group to assist us in ILL and document-delivery efforts.

This personal account of the genesis for pursuing resource-sharing relationships sets the stage for the remainder of this chapter. We realized that collaborating with internal and external groups, formally or informally, was going to be critical in the beginning stages of our disaster-recovery efforts, particularly relating to providing services and resources to our users.

REVIEW OF THE LITERATURE

It appears that very little has been written in the literature concerning disaster-recovery efforts involving partnerships, collaboration, and/or resource-sharing in libraries. And yet, there probably has not been a disaster of any magnitude that did not include most of these aspects. It is when a disaster occurs that there seems to be more cooperative sharing of resources: facilities, personnel, expertise, equipment, funds, etc.

From a more generalized scope of the business community,

Duncan (1973) wrote about how generations of business promoted individualism, independence, and self-sufficiency. However, the move towards solving problems regionally has produced more complex functions with which to deal and has required more co-operation and collaboration. Additionally, there has been a move by the public sector to enlist the assistance of the private sector to help accomplish various goals, especially those for the common good. It is this philosophical move from maintaining traditional self-sufficiency toward establishing affiliations, partnerships, coalitions that establish the basis for resource-sharing and cooperation among public/private organizations and institutions in disaster recovery.

More specifically dealing with academic library resource-sharing is Potter's (1994) article which discusses resource-sharing as the primary reason for the establishment of academic library consortia. He defined resource-sharing as maximizing an academic library's buying power because combined resources are better than resources from a single library. Additionally, consortia have expanded their definition of resource-sharing to include efforts in establishing union catalogs, courier services, and expedited Interlibrary Loan/document delivery.

Potter (1994) identified the most recent trend in consortial alliances, which is dealing with common information technology needs—the virtual library, Internet and the World Wide Web, the shared use of electronic databases, etc. He recognizes that many consortia have gone statewide to pool resources and cooperate to control costs. All of the above characteristics justify the existence of the Colorado Alliance of Research Libraries. However, it can now add disaster-recovery activities as another area of cooperation and collaboration. ARL's purpose is similar in that it is organized to provide various services and resources to its member libraries.

From a business, private-sector point of view, one example in the literature of an organized effort to collaborate systematically in disaster recovery is the Franchise Emergency Action Team (FEAT). This is an organized group of volunteers representing many business franchises who have set a goal of assisting in or around a disaster area in attempts to help in disaster response and recovery efforts. These business franchises provide resources which could include anything from food, lodging, construction, etc., depending on the franchise's expertise, products, and capabilities (Garrett, 1994).

In the Colorado State University disaster-recovery efforts, a prime example of this FEAT organization was Cellular One's assistance. Cellular One provided cellular phones and free phone service to the campus for affected units to use for internal/external communications since many of the buildings that were damaged did not have any telecommunications services in place. Another example of such an effort was a local company that provided free bottled water to folks working on disaster response and recovery on campus. These are great illustrations of resource-sharing and collaboration among the public/private sectors in disaster-recovery activities.

The most comprehensive bibliographic resource found on disaster recovery and collaboration was written by Gillespie (1993). He advocated the development of a disaster preparedness network to be in place before a disaster occurs. This network would be an established relationship between organizations who would be prepared to provide services and/or resources. It could include providing resources such as funds, personnel, facilities, personal contacts, joint planning, and coordination. Without prior planning for disaster recovery, communications and delivery services usually become problems. Fragmented responsibilities due to the differences of contributing organizations such as organizational size, type, and specialty can cause these problems. Gillespie maintains that disaster recovery is much more effective if disaster responsibilities are planned and assigned to different participating organizations.

Based on Gillespie's recommendations and on the Morgan Library disaster, libraries need to address, ahead of time, the possible roles and relationships of organized alliances, consortia, associations, and/or partnerships in disaster readiness. The planning results might be more global in nature until such time that a disaster might hit; but it is a start and it makes participants aware of their potential role in disaster recovery.

I asked myself if I thought the Alliance could have assisted us in interlibrary coordination for disaster planning beforehand, given our experience. My response was absolutely yes. One of the biggest advantages of our consortium's involvement would be the development of general planning principles relative to disaster recovery and then putting those principles into practice. For example, had the Alliance staff and its members had a disaster-readiness plan in place, the mechanics of getting the group together and the response time might have been different and definitely could have fallen on the shoulders of someone other than myself and/ or my staff who were already working long hours on emergency-disaster response.

Gillespie (1993: 5) asserts that "mutual aid agreements, policies of assistance, and other forms of cooperation increase access to resources both within the community and outside the community." Additionally, he discusses how communications can be affected in disaster readiness.

According to Gillespie and others, communication theory says that an organization linked to many others can pass on information through a minimum number of steps. He referred to the use of a star network where communication comes from one central unit within that network and that same unit is responsible for contacting members in time for adequate response.

I could not agree more with Gillespie on establishing effective communications. Earlier in this chapter, when I was sharing my personal account, I mentioned that the Alliance executive director and his management team became responsible for being our communication hub (star). It wasn't because I was so aware of communication theory, it was due to desperation and a little common sense. We didn't have the telecommunications in place to coordinate communications nor could we respond in a timely manner to colleagues trying to reach us out of concern and to express their willingness to help. The same thing happened with ARL staff. The ARL office became our star network, took over communicating with ARL libraries, and helped to establish cooperative activities to assist us through disaster response and recovery.

Gillespie and others identify the stages of coping with a disaster. First is disaster mitigation which includes all the activities that would eliminate or reduce the probability of a disaster. For example, in the original design of Morgan Library's new addition, which included a garden level (the lower level), landscape mitigation was approved. However, the mitigation for a water disaster was designed for a 100-year flood. What happened on the night of the disaster would have been avoided had the landscape mitigation been designed for a 500-year flood. Ironically, now there is a new mitigation wall for the library's garden level that was built for a 500-year flood.

The second stage is disaster preparedness which includes all activities developed prior to and in preparation for a disastrous event. Disaster preparedness strongly affects how an organization deals with stages three and four: disaster response and disaster recovery. According to Gillespie, disaster response incorporates providing assistance after the disaster happens; and disaster recovery is the rebuilding to return to normal conditions.

These same authors do an excellent job of dissecting the term, *disaster preparedness network,* in order for the reader to fully understand the concept in a working relationship. First they define disaster preparedness as the "degree of readiness to deliver services in response to a disaster" (Gillespie, 1993: 36). They further describe preparedness as the ability to identify weak links and deal with them and then to determine the overall capability of the community (in our case, the Alliance) to respond.

The authors then describe a network as consisting "of potential partners in a specific resources exchange" (Gillespie, 1993: 67). A disaster-preparedness network, according to Gillespie, is made up of the relations among organizations considered to be strategic for disaster planning and response. Not all participants in the network may be considered strategic. For example, our *FastFlood* project that provided rapid document-delivery services to our users during disaster recovery included only four of the Alliance libraries and two ARL libraries. These libraries were selected on the strengths of their collection in subject areas that were damaged and packed-out in our collection.

The authors cited the major disadvantages to operating a disaster-preparedness network. These disadvantages included recognition that:

- various organizations may operate on different philosophies;
- costs can be unevenly distributed; and
- risks can occur relative to negative consequences (e.g., law

suits). Additionally, if a written inter-organizational agreement is developed, it can be lost either in organizational restructuring or in leadership change within a participating organization.

However, in the realm of academic library networking, these disadvantages may not be as prevalent as they are when various diverse organizations try to work within a community.

This review of the literature supports the idea that some type of consortial and/or partnering network be established prior to the occurrence of a disaster. The more a network is organized as a working group, the greater the preparedness. Our experience within the Alliance was that we were not as prepared as the literature says we should have been because there had not been any disaster-preparedness activities within the Alliance. However, we cannot imagine how much more devastating it would have been without our participation in a consortium and in an association like ARL.

STRATEGY DEVELOPMENT FOR POTENTIAL RESOURCE SHARING

Plan For the Disaster

Learn from our disaster experience. If you already have a disaster-recovery plan in place for your organization, great. However, along with your disaster-recovery plan, you should develop a disaster-preparedness plan that includes possible resource-sharing activities with other libraries. This requires inter-organizational planning of activities. It also depends on whether or not your institution is formally involved in some type of network like a consortium, alliance, or association.

If you are formally involved in some kind of organizational networking already, half the battle is won. You have a mechanism already in place with the consortium leadership and membership already identified.

Initiate discussions within the consortium membership on disaster preparedness and develop a preparedness plan. It is Morgan Library's intent, after disaster recovery, to initiate the beginnings of a more formal process for disaster preparedness within the Alliance. Even if it only means examining and evaluating what was done in our recovery process relative to the Alliance membership's resource-sharing participation, that is a start. From those discussions, we should be able to develop the basics of a disaster-preparedness plan for the entire Alliance membership.

If your library or institution does not belong to a formal consortium or alliance, you can still work on inter-organizational cooperation. Start with informal contacts; that is, identify all the libraries (public and academic; publicly-supported and private) that you think would have an interest in the disaster-preparedness planning. Be prepared during your initial contacts to have other libraries/organizations mentioned as possible participants.

Based on your informal canvassing, organize the first meeting to discuss 1) all the ramifications of a possible disaster; 2) the potential effect of a disaster on your respective library programs, and 3) the development of a resource-sharing plan. Make sure that the appropriate players are involved in these discussions. They should include the decision makers—the library director, the heads of public and technical services, and the head of the disaster-recovery team as identified by your disaster plan, if you have one.

From those discussions, move onto a clearly understood verbal agreement which can be put into a written draft and taken back to your respective institutions for discussion. Reconvene in a timely manner to discuss possible additions/deletions and other changes. At some point, be prepared to finalize a well-defined written agreement among all the participants.

Components of a Disaster-Preparedness Plan

Using our personal experience and Gillespie's (1993) suggestions, we formulated several component and factors to be considered in a partnership-type, disaster-preparedness plan. These factors can be based on both scenarios: involvement in some kind of consortium/alliance or non-involvement in any official consortium. Remember that you are discussing the potential for resource-sharing, realizing that not until a disaster happens to a consortium member will you be able to apply what is defined in the disaster-preparedness plan. There will be a definite need to be flexible. The factors to consider include:

- physical facilities at each participating library;
- resources and services available at each library (resources include tangible benefits such as books and equipment while services include intangible benefits such as volunteers, training, information, and communications);
- a communication plan focusing on the star-network concept;
- personnel expertise available;
- training; and
- financial possibilities (for example, three members of the Alliance donated their share of grant funds for unmediated document delivery to Colorado State University Libraries to help pay for UnCover transactions).

WHAT TO DO WHEN A DISASTER OCCURS AND THERE IS NO INTERLIBRARY PLAN IN PLACE (AKA, THE COLORADO STATE UNIVERSITY EXPERIENCE)

If disaster preparedness at your library only includes a library-disaster recovery plan, then a different approach is necessary in the strategic development for potential resource-sharing. The first thing that needs to be done (after the disaster but before the discussions and development of resource-sharing activities among other libraries) is an assessment of the damage to your library program relative to library resources, services, and facilities.

Once that initial, preliminary assessment is completed, members of the disaster-recovery team—especially the heads of public and technical services—must develop internal strategies to present to external libraries. If you belong to a consortium or an association like ARL, your job will be easier.

The bad news in this strategic development scenario is that there is no interlibrary disaster-preparedness plan within the consortium/association. The good news is that, when you develop your internal strategies, you will know exactly what you need in terms of library resources and services to which consortium members can respond.

If you find yourself in a position, for whatever reasons, where you cannot enlist the support of other academic and public libraries, contact your state library immediately. The state library should take a leadership role in developing resource-sharing activities to assist you in disaster recovery and could be your communication link using the star-network concept. I have no doubt that had Morgan Library not had access to the Alliance or ARL, I could have relied on the State Librarian and members of the Colorado State Library's management team to assist us somehow in the development of resource-sharing activities.

CONCLUSION

The strategic development of resource-sharing partnerships between libraries in your state and region is essential to successful disaster response and recovery efforts. The intent of this chapter was not only to provoke thought but also to provoke action. This chapter covered a personal account of working with established resource-sharing connections and discussed strategic development of disaster preparedness for resource-sharing networks already in place and strategic development if no network/consortium is in place.

Although Morgan Library at Colorado State University was well prepared with a library-disaster plan in place and with practice drills held, we were not prepared for the extent of massive damage to our collection and, consequently, to our services. Neither was the Alliance's Member Council prepared with a disaster-preparedness plan to accommodate a member's most immediate emergency needs. Again, learn from our disaster. Resource sharing external to your immediate library is not a given unless it is planned beforehand. Be prepared.

Library Disaster Planning and Recovery Handbook

KEY RECOMMENDATIONS

Resource Sharing

- Do not wait for a disaster to happen. Make sure you have a library-disaster plan in place. However, that is not enough. Initiate discussions among your consortium members relative to disaster preparedness and resource-sharing within the consortium.

- If you have no organized consortium or alliance, work with your state library to initiate the same discussions mentioned in the previous recommendation.

- Have a communications system based on the star-network concept in place where there is only one communication link between your library and the outside world.

If you have not started or completed the above three items and if you are hit by a disaster, the following recommendations will help:

- Determine internally the extent of the disaster damage on your library facilities, services, and resources as soon as possible.

- Develop proposed strategies based on your immediate and possible long-term disaster recovery needs to present to consortium members and others relative to resource-sharing services and resources.

- Work with your consortium office staff to initiate emergency resource-sharing discussions and action plans.

- If you are not affiliated with a consortium or alliance, work with the state library to develop emergency partnerships with other libraries in resource-sharing efforts.

REFERENCES

Duncan, Joseph W. 1973. "Practical Requirements for Relating Private and Public Decision-Making on Regional Problems." *Business Economics* 8 (May): 22–27.

Garrett, Echo M. 1994. "Franchises that Capitalize on Solving Our Problems." *Inc* 16 (September): 106–109.

Gillespie, David F., et al. 1993. *Partnership for Community Preparedness.* Boulder, CO: University of Colorado.

Potter, William G. 1994. "Recent Trends in Statewide Academic Library Consortia." *Library Trends* 45 (Winter): 416–417.

27 The Role of the Colorado Alliance of Research Libraries in Colorado State University Libraries' Disaster Recovery

Alan N. Charnes and George Machovec

THE ALLIANCE: AN OVERVIEW

The Colorado Alliance of Research Libraries (the Alliance) was formed in 1974 as a five-institution cooperative searching for ways to provide improved service at lower cost through the sharing of resources. Hardly unique to Colorado, the Alliance was one of a number of library cooperatives around the country working to become bigger than the sum of its parts. The promise lay in automation, particularly the computerized library card catalog. But the cooperative also saw promise in the sharing of expensive but little-used library materials.

Colorado State University is one of the original five institutions. The others are the University of Denver (including its law school), the University of Colorado at Boulder, the University of Northern Colorado, and the Denver Public Library. Two additional libraries were added in 1976, the Colorado School of Mines and Auraria. Colorado State University withdrew from the Alliance in 1984 and rejoined in 1990. The University of Colorado Health Sciences Center was added in 1989, the University of Wyoming in 1990, and, finally, Regis University in 1993.

The Articles of Incorporation state that the Alliance "is organized exclusively for educational purposes within the meaning of Section 501 (c) (3) of the Internal Revenue code to promote the progress and advancement of Colorado Research Libraries." The specific purposes stated in the Articles are:

- sharing information concerning acquisitions, services, and procedures;
- increasing patron access to collections of Colorado Research Libraries;
- sponsoring research into areas of common problems and common interests;
- encouraging a high quality of library services to patrons;
- supporting the efficient utilization of available library funds; and
- such other appropriate means as approved by the Board of Directors.

All policy and financial matters are the responsibility of the Board of Directors. Although at present there are eleven Alliance libraries, the Alliance Board of Directors is comprised of eight institutional representatives. The institutions are the University of Colorado System, Colorado School of Mines, Colorado State University, Denver Public Library, University of Denver and University of Denver Law School, Regis University, University of Northern Colorado, and University of Wyoming.

By virtue of its membership, Colorado State University sits on all governing bodies and developmental task forces of the Alliance. A CSU representative is one of the eight members of the Board of Directors responsible for overall policy and financial affairs. The CSU Dean of Libraries sits on the 11-library Members Council, responsible for cooperative activities and recommendations to the Board of Directors.

In 1983, the Alliance, then known by the acronym CARL, made its Public Access Catalog prototype available and began installing the system in member libraries. Believing it to have general applicability, an agreement was signed in 1985. In 1988, "CARL Systems Inc. (CSI)," a for-profit subsidiary was created. The CARL Integrated Library System (ILS) was the principal product of CSI. In that same year, UnCover, a unique online document-delivery service, was launched as CSI's second major product. In 1995, CARL Corporation, The UnCover Company and the "CARL" name were sold to Knight Ridder Information, Inc. As part of the sales agreement, the consortium named "CARL" became "the Alliance."

A number of other changes occurred during this period. In the past, every Alliance library used the centrally-operated CARL System. Indeed, the system was said to be the glue that held the consortium together. However, in 1994, the University of Colorado at Boulder and the University of Colorado Health Sciences Center migrated to a different ILS: Innovative Interfaces' Innopac (III). That migration to III was followed in 1995 by Colorado State University and in 1997 by Auraria, the University of Northern Colorado, and the University of Denver at the main campus and the law school. At present, four Alliance libraries remain on the CARL System, operating centrally on hardware located at the Alliance central office.

Another major change for the consortium during this period was the attention given to the collective acquisition of electronic databases. When print was the principal database medium, acquisition was relatively simple. The product was well-known; price, terms, and conditions were well understood; and renewal was an essentially automatic annual event between the library and the vendor. As electronic database alternatives proliferated, the historical cost squeeze became more pronounced, the contractual requirements more perplexing, and issues of authentication and verification more important. Increasingly, the Alliance centralized the purchase of electronic databases on behalf of its members.

The Alliance also handled these changes and many others that accompanied the evolution of the organization from its CARL System roots to a multi-purpose, multi-vendor service provider and system operator. New staff capabilities were added at the central office.

Additionally, the Alliance has clustered its purchases, forming ad hoc groups of libraries to acquire specific databases. The objective is always the same, to provide the Alliance institutions with the services they need at the best price and most favorable terms and conditions. Currently, there are 26 clusters. Colorado State University has been a strong advocate of this approach, participating in 18 of these clusters. It enjoys a reputation as a careful buyer. In fact, seeking a better ILS at lower cost, CSU left the CARL System and the Alliance in 1984, only to return in 1990. Over time and with thoughtful analysis, CSU has embraced the consortial approach as the most effective way to meet its institutional needs. So have many others.

WHAT ROLE CAN A CONSORTIUM PLAY IN DISASTER RECOVERY?

The First Days

> Colorado State University Libraries is closed due to a disaster. Power is off and the basement is damaged due to heavy rains. As of this notice, the basement is being pumped. All bound periodicals and half of the book collection is affected. Telecommunications are down. SAGE is temporarily unavailable and ILL is suspended until damage is identified. Disaster recovery is in place. The library is closed until further notice. Updates will be through the Alliance.

This was the note sent to the Colorado Alliance of Research Libraries via the listserv the day after the disaster. Clearly a disaster of unprecedented magnitude had occurred, and some Alliance members were going to play a critical role in disaster recovery.

Provide Communications

The initial role a consortium office can play is to assist in communications. Most likely, the library's telephone system and electric power will be inoperable. E-mail may be out. For the first few days, a consortium office can serve as a communications clearing house, forwarding messages to and from library staff members using cellular phones. After a few days, as the recovery strategy begins to unfold, the consortium staff can assume specific assignments that can best be performed in the consortium's office(s) outside of the disaster area.

Acquire Free Access To Electronic Databases

The most visible consortium contribution will be in obtaining free use of important electronic databases to replace paper material lost in the library's disaster.

As executive director of the Alliance, I (Charnes) talked to each vendor on the CSU electronic database priority list. In each case my request was simple, one year's access to their electronic product . . . gratis. The seriousness of the disaster was by then well-understood around the library community. The vendors that I contacted all knew that this was the worst natural disaster ever at an academic library. In a few cases, it took several days for the vendor to determine exactly how it could meet my request, but no one turned us down.

Within a few days, Colorado State University was online with Project MUSE from Johns Hopkins Press, LION from Chadwyck-Healey, JSTOR, Lexis-Nexis, ECO from OCLC, and, later, backfiles of the 175 journals of the Academic Press electronic service. The estimated value of these contributions was $275,000. In my mind, the willingness of these vendors to provide these services speaks to a special code of conduct that I believe exists in the library business community. These were not trial periods offered in the hope that a sale would result. I believe that these vendors simply wanted to help.

Provide Off-Site Technical Support

If your consortium's breadth of skills available includes off-site technical support, you can provide that at no cost to the library affected by the disaster and give it top priority. The principal contribution will be in programming.

The Alliance created the Emergency Information Website, developed the system for receiving donations online, and built the Loss Management System (LMS). More information on all this is covered later in this chapter under "Technical Support."

Coordinate Consortium Member Libraries' Willingness to Help

Member libraries will respond in the most collegial ways possible. Without fail, your consortium needs to serve as the coordinator/liaison for those libraries and the library suffering through the disaster. Suggestions will flow into the consortium office and the affected library about various ways on how member libraries can assist.

On August 7, 1997, an emergency meeting of Member Council was held at CSU. Because of the unavailability of meeting space in the library, the meeting was held off-campus. By this time, the recovery strategy had been formulated and the other Alliance libraries were prepared to respond. Each member said to CSU Libraries, "Tell us what you need and we will deliver." Suggestions flowed into the Alliance office and directly to CSU on ways that the other libraries could assist.

That assistance included:

- Providing Colorado State University students and faculty with full library privileges at nearby institutions.
- Establishing and staffing *Ariel* workstations at selected Alliance libraries.
- Donating significant amounts of duplicate material to CSU. The University of Wyoming, Colorado School of Mines, the University of Colorado–Boulder, and the University of Denver sent large collections of bibliographic material to CSU.
- Giving first priority to CSU for the use of Serial UnMediated Ordering (SUMO). This is an UnCover project that permits an institution to subsidize the electronic acquisition of journal articles by students and faculty. UnCover is an ideal replacement for paper periodicals and instantly provides significant breadth of coverage. Alliance funds previously had been committed to providing SUMO service to four libraries: Colorado State University, the University of Colorado at Boulder, the University of Colorado Health Sciences Center, and Auraria. The library deans at these three University of Colorado libraries waived access to these funds and dedicated it all for Colorado State University use.

ALLIANCE TECHNICAL SUPPORT

This entire section on specific technical support provided by the Alliance concentrates on particular projects. Those projects are described in detail, giving you, the reader, a clear example of how a consortium office can be crucial in assisting a member library through disaster recovery.

Colorado State University Library Assistance Center (Website)

Since the university was beginning its fall term only weeks after the disaster, it was crucial that the campus community, surrounding region, and the broader library community be informed of the disaster and of Colorado State University's needs. To facilitate this, Colorado State University Libraries asked the Alliance to create a Website called the "Colorado State University Library Assistance Center" which would act as a central point of information and would provide information on the most critical needs as well as other auxiliary services (e.g., shuttle services from Colorado State University to nearby academic libraries in Colorado and Wyoming). (See Appendix 27-A.)

FEATURES OF THE WEBSITE

- A story of the disaster along with photographs taken within the first few days of the aftermath.
- Colorado State University student services section which included shuttle van schedules to regional academic libraries, information on how to request materials through interlibrary loan, directions to regional libraries, and even parking information.
- A Web donation form that could be used by either individuals or libraries to make offers. This form created a structured e-mail message that went to the collection-development department at Colorado State University for their consideration.
- A listing of the most needed monographs and serials which were lost in the disaster. This was searchable by title and call number.

HOW IT WAS BUILT

The Colorado State University Library Assistance Center Website was developed in standard HTML so that it could easily be accessed by both older and newer browsers as well as Lynx browsers. The most interesting feature was the list of most needed monographs and serials as part of the Colorado State University Libraries' donation process. Within a month or so after the disaster, it was clear that top priority must be given to building a robust donation program since materials returning from the freeze-drying process would take a long time to get back on the shelf and would have a higher number of materials declared a total loss than origi-

FIGURE 27–1
Web-Based Sample of Monograph Record

Landscape vocabulary

Author:	Marsh, Warner L.
Title:	Landscape vocabulary.
Publisher:	Los Angeles, Miramar Pub. Co. [1964].
	[1st ed].
	Landscape architecture—Terminology
Call Number:	SB 476 M37

nally expected. Additionally, there was great interest in having better quality copies back on the shelves instead of freeze-dried but still-damaged materials.

Through the Innovative Interfaces Inc. (III) Innopac system, which Colorado State University used as their library automation system, the library was able to use the *create lists* function to generate lists of lost materials in the most high-demand call number ranges. This was possible because the library knew that virtually all of the bound periodicals and the monograph call number ranges that were in the lower level when it filled with water. Through using statistics and knowledge of the collection and the academic programs on campus, a list of top-priority monographic and serials titles could be created. Fortunately, the library's III Innopac system was not in the lower level during the disaster so that this type of work could begin fairly quickly after power and appropriate segments of the network could be restored.

CSU delivered to the Alliance approximately 20,000 MARC records of high-priority materials that were lost in the disaster. Through the Alliance programming staff and some outside contract assistance, the CSU Library Assistance Website was created. A program was developed which transferred key elements from each MARC record into a discrete miniature HTML document. Figure 27-1 provides an illustration of a sample monograph record placed on the Website that was developed by the Alliance staff.

These documents were then indexed under the ht://Dig 3.0 search engine which is a shareware Web indexing program available from San Diego State University (*http://htdig.sdsu.edu*). In addition, title browse and call-number browse indexes were created so those users could look for specific titles or call numbers more easily. Much of the work for this project was modeled after some development work for the Alliance Electronic Journal Access project (*www.coalliance.org/ejournal*) that is a comprehensive index to electronic journals on the Web.

The ht://Dig system is a complete World Wide Web indexing and searching system for a small domain or intranet. This system is not meant to replace the need for powerful Internet-wide search systems like Lycos, Infoseek, Webcrawler, and AltaVista. Instead it is meant to cover the search needs for a single company, campus, or even a particular subsection of a Website. As opposed to some WAIS-based or Web-server based search engines, ht://Dig can span several Web servers at a site. The type of these different Web servers doesn't matter as long as they understand the HTTP 1.0 protocol. The ht://Dig system was developed as a way to search the various Web servers on the campus network. San Diego State University makes this product available on a free basis for non-profit applications.

After a user identified a high-priority monograph or serial, a hotlink on each record offered a donation form where the user could enter both bibliographic, personal, and contact information. (See Chapter 12, Appendix 12-A.)

UNEXPECTED CONSEQUENCES

The Web donation form generated approximately 4,000 e-mail messages that were sent to CSU. During the peak 90 days of this Web service (January through April 1998), the Website was hit about 500,000 times from 135 different countries. This was an intended consequence, although early in the program it overwhelmed CSU with volume of public support. However, the design of the CSU Library Assistance Center Website, although modeled after the highly successful Alliance Electronic Journal Access project, had several unexpected consequences.

Because the Website was completely indexed by major search engines such as AltaVista, Northern Light, and others, it came to have a high profile on the Web. The thousands of mini-cataloging records were being retrieved out-of-context via general Web engine searches with interesting results—both good and bad. Many new individual donors were found who would not have otherwise known or cared about the disaster. On the other hand, because many of the MARC records were referencing specific CSU titles that were lost in the disaster, the Alliance office received large numbers of peculiar e-mail. In most cases these were e-mail that were caused by an individual finding a specific book or journal title out of context and assuming that the Alliance were experts in areas. In each case, we would respond in a polite manner explaining the situation, but there were hundreds of these messages.

After running this disaster information and delivery system for about nine months, Colorado State University Libraries decided that this program had run its course and would close down the public portion of this operation on the Alliance Website. After putting this entire section under an IP filter (at this point it was left operational only to CSU staff who wanted access for internal purposes) it was closed to the public . . . almost! We discovered that many of the Web search engines which had indexed the Website and the accompanying MARC records do not quickly de-index these materials. Although the pages were put under an IP filter and the directories in which these records were stored were put in a robots.txt file (which most Web spiders consult before indexing a Website), it took many months for the records to be removed from most search engines (AltaVista was especially problematic). Notification was given to the major search engines to de-index these records, but in most cases it took several months for their spiders to re-visit and get rid of these HTML pages from their search engines. This caused an entirely new disaster of responses of why these HTML pages were not available!

Developing Software Systems for Disaster Recovery

Need for a system

Very early after the disaster, the CSU university administration hired several consultants to assist the aftermath. One of the early recommendations of the contractor hired to operate the Processing Center was that the library needed to build a Loss Management System (LMS) for tracking volumes as they were returned from the freeze-drying process. The challenge was how to do this. Because Colorado State University was engaged in managing many other aspects of the disaster, they decided to outsource this development process to the Alliance, an obvious partner since we had worked so closely with them on other library automation projects.

After several meetings with the contractor, CSU library personnel, and Alliance personnel, it became clear that this project was going to become very detailed and complex. A project that CSU Libraries originally wanted done in just a month or two was to end up taking almost a year. This was partially due to the complex and changing nature of the specifications for the project and due to the fact that the donations project was given first priority along with a Web-based bindery project. Both were projects which CSU Libraries wanted to put in front of the LMS system.

On September 8, 1997, CSU called for a meeting with the Alliance office to discuss the concept of an inventory control system to handle returning materials. Over the next few months a very complex set of specifications arose through a series of meetings and quickly changing specifications as needs evolved.

What emerged, as the top priority by the end of October 1997, was the need for two discrete projects: A Non-Matching Gifts Program and a bindery interface. The Non-Matching Gifts Program would create a Web-based inventory system whereby gifts (donations) could be entered into an inventory file and accessed by all library staff via an internal intranet. This means that anyone in the library could access one simple inventory interface via a Web browser to add, delete, or modify records, or just to look something up. This was up and running by the end of November 1997, within three days after receiving the specifications. Tweaks, updates, additions, and bug fixes for this project continued for many months, but it was up and running.

A second sub-project was the development of a bindery interface for managing the bindery ship transactions. This product was never used—even though it was developed—as another system proved adequate for the task. These two sub-projects were quick and successful because they were well-defined, simple, and met a high-priority need.

The need for a broader Loss Management System (also called the Processing Center database, or Center Information Management System [IMS]), continued to proceed during the fall of 1997. The major accomplishments were the development of a very comprehensive and complex set of specifications which would allow staff to track the progress of materials that were returned. The development of this more comprehensive system was completed in the spring of 1998. However, the LMS system was never used as originally intended. After its completion, it was decided by the contractor that what was really needed was a quick way to provide a look-up system to be used at the freeze-drying facility. It turned out that because a higher-than-expected percentage of materials was not going to be returned to the library, what was really needed was a quick way to indicate if a title was total loss while in the field. This way the badly damaged volumes would not even be shipped back to the library.

The software development for building the Non-Matching Gifts Program, the Bindery Module, and the Loss Management System was a group effort. CSU Libraries was the primary developer of the specifications for each of these systems. They worked with the contractor on various aspects of the process since he was responsible for broader disaster-recovery issues at the university. These specifications were then submitted to the Alliance who performed some of the programming in-house and also outsourced several aspects of the development to an outside programmer whom the Alliance has used on this and several other contracting projects. The project was built in an iterative fashion since specifications in the abstract did not always yield the results which the library contractor wanted. However, as each release of software was developed, feedback provided information for refining the functionality and interface.

How the Systems Were Designed

The Non-Matching Gifts Database and the fuller Loss Management System all shared some common design characteristics. The user interface was Web-based and designed to work with any standard browser. This was done because of the ease of Web-based interface development, a widely available set of design tools, and the ubiquitous nature of the Web browser. It was decided to develop a solution which ran on Unix-based servers because of the robust nature of Unix in a Web-environment. The databases would be built around an SQL database structure. To keep costs low, a shareware package called Mini SQL was chosen from Hughes Technologies (*www.Hughes.com.au*). Mini SQL is free to educational and non-profit organizations, and it had the required functionality. In addition to basic relational database functionality, the product also features W3-mSQL, the WWW-to-mSQL interface package. This allowed the package to be interfaced with the World Wide Web. A Free-BSD Unix operating system was used on an Intel Pentium server acquired by the contractor for the development of the LMS.

AFFIXING COSTS FOR SYSTEM TECHNICAL SUPPORT

The Non-Matching Gifts Database and Bindery Module we developed in the Alliance with Mini SQL was transferred to the main IBM AIX Unix server at Morgan Library for actual operations. This allowed for fast in-house response times since the IBM AIX system was connected to the 100-Mbps library network.

The costs for building the Non-Matching Gifts Database, Bindery Module, and the broader LMS were primarily in staff and some hardware expense. Staffing costs were: specification development by CSU Libraries; Alliance staff time for research for the project, setting up the server (installing the operating system, Mini SQL database setup, and Apache Web Server configuration), and software development; and outside contractor work. The contractor purchased the Pentium server from a local PC builder and wrote a check to the Alliance for initial outsourced software development. Since CSU Libraries is a member of the Alliance, the in-house staff development for this project (which was substantial) was of no direct cost to CSU. However, the outside contract work was paid by the contractor.

The development for the project spanned over a year in terms of work done in the Alliance office and its contractor. As would be expected, there were times of intense development and long periods of no action while awaiting feedback or specifications. The story is not yet finished.

CONCLUSION: THE DISASTER AND THE DIGITAL LIBRARY CONCEPT

There is an energetic consortia movement among libraries in the United States and overseas. Although the majority of consortial activities revolve around the shared licensing of electronic resources, shared system operations and training, and education, clearly consortia can help play an important role in disaster recovery. The Alliance's efforts on behalf of the Colorado State University Libraries were centered on early post-disaster communication, assisting in arranging access to additional electronic resources, and in special project programming to support the recovery effort. These support activities took considerable commitment for each party but played an important role in the recovery of library services.

The Colorado State University experience created an opportunity to test the reach of the digital library in today's real world. In other words, how far can electronic media currently go to supplant print material? The answer to that question is not far, especially in terms of retrospective runs of serials and monographic material. Colorado State University Libraries proved that, at the present time, electronic services are vital and rapidly expanding but they remain a limited library alternative. Colorado State University was able to get a suite of basic services back in operation in a timely manner as a result of the Alliance's efforts, along with the contributions of its member libraries, and with timely and generous contributions from several electronic-database vendors. But the digital library vision of "one user, located anywhere, accessing all digital material" still requires much work. Print is still king in many areas.

There are hundreds of consortia in the U.S. and many more worldwide. Their organizational structure and available resources vary widely. Some will not be able to offer any assistance in a disaster, while others, centralized and well staffed, could match or exceed the services provided by the Alliance in the CSU disaster. Based on the Alliance's experience, and to the extent possible, it is recommended that a consortium consider the following recommendations when responding to a member library's disaster:

Library Disaster Planning and Recovery Handbook

KEY RECOMMENDATIONS

The Consortium's Role

- Assist in communications and, if necessary, serve as the communications center. Particularly in the first few days after the disaster, while the library is still evaluating the situation and the outside library community is requesting status reports and coming forward with offers of assistance, the consortium should divert communications traffic away from the impacted library. The communications should be proactive, getting a consistent message out to all likely interested parties. If feasible, a single point of contact should be established between the institution and the consortium.
- Give first priority to disaster recovery efforts. The consortium should obtain broad permission from its members to use their resources to aid in the recovery. Library policies should be modified at each institution to facilitate resource sharing. The staff workload should be prioritized to deal with the emergency.
- Make a full range of library services available, including:
  * Full borrowing privileges at all nearby academic and public libraries.
  * Free use of electronic databases that might offset lost print material.
  * The commitment of all libraries to provide immediate turnaround on all Interlibrary Loan requests.
  * Dedicated Ariel workstations where appropriate.
  * Donations of duplicate collections.
- Provide technical support.
  * Create a Website containing information about the disaster, library services currently available on- and off-campus, and instructions on how individuals and libraries could assist.
  * Develop a donation and gift receipt system.
  * Support the long-range recovery strategy adopted by the institution.
- Provide management support. Because of a consortium's independent status, it may be able to move more quickly than the impacted institution. If possible, the consortium should:
  * Develop and negotiate clear and enforceable contracts with all outside contractors involved in the disaster recovery.
  * Where there are several parties to a contract, insure that the lines of communication are open and each party understands its role and responsibilities.
  * Develop cost estimates on outside services.
  * Participate in developing the long-range recovery strategy.
- Get out of the way. The consortium should be sensitive to the stress associated with the disaster, particularly during the first few days. Every step should be taken to insure that the proffered assistance is timely, effective, and welcome.

APPENDIX 27-A
WEB-BASED SAMPLE OF TEXT FOR ASSISTANCE CENTER

THE CSU LIBRARY ASSISTANCE CENTER

The Story of the Flood	Current Needs
The Damages	Search for Needed Titles
Gifts Received	Offer titles for donation to CSU
CSU Student Services (shuttle schedule, ILL, ...)	

On July 28, 1997, the Morgan Library at Colorado State University sustained considerable damage from flash flooding when a wall in the library basement broke admitting up to 5,000 cubic feet of water per second. Shelves were twisted and books forced into the water. The water rose above the drop ceiling causing the ceiling tiles to collapse. Due to the recent library renovation, much of the collection was located in the basement which was totally submerged.

Two days were required to pump out the water. A restoration company began the book "pack-out" on July 31st. Some 230,000 pieces had been removed by August 5th. Materials which were badly twisted or dissolved were left behind. 10% of the collection is totally destroyed; the restoration company is optimistically hoping to salvage 80% through freeze drying. The freeze-drying process will take at least six months before the first materials are ready to return to the library. The entire process will take up to two years. Some 425,000 titles will have to be reprocessed. Due to the fact that rapid removal of the materials was critical and many books were thrown from the shelves, an inventory of the damaged items was impossible. An inventory and selection process will be needed as the items are returned.

Current periodicals, government documents, and special collections were not affected by the water. All curriculum and oversized materials were damaged. All current-awareness browse materials were also damaged. All the bound periodicals were damaged along with many monographs. The areas that sustained the most damage are:

- Business (HG, HJ)
- Sociology (HM, HN, HQ)
- Urban/Cities (HT)
- Social Work, including Animal Rights, Women's Studies, Gay & Lesbian, and Disability (HV)
- Political Science (J)
- Law (K)
- Education (L)
- Music (M)
- Science, including Astronomy, Geology, Chemistry, Physics,

Mathematics, Zoology, Biology, Ecology, Botany, Physiology, Atmospheric Sciences, and Statistics (Q)
- Medicine (R)
- Agriculture, Forestry, Vet Science, and Soil Science (S)
- Engineering (T)
- Military Science (U-V)
- Library Science and Bibliography (Z)

Eleven of the thirteen programs of excellence were also affected:

- Animal Reproduction & Biotechnology Laboratory
- Department of Biochemistry & Molecular Biology
- Department of Chemistry
- Center for Environmental Toxicology & Technology
- Infectious Diseases Program
- Program in Meat Science
- Natural Resources Ecology Laboratory
- Program in Neuronal Growth & Development
- Optoelectronic Computing Systems Center
- Radiological Sciences & Cancer Research
- Water Resources Research

CSU Libraries have identified four primary areas of need in which other libraries can be of assistance:

1. Journal Article Delivery
   Other member libraries from the Colorado Alliance of Research Libraries will set up Ariel stations in their libraries to help CSU provide journal article delivery. The participating Alliance libraries are:

   - Colorado School of Mines
   - University of Denver
   - University of Colorado at Boulder
   - University of Northern Colorado

2. Interlibrary Loan Preference
   All the member libraries from the Colorado Alliance of Research Libraries have committed to giving CSU priority fill status for interlibrary loan. CSU is seeking such an arrangement with other ARL libraries and the Big 12 Plus Libraries.

3. Services at other libraries for CSU "walk-in" patrons
   Alliance libraries have committed to provide library services to CSU patrons that physically come into the library with the most generous circulation policies possible. In many instances the libraries are providing the same privileges as they would for their home patrons.

4. In-Depth Reference Services
   CSU is able to provide ready-reference and electronic-reference services. However, in-depth reference assistance in specialized areas is needed. The Colorado Alliance of Research Libraries librarians, as well as librarians throughout the country, have offered to provide in-depth reference services either on-site or through electronic means. The Alliance office is setting up a Web-based "Skill Bank" to help identify reference personnel resources. The possibility of shuttle service between CSU and other Alliance libraries is also under investigation in order to allow CSU students and patrons to browse a physical collection.

Due to the situation at Colorado State University, the library has suspended lending to outside libraries.

We wish to thank the library community for all the concern and offers of help that have been expressed. Monetary and other donations are being coordinated through the Morgan Library Flood Relief Fund. The phone number is 970-491-7328.

A set of databases is available through this Website which allows you to search the lists of serials and monographs that are still needed at CSU. If you have any materials on these lists or other materials that you would like to donate to CSU, please use the Offer Titles for Donation to CSU online form. The offer will be sent directly to CSU staff for evaluation and processing.

CSU Student Svcs	Search for Needed Titles	Gifts Received

Bibliography

American Library Association. 1994. Special Committee on Public Awareness. *Americans Can't Wait—Library Advocacy Now!* (Training Notebook).

Barber, Giles. 1983. "Noah's Ark, or Thoughts Before and After the Flood."
Archives 16, No. 70 (October): 151–161.

Barton, John P., and Johanna G. Wellheiser. 1985. *An Ounce of Preven-
tion: A Handbook on Disaster Contingency Planning for Archives,
Libraries and Record Centres.* Toronto: Toronto Area Archivists Group
Education Foundation.

Bennon, Barbara A. 1967. "Book Restoration in Florence." *Publisher's
Weekly* 192 (November 6): 27–28.

Berridge, John, Gary Cooper, and Carolyn Highley-Marchington. 1997.
Employee Assistance Programmes and Workplace Counselling. New
York: John Wiley and Sons.

Blythe, Bruce T. 1992. "HR . . . Home Run or Strike Out." *HR Focus* 69
(April): 13–14.

Buchanan, Sally. 1979. "The Stanford Library Flood Restoration Project."
College & Research Libraries 40, No. 6 (November): 539–548.

————1988. *Disaster Planning, Preparedness and Recovery for Libraries and Archives: A RAMP Study.* Paris: UNESCO.

————1992. "Drying Wet Books and Records." *Northeast Document
Conservation Center Technical Leaflet.* Andover, MA: Emergency Management.

Bunge, Charles A. 1989. "Stress in the Library Workplace." *Library Trends*
38 (Summer): 92–102.

Cerullo, Michael J., and Virginia Cerullo. 1998. "Key Factors to Strengthen
the Disaster Contingency and Recovery Planning Process." *Information Strategy: the Executive's Journal* 14, No. 2 (Winter): 39–43.

Chadbourne, Robert. 1994. "A Post-Disaster Primer: Elba on the Rebound."
Wilson Library Bulletin 68 (May): 24–25.

Colorado State University Libraries. 1996. *Disaster Recovery Manual.*

Colorado State University Libraries. 1997. *LTS Disaster Plan.*

Cortez, Edwin M. 1983. "Library Automation and Management Information Systems." *Journal of Library Administration* 4, No. 3 (Fall): 22–28.

Cunha, George Martin. 1992. "Disaster Planning and a Guide to Recovery Resources." *Library Technology Reports* 28: 533–624.

Davies, Jean S. 1990. "Crisis Management: Working in the Media." *The Camping Magazine* 62 (April): 31–34.

"Disasters: Prevention & Coping." 1981. *Proceedings of the Conference, May 21-22, 1980.* Palo Alto, CA: Stanford University Libraries.

Drabek, Thomas E. 1987. *The Professional Emergency Manager: Structures and Strategies for Success.* Boulder, CO: Institute for Behavioral Sciences, University of Colorado.

Duitch, Dennis, and Terri Oppelt. 1997. "Disaster and Contingency Planning: A Practical Approach." *Law Practice Management* (January/February): 36–39.

Duncan, Joseph W. 1973. "Practical Requirements for Relating Private and Public Decision-Making on Regional Problems." *Business Economics* 8 (May): 22–27.

England, Claire and Karen Evans. 1988. *Disaster Management for Libraries: Planning and Process.* Ottawa: Canadian Library Association.

Federal Emergency Management Agency. 1996. "Basic Public Information Course." Chapter 1: 4. Available: *www.garlic.com/oes/pio.txt.*

Fortson, Judith. 1992. *Disaster Planning and Recovery: A How-To-Do-It Manual for Librarians and Archivists.* New York: Neal-Schuman.

Foster, Constance L. 1996. "Damaged Periodicals: A Wet Trail Yields Dry Results." *Serials Review* 22, No. 1 (Spring): 33–38.

Gallup, George, Jr. 1996. *The Gallup Poll: Public Opinion 1995.* Wilmington, DE: Scholarly Resources.

Garrett, Echo M. 1994. "Franchises that Capitalize on Solving Our Problems." *Inc.* 16 (September): 106–109.

George, Susan C. 1994. *Emergency Planning and Management in College Libraries.* ACRL CLIP Note #17. Chicago, IL: Association of College and Research Libraries.

Gillespie, David F., et. al. 1993. *Partnership for Community Preparedness.* Boulder, CO: University of Colorado.

Graham, Alan. 1998. "When the River Ran Wild." *Security Management* (March): 46–51.

Griffith, J.W. 1983. "After the Disaster: Restoring Library Services." *Wilson Library Bulletin* 58, No. 4 (December): 258–265.

Grosser, Kerry. 1985. "Stress and Stress Management: A Literature Review, Part III." *LASIE* 16 (July/August): 2–23.

Hamilton, Marsha J. 1993. *Guide to Preservation in Acquisition Processing.* Chicago: American Library Association (Acquisitions Guidelines, No. 8).

Harrington, Gary. 1993. "Flood! Or, Disasters Always Happen on a Weekend." *Southwestern Archivist* 16, No. 4 (Winter): 1–5.

"Health Concerns for Flood Recovery." 1993. *Colorado Preservation Alert* 3, No. 4 (Winter).

Henry, Walter. 1988. *A Brief Bibliography on Disasters.* Palo Alto, CA: Stanford University Libraries.

Higginbotham, Barbra Buckner. 1996. "'It Ain't Over 'Til It's Over': The Process of Disaster Recovery." *Technicalities* 16 (May): 12–13.

Horton, Carolyn. 1967. "Saving the Libraries of Florence." *Wilson Library Bulletin* 41, No. 10 (June): 1034-1043.

Hudgins, V. Lavoyed. 1996. "Crisis Management and Media Relations for Small Agencies." *The Police Chief* 63 (February): 50-52.

"Insurance for Libraries: Part II." 1985. *Conservation Administration News* (CAN) 20 (January): 10–11.

Kahn, Miriam B. 1994. "Fires, Earthquakes, and Floods: How to Prepare Your Library Staff." *Online* 18, No. 3: 18–24.

————— 1998. *Disaster Response and Planning for Libraries.* Chicago: American Library Association.

Kane, Laura Townsend. 1997. "Access vs. Ownership: Do We Have to Make a Choice?" *College and Research Libraries* 58 (January): 59–67.

Kelin, Norman. 1986. "Counting the Losses." *Communicator* 19, Nos. 11-12 (Nov/Dec): 49–52.

Kempner, David. 1995. "Reputation Management: How to Handle the Media During a Crisis." *Risk Management* 42 (March): 43–48.

Leighton, Philip D. 1979. "The Stanford Flood." *College & Research Libraries* 40, No. 5 (September): 450–459.

Lenzuni, Anna. 1987. "Coping with Disaster: Preservation of Library Materials." Conference held at the National Library of Austria, Vienna, April 7-10, 1986. *ILFA Publications* 2: 98–102.

Levitt, Alan M. 1997. *Disaster Planning and Recovery: A Guide for Facility Professionals.* New York: Wiley.

Lustberg, Arch, and Beverly Silverberg. 1995. "Sending the Right Message when Crisis Strikes." *Association Management* 47 (July): 3–4.

McCracken, Peter. 1995. *The Crucial Inadequacy: Disaster Planning in Libraries and Museums*. Master's Paper. School of Information and Library Science, University of North Carolina at Chapel Hill, NC: (April).

Menkus, Belden. 1994. "New Importance of Business Continuity in Data Processing." *Computers & Security* 13, No. 2: 115–118.

Mileti, Dennis, and John Sorensen. 1987. "Determinants of Organizational Effectiveness in Responding to Low Probability Catastrophic Events." *Columbia Journal of World Business* 22, No. 1 (Spring): 13–19.

Moon, Myra Jo. 1981. "A Report on the Colorado Disaster Prevention and Preparedness Workshop." *Colorado Libraries* 7, No. 3 (September): 39–43.

Moreau, Michael. 1987. "Putting It Back Together: Los Angeles Central Library." *Wilson Library Bulletin* 61, No. 7 (March): 35–39.

Morris, Dilys E., Pamela Rebarcak, and Gordon Rowley. 1996. "Monographs Acquisitions: Staffing Costs and the Impact of Automation." *Library Resources and Technical Services* 40, No. 4 (October): 301–318.

Morris, John. 1986. *The Library Disaster Preparedness Handbook*. Chicago: American Library Association.

Murphy, Joan H. 1991. "Taking the Disaster Out of Recovery." *Security Management* 35, No. 8: 60–66.

Murray, Toby. 1987. "Don't Get Caught With Your Pants Down." *Records Management Quarterly* 21, No. 2 (April): 12–41.

Naslund, Cheryl T., and Susan C. George. 1986. "Insurance Settlement Negotiation." *C&RL News* 47, No. 5 (May): 325–328.

Nelms, Willie. 1984. "One Library's Response to Disaster." *North Carolina Libraries* 42 (Fall): 140–142.

Nemzow, Martin. 1997. "Business Continuity Planning." *International Journal of Network Management* 7: 127–136.

O'Connor, Patrick V. 1988. "Debris Removal: Planning for the High Cost of Post-Emergency Cleanup." *Emergency Management Quarterly* (2nd Quarter): 2–3.

O'Mara, Lisa. 1991. "Openness and Quick Response Critical When Working with the Media in a Crisis." *Occupational Health and Safety* 60 (March): 28–30.

Ogden, Sherelyn. 1979. "The Impact of the Florence Flood on Library

Conservation in the USA: A Study of the Literature Published 1956–1976." *Restaurator* 3: 1–36.

Page, Julie A. 1993. "Exercising Your Disaster Plans: A Tabletop Drill." *Conservation and Administration News* 54 (July): 8–9.

Potter, William G. 1994. "Recent Trends in Statewide Academic Library Consortia." *Library Trends* 45 (Winter): 416–417.

"Protecting Book and Paper Against Mold." (Technical Leaflet) 1994. Andover, MA: Northeast Document Conservation Center.

Quarantelli, E.L. 1997. "Ten Criteria for Evaluating the Management of Community Disasters." *Disasters* 21, No. 7: 42–51.

Records Management. 1997. "Part C-Disaster Recovery-A Planned Approach." Available at: *www.system.missouri.edu/records/partc.html.*

Reinsch, Mary. 1993. "Library Disasters and Effective Staff Management." *Conservation Administration News* 55 (October): 4–5, 31–33.

Revenue Ruling. 87-41, 1987-1 C.B. 296.

Rothstein, Philip Jan. 1990. "Put it to the Test." *Contingency Journal* 1, No. 3 (July-September): 51–52.

Ruyle, Carol J., and Elizabeth M. Schobernd. 1997. "Disaster Recovery Without the Disaster." *Technical Services Quarterly* 14, No. 4: 13–24.

Sanders, Nancy P. "The Automation of Academic Library Collection Management: From Fragmentation to Integration." Quoted by Mary F. Casserly and Anne C. Ciliberti "Collection Management and Integrated Library Systems" in *Collection Management for the 21st Century: A Handbook for Librarians*, edited by G. E. Gorman and Ruth H. Miller. Westport, CT: Greenwood Press, 1997. Originally published in *Collection Management for the 1990s*, edited by Joseph Branin. Chicago: American Library Association, 1993.

Solomon, Charlene. 1994. "Bracing for Emergencies." *Personnel Journal* 73, No. 4: 74–83.

Spawn, Willman. 1979. "Disasters: Can We Plan for Them? If Not, How Can We Proceed?" *A Manual of Archival Techniques.* Harrisburg, PA: Pennsylvania Historical and Museum Commission.

Stanford-Lockheed Meyer Library Flood Report. 1980. Stanford University Libraries (May).

Strouse, Karen G. 1995. "What If Your Office Vanishes? Practical Advice on What To Do if Disaster Strikes." *Industry Week* 244 (July 3): 60.

Sung, Carolyn Hoover, Valerii Pavlovich Leonov, and Peter Waters. 1990. "Fire Recovery at the Library of the Academy of Sciences of the USSR." *American Archivist* 53 (Spring): 298–312.

Switzer, Teri R. 1998. "The Crisis Was Bad, But the Stress Is Killing Me!" *Colorado Libraries* 24 (Fall): 19–21.

Tinker, Chauncey B. 1948. "The Library" in *Readings for Liberal Education*, edited by Louis G. Locke, William M. Gibson, and George Arms. New York: Rinehart and Company.

Toigo, Jon William. 1996. *Disaster Recovery Planning for Computers and Communication Resources.* New York: John Wiley.

Ungarelli, Donald L. 1990. "Insurance, Protection and Prevention: Are Our Libraries Safe from Losses?" *Library and Archival Security* 10, No. 1: 56.

Walsh, Betty. 1988. "Salvage Operations for Water-Damaged Collections." *WACC Newsletter* 10, No. 2 (May): 2–5.

Waters, Peter. 1970. "Requirements for An International Center for Preservation of Books and Manuscripts." *Bollettino dell'Istituto di patologia del libro.* 60–84.

———1990. "Phased Preservation: A Philosophical Concept and Practical Approach to Preservation." *Special Libraries* (Winter): 35–43.

———1993. *Procedures for Salvage of Water-Damaged Library Materials.* Washington, D.C.: Library of Congress.

———1996. *Bibliography on Disasters, Disaster Preparedness and Disaster Recovery.* Tulsa, OK: Murray.

Wellheiser, Johanna G. 1992. *Nonchemical Treatment Processes for Disinfectation of Insects and Fungi in Library Collections.* London: K.G. Sauer.

Wexler, Jim. 1993. "Using Broadcast Television to Control a Crisis." *Communication World* 10 (November): 30–31.

Wrotenbery, Carl R. 1972. "Recovery from Disaster: The University of Corpus Christi Library Recovers from Hurricane Celia." *Libraries and Archives Conservation.* The Boston Athenaeum's 1971 Seminar on the Application of Chemical and Physical Methods to the Conservation of Library and Archival Materials, 221–227.

Zerman, David. 1995. "Crisis Communication: Managing the Mass Media." *Information Management* 3: 25–28.

Zoch, Lynn, and Sonya Forte Duhe. 1997. " 'Feeding the Media' During a Crisis." *Public Relations Quarterly* 42 (Fall): 15–18.

Index

About the Editor

Dr. Camila Alire is the Dean of University Libraries at Colorado State University. She has been very involved in various divisions of the American Library Association and Colorado Library Association. Her other areas of research include library services to underserved communities, leadership development, job search strategies, and library management. This is her second book with Neal-Schuman.